WOMEN AND LITERARY CELEBRITY IN THE NINETEENTH CENTURY

Focusing on representations of women's literary celebrity in nineteenth-century biographies, autobiographical accounts, periodicals, and fiction, Brenda R. Weber examines the transatlantic cultural politics of visibility in relation to gender, sex, and the body. Looking both at discursive patterns and specific Anglo-American texts that foreground the figure of the successful woman writer, Weber argues that authors such as Elizabeth Gaskell, Fanny Fern, Mary Cholmondeley, Margaret Oliphant, Elizabeth Robins, Eliza Potter, and Elizabeth Keckley helped create an intelligible category of the famous writer that used celebrity as a leveraging tool for altering perceptions about femininity and female identity. Doing so, Weber demonstrates, involved an intricate gender/sex negotiation that had ramifications for what it meant to be public, professional, intelligent, and extraordinary.

Weber's persuasive account elucidates how Gaskell's biography of Charlotte Brontë served simultaneously to support claims for Brontë's genius and to diminish Brontë's body in compensation for the magnitude of those claims, thus serving as a touchstone for later representations of women's literary genius and celebrity. Fanny Fern, for example, adapts Gaskell's maneuvers on behalf of Charlotte Brontë to portray the weak woman's body becoming strong as it is made visible through and celebrated within the literary marketplace. Throughout her study, Weber analyzes the complex codes connected to transatlantic formations of gender/sex, the body, and literary celebrity as women authors proactively resisted an intense backlash against their own success.

Ashgate Series in Nineteenth-Century Transatlantic Studies

Series Editors: Kevin Hutchings and Julia M. Wright

Focusing on the long nineteenth century (ca. 1750–1900), this series offers a forum for the publication of scholarly work investigating the literary, historical, artistic, and philosophical foundations of transatlantic culture. A new and burgeoning field of interdisciplinary investigation, transatlantic scholarship contextualizes its objects of study in relation to exchanges, interactions, and negotiations that occurred between and among authors and other artists hailing from both sides of the Atlantic. As a result, transatlantic research calls into question established disciplinary boundaries that have long functioned to segregate various national or cultural literatures and art forms, challenging as well the traditional academic emphasis upon periodization and canonization. By examining representations dealing with such topics as travel and exploration, migration and diaspora, slavery, aboriginal culture, revolution, colonialism and anti-colonial resistance, the series offers new insights into the hybrid or intercultural basis of transatlantic identity, politics, and aesthetics.

The editors invite English language studies focusing on any area of the long nineteenth century, including (but not limited to) innovative works spanning transatlantic Romantic and Victorian contexts. Manuscripts focusing on European, African, US American, Canadian, Caribbean, Central and South American, and Indigenous literature, art, and culture are welcome. We will consider proposals for monographs, collaborative books, and edited collections.

Women and Literary Celebrity in the Nineteenth Century

The Transatlantic Production of Fame and Gender

BRENDA R. WEBER
Indiana University, USA

ASHGATE

Published by
Ashgate Publishing Limited
Wey Court East
Union Road, Farnham
Surrey, GU9 7PT   England

Ashgate Publishing Company
Suite 420, 101 Cherry Street
Burlington
VT 05401-4405   USA
www.ashgate.com

British Library Cataloguing in Publication Data
Weber, Brenda R., 1964–
Women and literary celebrity in the nineteenth century: the transatlantic production of fame and gender. – (Ashgate series in nineteenth-century transatlantic studies)
   1. English literature – Women authors – History and criticism. 2. American literature – Women authors – History and criticism. 3. English literature – 19th century – History and criticism. 4. American literature – 19th century – History and criticism. 5. Women and literature – History – 19th century. 6. Women in literature – History – 19th century. 7. Feminism and literature – History – 19th century. 8. Fame – History – 19th century.
   I. Title II. Series
   820.9'9287'09034–dc23
Library of Congress Cataloging-in-Publication Data
Weber, Brenda R., 1964–
   Women and literary celebrity in the nineteenth century: the transatlantic production of fame and gender / by Brenda R. Weber.
      p. cm.—(Ashgate series in nineteenth-century transatlantic studies)
   Includes bibliographical references and index.
   1. English literature—Women authors—History and criticism. 2. American literature—Women authors—History and criticism. 3. English literature—19th century—History and criticism. 4. American literature—19th century—History and criticism. 5. Fame—History—19th century. 6. Sex role—History—19th century. 7. Women authors—Biography—History and criticism. 8. Women authors in literature. 9. Authorship—Social aspects—Great Britain—History—19th century. 10. Authorship—Social aspects—United States—History—19th century. I. Title.
   PR115.W43 2012
   820.9'928709034—dc23
                                                                                    2011046387
ISBN 9781409400738 (hbk)
ISBN 9781409400745 (ebk)

Printed and bound in Great Britain by the
MPG Books Group, UK

To Jacob David Waller,
a miraculous testimonial to perseverance

Contents

List of Figures

Acknowledgements

In this book I discuss the use of a metaphor in which the books women wrote often came to function as textual children. If that is the case for me, the gestation of this book from beginning idea to publication constitutes a mighty long pregnancy. When this project began, I was preparing for my comprehensive doctoral exams. Now that it is being published as a book, I am an associate professor with tenure. In the intervening years, I researched, wrote, and published an entirely different book on makeovers and contemporary television, but I never lost sight of this first major project on Victorian literature or my commitment that it live a life beyond the dissertation.

It is, indeed, because of this book's long developmental period and its steady maturation from a dissertation on the politics of Victorian codes of representation to a book that addresses the transatlantic workings of literary celebrity that I have so many people to thank. Of these, my foremost thanks and appreciation go to my former dissertation advisor and present friend and colleague, Mary Jean Corbett, who not only helped shape this project and give it direction and meaning but whose kindness and counsel helped me develop it into its present form. Mary Jean was formative for me intellectually, and I have profited greatly not only from her scholarship but from her careful editing of my work. Perhaps even more importantly, Mary Jean is an incredible advisor, and now, as I find myself in the role of guiding my own graduate students, I see how extraordinary her gifts to me truly have been. Mary Jean was in all ways reliable, insightful, and supportive, and I can only hope to repay the enormous debt I owe her through a continued conscientious attention and mentoring of my own students, present and future. Paying it forward is perhaps a clichéd form of gratitude, yet in many ways it is the only kind of payment that matters.

In addition to Mary Jean, I'd like to think the wonderful professors who worked with me at Miami University of Ohio, in particular Lori Merish, Lu Ming Mao, Kerry Powell, Laura Mandell, Mary Frederickson, and Whitney Womack. I'd also like to thank Miami University of Ohio for a doctoral dissertation fellowship and other graduate support that helped expedite my time to degree. My thanks to others who helped solidify my grad school cohort: Yvetta Jusova, Jill Swiencicki, Kevin Mahoney, Rich Zumkhawala-Cook, Ed "Kofi" Sackey, and, most important and indispensably of all, the magnificent Judith Wenger.

At Ashgate, I'd like to express my thanks to Ann Donahue, the editors of the Nineteenth-Century Transatlantic Studies Series Kevin Hutchings and Julia M. Wright, and the anonymous reviewers, all of whom offered insightful guidance and support. Kathy Bond Borie was an excellent editor.

Portions of this book have been published in different forms in either journals or edited volumes. I thank the editors of *Feminist Studies* and Ohio University Press, publisher of *Other Mothers*, for their permission to republish portions of Chapter 5. I thank the University of New Hampshire Press, publisher of *Transatlantic Women*, for their permission to republish brief sections of the introduction and the gendered discourse manifest through Fanny Fern's representation of Harriet Beecher Stowe. Thank you to the editors of *Women's Writing* for permission to publish materials in relation to Elizabeth Robins's *White Violets* and thank you to the editors of *PMLA* for their permission to republish some of the material on celebrity, gender, and motherhood. I also thank Indiana University's College of Arts and Humanities Institute (CAHI) for two research travel grants that allowed me to visit the Fales Special Collections Library at NYU, the Bodleian Library at Oxford University, and Haworth, the Brontës' home in Yorkshire. I also appreciate and benefitted from the support of Indiana University's Associate Provost for Research. Since an archival project is only as good as one's librarians, I thank the very capable research staff particularly those in special collections and inter-library loan at Miami University of Ohio, the University of Kentucky, Transylvania University, Indiana University, New York University, the University of Michigan, and the Harry Ransom Center at the University of Texas at Austin. In particular, I thank Angela Courtney at Indiana University, whose capacious imagination and capable library skills have ably stretched from Victoriana to Reality TV and back again.

At Indiana University I thank, as always, the members and affiliates of my department in Gender Studies, who provide such a rich haven for reflection and intellectual stimulation, most specifically Karma Lochrie, Judith Allen, Purnima Bose, Colin Johnson, Sara Friedman, Lessie Jo Frazier, Jen Maher, Marlon Bailey, Alex Doty, Mary Gray, Stephanie Sanders, Susan Seizer, and Rick Wilk. I am also grateful for the assistance and general good humor of our exceptional office staff, Nina Taylor and Barbara Black-Kurdziolek.

I have profited greatly from conversations and connections with the Indiana University Nineteenth Century Studies group, and in particular, I would like to thank Andrew Miller, Ivan Kreilkamp, Susan Gubar, Pat Bratlinger, Steve Watt, Jennifer Fleissner, and Christoph Irmscher for their advice, suggestions, and reflections. Without a doubt, my greatest debt is to Joss Marsh, who is an extraordinary interlocutor on matters related to literature, celebrity, the nineteenth century, and practically any other topic that arises. Joss did me the extraordinarily generous favor of reading several chapters of this book while in development, and I credit her for helping to draw out points of richness that reminded me of just how fascinating these matters can be. My other book might theorize the meanings of the makeover, but were it not for Joss and her extraordinary makeover skills, this book would be a much dimmer Before-body rather than what I hope is a celebratory After-body.

I owe a strong debt to those many scholars who have contributed to this book through conversation, feedback, and the generous sharing of archival materials. Those of particular note include Elaine Showalter, Suzanne Raitt, Rynetta Davis, Dana Nelson, Ellen Rosenman, Claudia Klaver, Helena Michie, Whitney Womack, Beth Lueck, Chris Holmlund, Su Holmes, Courtney Berger, and Sarah Meer.

Thanks to all of my students, but in particular those in my undergraduate and graduate celebrity and gender seminars, who, as ever, are a source of fascination and inspiration. Specifically, I offer my gratitude to Katie Schweighofer and Julie Campbell, who masterfully helped edit the text, and to Karolyn Steffens, Andy Lewis, and Spring Serenity Duvall, whose interest in literature, gender, and the politics of celebrity has been a nourishing source for the continuance of this project.

Thank you so much to my friends, who create the loving and supportive network that makes this sort of work possible: Patti Peplow, a teacher of integrity and serendipity; Suzanne Bresina Gripenstraw, a model of how to engage with the world with passion and joy; Jean Ward, the possessor of both a warm heart and wry sense of humor; Chantal Carleton, a sister in the scholarly struggle but also sister to my heart; Georges-Claude Guilbert, BFF in word and deed; and, Lara Monaghan, a comedienne par excellence for making me laugh when you said you'd rather eat this book than write it. Thanks to my wonderful group of friends who have nurtured this project: Sara Friedman, Gardner Bovingdon, Radhika Parameswaran, Barb Klinger, Richard Angelo, Karen Tice, Sarah Knott, Catherine Guthrie, Sharon Hamilton, Jennifer Philpot, Jan Isenhour, Sue Bonner, and Linda Blackford.

During a portion of the time I was writing this book, I served as the executive director of the Kentucky Women Writers Conference, and I thank the many people who attended and presented at the conference as well as my colleagues, teams of mighty interns, and stalwart volunteers who all helped reinforce to me the importance of women's writing. In particular, I thank James Baker Hall and Mary Ann Taylor-Hall, who didn't much care *what* I wrote only *that* I wrote. At one of those conferences, the Kentucky novelist and poet laureate Sena Jeter Naslund pulled me close to her and whispered, "You have books inside of you waiting to get out." Would that we could all midwife each other's thoughts into being.

Some of the family mentors who were present at the start of this book have now passed away, but their influence is much remembered and appreciated. In particular, I thank my grandmother, Marion Jones Weber, the world's most consummate reader, and her daughter, my aunt Margaret "Margo" Weber, who also loved books. Somewhere the spirits of these two library ladies are smiling at this most recent addition to the card catalogues (and computer databases). I also thank my great aunt and uncle Mina Rea and Gilbert Perlow, who were extraordinary models to me of what academic life might look like. In the land of the living, I offer my thanks and appreciation to my brothers and their families: John, Becky, Robert, Heather, Alex, and Ciara. I also thank my sisters-in-law, Andrea Waller and Beth Kamhi. But above all, I thank my parents, David and Mary Weber, who never failed to remind me that I could do things in the world. Thank you Mom (Grammy) and Dad (Ba-Pa!) for your love, support, and encouragement.

In a project as long in the making as this has been, spirits and familiars factor largely. In that vein, I therefore thank two creatures of my heart, sweet Zu-Zu and rambunctious Bud-Bud, always there for clarifying walks and consoling ear rubs. Finally, I offer my thanks to little Baby Jakey, now wiggling and squiggling on my lap, and to Greg Waller, who has truly been a resource and sounding board for each and every step in this journey, providing me nourishment of the body and of the mind. Elizabeth Barrett Browning has said, "Of writing many books there is no end." If that is the case, Gregy, let it always be with you by my side.

Brenda R. Weber. Bloomington, Indiana. September 2011

Introduction:
A Right to Call Herself Famous

The practices of femininity can readily function in certain contexts that are difficult to ascertain in advance, as modes of guerilla subversion of patriarchal codes, although the line between compliance and subversion is always a fine one, difficult to draw with any certainty. All of us, men as much as women, are caught up in modes of self-production and self-observation; these modes may entwine us in various networks of power, but never do they render us merely passive and compliant. They are constitutive of both bodies and subjects.

—Elizabeth Grosz, *Volatile Bodies*

[W]e think that when a lady has had a mud-scow and a hand-cart, a steamboat and a hotel, a perfume and a score of babies, not to mention tobacco and music, named for her; and when she is told what her name is, wherever she goes, till she is sick of the sound of it, that she does not earn for herself a boxed ear when she couples with it the word "famous."

—Fanny Fern, December 10, 1864, *New York Ledger*

In 1913, *The New York Times* reported on the findings of Cora Sutton Castle, an American academic who, as part of her doctoral dissertation, had compiled a statistical calculation of the world's most famous women.[1] Spanning a 26-century period, Castle's study identified 27 "fields of celebrity" in which women had achieved eminence. These fields included both the notorious and the meritorious—mixing marriage, beauty, and fame for being a mistress with political influence, scholarship, and eminence for social reformation. Through the means of her exhaustive study on celebrity, Castle concluded that in the history of the (primarily Anglo-European-American) world, there had been 868 women who qualified for eminence, the large majority of these being nineteenth-century professional authors who claimed national identities in either Britain or America.[2]

---

[1]   Written at Columbia University, Castle's dissertation, *A Statistical Study of Eminent Women*, was published in 1913 as a book of the same name through The Science Press. As a statistical analysis, Castle's book was positioned as qualitatively different from other surveys of famous women, such as Sarah Josepha Hale's *Woman's Record: or Sketches of All Distinguished Women, from "The Beginning" till AD 1850*. To garner a fuller sense the particularities of Castle's study or the extraordinary sweep of encyclopedias of eminent women, particularly as rendered in biographical formats, consult the "Bibliography of Collective Biographies of Women, 1830–1940" in Alison Booth's *How to Make it as a Woman* (347–87).

[2]   Literary practitioners by far lead the list with 337 people, followed next by women made famous by marriage (87), religion (64) acting (56), sovereignty (59), music (49), and birth (39). Mistresses (29), those made famous by tragic fate (11) and those famed for

Castle noted that such low overall numbers in comparison to the 1,000 eminent men identified by Professor J. McKeen in a similar study proved not that women were less deserving of fame but merely that they had experienced reduced opportunities for asserting their eminence. Speaking to the *Times* reporter, Dr. Castle noted, "I believe that the increase of eminent women in the past two centuries is due largely to the increase in the opportunities for them to become eminent. There is, as everywhere recognized, a wholly different attitude toward women to-day, and the reason that the number of eminent women is less than a thousand is perhaps not so much innate inferiority to man as of the prohibitive attitude of civilization toward her" ("Twenty Most" SM7). Castle speculated that the clear predominance of literature as a domain to establish women's fame was probably due to the fact that literature offered women opportunity for free expression, in opposition to the way a woman's "actions have been restricted" and her "thought has been regulated" in other lines of work ("Twenty Most" SM7).

Castle's findings illuminate some telling points of value to this consideration of women and literary celebrity in a transatlantic context. A point tacitly suggested by Castle is that fame confers unquestioned cultural value on those who hold it, so that fame is imagined as primarily a positive reward. As Castle's choice of words indicates, fame is something that one deserves rather than, as is sometimes perceived to be the case in our contemporary context, an indication of popularity and even superficiality in a postmodern media-saturated age. Further, fame serves a nation-building function. As Alison Booth has noted, Castle's compilation joined with a host of other encyclopedias and catalogs that were often marshaled to "measure progress" and argue tacitly for "national superiority in terms of race and gender" (*How To* 212). Fame could thus serve as a benchmark for comparison, indicating not only the individual but also the nation as superior in taste and ability. The predominance of Americans on her list, Castle opined, "reflects credit on the physical vigor of the American people as well as upon our hygienic and sanitary conditions and the skill of American physicians and surgeons" (*A Statistical Study* 89).

Castle's optimistic sense that women will continue to achieve fame as their opportunities expand speaks directly to shifting attitudes about the transatlantic politics of gender and visibility. Though Castle could praise eminent literary women in 1913, the very authors she cites as famous often struggled with the tensions between celebrity and gender. For instance, Castle ranks Harriet Beecher Stowe (who ties with Cleopatra) in her top-twenty list; yet, during her own lifetime, Stowe professed what she herself termed a "natural modesty" that made fame an unnatural phenomenon that one experienced with great reluctance.[3] After the intense public acclaim following the publication of *Uncle Tom's Cabin* (1852),

---

beauty (6) or immortalized in literature (6) also make Castle's list. Alison Booth points out that Castle's list "becomes increasingly eccentric as eminence decreases through fifteen fine-type pages" (*How To* 212).

    [3]   Stowe used this phrase in a letter to her friend Eliza Cabot Follen, December 16, 1852. Quoted in Hedrick, 240.

which constituted the apogee of celebrity experienced in Stowe's own lifetime, the author set sail to Britain for an extensive publicity tour in England and Scotland where she was greeted by masses of fans.[4] Though Stowe possessed undisputed international celebrity, on this speaking tour she often sat quietly in the "'ladies' gallery,' separated from the main hall by a lattice, [which] enabled ladies to 'see and not be seen'" while her husband and brother spoke for her (Hedrick 238). Letters and newspaper accounts suggest that Stowe chose such retiring behavior in response to an injunction that precluded middle-class white women from eagerly claiming public roles. So, though celebrity offered a form of cultural currency, it was a coin that women spent at great cost.

Even given the potential handicaps, however, the risks of fame did not wholly lessen its desirability. Lord Byron wrote in *Childe Harolde* that, "fame is the thirst of youth" (Canto III, CXII, 185). And while Byron probably had thirsty young men in mind, many women also desired to quench their desires with public acclaim. Louisa May Alcott declared as a child, for instance, that her great ambition was to be "rich, famous, and happy before I die" (Reisen 4). It was a goal she would make good on, but not without some frustration brought by the spoils of success, details Alcott built into her fiction, particularly *Jo's Boys* (discussed in Chapter 2). Like Alcott, many men and women worked to establish careers and public lives that might make them rich but would also qualify them for the kind of posterity that turns short-term celebrity into everlasting fame, perhaps agreeing with Elizabeth Barrett Browning's *Aurora Leigh* that, "Fame's smallest trump/ Is a great ear-trumpet for the deaf as posts/ No other being effective" (Book 7, 560–62). Fame was desirable, then, not only because it conferred value, legitimacy, and consummation as a love-object but also because it made even the dullard take note. Fame, in other words, draws attention to itself; it cannot go unmarked.

Whether male or female, it was important for all celebrity-aspirants that they not signal their desires for fame too obviously. Such an attitude of cloaked desire corresponds with what Leo Braudy has theorized as a foundational principle of the workings of fame in a Western tradition. To be "famous for yourself, for what you are without talent or premeditation," Braudy argues, allows for the terms of fame as one's "rightful inheritance," thus allowing star aspirants to shirk the stigma of hubris connected to calculation (7). Despite such injunctions, however, to strive toward greatness could in many ways be a gender-affirming process for men, since it reinforced a code of masculinity predicated on competition, singularity, and aggrandizement. These same qualities when applied to women laid bare a sexual double-standard still largely operative today, where ambitious women with opinions are more frequently read as difficult than as possessing the qualities of greatness. As Castle's study indicates, in the broad sweep of history, women who

---

[4]   Margaret H. McFadden reports, "Three thousand copies of *Uncle Tom's Cabin* were sold on the first day of its publication in 1852. Within a year more than 300,000 copies had been sold in the United States and 1.5 million copies in Great Britain" (68). *Uncle Tom's Cabin* was also hugely popular internationally (see McFadden 68–70).

achieved the heights of fame often did so by virtue of their affective relationships—
as mothers, handmaids, wives, and mistresses to great men.

The great nineteenth-century surge in transatlantic publishing opportunities
opened new fields of possibility where a woman could not only earn her own bread
but could actively build her own reputation—a reputation, which for many authors
such as Stowe, extended internationally. As Ronald Weber notes in *Hired Pens*,
the mid-nineteenth century witnessed the emergence of a number of American
and British periodicals that offered new authors, many of them women, a shot at
a literary livelihood and celebrity. Public acclaim and the threat it represented to
men, however, also fostered what Ronald Weber calls "a chorus of critical lament"
that included intense "critical scorn" (43). To perpetuate a sense of women's
"natural modesty," famous female authors (or their alter-egos in print) learned to
ever more skillfully deflect the appearance of actively desiring celebrity. As such,
it was permissible to recognize oneself as famous—as Fanny Fern's epigraph
starting this chapter indicates—but one's fame had to arrive passively, like a
guest in the night, the unsought dividends of more humble aspirations. Putting
fame into this metaphorical context allowed a woman's notoriety to be a matter
of fate rather than of design, of rewards passively received rather than conquests
actively pursued.[5]

Women and Literary Celebrity in the Nineteenth Century examines the
tensions built into Anglo-American Victorian representations of gender, fame,
and professionalism, noting that fame constituted a significant public achievement
that often had complex and vexing consequences for women. This book is
consequently not so much a study of famous people as of the phenomenon of
fame itself, considering in particular how the gendered connotations attached
to celebrity both limited and ultimately authorized new codes of femininity and
womanhood in a transatlantic Victorian worldview. I focus on the representation
of the condition of celebrity as traceable in fictional texts and as augmented by
newspaper and periodical paratexts, so that I might more fully elucidate the "idea"
of a person expressed through celebrity, rather than to glean a more "accurate"
sense of nineteenth-century practices or a particular historical person's biography.
In so doing, I aim to demonstrate that the representation of famous women authors
often functioned as a conceptual device that allowed for a shift in the broader
meanings of gender identity.

Linda H. Peterson has noted that, "As social norms for women changed during
the nineteenth century, so too did attitudes toward women's writing, yielding a
greater range of possibilities in the profession of letters" (10). *Women and Literary*

---

[5]   In the second volume of his extraordinary biography of Margaret Fuller, Charles
Capper presses on this idea that Fuller reconciled her public image and her private identity
by assuring herself she was the inheritor of a fated stature rather than the seeker of celebrity.
In a similar vein, Anne Firor Scott notes that Emma Willard, the founder of the Troy Female
Seminary, was subjected to "slanderous aspersions" through accusation claiming that her
"work on the Greek project had been less for the benefit of Greece than for her own fame" (50).

Celebrity in the Nineteenth Century takes this claim and reverses it, asking how attitudes toward women's popularity as famous writers might have given rise to new ways of conceptualizing social norms for women in the nineteenth century. Each of the authors considered here created female author-characters who leave domestic roles, toil at professional writing, and—seemingly through no desire of their own—become famous. Doing so involved an intricate gender/sex negotiation that had ramifications for what it meant to be public, professional, intelligent, and publicly known. As cultural producers, these authors helped forge an intelligible category of the professional and famous author, who could also uphold Anglo-American Victorian mandates for gendered middle-class legitimacy; in their characters, they performed what the British author Mona Caird in *The Daughters of Danaus* called "guerilla warfare," by enacting the values of the class- and race-coded lady even as they broke the very rules on which such norms were established.

Since the 1980's, feminist scholars have created a rich archive for theorizing the importance of the woman writer, including the relation between a private self and public persona. Studies such as Elaine Showalter's *A Literature of Their Own* (1977) have been fundamental in recovering works by women lost through the politics of canon formation. Sandra Gilbert and Susan Gubar's *The Madwoman in the Attic* (1979) worked to place women in coherent relationship to pre-existing masculinist modes of analysis, examining, for instance, how the woman writer contended with the Freudian dilemma of the phallogocentric pen; Mary Kelley's *Private Woman, Public Stage* (1984) also sought to establish the cultural and psychological battles that actual women fought in order to write. A critical generation removed from these first texts, a new wave of scholarship implicitly critiqued the assumptions of their originary claims. Informed by post-structuralist and Foucauldian discourses, studies such as Jane Tompkins' *Sensational Designs* (1985), Mary Poovey's *Uneven Developments* (1988), and Nancy Armstrong's *Desire and Domestic Fiction* (1987) sought to define the manner in which ideologies are encoded into the text as artifacts bearing cultural power. Another generation, one still forming, is self-conscious of political, historical, and material investments in modes of analysis that reinscribe hegemonies. Scholars such as Robyn Wiegman (*American Anatomies*, 1995), Pamela Gilbert (*Disease, Desire, and the Body in Victorian Women's Popular Novels*, 1992) and Ann Cvetkovich (*Mixed Feelings*, 1992) seek to trace out the many contortions and contingencies of ideology as mapped onto social practice.[6]

Women and Literary Celebrity in the Nineteenth Century is situated in analyses of the woman writer over the past 20 years, but it extends existing scholarship in several significant ways. This book is governed by the idea, as offered by Richard

---

[6]   I have highlighted the work on authorship that has been particularly influential to my own practice. For a much broader indication of the depth of scholarship on women writers, the gendered politics of canon formation, and the literary marketplace, consult the full bibliography at the end of this book.

Brodhead and Mary Poovey, that both celebrity and authorship are socially constructed categories that emerge out of specific conditions and particular historical moments. Because my focus is on the representation of the famous female author rather than the socio-historical circumstances of the condition of women in the nineteenth century, it is the discursive manipulation of fame and professional authorship that governs my analysis. To theorize my findings, I turn to recent work on the meanings of the body, gender, and celebrity, offered by such scholars as Elizabeth Grosz, Judith Butler, and Richard Dyer. Since my analysis seeks to identify the way in which literary practitioners were able to make the subversive more legitimate, the body as semiotic text is critically relevant to my discussion in its function as a register of social values. The bodies I examine here are not so much physical forms, but the discursively constructed body, or, as Helena Michie puts it, "the flesh made word." In theorizing the body and how it is situated in these texts, I also work through issues of the discursive construction of subjectivity. Throughout the texts I analyze, I see many moments of postmodern and queer subjectivity(ies). This does not suggest to me that the women I analyze were necessarily postmodern or queer, but that the competing ideologies of the Victorian period contained within themselves resources for radical alterity.

In its examination of the development of the artist, my book could well be considered literary criticism on the *Künstlerroman*. And while many of my case studies depict the development of the artist from childhood to maturity, I am much more interested in the interworkings between gender and literary celebrity than I am in the particular genre that marks the *Künstlerroman*. Further, I very specifically target authors over other nineteenth-century avatars of fame, such as politicians or actors. It is the literary professional, I argue, even more than the famous actress or notorious suffragette, who occupied a position most suitable for using celebrity as a touchstone for gender change in the nineteenth century. In this, I concur with Maura Ives who argues that "*literary* celebrity" illustrates a longer history to fame and notoriety that is "rooted in earlier media technologies, primarily the technology of print as it developed in the nineteenth and early twentieth centuries and perhaps even earlier" (2, italics in original). Extending the significance of the literary famous to a transatlantic frame, I argue that the importance of the professional author's representation of gender and celebrity is not due to her greater fame at the time or legendary status in our own moment. Indeed, although Charlotte Brontë or E.D.E.N. Southworth were famous in their own day, other women of the age—such as the Swedish opera singer Jenny Lind, the French actress Sarah Bernhardt, or the British socialite and authoress Caroline Norton—arguably possessed greater acclaim.[7] I argue here, rather, that literary character studies of the famous female author allowed for a distinct kind of conceptual change, one predicated on nuanced, intertextual, and long-lasting

---

[7]   For insightful discussions on the celebrity experienced by the nineteenth-century actress Fanny Kemble, see Deirdre David's *Fanny Kemble: A Performed Life* and Rebecca Jenkins's *Fanny Kemble: A Reluctant Celebrity*.

discursive links between readers, historical moments, and political conditions predicated on a sense of a familiar intimacy fostered in both media accounts and fictional representations. As I demonstrate in Chapter 1, for instance, Elizabeth Gaskell's *The Life of Charlotte Brontë* provided inspiration and affective bonding not just for readers in the 1850s but for a transatlantic audience that extended through the nineteenth century and into the present day.

In her review of Mary Kelley's important book *Private Woman, Public Stage*, Carroll Smith-Rosenberg argues that in response to the widespread success and popularity of women's publishing in mid nineteenth-century America, authors such as Harriet Beecher Stowe, Sara Parton (Fanny Fern), and Augusta Evans Wilson became "darlings of the public." Yet Smith-Rosenberg concedes, "these writers constituted an anomaly in the rigidly gender-ordered world of Victorian America" since a larger transatlantic society responded to their success with ambivalence. "While clamoring for ever more of their novels," Smith-Rosenberg reflects, societal ambivalence "taught them to suspect their own talents and to deny their real accomplishments …. above all, the plots of their novels indicted their private lives by condemning women who desired literary fame and economic autonomy" ("Their Writing"). It is the work of this book to suggest that such condemnatory representations of gender and literary fame cannot be taken at face value, that they often functioned rhetorically, as Virginia Woolf phrased it, as lies told to succeed. For indeed, as Smith-Rosenberg herself notes in her review of Kelley, both professional and domestic women seized on and manipulated multiple ideological imperatives in order to invert "male bourgeois myths" of order and domination.[8] Gender is, thus, a critical key to reading these multiple manipulations. To differing degrees, the texts examined here build the gendered infrastructure of celebrity into the narratives that their author-characters experience, in the process troubling popular representations of famous women as man-ish or unsexed.

Gender thus bears an important relation to the symbolic currency that celebrity affords; it also has important bearing on separate spheres typologies that gendered spaces in the Victorian imagination. Women authors in the nineteenth century often functioned as cultural flashpoints for debates about separate spheres, since their work and their sexed identities put them in direct proximity to clashes between ideologies and actualities. Although we are aware that binary arrangements (public/private, man/woman, masculine/feminine) are social mythologies rather than descriptive realities, it is equally true that their ideological appeal held (and often still holds) a particular coercive authority.[9] Linda Hughes tells us, for

---

[8]   In *Poets in the Public Sphere*, Paula Bernat Bennett offers a somewhat similar argument that the publication of women-authored poetry in postbellum American periodicals fostered a broader discursive culture that allowed "ordinary women" to engage in conversations about abolition, Indian removals, economic and racial injustices, the Civil War, and their own status as subjects.

[9]   For more on the separate spheres debate, see Monika Elbert, ed., *Separate Spheres No More*; Cathy N. Davidson and Jessamyn Hatcher, eds., *No More Separate Spheres!*;

instance, that at the end of the nineteenth century, women's coming together in professional literary clubs elicited uproar from a male literary establishment that had worked assiduously to preserve the sanctity of all-male clubs (and literary achievement). "[A] woman's literary dining club," Hughes notes, "represented a collective female incursion into public urban spaces" and was thus threatening since it represented a "claim to equal status and privileges enjoyed by male authors" (235, 236).

The point here, then, is that we might recognize a separate spheres typology as an outmoded fiction describing a moment that never actually existed, but we cannot fully do away with the governing metaphor entirely. The domains of the public and private were never separate and non-permeable spaces, but the ideology of separation and difference created a fantasy of a sex- and class-segregated order that called for prescriptive divisions between actors, bodies, and identities. Caroline Levine argues, in this vein, that "scholars have successfully unsettled the notion of a rigid divide between public and private, showing that Victorian women played significant roles outside of the home, while men struggled to find their proper places within the domestic sphere" (627). But Levine urges us not to dismiss the prescriptive notions of separate spheres altogether since the discourses themselves wielded considerable ideological influence.

In this study about literary celebrity, I demonstrate how disagreements about "women's rightful place" could actually serve as a ruse for celebrity, since the amalgamated signifier of a famous female author developed complex gender fluidities even as it reified conventional dimorphic separations. Hedrick notes about Harriet Beecher Stowe and her "silent" visit to Great Britain, for instance, that the author was an agent in her own separation, since she was eager to retain (or perpetuate) a sense of her "modesty" and to "do nothing that would upset this delicate standoff between ideology and reality, for it allowed her to move back and forth between the private and the public realms and to have an influence in both" (238).[10]

Telling Lies to Succeed

Toward the end of the American newspaper columnist and novelist Fanny Fern's transatlantic best-selling *Ruth Hall* (1855), Ruth's young daughter Nettie, who has seen her mother struggle to break the grasp of poverty through arduous nights of writing, asks, "When I get to be a woman shall I write books, mamma?" Ruth responds with a shudder, "God forbid, no happy woman ever writes" (*RH* 175). Though Ruth tells her daughter she despises writing, Fern's depiction

---

Linda Kerber, Alice Kessler-Harris and Kathryn Kish Sklar, eds., *U.S. History as Women's History*; and Clare Midgley, *Women Against Slavery*.

[10]   Nicole Tonkovich observes, "For all their advocacy of women's right to speak in public, [Harriet] Beecher [Stowe], [Sarah Josepha] Hale, [Fanny] Fern, and [Margaret] Fuller customarily avoided the podium, preferring to style themselves not as lecturers but as conversationalists" (124).

of Ruth suggests she thrives on literary work, a fact rewarded in the novel by enormous celebrity (and a good deal of money). Ruth makes quite clear, however, "those articles were written for bread and butter, not fame" (*RH* 136).[11] Such statements fulfill what Rachel Blau DuPlessis describes as a "mid-century base line of attitudes, in which a woman's entry into public discourse elicits a shudder of self-disgust and is allowable only if it is undertaken in mourning and domesticity" (87). ✓ This scene between Ruth and her daughter underscores that her celebrity comes to Ruth passively, not as the consequence of her ambition or desire but as the unsought dividends of her domestic labor and sacrifice. In exemplifying the heroic quotidian, Ruth becomes extraordinary. Fame is thus a merited reward for Ruth's tenacity and domestic responsibility rather than a marker of hubris or vanity.

Fern managed the terms of her own literary celebrity differently, as evidenced in the epigraph that starts this book. Having perfumes, steamboats, babies, and cigars named after her was an unquestioned form of status, which afforded her an obvious fame. Why should she be punished, Fern argued, if she claimed the adjective "famous" for herself?[12] Even here we can see that if the author must defend herself from charges of too-eagerly claiming her fame, then the meanings of fame carry connotations of both shame and avarice.

Fern's double denunciation of professional authorship and fame through Ruth strikes me as the sort of guerilla warfare that Mona Caird called for in a late-Victorian context, as well as a strategy for subversion championed by the modern-day feminist Elizabeth Grosz as a mode of gender practice. It is also one of the lies told for success that Virginia Woolf evokes in "Professions for Women." A woman could not "put pen to paper," Woolf bemoaned, without battling an internalized injunction to be good. And yet, she opined, because one "cannot review even a novel without having a mind of your own, without expressing what you think to be truth about human relations, morality, sex," it was impossible to write incisively in the context of a gender identity that precluded women from dealing "freely and openly" with the matters of living. "[Women] must charm, they must conciliate, they must—to put it bluntly—tell lies if they are to succeed" (212).

"Professions for Women" was not published until 1942, yet Woolf's internalized agent, what she called "the Angel in the House" in reference to Coventry Patmore's 1854 poem of the same name, has long been taken as an emblem for the situation of white, heterosexual, middle-class Anglo-American women in the nineteenth century—tied to hearth and home, to children and husband, their voices unheard

---

[11]   Linda H. Peterson notes that Harriet Martineau claimed the "need for utterance," rather than the necessity of money, as her motivating rationale for authorship. However, in Martineau's case she also eschewed fame as a legitimate reason for writing (Peterson 67).

[12]   These gendered prescriptions have, unfortunately, not changed much, as evidenced by a December 2006 *New York Times* feature article on women C.E.O.'s that began its profile of Carol Bartz by noting that she "did not harbor secret desires to run her own company or become chief executive of a large corporation. She just wanted to do a good job" (Creswell 3–1). In this regard, eminence is allowable, but ambition is not.

Fig. I.1   Fanny Fern Cigars. Author's collection.

and unrecognizable in the spheres of commerce, politics, and ideas. With her angel, Woolf voiced a frustration grounded in perceived gender/sex dichotomies, a sense that her ontological state as woman limited her gendered abilities. In this case a woman's sexed body compromised the perceived merit of that produced by her mind. And yet Woolf, like many other professional writers, found a place of influence in an intellectual society that made little room for her. She and others found this place by making it appear, by actively rendering strong, imaginative, visible, and sometimes famous women in the texts they constructed. Woolf credits others for the relative ease of her own literary career. "Many famous women, and many more unknown and forgotten, have been before me, making the path smooth, and regulating my steps" ("Professions" 227).

Understanding how these nineteenth-century authors "cut the road" is the overall objective of this book. More specifically, *Women and Literary Celebrity in the Nineteenth Century* suggests that in the construction and embodiment of fictional author-characters, actual writers exploited the idea of celebrity to reconstitute the terms of both professional success and of the meanings attached to gender and sex. In this telling of stories, this "lying to succeed," these authors were able to create new modalities of expression, demonstrating, as Grosz suggests, that though we are entwined in various networks of power, never are we rendered "merely passive and compliant" (147).

Centered on representations of famous author-characters, this book spans American and British publications and cover a time period from roughly 1850 to 1900. *Women and Literary Celebrity in the Nineteenth Century* thus analyzes texts produced within an historical moment in which remunerated writing became an occupation for women that could, in turn, give rise to celebrity. As Weber notes in *Hired Pens*, the mid-nineteenth century witnessed the emergence of a number of American periodicals that offered new authors, many of them women, a shot at a literary livelihood and celebrity. It is also in this second half of the nineteenth century with the 1848 Declaration of Sentiments and the rising abolition and suffrage movements, that a visible American feminism found its voice. These American social justice campaigns joined consolidated women-led crusades in England to dispute all manner of social ills, from slavery to disenfranchisement to the Contagious Diseases Acts, thus furthering a rich transatlantic network that bolstered feminist consciousness raising and women's visibility.

I have selected texts less because they were generated by famous authors, though many of the authors considered here were quite famous in their own lifetimes, than because their discursive treatment of fame provides a perspective through which to reconsider and expand a nineteenth-century sense of women's "natural" abilities. Specifically, I offer close readings of Fanny Fern's newspaper columns as well as her novel *Ruth Hall* (1855), Elizabeth Gaskell's *The Life of Charlotte Brontë* (1857), Eliza Potter's *A Hair-dresser's Experience in High Life* (1858), Elizabeth Keckley's *Behind the Scenes, or, Thirty Years a Slave and Four Years in the White House* (1868), Rhoda Broughton's *A Beginner* (1894), Elizabeth Robins's *George Mandeville's Husband* (1894), Mary Cholmondeley's

Red Pottage (1899), and Margaret Oliphant's *The Autobiography* (1899). I supplement close readings with contemporary published responses and reviews, showing how periodicals like *The Ohio Farmer* joined with more august journals, such as *Blackwood's Edinburgh Magazine, The Athenaeum, Harper's Bazaar*, or *The Saturday Evening Post*, to perpetuate the codes through which gender and literary celebrity gained intelligibility.

Although the focus of my examination is primarily on these authors and their writings, many others merit extended discussion within the respective chapters of *Women and Literary Celebrity in the Nineteenth Century*, including English authors such as Rhoda Broughton, Harriet Martineau, Mona Caird, George Egerton, George Eliot, Elizabeth Barrett Browning, Mary Augusta Ward, Eliza Lynn Linton, Marie Corelli, and Sarah Grand, and American authors such as Gail Hamilton, Harriet Jacobs, Margaret Fuller, Grace Greenwood, Charlotte Forten Grimké, Harriet Beecher Stowe, Louisa May Alcott, and Augusta Jane Evans Wilson. I have allowed the content of their books to determine the attention I offer them in my book, privileging those texts, such as *Ruth Hall*, where successful authorship is the desired narrative outcome, over other writings such as Browning's *Aurora Leigh* (1856), Wilson's *St. Elmo* (1868), Grand's *The Beth Book* (1897), Jewett's *The Country of Pointed Firs* (1896), or Corelli's *The Murder of Delicia* (1896), where the narrative build for the writer-heroine is toward heterosexual union and marriage rather than success as marked by fame and career, the writer-protagonist story is drowned out by competing plot lines or commitments to regional description, or the author-character begins the novel famous and ends it dead.[13]

Taken together, the books I analyze in depth represent a critical grouping of literary documents that use the representation of celebrity to de-stabilize Anglo-American prescriptive norms about gender in the last half of the nineteenth century. I don't mean to suggest that authors I examine necessarily engaged in this representational re-organization deliberately; rather I believe that the authors considered here made use of broader cultural memes about womanhood, visibility, professionalism, and literature, often putting concepts in a discursive ideological conflict that resulted in expanded codes of gender. The non-autobiographical relation of Fanny Fern to her creation, Ruth Hall, offers a good example of this productive tension. Fanny Fern (Sara Payson Willis Parton)[14] was an enthusiastic writer who sustained a literary career long after the state of her finances required

---

[13]   A number of better-known novels by male authors also feature interesting vignettes of professional women writers, such as George Gissing's *New Grub Street* (1891), Anthony Trollope's *The Way We Live Now* (1875), and Henry James' *Portrait of a Lady* (1882). All of these professional women writers function in minor roles, playing secondary and even tertiary parts relative to the ongoing direction of the narrative.

[14]   Nicole Tonkovich is a bit more thorough in her recounting of Fern's "real names," which, because of multiple marriages and deliberate changes of spelling, were: Grata Sara(h) Payson Willis Eldrege Farrington Parton. Fern also used the pseudonyms Tabitha and Olivia.

that she do so. She was immensely popular, read widely in both America and Britain, and, for a time, the highest paid journalist, male or female, of the mid- to late-nineteenth century, noting in her weekly columns that her passion for writing drove her to the pen daily. Fanny Fern, as both a once-desperate woman compelled to write and an enthusiastic and well-paid literary celebrity, is a richly nuanced and seemingly contradictory model for what it means to be a literary professional in the nineteenth century. The character she creates in her literary double Ruth Hall, however, contains little of this complexity. Fern represents Ruth as pious, good, generous and gracious, unambitious, and deeply troubled by her rising fame as authoress. Significantly, Ruth is delicate, frail, and sensitive, her body thin, her looks luminous. Ruth's complaint that no happy woman writes stems from the idea that her sadness and her poverty sprang from her dead husband's grave. Thus, tragedy gave birth to "Floy," Ruth's literary persona. Ruth contends that writing professionally is an occupation that only the most desperate of women will attempt, and then only after she has exhausted every other option for self-support. But since Ruth's ideas are voiced through the famous author Fanny Fern, most contemporary readers would surely have perceived Ruth's resignation as double-coded—the expressions of the sentimental heroine as amplified by the irascible, highly paid, immensely popular newspaper columnist, essayist, and novelist. Ruth as author-character thus provides a "corrective" version of the female literary celebrity, a fiction that embodies those precise virtues of humility and delicacy so highly prized as essential to hetero-normative notions of [white] race, [middle] class, and [feminine] gender.

The fictional Ruth and Floy are both foils, elaborately constructed authors designed to "charm" and "conciliate" rather than to incite public anxieties and curiosities. Importantly, they are concrete yet abstract textual bodies that serve as shield and decoy to the "real" author. This is not to suggest that the flesh and blood of the living author is any more "real" than the chimera of the fictional writer. Indeed, these representations, whether of character in fiction or of famous author in the cultural imaginary, circulate as similar currency; it is therefore not weeding the "unreal" from the "real" that concerns me, but working through gendered semiotic codes articulated through literary celebrity. Indeed, the workings of celebrity are critical since fame afforded these authors both a set of tools for tinkering with and a public platform for commenting upon their own visibility, and thus with the symbolic codings of "author" and "woman."

These codes reveal themselves through the bodies and behaviors of author-characters who are constructed as famous within the texts in which they function. The particular books I examine make visible several telling factors. Though all of the texts reference an ideal body type that is wan, white, and waiflike, not all of them contain author-characters who conform to this ideal. By creating strong, sympathetic protagonists who do not always reside comfortably in ideal bodies, the writers disallow the totalizing power of hegemonic ideologies of embodiment. Eliza Potter and Elizabeth Keckley, for example, underscore their identity as black women, choosing not to accentuate (or even mention) their "mulatta" complexions, and so resist a common sentimental trope that afforded sympathy to mixed-raced women. Elizabeth Robins's George Mandeville is obese, animalized, and obsessive, yet she clearly provides the indomitable energy that fuels the novel. Fanny Fern's many representations of the famous female author depict her in every register from sentimentally violet-strewing to unfashionably black-shod, but no matter the guise her personae adopt, the pen behind the portrait is resolved and intrepid. Elizabeth Gaskell's Charlotte Brontë is from the pale waif school, but hers is a physical delicacy punctuated with bursts of frenetic genius. Margaret Oliphant's writerly persona is old, sad, and humble, but one of the fiercest literary critics in all of England. Mary Cholmondeley's author-character Hester is pale and diminutive, but her thoughts and behavior are bold and decisive, suggesting a discordance between the sign of the weak female body and the strength it renders in the body of the text. These diverse embodiments interrupt essentializing narratives of the author that locate her as either largely frustrated, troubled, and neurotic and as white, middle to upper class, and heteronormative. Instead, they allow for a varied and finely nuanced spectrum, where the famous female author, like the woman herself, is allowed to occupy many potential roles and bodies. Such challenges forward social change, even if by inches, by displacing limiting designations, pluralizing legitimate possibilities for identity through the means of "self"-representation.

Through their depiction of bodies and behaviors, the authors I consider use celebrity as a means of making gender more performative. The strategy for doing so can be broadly generalized into three-parts. The first part of this strategy occurs through the representation of pluralization. One way that Fanny Fern throws off her critics (and her fans) is to flood the marketplace with images of herself, thus making it impossible to fully locate and contain her or her many personae. Augmenting this strategy is a second device that keeps a ready model of the "ideal" in place, a facade construction that allows for a perpetuation of the myth even as that myth is altered. Eliza Potter, for example, constantly critiques her white upper-class employers, suggesting quite baldly that they are social climbers and hypocrites, but she never critiques the notion of the lady itself. The ladies are undone, but the category is not, thus raising the possibility that the category of lady (and its legitimating ideology) might expand to accommodate those who are more worthy rather than those who fit a particular racial or class-based type. These two strategies are, in turn, augmented by a third device that sustains the dialectics of dualism, even as representation allows the famous author-character to transcend the either/or binary imposed by duality. When Cholmondeley figures the textual product as a child, for instance, she reinforces a glorification of Victorian motherhood that assumes an incompatibility between professional work and motherhood, allowing the author-mother to fulfill her maternal obligation to a text-as-child. More broadly, the mutually exclusive dilemma that Ann Douglas Wood posed nearly thirty years ago, that "women writers wanted to have their cake and eat it too: to stay 'feminine' and write successful best sellers" (6), is no longer relevant in this third strategy since it positions professional success as critical to hegemonic femininity. For really, what's the point of having cake if you can't eat it?

In the texts featured here, the represented author-character, her body, and her fame are crucial to both the logic of the narrative and the ethos of the text. We cannot overlook these protagonist figures or disregard their professional status. They are insistent characters, women who earn money and hold professional public positions in the contested domain of the Victorian literary marketplace. They are women who demand to be seen. They are also, somewhat ironically, heroines in non-canonical texts by lesser-known writers—literary producers whom, in an historical sense, fame has largely forgotten. Of the books included here, Elizabeth Gaskell's *The Life of Charlotte Brontë*, and increasingly *Ruth Hall*, are perhaps the most widely known. None of the handful of women to whom posterity has ascribed greatness—Charlotte Brontë, George Eliot, Jane Austen, Emily Brontë—wrote texts that imagined and embodied the woman writer as a central character. Elizabeth Barrett Browning's epic poem *Aurora Leigh* (1856) comes closest, and indeed, many of the elements she lays out in her poem are picked up and developed in the works I examine, particularly a resistance to norms of the conventional.[15] Overall in this study, it is not the star who tells the story of her own fame, but the supporting actress watching from the wings of the stage who crafts the narrative of celebrity and gender.

Literary Celebrity and the Gender Trick of Fame

Celebrity is commonly theorized as the by-product of a twentieth- and twenty-first-century media-driven culture that inundates us with indiscriminate images of stars, thus allowing for consumer fetishization through fanzines, web sites, entertainment programming, celebrity talk shows, inside editions, etc. Graeme Turner has argued, for instance, that it is the constantly proliferating possibilities inherent in an ever-changing twentieth and twenty-first-century mediascape that have given rise to so many possibilities for, and so much obsession with, celebrity. Yet, in the centuries before our own, celebrity was experienced with no lesser intensity. Ghislaine McDayter notes, for instance, that in the early nineteenth century, Byromania swept through England, generating the sort of fan hysteria commonly associated with the Beatles or Elvis (2). In mid-nineteenth century America, Henry Ward Beecher of the famous Beecher family preached twice each Sunday to standing-room-only crowds of 3,000 people (Applegate 4). The aspirational fantasies and cautionary tales that rely on notions of fame found shape and intelligibility long before the rise of moving images and mass mediation.

The gendered dynamics of fame are critical in determining the cultural work performed by notoriety, particularly since gender is so infrequently considered as an important modality in the theorization of celebrity. As Claire Brock notes, it is

---

[15] For an excellent reading of the American poetic response to and adaptation of Browning's *Aurora Leigh*, see Mary Loeffelholz, "Mapping the Cultural Field."

a "critical commonplace" to trace out the phenomenon of fame only in relation
to men. "Women have been relegated to occasional footnotes in the history of
fame," Brock observes, even when in practice women in both an eighteenth and
nineteenth-century context dominated literary production (1). Though academic
studies of fame and celebrity sometimes acknowledge the absence of women,
they quite often leave it at that, perpetuating a reading of "great men" that only
minimally considers the social construction of gender, be it either masculinity or
femininity, particularly in the nineteenth century.[16] One must move to the early
twentieth century and the advent of moving pictures, before discussions on
celebrity and gender take hold.[17] In this respect, *Women and Literary Celebrity
in the Nineteenth Century* can be considered a prequel of sorts to the fine work
on women and celebrity in early Hollywood offered by such scholars as Marsha
Orgeron, Mary Desjardin, Diane Negra, Jennifer Bean, and Amelie Hastie.

In this study, I am interested in how women negotiated (and modified) gender
imperatives through the representation of fame. Since the nineteenth century
offered a marked rise in opportunities for women to occupy public and celebrated
positions, particularly through authorship, the question is not: were women
famous; they most certainly were and in growing numbers. The question is: how
did celebrity offer a conceptual tool for reworking the meanings of gender in
a transatlantic context? Fame for women could be vexed. Alison Booth argues
that "negative modeling" often positioned famous women in ways that heighted
the "proximity between fame and vice," thus underscoring a "suspicion of
female fame," even as fame functioned as a tautology that made its possessor
seemingly deserving of attention and accolades (*How to Make it as a Woman* 68).
As many historical and biographical accounts make clear, public visibility
for women in the nineteenth century could itself be a gender-problematizing
phenomenon. Ellen Rosenman and Claudia Klaver note, for instance, that the
professional woman writer "circulated her name in public, a form of visibility
that could also be pathologized as indecent, akin to the physical display of
actresses and prostitutes" (5–6). A prevailing truism indicated that no "decent"
woman occupied (or desired) a publicly visible position, leading to what Virginia
Woolf critiqued in 1929 as a culture of shame where important women veiled
themselves and their talents due to a misguided notion that "publicity for women

---

[16]   There are many helpful studies on fame and celebrity, including Leo Braudy's *The
Frenzy of Renown*, Richard Dyer's *Stars* and *Heavenly Bodies*, P. David Marshall's *Celebrity
and Power*, Frank Donoghue's *The Fame Machine*, and Joshua Gamson's *Claims to Fame*.
Gamson notes in a parenthetical statement, "(Women, almost entirely excluded from public
life, were also excluded from this early mythology of public greatness)" (19). For specific
discussions on literary celebrity, see early chapters of Joe Moran's *Star Authors* and Loren
Daniel Glass's *Author's Inc.*, as well as Philip Waller's *Writers, Readers, and Reputations*
and John Rodden's analysis of George Orwell in *The Politics of Literary Reputation*.

[17]   Although not on celebrity, per se, there is much fine scholarship on gender and
genius. See Alison Booth's *Engendering Greatness* and Christine Battersby's *Gender
and Genius*.

is detestable" (*A Room of One's Own* 65). Or, as Dorothy Mermin phrases it, "for women, all fame was ill fame" (18).[18]

The Victorian bias against literary celebrity for women was potent, as evidenced in just one case by the Poet Laureate Robert Southey's advice to Charlotte Brontë that "literature cannot be the business of a woman's life, and it ought not to be" since it will fill her mind with daydreams that make her unfit for her domestic duties (Gaskell *Life* 102).[19] Southey encouraged Brontë to continue writing, but for its own sake, "not with a view to celebrity" or career (Gaskell *Life* 103). Within such a prescriptive ideological system, the question then became: how is it possible to claim fame, which, by definition indicates a position of prominence and visibility, in the midst of gendered imperatives that mandate modesty, privacy, and humility?

Brontë's solution was to be all things: domestic and devoted as well as artistic and passionate. She responded to Southey, "You do not forbid me to write....you only warn me against the folly of neglecting real duties" (Gaskell *Life* 104). Brontë reasoned that as long as she fulfilled her domestic obligations and eschewed desires for public fame, she could circumvent a gendered mandate that she shrink into the shadows. "I shall never more feel ambitious to see my name in print," she assured Southey (Gaskell *Life* 104). Since as Lucasta Miller observes, "Charlotte's early ambition was not merely to write but 'to be for ever known,'" we can only assume that Brontë's response to Southey, in Virginia Woolf's parlance, told lies to succeed (3). The consequence of her actions, as with the other authors considered in this book, was to perform what Ruth Bernard Yeazell has termed "fictions of modesty" even as Brontë worked to develop a craft that would give her lasting visibility.

By altering a public understanding of gender through the discursive management of self/persona/character that celebrity made possible and indeed required, the authors and texts I examine here work to assure that the "true woman" would be pious, pure, submissive, and domestic (Welter 6). These authors also, however, complicate such simple categories, suggesting that the version of white middle- to upper-class privilege encoded into the true woman ideology could no longer automatically exclude women of color, women of excess, women who love women, women who work for a living, or women who seek and possess fame. Elizabeth Gaskell, for instance, dismantles the ideology of the "true woman," only to rebuild it so that genius and poetic fire figure prominently in her construction of

---

[18] Mermin ends her chapter titled "Travels, Trials, Fame" with the optimistic, though briefly argued, statement that, "In fact fame proved no worse for women than for men." Exempting those with "less exalted reputations and more scandalous private lives," Mermin contends, "women of genius could achieve fame and escape its penalties" (39). The elaborate representational politics I address in this book whereby women authors created famous author-characters who worked to situate the meanings of their fame in relation to their gender, suggest that Mermin's optimistic conclusions about fame for literary women in the mid-nineteenth century were somewhat premature.

[19] For greater discussion on the tensions between authorship/artistry and gender mandates, see Mary Poovey's *The Proper Lady and the Woman Writer*, Mary Kelley's *Private Woman, Public Stage*, and Anne E. Boyd's *Writing for Immortality*.

the famous Charlotte Brontë; for Elizabeth Keckley, it becomes not only possible but self-evident that a black woman who works for her living can be more of a lady than the famous First Lady of the land. These texts do not overtly suggest the Cult of True Womanhood is bankrupt. Far from it. They undergird it, play it up, speak on its behalf, and in so doing, the authors claim for themselves and their characters the right of expertise and celebrity. These writings thus perform what Grosz has identified as "modes of guerilla subversion of patriarchal codes" by surreptitiously undoing the rigid logic behind those codes and replacing them with more fluid possibilities (144). As such, these texts, and their authors through them, become interpreters of ideology. And since to transmit a story can often yield the power to determine its meaning, literary invention in this case serves as cultural intervention.

A final note in this section on terminology. Thus far, I have referenced fame and celebrity as synonymous terms, but it is helpful to parse out their meanings a bit more since the scholarly study of fame and celebrity largely considers the words to hold vastly different meanings. Leo Braudy, for instance, considers fame to be the reward offered to those who perform great and wonderful deeds (like walking on the moon or becoming a political leader); celebrity, by contrast, indicates the flash-in-the-pan personalities who entertain us for a short period of time but ultimately sink into obscurity (see also Turner 2010). In this nomenclature, fame stands for the high, celebrity for the low. Fame marks aspiration; celebrity brands ambition. Fame indicates valor; celebrity stains scandal. And, since the machinery of fame is often the elite masculinist theatre of politics, war, and heroism, whereas the workings of celebrity often engage with the feminized domains of rumor and innuendo, the divide between fame and celebrity clearly conveys both classed and gendered distinctions. In this book as well as in my other published work that analyze fame and celebrity, unless the materials I am discussing are specific in their understanding and references, I deliberately move back and forth between the terms fame and celebrity so as to problematize the gender bias that stands at the heart of the fame/celebrity distinction. Also, as a sheer matter of pragmatics, it seems to me that the difference between fame and celebrity is rather porous, since it is not always clear what constitutes the legendary stuff of fame as distinct from the momentary fluff of celebrity. Indeed, in the nineteenth-century materials that I analyze here, fame and celebrity are equally pejorative terms for women, and so it is not always the distinction between fame and celebrity that is most at stake in these texts but how one came by her fame/celebrity. As I've noted, particularly for women, fame could be had but it should not be sought. If a woman were passive in her celebrity (it simply came to her without her bidding), she could be forgiven her fame. But if she schemed and plotted to achieve her fame, the avarice for celebrity was a scathing social stigma.[20]

---

[20]   For more on "reluctant celebrity" and the social punishment that meets women who too actively court their own fame in both a nineteenth-century and contemporary context, see Weber, "Always Lonely: Celebrity, Motherhood, and the Dilemma of Destiny."

Complicating Ontologies: A Transatlantic Approach

In September 1890, the British humor and politics magazine *Punch* ran a poem and cartoon, titled "The American Girl." The piece carried no identifying information about its author or artist but is attributed to "an American Correspondent of *The Galignani Messenger*" who is "very severe on the matters of his fair countrywomen."[21] The satiric piece catalogues the flaws and failings of a certain breed of anonymous American woman, here lifted into stereotype as the American Girl. She is vain, gaudily dressed, yellow-haired (suspiciously as the consequence of dye), nouveau riche, a bit garish, and apparently suffering from Attention Deficit Disorder ("She did Rome in a swift two days, gave half the time to Venice, But vows that she saw everything, although in awful haste"). She speaks with an "alarming" accent and is so superbly "dediamonded" that one "scarce can see her fingers for the multitude of rings." The American Girl is set on snaring for herself a titled husband, an intent underscored by the image of her in profile, looking determined as she carries a parasol, the shaft and handle of which are a club. The parasol's decorative pom-poms are a ball and chain. While the attribution for "The American Girl" cartoon is not certain, its image and tone fit fully within the trope of representation established over decades of publishing in *Punch*, as led by the drawings of George du Maurier (author of *Trilby*, 1894). Writes Marion Harry Spielmann in his 1895 history of *Punch*, "[du Maurier's] misrepresentation of that divinity – the American Girl – is beyond all hope of pardon, beyond contrition, beyond all penance. He does full justice to her refined and splendid loveliness and her magnificent proportions; but he seems to regard her, if one may say so, as a sort of Kensington-Town-Hall-Subscription-Dance young lady, a little more outré and free and slangy and vulgar" (511). Clearly, the American Girl faced an image problem redolent with class and gender violations, and her celebrity only served to exacerbate these issues.

Punch itself tells us much about celebrity. Founded in London in 1841 by Henry Mayhew and Joseph Stirling Coyne, *Punch* functioned as a veritable icon of Victorian culture that spread far beyond British readers. *Punch*'s circulation figures would vacillate throughout its existence in the nineteenth and twentieth centuries, yet it dominated the Victorian literary world in prominence and popularity, no doubt aided in the 1840s through the editorship of Charles Dickens when its circulation peaked to 175,000. Historian Richard Altick writes, "To judge from the number of references to it in the private letters and memoirs of the 1840s, *Punch* had become a household word within a year or two of its founding, beginning in the middle class and soon reaching the pinnacle of society, royalty itself" (*Punch* 17).

---

[21] Established in 1814 by Giovanni Antonio Galignani, *The Galignani Messenger* was a daily paper founded by an Italian, based in France, published in English, and dedicated to creating good will between England and France. In 1884, the Galignani family sold controlling interest in the paper, and from that time until 1904, when it went fully out of print, the paper was known as *The Daily Messenger*.

THE AMERICAN GIRL.

[An American Correspondent of *The Galignani Messenger* is very severe on the manners of his fair countrywomen.]

She " guesses " and she " calculates," she wears all sorts o' collars,
  Her yellow hair is not without suspicion of a dye; 
    Her " Pàppa " is a dull old man who turned pork into dollars.
    But everyone admits that she's indubitably spry.

    She did Rome in a swift two days, gave half the time to Venice,
    But vows that she saw everything, although in awful haste;
    She's fond of dancing, but she seems to fight shy of lawn-tennis,
    Because it might endanger the proportions of her waist.

    Her manner might be well defined as elegantly skittish;
She loves a Lord as only a Republican can do;
And quite the best of titles she's persuaded are the British,
  And well she knows the Peerage, for she reads it through and
    through.

She's bediamonded superbly, and shines like a constellation,
  You scarce can see her fingers for the multitude of rings;
She's just a shade too conscious, so it seems, of admiration,
  With irritating tendencies to wriggle when she sings.

She owns she is " Amur'can," and her accent is alarming;
  Her birthplace has an awful name you pray you may forget;
Yet, after all, we own " *La Belle Américaine* " is charming,
  So let us hope she'll win at last her long-sought coronet.

Fig. I.2   "The American Girl." *Punch*. September 20, 1890, 136.

Altick notes that soon after its launch, "Punch vaunted its international circulation" and was recognized and read across the Atlantic world, assisted by a large cadre of Anglo-American literary celebrities, such as Elizabeth Gaskell, Elizabeth Barrett Browning, Charlotte Brontë, Henry Wadsworth Longfellow, and Ralph Waldo Emerson, who referenced the ongoing caricatures and political intrigues featured in the magazine in their own writings (*Punch* 22, 24–9). As such, *Punch* carried its own form of transatlantic literary celebrity and offers a helpful illustration of the international flow that is endemic to fame since a periodical so coded with British-ness conveyed meanings and messages to many foreign lands (a geography sometimes never so foreign as its own home soil).

Due to its prominence within *Punch*'s pages and its citation of an embodiment of femininity that codes as gauche and unrefined, "The American Girl" cartoon in many ways serves as emblem for the transatlantic meanings of gender and celebrity that guide my analysis in this book since *Punch*'s satire suggests how fully gender is inculcated into representation. Prescriptive gender codes are, of course, important indicators of nationalized ideologies. And so here, *Punch*'s satire of the American Girl tacitly calls forth a better kind of non-American girl who is refined, cultivated, and elegant. It would be an error to assume, however, that the "better" girl is an actual English lass, for *Punch*'s pages suggest that British women were also targets for public scolding and redirection. Indeed, it is safe to assume that the "better" girl is not nationalized or "natural," in that she doesn't exist without specific crafting through the disciplinary gendered discourses provided, in this case, by nineteenth-century social media. Carried through the transatlantic auspices of the British *Punch*, this critique of the American Girl (perhaps created by a French artist) stands in for English commentary on the United States and instantiates a code of gender that is both dependent on national difference and seemingly transcendent to these distinctions. For certainly, the point of this "severe" assessment of American women by her "countryman" is not to put a different national female body in her place but to force a disjunction between material bodies and represented ideals that can never be reconciled. This dislocation between the real and the imagined, between the normal and the normative, between the anonymous/actual and the conspicuous/imagined is precisely the North Star from which gender and celebrity take their bearings. For as I note throughout this book, it is not the "real" person but the "idea" of a person that animates the salience of celebrity, and it is not "real" gender as enacted in a socio-historical context but prescribed gender as inculcated through such print materials as "The American Girl" that provide the evidence through which to read for the presence of ideology in the politics of representation.[22]

---

[22] Alexis Easley makes a compelling argument in *Literary Celebrity, Gender, and Victorian Authorship* that the intense British fascination with literary celebrity after 1850 performed the cultural work of bringing "coherence and meaning to modern experience" by "recovering a unified British national culture," a task, she notes, that was "inherently unattainable" and so "always incomplete and unfulfilled" (21). Drawing from a rich trove

Although "transatlantic" is a broad term that encompasses the transnational and international history of the Atlantic world, in this study I primarily examine Anglo-American materials and relationships due to the tight network that existed between the United States and Great Britain in literary production, distribution, and consumption.[23] To chart the workings of Anglo-American celebrity and its relation to gender, I examine works produced by both U.S. and British women and materials written about those authors and their writings in U.S. and British encyclopedias, biographies, journals, magazines, and newspapers. Yet, as I suggest at the beginning of this section through the cartoon of "The American Girl," Anglo-American as a term insufficiently suggests the scope of my archive since neither writers nor readers were necessarily confined to the respective national geographies in which they were born, lived, worked, or claimed citizenship. And certainly, the cultural product—the novel, the poem, the written idea—potentially travelled a broad international journey that helped create the pedagogies that made celebrity recognizable and gender meaningful. For my purposes, then, the "transatlantic" indicates the specifics of both nation and geography, but it also references a metaphoric epistemology that Daphne Brooks has termed a "transatlantic imaginary" that functions as a "lively cultural space owing less to geographical cartography and more to the landscape of popular culture" (7).

There are other compelling reasons to adopt a transatlantic frame in the study of gender and celebrity. As in our own moment, national divisions did not tightly

---

of evidence, Easley writes, "the cult of literary celebrity" allowed for a simultaneous synthesis and distortion of "national ideals and cultural anxieties," mapped out through the concomitant idealization of celebrity and codification of a canon of English literature (195–6). While Easley sees these practices as primarily illustrative of British ideas of the nation, I believe that the figure of the celebrity, the hegemonic codes of gender, and the geographic reach of literary products exceeded the nation-state boundaries of either the UK or the US, thus calling for an interstitial approach that can account for the flow and contradiction of both ideology and discourse.

[23]   For more on the meanings of transatlanticism in particular reference to literary studies, see Kevin Hutchings and Julia M. Wright, eds., *Transatlantic Literary Exchanges, 1790–1870*; Meredith L. McGill, ed., *The Traffic in Poems*; Joselyn M. Almeida, *Reimagining the Transatlantic, 1780–1890*; Sigrid Anderson Cordell, *Fictions of Dissent*; Anna Brickhouse, *Transamerican Literary Relations and the Nineteenth-Century Public Sphere*; Susan Manning and Andrew Taylor, eds., *Transatlantic Literary Studies, A Reader*; Philip Schwyzer, *Archipelagic Identities: Literature and Identity in the Atlantic Archipelago, 1550–1800*; Beth L. Lueck, Brigitte Bailey, and Lucinda L. Damon-Bach, eds., *Transatlantic Women*. In claiming an Anglo-American lens, I'm aware of reminders from such scholars as Joselyn Almeida and Kirsten Gruesz that it is not only the United States or English-speaking peoples that inform scholars about the meanings of America or Americanness. As Gruesz cautions, "Part of what has been repressed in the United States is its location within a hemisphere also known as America (or, to inflect it with an appropriate Spanishness, América), a name which has been appropriated synechdochically into itself" (10). I default to the use of America to designate the United States primarily because the nineteenth-century texts I'm examining used such terminology.

bind authors, readers, and texts in the nineteenth century, and so to study them through imposed state boundaries often creates a too-tidy fiction of their separation. This is not to say, however, that differences in national character were not thought to exist in the nineteenth century. The United States and Britain were very much divided in their political policies and public identities, the former standing for (even if not always meting out) meritocratic egalitarianism, the latter indexing a hide-bound traditionalism and severe class division that created what Benjamin Disraeli termed "the two nations" (*Sybil* 1845).[24] The United States and Britain also held very different investments in terms of democratic rights to privacy and autonomy, though these differences manifested more for white, land-holding male citizens (eligible for civic entitlements such as the vote) than they necessarily did for subaltern subjects, such as women and people of color, who were blocked from participation in the credos of egalitarianism.

Indeed, it is largely due to the fact that my work is so indebted to the social history of women's uplift and feminist consciousness that I flatten specific national differences between the United States and the United Kingdom in order to engage with commonalities that expressed themselves through tacit ideological imperatives about gender. Again, "The American Girl" illustrates this point nicely, since its critique denigrates a certain breed of American women while tacitly referencing an ideal of womanhood that is without specific national affiliation. While many other portraits would depict both American and/or British women as the zenith or the nadir of womanhood (depending on what sort of contrastive bad model were evoked), these glorified portraits established a fictional hegemonic ideal that was both compelling and coercive. Indeed, my study could well be understood as how a set of literary practitioners fought fire (the representation of famous women as "unsexed") with fire (the counter-representation of famous women as the epitome of womanhood).

The need for a transatlantic reading is particularly insistent in the context of the complex relationship between the United States and the United Kingdom, which, as Janet Beer and Bridget Bennett contend, has been historically sutured through equal parts amity and antagonism. Largely due to a shared language and assumed sense of common heritage as well as a publishing and circulation network that trafficked in similar notions of the bestseller and the cultural masterpiece, even as it made distinctions between American and British tastes, the literary legacies of Britain and America are forever entwined, particularly when in antagonism. Kevin Hutchings and Julia M. Wright observe in their introduction to *Transatlantic Literary Exchanges* that beginning in the early nineteenth century, Britain and the U.S. engaged in a fierce rivalry over the respective value of their national literatures. Americans, claimed Sidney Smith writing for *The Edinburgh Review* in 1820, had "produced nothing worthy of lasting fame 'their chief boast for many

---

[24] Novelist/politician Benjamin Disraeli was not the first to coin this idea. It appears in print almost simultaneously in Friederich Engels's *The Condition of the Working Class in England* (1844), as well as in earlier publications, including those by Plato.

generations to come, that they are sprung from the same race with Bacon and Shakespeare and Newton'" (qtd. in Hutchings and Wright 3). Americans, on the other hand, lambasted the British as being old-fashioned and unmodern. On either side, national literary value was marked by fame and those literary masterpieces cited as evidence of national superiority were produced by men. While both British and American women far outsold their male contemporaries and earned through their labors significant celebrity, their writings were often denigrated as public pablum rather than venerated as national treasures. As I discuss throughout this book, these gendered biases about aesthetics, canonization, and what constitutes genius are at the very heart of a discussion on women and celebrity, since all of these defining features of value factor differently when women occupy the figure of fame.

It is not only the enmeshed relationship between gender and aesthetics that calls for a transatlantic reading but the practices of cultural producers and readers that makes such a frame relevant. We know, for instance, that Charlotte Brontë and Elizabeth Gaskell read and admired *Uncle Tom's Cabin*, and indeed, such recent academic contributions as *Transatlantic Stowe* trenchantly demonstrate the degree to which neither Harriet Beecher Stowe nor *Uncle Tom's Cabin* can be adequately understood if focalized exclusively through an American literary and historical lens. Equally, American authors such as Louisa May Alcott and Charlotte Forten Grimké were deeply moved by *The Life of Charlotte Brontë*. Grimké wrote in her journal that she found Gaskell's portrait "very beautifully written, and, of course, deeply interesting. There is in it a portrait of Charlotte, a noble face – which the light of the soul beautifies. Just such a face as one might imagine in Jane Eyre's" (220).[25] The transatlantic fascination with all of the Brontë sisters helped further the literary reputations and fill the coffers of those authors who attached their names to the Brontës' collective and individual works. Mrs. Humphry Ward, for instance, wrote the preface to the Haworth Edition of the Brontës' novels (published 1899–1900), earning for herself £1,000 in royalties, 400 guineas of which came from American sales (Sutherland 231).

Travel and migration altered many of the national voices that any one author might have evinced, as, for instance, in the case of Elizabeth Robins, who was born in Louisville, Kentucky but moved to London, England in her thirties, while sustaining a dynamic career where she was recognized on both sides of the Atlantic as an actress, novelist, journalist, travel writer, and suffragette. Many other authors, like Harriet Beecher Stowe and Grace Greenwood, also traveled widely in England and Europe; and, as Jennifer Cognard-Black notes, American

---

[25] In *Women, Celebrity, and Literary Culture Between the Wars*, Fay Hammill pursues this fuzzy relation between character and author in an early–twentieth-century context where literary celebrities and silent film stars negotiated the terms of the same fame-making apparatus. Such literary stars as Lucy Maud Montgomery (*Anne of Green Gables*) and Anita Loos (*Gentlemen Prefer Blondes*), Hammill argues, adopted personal styles that mirrored their famous heroines, Anne Shirley and Lorelei Lee.

authors like Stowe and Elizabeth Stuart Phelps had intense, even mentoring, relationships with such English authors as George Eliot and Elizabeth Barrett Browning. Anne E. Boyd argues that several American authors, such as Louisa May Alcott, drew material from their travels abroad, feeling that the culture of Europe lent an artistic validity to their work.[26] In like manner, the "untamed" spaces and stories of America figured as a great untapped land of narrative, filled with all manner of curious characters to satisfy English and European curiosities for the exotic and rustic. If such literal and metaphoric travel sometimes reified differences between English and American temperaments and sensibilities, it also effaced clear separations between producer, product, and audience, since, even in the context of lax copyright regulations, English and European readers offered a significant corollary market to American authors (and vice versa).

Celebrity factored critically into this transatlantic flow. As my use of Anglo-American newspapers and periodicals makes clear, cultural production and literary celebrity were recognized (and created) on both sides of the Atlantic. The constant flow of texts and authors back and forth across the Atlantic suggests that a form of cross-pollination was inevitable. As Amanda Claybaugh reminds us, "Nineteenth-century novelists and critics took for granted what present-day scholars have only recently begun to acknowledge: that the literatures of Great Britain and the United States should not be read in isolation from one another" (440).[27] Visits between authors—such as Margaret Fuller's meeting with Harriet Martineau—paved the way for a larger recognition of and saliency to the female literary professional, each woman offering legitimacy and increased visibility to the other.

Since so many scholars have argued that national identities are seldom wholly coherent but often emerge from the demand for clear distinctions between (national) self and (colonial) other, it is also important to ask just what it means to write within a national tradition. In delineating a national canon, this practice becomes even more problematic. As scholars from Gerald Graff to Robert Crawford to Gauri Viswanathan adeptly show, the very notion of a literary canon emerges from the belief that cultural hierarchies are apolitically formed in accord with norms of common sense and intrinsic aesthetic properties.[28] Instead, as Graff notes, literary texts "are not neutral principles of organization, but agents that transform the cultural and literary-critical 'ism' fed into them, often to the point of subverting their original purpose, or so deflecting them that they become unrecognizable

---

[26] In *Private Sphere to World Stage from Austen to Eliot*, Elizabeth Sabiston has juxtaposed Harriet Beecher Stowe against Elizabeth Gaskell, feeling that the lives and writing of one illuminates the other.

[27] Claybaugh does address, however, a nineteenth-century preoccupation with "British preeminence" announced through a sort of deafening silence. She notes, "literary reviews … devoted little or no space to works by American or Canadian authors" (440).

[28] For more on the necessity of adopting transatlantic considerations, see Lawrence Buell, "Rethinking Anglo-American Literary History"; Paul Giles, *Virtual Americas*; Susan Manning, *Fragments of Union*; Christopher Mulvey, *Transatlantic Manners*; and Robert Weisbuch, *Atlantic Double-Cross*.

to outsiders" (5). Given this contested ground, moving between the borders of British and U.S. literatures interrogates scholarly positionality, thus exposing issues of textual agency and authority in a way that foregrounds literature's connection to practice and ideology without entirely reducing literature to either of these. Such is a position borne out by other transatlantic scholars including Stephen Greenblatt and Giles Gunn, who argue that redrawing lines of analysis "remind[s] us that literature is not something given once and for all but something constructed and reconstructed, the product of shifting conceptual entitlements and limits" (5).[29] Greenblatt and Gunn also argue that remapping the traditional boundaries of literature allows scholars to recognize and articulate important ontological questions: Of what material are disciplinary maps made? On what principles are they based? Who makes and maintains them? What institutions and practices do they serve? (3). And, of course, what sorts of gendered investments are at stake in the production of literary texts and celebrated personae?

In addition to these points, there are important symbolic and historical reasons for not adhering to the separatist tradition of cordoning off the work of American from British writers. As feminists have clearly demonstrated, a masculinist rendering of history has long characterized the past as being largely about political, economic and military skirmishes that resulted in revised ruling boundaries, bodies, and practices, and as I've already suggested, these masculinist values link to cultural norms about value (and hence fame). The formidable work of women historians from Gerda Lerner to Linda Kerber to Joan Scott demonstrates that prior to the second wave of feminism in the 1960s, history was "rigidly limited. It paid little attention to social relationships, to issues of race, to the concerns of the poor, and virtually none to women" (Kerber 1). Considering alternative narratives, then, also helps complicate other perceptual domains, for, as Jennifer DeVere Brody points out, a "reconfigured genealogy," that challenges the "discrete boundaries between 'Victorian' and 'African American' or 'Black' studies," reveals what historical memory often glosses over (6–7). This, in turn, authorizes new possibilities for contiguity, so that national distinctions become not impermeable divisions but arbitrary concepts that reveal the "tenuousness of … sociopolitical, ideological, and even economic boundaries" (Brody 7). Claybaugh notes that issues of social reform such as abolition, temperance, suffragism, and world peace—issues, not incidentally, that gave women opportunities for collective consciousness building, argument making, and speech giving—"point to the need for a transatlanticism that is as attentive to the connections across national boundaries as to the differences between nations …" (439). In this study of gender and the literary marketplace as expressed through the polyvalent representations of celebrity, it seems equally appropriate to look to both sides of the Atlantic.

---

[29]   Meredith L. McGill argues that even in the context of this new interest in transatlantic scholarship, "it would be hard to underestimate the power of the idea of a national literature over the discipline of literary study, structuring as it still does undergraduate instruction, graduate training, and professional formation" (2).

In sum, all of these points reinforce Alison Booth's contention that the traffic in nineteenth-century "Anglophone discourses was all-encompassing, far beyond such well-publicized visits as Dickens's to America" (qtd. in Rosenman "Gender Studies"). An informed scholarship that hopes to trace these discourses, then, must cut across and blur national boundaries.

As I have noted, particularly at mid-century onward with what has been called the first generation of the feminist wave, women took a more active and often militant role in carving out rights, responsibilities, and roles for themselves. Indeed, Bonnie Anderson's work on emergent feminist collectivities in the nineteenth century demonstrates the manner in which feminist change functioned in transatlantic and even global ways, since early feminists "considered themselves to be joined in working toward a universal cause" (2).[30] Meredith McGill eloquently reinforces this point when she notes the "importance of women to a transatlantic history of nineteenth-century" literature and poetry (3). The ongoing "civic disenfranchisement of women in a period in which the right to vote was gradually extended to unpropertied and non-white men," McGill reminds us, "made literature a particularly charged site for women's critiques of stage policies" (3–4). The texts I consider are aware of and in great degree converse with a larger mandate for improved conditions for women. From finance to physiology to enfranchisement, women demanded a say in the governance of their own lives, and they were sustained in their efforts for change by complex communities within and between national entities, particularly in the production and consumption of cultural materials.[31]

The Figures of *Women and Literary Celebrity in the Nineteenth Century*

For both British and American authors and audiences, Charlotte Brontë's life and career stood as the touchstone for what it meant to be a famous woman in the Victorian period. Though Brontë herself published no extended piece commenting on her fame or profession, much was written about Brontë, both in her own lifetime and after her death (continuing to the present day). Charlotte Brontë is thus critical to the transatlantic concepts of fame and femininity, of gender and genius, that are negotiated by the authors of *Women and Literary Celebrity in the Nineteenth Century*. As a consequence, Brontë figures prominently throughout this book, in particular in the first three chapters. The materials analyzed in these chapters respond to (and help create) the myth of "Charlotte," each devising different rationales to accommodate and expand the perceived anomaly of famous female genius. I put "Charlotte" in quotes to underscore her discursive construction; these texts refer not to the biography of Charlotte Brontë, but to fame and gender as expressed through the idea of Charlotte. The first three chapters consequently make

---

[30] See also Margaret H. McFadden, *Golden Cables of Sympathy*.

[31] Martha Vicinus offers an illuminating history of women's intimacy in a transatlantic context in *Intimate Friends*.

Fig. I.3   *Days With the Great Writers*, 1911. Author's collection.

clear that Charlotte Brontë is often evoked as a reference point for gendering fame and authorship. The writers in these chapters do not all focus on Brontë equally, but each of them uses the figure of Charlotte Brontë as a key to discussions on literary celebrity and artistic genius.

It is worth asking why Charlotte Brontë should be the touchstone. Why Charlotte, rather than some other august woman writer such as George Eliot, Jane Austen, Harriet Beecher Stowe, or either of the other Brontë sisters? Although it is true that George Eliot makes a fair number of appearances in nineteenth-century references to famous woman authors, the discursive Charlotte clearly held a greater popular fascination than these other authors, a trope Patsy Stoneman adeptly maps in *Brontë Transformations* and Lucasta Miller persuasively supports in *The Brontë Myth*. One reason for Charlotte's iconicity is surely due to the fact that her talent inspires, but her life can be represented as tragic but ordinary. In addition to her compelling life story, Charlotte's writings also play upon the heart, whereas Eliot's novels were considered exercises for the intellect. Elaine Showalter speculates that Charlotte's membership in a sisterly triumvirate further heightened her appeal, particularly to American women, whose feelings for Charlotte were "intimate, sisterly, and affectionate" ("English Fruits"). As just one example of a transatlantic and transracial affective response to Charlotte, in the 1850s the African American Charlotte Forten Grimké reflected on the inspiration found in the story of Charlotte Brontë's life: "Poverty, illness; many other difficulties which would have seemed insurmountable to a less courageous spirit were nobly overcome by one, who was yet as gentle and loving as she was firm. Such a life inspires one with faith and hope and courage 'to *do* and to *endure*'" (220).

In a twenty-first century context, English author Julie Noble has dedicated *Talli's Secret* (2004), a novel for teenagers that has Charlotte's portrait on the front and is sold in the Brontë Parsonage Museum gift shop, to "everyone who knows what it is to struggle," and in her acknowledgements, she thanks, "Charlotte Brontë and her family, for having a dream and following it" (vii).[32] Not to be outdone, Japanese-American author Laura Joh Rowland, creator of the Sano Ichiro novels that popularize the samurai, writes Charlotte Brontë into a crime series, taking elements of Brontë's fiction, intermingling them with scenes from Brontë lore, and then throwing in a murder mystery. In *The Secret Adventure of Charlotte Brontë*, the character Charlotte goes to London to settle with her publisher the matter of her identity, as the historical Charlotte did, only to encounter a Byronic love

---

[32]   In truth, I myself am more than a little awed by what the Brontë sisters endured professionally. For instance, their initial money-making option of running a school was a complete failure. Though they had brochures printed to advertise their school, they never enrolled a single pupil. Their first book, the collected poems of Currer, Ellis, and Acton Bell, was self-published and sold only two copies. Charlotte's first novel, *The Professor*, was never published in her life time. In the Foreword to *Popular Nineteenth-Century American Women Writers and the Literary Marketplace*, Lisa West offers an important reminder relevant to the transatlantic literary marketplace: "[T]here were many more women (and men) aspiring to publish in nineteenth-century venues than there were successes" (ix).

interest, as Jane Eyre did, and then to switch genres altogether into a Nancy-Drew-meets-Sherlock-Holmes crime story.[33] For these reasons, as well as Charlotte's easy appropriation into the trope of Victorian decorous womanhood (something George Eliot's lifestyle and appearance resisted), Charlotte has been resourcefully reconstructed, and this dialogic energy, channeled through the cultural cachet of celebrity, allows for a re-inventing of the terms of gender and authorship.

Chapter 1 begins *Women and Literary Celebrity in the Nineteenth Century* by offering a close reading of Gaskell's *Life*, as augmented by contemporary transatlantic publications. Certainly the touchstone for all Brontë ruminations, Elizabeth Gaskell's *The Life of Charlotte Brontë* reclaims and reconstructs an author who had so taken the literary world by storm with her 1848 *Jane Eyre* and subsequent novels. Published two years after Charlotte's death in 1855, Gaskell's biography carefully crafted the author, transforming Charlotte from one of the "wild Brontë sisters of the moors," filled, as Matthew Arnold said, with "hunger, rebellion, and rage," to a more conventional, palatable, religious, and refined lady, worthy of respect and emulation. As Linda K. Hughes and Michael Lund note, Gaskell's portrait of Brontë provided a formative model that accommodated both the female writer and the sphere of domesticity (137). Gaskell's *Life* was for many years the definitive reflection on Charlotte, but a number of other biographical and reconstructive works were published between 1860 and 1901, making Charlotte Brontë one of the most frequently represented female figures of the Victorian period. In this chapter I argue, in opposition to other scholars, that regardless of what Gaskell's intention might have been, the effects of the publication of the biography were not primarily competition or redemption. Through her fictionalized Charlotte Brontë, Gaskell forms a model of literary celebrity that occupies the same (female) body as the genius writer, thus serving as an important legitimation of the "public woman," a term that can no longer exclusively indicate the actress or the prostitute.

Chapter 2 attends to Fanny Fern's discussion of her writing peers, showing that in the movement from biography to fiction—from Charlotte Brontë, through Gail Hamilton and Harriet Beecher Stowe, to the heroine of Fern's novel *Ruth Hall*—there is a collapse of the fictive and the real. Fern often used seemingly counter-intuitive ploys, such as calling the woman writer a "sort of monster," in order to mock popular stereotypes. By juxtaposing the ridiculous with the matter-of-fact while highlighting the physicality (and vulnerability) of the public woman's body, Fern leveraged new conceptual space for the famous author. This reconstituted sense of the woman of celebrity allowed her to be imagined in a more diverse

---

[33]   Much like Jane Austen, Charlotte Brontë reigns supreme in a twenty-first-century world of spin-offs and fan fiction that feature her or her characters in new genres, settings, and situations. My particular favorite: Michael Thomas Ford's series of novels about Jane Austen as vampire, nefariously turned to the cause by fellow author and vampire Lord Byron, and competing violently against the evil, deranged—and also a vampire—Charlotte Brontë.

register than typically accorded middle-class women (white or of color). In Fern's styling, the "sort of monster" resists easy categories: she does not always walk through rose gardens in pools of light (though she may); she does not always appear with stained fingers and in blue stockings (though she may do this as well). She is, however, always fully competent and, above all, interesting. Fern subverts easy dichotomies that limit female agency—suggesting that progressive change comes not in new dualistic pairings but in an expanded semiotic register that can allow for multivalence.

Chapter 3 turns to Margaret Oliphant and her reflections about fame and gender. Though Oliphant had a career extending more than fifty years in which she authored a bounty of novels, biographies, histories, and articles, in her posthumously published *The Autobiography*, she portrays herself as a humble failure, who could not aspire to the heights achieved by such literary luminaries as Charlotte Brontë, George Eliot, or George Sand. Her comments in both *The Autobiography* and across her voluminous range of published materials, however, point to a keen investment in influencing where she would stand in the halls of literary greats. In her reflections about other famous women, Oliphant used a method of critical comparison through which she contrasted herself unfavorably to "better" authors, only to critique the talents of those writers and thus re-establish her better sense, decorum, and, ultimately, talent. In so doing, Oliphant sustains the sense that a great author can also be a worthy woman, using the treatment of her own and others' celebrity to exert claims relevant to gender.

Chapters 4 and 5 more fully lay out the performative function of gender and celebrity. When Fanny Fern writes in her November 19, 1870, *New York Ledger* column, "If you were my husband, and your health failed, and you could not work, I could go out into the world and earn your living and mine too," she expresses a material fact desired, if not always fully experienced, by many professional women of the period (qtd. in Warren, *Ruth Hall*, 372). Yet, as I've noted here, women had to be crafty about occupying and deploying a public identity. Extending past Charlotte Brontë, Chapters 4 and 5 look closely at representations of the pluralized author personae in the works of Elizabeth Keckley, Eliza Potter, Elizabeth Robins, Rhoda Broughton, and Mary Cholmondeley. These chapters develop the idea that representation(s) of one's "self" can offset interpellated reading positions and thus afford validity without full conformity to gender ideology. In different ways, these authors play with issues of the "authentic" self, and in so doing they obliquely question seemingly stable identity rationales. For each writer, generic mode plays a part, as their texts combine elements of memoir, poetry, autobiography, the novel, sentimental fiction, and/or slave narrative, thus heightening a commitment to eradicating boundaries through the embodied generic complexity of the textual body.

In the conclusion, I return again to Robins, whose writings help establish what is at stake in the conception of the exceptional, which is often to say the famous, woman. In her 1913 essay "Woman's Secret," for instance, Elizabeth Robins writes, rather sardonically, that the women of England and America should take heed, for at "some unwary hour you, too, may become exceptional, and so, by a well-known philological necessity, decline through 'singularity' to 'egregiousness' and 'insolence'" (15). Though Robins's quip is a laugh at the so-called slippery slope from the exceptional to the subversive, it is also an apt descriptor of the social pressure ambitious and talented women endured. To be branded singular or insolent was a coded label that might well have read as un-gendered and un-sexed, "three quarters male" as one of Robins's characters says in *George Mandeville's Husband*. Given this descriptive link to two sexes, women authors often occupied a metaphoric hermaphroditic role that, when adroitly manipulated, could offer greater artistic legitimacy and public viability. In the conclusion, therefore, I argue for a reconstitution of the "exceptional woman" made possible by complicating modes of gender/sex and literary celebrity, thus tying together debates about women and the politics of celebrity that serve as the conceptual core of the entire book.

Finally, I conclude the book in an afterword, in which I narrate my own journeys to Haworth, the Yorkshire home of the Brontës, commenting on the vestiges of literary celebrity still present in what has become a major British tourist attraction. Charlotte's fame remains very much a salient feature of her presence in this small town on the moors, but her legend manifests in a form of commodification that might strike one as enigmatic, if not surprising. So, for instance, the chemist shop where Charlotte's brother, Branwell, bought his opium is as much as a must-see destination as the actual vicarage where the Brontë family lived. Departing a bit from classic academic discourse, I use the last section of the conclusion to comment on and observe what we might arguably term "ground zero" for the place of women's literary celebrity in Anglo-American nineteenth-century culture.

Chapter 1
Reconstructing Charlotte:
The Making of Celebrated "Female Genius"

Charlotte Brontë is without doubt a most remarkable woman. Up to the publication of *Jane Eyre* three or four years ago, she was unknown. That wonderful story and its no less wonderful successor have fixed the fame of the author forever. Wherever men and women speak and read the English language, she is known – the thin disguise of "Currer Bell" having long since parted from her form – as the most powerful female writer of fiction that employs that language at all. We might go further. We might call her the most powerful now living. With the single exception of that frenzied Circe of French romance – Madame Dudevant – we know no woman who works so strongly upon the feelings as this Charlotte Brontë.

—*The Southern Literary Messenger*, 1853

The above testament to Charlotte Brontë's talent and renown may strike us today as obvious. Of course, this author of *Jane Eyre*, *Shirley*, *The Professor*, and *Villette*, this suffering sister of the moors, this writer who is read widely in the Anglophone world would be considered one of the most revered writers of fiction who ever lived. More surprising than the hyperbole of the above epigraph, then, is the fact that this American literary magazine based in Richmond, Virginia, published such a statement in 1853, four years before Elizabeth Gaskell's biography paved the way for Charlotte's genius to be perceived as a commonplace. Indeed, though Brontë's works were best-sellers in her own time and the mystery surrounding her sex and identity incited great curiosity in both Britain and the United States, she was more frequently considered notorious than meritorious. It was not until her death in 1855 and Gaskell's *The Life of Charlotte Brontë* in 1857 that Charlotte achieved a level of genius that would forever secure her fame. As the above epigraph attests, in her own lifetime Brontë already constituted at least one literary journal's conception of "the most powerful female writer of fiction" and as such, she possessed considerable notice due to the force of her talent, even if such celebrity did not also credit the goodness of her character. It will be the work of this chapter, however, to argue that Charlotte Brontë's lasting fame earned its saliency through Elizabeth Gaskell's biography that fixed Brontë in the public imagination as the perfect embodiment of both female genius and feminine literary celebrity, in turn recalibrating a transatlantic conception of gender through fame.

In his introduction to the second edition of *Myths of Power*, Terry Eagleton regrets that he did not more fully engage with the Brontë myth. "The Brontës, like Shakespeare," he observes, "are a literary industry as well as a collection of literary texts, and it would have been worth asking why this should be so and

Fig. 1.1   Illustration from the American printing of *The Life of Charlotte Brontë*. Author's collection.

how it came about" (xix). In 2005 Lucasta Miller heeded Eagleton's call for a discussion on the celebrated significance of this literary family with *The Brontë Myth*, which offers an impressive overview of the British fascination with the lives, works, loves, and tragedies of the three Brontë sisters. Miller notes that all of the sisters, but Charlotte in particular, have been appropriated to serve a wide array of political and ideological agendas, from domestic femininity to radical feminism, their representations becoming "fictionalizations" largely "unconcerned with historical precision" (168). Miller's analysis is important for its careful charting of social myth, but it largely discredits the significance of such myth, instead wanting to reclaim the *real* authors from behind the veil of created personae. Miller acknowledges the significance of Gaskell's biography but gives little credit to Gaskell's artistry. Though she concedes that Gaskell possessed literary talent, Miller contends that Gaskell's biography was "misleading" (33), filled with countless "inaccuracies and half-truths" (40) and "literary trickery" (68). Miller argues that Gaskell herself was two-faced (34) and "gossipy" (37), her lesser talent clearly manipulated by Charlotte's superior genius. Given this, Miller reflects, "We have to wonder to what extent Charlotte actively promoted the exaggeratedly tragic, and thus exonerating, view of her own life which Gaskell later transmitted" (45).

My position on this material is that, as far as it concerns gender and celebrity, there is no productive difference to be made between the fiction and the fact of Charlotte Brontë. As John Fiske has theorized, in an age of mass communication "we can no longer rely on … a clear distinction between a 'real' event and its mediated representation" and so a mediated event is "not a mere representation of what happened, but it has its own reality" (2). Although different from our present high-tech moment, the discursive climate the Victorians experienced contained its own multiply-layered forms of information transfer as aided by increasingly affordable printed materials circulated through and between transatlantic distribution networks. Thus the "exaggerated" and "historically inaccurate" personae of Charlotte Brontë—as mutually created by Brontë, Gaskell, other authors of the time, and a larger transatlantic discursive climate—constitute an *idea* of Charlotte that is, in itself, an authentic, if not necessarily an accurate, figure of fame.

In order to accept such a claim that representation is its own reality, we must also resist the reification of Romantic artistry, which holds that genius grows in isolation and earns fame only through the force of its own talent, rather than through machination or self-promotion. Instead, we must perceive fame as the by-product of historical circumstances, biographical representations, and media portraits. "Inaccuracies" in this regard, only serve to make those representations more striking. If the *Life*, as Miller argues, "evolved out of a subtle interplay between Gaskell's preconceived assumptions and Charlotte's own self-projection," so much the better for my project (31). My aim, consequently, is not so much to sort out what was accurate from what was fiction and thus to reveal the "real" Charlotte Brontë, but to attend to the texture of representation in the *Life* so as to better see how it established a register for later iterations of women's fame and genius.

Gaskell's depiction of Brontë, much like the coverage of contemporary entertainment celebrities, relied on the personal, perhaps presciently foretelling Graeme Turner's claim in *Understanding Celebrity* that a public figure first turns into a celebrity at the moment when interest turns from public acts to private lives. Gaskell spoke of Brontë's desires and hopes, her disappointments and trials, her great suffering and forbearance. We learn of Charlotte's weak body, her glowing jewel-like eyes, her captivating plainness. We learn, too, of the character of her family, her overbearing father, her spirited and stubborn sister, Emily, her meek and comely sister, Anne, her incorrigible brother, Branwell. Indeed, the personal nature of Gaskell's biographical treatment caused the *National Review* to upbraid Gaskell, stating their frank conviction that she was mistaken in being so forthcoming about the private matters of Brontë's life: "The principles and the practice which in England make it indecorous to withdraw the veil from purely domestic affairs, – the joys, the griefs, the shames of the household, – have a true basis in fortitude and delicacy of feeling, and are paramount to considerations of gratifying public curiosity, or even to that of securing a full appreciation for the private character of a distinguished artist" ("Miss Brontë" 129). This notion of a protected private zone where prying public eyes should not gaze was a frequent mandate of the period, a point Mary Jean Corbett elucidates in her discussion of Margaret Oliphant's critical reading of Harriet Martineau. Oliphant was also none too happy about what she considered to be Gaskell's indiscrete discussions of Brontë, a point I address further in Chapter 3.

It was this very tearing of the private veil, however, that transformed Brontë from a woman who wrote into a figure of fame. Gaskell thus made of Brontë a representative character, as S. Paige Baty uses the term, an exemplary figure that, through body and person, communicates culturally significant iterations of authority, legitimacy, and power. Baty notes that the representative character "embodies and expresses achievement, success, failure, genius, struggle, triumph" in cultural narratives that may be read as either cautionary tales or testaments to achievement (8–9). Constructing Charlotte as a representative character who could stand both for ideal gender and artistic excellence not only solidified Brontë's literary celebrity but also reinforced Gaskell's claims to fame, since she will be forever connected to Brontë studies and lore.

Gaskell's construction of Brontë was formative, yet we should be cautious about implying a too-simple causality between Gaskell's rendition of Brontë and all others that followed. Indeed, I believe Gaskell offered an influential template but not a concrete prescription. In this regard, it is important to heed Rosemary J. Coombe's reminder that the "celebrity image is a cultural lode of multiple meanings, mined for its symbolic resonances" (59). So, though it is possible to trace the polyvalence of the celebrity image, that image functions, in itself, as "a floating signifier, invested with libidinal energies, social longings, and political aspirations" (Coombe 59). Charlotte, as celebrity, thus stands as the direct creation of Gaskell but also as a free-floating and multiply-signifying idea, communally authored through a conglomerate of sources, as the opening epigraph attests.

Through a close reading of the *Life* as augmented by a study of Victorian Anglo-American periodicals, I aim to demonstrate how the making of the genius Charlotte not only fused womanliness and femininity to literary professionalism, it legitimated an idea of the writing woman as simultaneously fully feminine and deservedly famous. Ironically, in her construction of famous (and female) genius, Gaskell used the very indictments lobbed at Brontë: Charlotte's passion, which verged on frenzy; her unconventional family life and background; her enactment of gendered behavior, which often struck critics and readers as inappropriate, at best, and unsexed, at worst. One of Gaskell's primary devices for reconstructing Charlotte was her use of a compensatory body, a delicate, sick, and weakened physical Charlotte that worked to lessen the perceived threat of her literary genius. Anglo-American periodical and newspaper accounts created a version of Charlotte that was remarkably faithful to Gaskell's conception: the delicate and sick victim, Charlotte, who suffered through loss and pain, and whose womanliness and femininity merited her reputation as one of the most famous literary geniuses of all time.[1]

Inserting the Thin End of the Wedge

Of the many critiques of *Jane Eyre*, Elizabeth Rigby's December 1848 *Quarterly Review* piece has arguably generated the most attention. Writing anonymously, Rigby condemned both Jane and Rochester as models of "vulgarity" and "ignorance"; they were "singularly unattractive" characters, she wrote, who deserved little more than each other's perpetual, insufferable company. Rigby was even less complimentary when speculating on the identity of the androgynous author of *Jane Eyre*, known only as Currer Bell: "Whoever it might be, it is a person who, with great mental powers, combines a total ignorance of the habits of society, a great coarseness of taste, and a heathenish doctrine of religion …. [I]f we ascribe the book to a woman at all, we have no alternative but to ascribe it to one who has, for some sufficient reason, long forfeited the society of her own sex" (119–20).

---

[1]   Staking out Charlotte Brontë's claim to fame was a matter of particular concern to Anglo-American Victorian literary critics, who in a series of reflective pieces never fail to list Charlotte as deserving of great honors, even if doing so put Charlotte in a contestatory position against other writers with whom she must share the spotlight. So, for instance, in a tribute piece written about George Eliot, the *Dublin Review* noted that Charlotte held greater genius in matters of character construction (379). L.G. Moberly surveys the women and literature during Queen Victoria's reign and contends that "no one has called for such lasting homage" as Charlotte Brontë (132). Herbert Paul reminds the reader in his 1902 reflections on George Eliot, that Eliot's own companion, George Lewes, predicted that "Charlotte Brontë would be read by a discerning public with enjoyment and delight when *Daniel Deronda* had gone the way of all waxwork" (940). George W. Curtis, lecturing at New York's Astor Place, commented that "George Sand's genius was superb and impassioned, but Charlotte Brontë's was sweeter and stronger" ("Charlotte Bronte and the Jane Hyre [sic] Novels," *New York Daily Times*, 10).

Even in a twenty-first-century context, Rigby's criticisms have been denounced for the intensity (and seeming ignorance) of their attack on Charlotte Brontë's femaleness and femininity; yet, these same charges that Currer Bell had "long forfeited the society of her own sex" are often raised when talking about Charlotte Brontë (as I am doing now). Rigby's review functions as a variation on the return of the repressed—in this case, no one fully believes the claim that Brontë is vulgar, and yet no one is allowed to forget it. In *The Life of Charlotte Brontë*, Elizabeth Gaskell uses Rigby to articulate this same shock at and reminder of Charlotte's oddly engendered experience. Gaskell scolds Rigby's vain desire to "write a 'smart article,' which shall be talked about in London" (260), charging that the critic completely misses the pathos of this misunderstood artist who is not vulgar at all but a poor motherless waif. But Gaskell also devotes textual space to Rigby's review, quoting from it quite specifically, when she only paraphrases other contemporary reviewers. Thus, though Gaskell attacks Rigby, she also reproduces her claims.

This somewhat counterintuitive rhetorical turn also marked the genesis of the *Life*. Indeed, given that Gaskell casts herself in the role of savior to the misunderstood Charlotte, it is ironic that the very impetus for the *Life* arose from a different anonymous article on Charlotte Brontë, this one called "A Few Words about *Jane Eyre*" published in *Sharpe's* in 1855 soon after Charlotte's death. The *Sharpe's* article is less openly critical of Charlotte, though still acknowledging an abundance of "odd and incorrect" stylistic quirks replete with "real wicked oaths" (340), although the article fits with other tropes demonizing the tyrannical father, Patrick Brontë. Ironically or conveniently, the *Sharpe's* piece was almost certainly written by Elizabeth Gaskell herself.[2] The article was one of many remembrances published in honor of Brontë and as Hughes and Lund note, it helped cement the obituary as an important literary form. The ongoing discursive obituary of fan worship was also an important precursor to posthumous fame.

Indeed, Juliet Barker observes that soon after Brontë's death, a number of "self-important busybod[ies] got to work" to underscore their connection to the recently departed Charlotte Brontë (774). Specifically, Barker points to John Greenwood, the local Haworth stationer, who took on the task of notifying Brontë's "famous friends" of her recent passing. This list of famous friends included Elizabeth Gaskell and Harriet Martineau, both of whom responded with sympathy and public tributes. Barker explains that Martineau's "well-meant but highly coloured obituary" set off a trend of "prurient and speculative" notices feeding the Brontë legend (778). This legend was fueled by accusations of ill-treatment and abuse suffered by Charlotte and her sisters, as well as by exaggerated accounts of Patrick

---

2   Writing in 1970, J.G. Sharps seems to have been the first to hypothesize a connection between the *Sharpe's* piece and Gaskell's authorship (575–8). Brontë biographers Miriam Allot and Juliet Barker have cemented the claim (see Allott, fn 87, p. 53; Barker, *The Brontës*, pp. 780–81). Angus Easson contends in his introduction to the *Life*, however, that the *Sharpe's* article was written by novelist Frank Smedley.

Brontë's icy remove with his children (both of which are key components in Elizabeth Gaskell's rendition). As Martineau put it in a passage that blended the author with her character, after Charlotte's experiences at Cowan Bridge, "'Currer Bell' (Charlotte Brontë) was never free, while there (for a year and a half) from the gnawing sensation, or consequent feebleness, of downright hunger; and she never grew an inch from that time. She was the smallest of women, and it was that school which stunted her growth …. She was living among the wild Yorkshire hills, with a father who was too much absorbed in his studies to notice her occupations in a place where newspapers were never seen (or where she never saw any) and in a house where the servants knew nothing about books, manuscripts, proofs, or the post" (5). It is not difficult to see how Gaskell could improvise on this theme for her larger treatment of Brontë's life and how both Gaskell and Martineau's writings provoked a curiosity that grew into an insatiable hunger, enabling the growth of Brontë's celebrity status and her consequent construction and re-construction in the mass media.

After Charlotte's death, many authors sought to write of her life, but it was Gaskell who won the role of biographer.[3] The chain of events leading to her selection as the family's "official" biographer bears consideration. Following the publication of Gaskell's *Sharpe's* piece, Ellen Nussey, Charlotte's life-long friend, Patrick Brontë, Charlotte's father, and, eventually, Arthur Nicholls, Charlotte's husband of nine months, appealed to Mrs. Gaskell, as a friend of the deceased author, to set down the record of Charlotte's life in a manner allowing some degree of control in the production and thus reception of her image. For her part, Gaskell responded to their request with alacrity, and her eagerness has always clouded the issue of intent: was Gaskell self-serving in authoring the *Life*, having sought out an intimacy with Charlotte, jotted down notes of their conversations, logged the pithy anecdotes she knew would hold a reader's attention, or was she simply acting as a good friend should? Meta Gaskell felt her mother deliberately fostered an intimacy with Charlotte, intending to write a posthumous biography of the sickly author and thus further her own career (Wise and Symington 239). Deirdre D'Albertis argues for a literary rivalry between Gaskell and Brontë with the *Life* as the terrain on which Gaskell could best fight and win by turning the genius Charlotte into her subject. Alison Foster views the bond between Gaskell and Brontë as one of deep camaraderie, indicating they had an "intimate friendship" established in three days that "would continue through Charlotte's short lifetime and beyond it with the publication of her biography" (77).

---

[3]   One indication of why Martineau's version of Charlotte was influential but did not predominate public impressions of her is perhaps seen in the gender/sex polymorphism Martineau attributes to Charlotte, who possessed the "deep intuitions of a gifted woman, the strength of a man, the patience of a hero, and the conscientiousness of a saint" (5). Martineau herself battled gender legitimacy issues, since in 1902, Herbert Paul would still write of her, "Miss Martineau was as masculine as Mrs. Gaskell was feminine" (932). For more on antecedents to the *Life* in the form of Romantic and Early Victorian biographies of literary women, see Peterson, *Becoming a Woman of Letters*, 132–4.

None of these options strike me as mutually exclusive or as necessarily what's most at stake in the Brontë/Gaskell connection. Regardless of her intent, Gaskell's portrait of Charlotte took the teeth out of a good deal of contemporary literary criticism that either attacked or patronized female authors from the vantage point of their sex first and their books second. Because women who occupied remunerative public roles—from actress to governess to author to prostitute—were frequently criticized at the level of their womanhood, incursions into "forbidden spaces," be they actual or textual, invoked debates about gender propriety. Before the New Woman had become a recognizable term, cultural critics were already assailing what Eliza Lynn Linton in 1868 famously termed the "girl of the period," who with her ambitions and lack of modesty made men afraid of her. By the end of the century Linton's invective would become harsher, as she railed against the "wild women" who trafficked in social insurgency and public visibility, thus betraying their sex. "Unconsciously she exemplifies how beauty can degenerate into ugliness," Linton scolded, "and shows how the once fragrant flower, run to seed, is good for neither food nor ornament" ("The Wild Women: As Social Insurgents" 576).

Writing at mid-century, propriety and its gendered connotations were issues of much personal significance to Elizabeth Gaskell, largely because of her own position as published author and wife of a middle-class Unitarian minister, but also because she had a broad commitment to social justice. Gaskell repeatedly underscored her investment in fostering conversations about injustice that would, as she put it, provoke a "permanent state of change" by inserting "the short end of the wedge," but she had an equal investment in sustaining her image as conventionally feminine and maternal, as a writer who could be turned to with a "sense of love and gratitude" (Lyall 119).[4] Throughout her career, Gaskell would frequently assert her willingness to insert the short end of the wedge, forcing a consideration of topics previously considered unmentionable among the polite, such as the class conflicts she depicts in *North and South* (1854) and the reformed moral politics she models toward the fallen women of *Ruth* (1853) and *Mary Barton* (1848). Through her portraits of flawed but noble women in characters such as Ruth or, in this case Charlotte, Gaskell discursively imagined transgression in ways that made her female characters sympathetic. In this regard, Charlotte Brontë offered the perfect material for reforming public conceptions of femininity and fame.

Gaskell announces that her objective in the *Life* is to provide a "right understanding" of Charlotte Brontë and to make her "known and valued" to the reader (2). What is left unsaid, but seems to have been well understood, was that Brontë's reputation needed redeeming. Before the *Life*, Brontë's deviance was

---

[4]   Jenny Uglow notes that Gaskell used the phrase "the short end of the wedge" in letters following the scandal caused by her book *Ruth* (1853). After the first wave of criticism to her sympathetic portrayal of a fallen woman, Gaskell justified *Ruth* by arguing it had at least made people "talk and think a little on a subject which is so painful that it requires all one's bravery not to hide one's head like an ostrich and try by doing so to forget that the evil exists" (Uglow 339).

widely discussed—first as attached to her androgynous pseudonym, Currer Bell, and then later affixed on "the real" Charlotte Brontë. The gossipy representation of Charlotte circulating from London to Liverpool to Louisville positioned her as willful, strongly sensual, and subversive; a woman—though only doubtfully a lady—who cared little for social sanction or convention and who must have enjoyed a coarse life to evoke such passion in her texts.[5] In his introduction to Brontë's last book, an unpublished fragment called *Emma*, William Thackeray spoke of the author as brash and angry, with an "impetuous honesty" that caused her to jump "too rapidly to conclusions" (Ward, Vol. III, 203). Though Thackeray was quick to equate this anger with a moral fortitude, others did not give her such credit. The mystery of Currer Bell combined with a reputation for coarseness and the emotional appeal of the novels themselves, both created and fed the public's fascination with the "real" author's sex and gender.

Indeed, Gaskell was attentive to the degree that the notion of womanhood stood at the crux of Charlotte's legend. Despite the fact that Gaskell raised issues related to religion, race, nationality, class, and, to a very minor degree, sexuality in the *Life*, it is gender that merits her fullest and most careful consideration. In her portrayal, all elements of Brontë's character serve to underscore an idealized femininity through descriptions of Charlotte's "gentle unassuming manner" (377), her "delicate cleanliness" (43), and her patient endurance (97). Gaskell's portraiture of Brontë perpetuates those class-specific gender codes fully integrated into Victorian mores at this moment. Indeed, her treatment naturalizes the relation between Brontë's female body and her "feminine" qualities of humility, patience, and tidiness. Of particular note to me in this string of qualifiers is the manner through which Gaskell's descriptions position gender itself as monologic and stable. For indeed, though gender in a nineteenth-century context was in practice as malleable and fluid as in our own moment, prescriptive edicts tightly regulated male and female behaviors and tacitly argued for gender's innate and inalienable relation to sex.[6] It seems clear from Gaskell's usage, however, that her objective is better served by making the terms for gender appropriateness *appear* rigid. In this case, if the codes for constituting femininity were inflexible, her task was to cut and shape the character of Charlotte to fit the mold. In other words, in choosing to deploy a version of gender that was prescriptively narrow and in crafting the consequent character of Charlotte so that she conformed to conservative manifestations of femininity, which as Miller has noted, were "self-denying, dutiful, and passion-free," Gaskell could lay claim to Charlotte's redeemed womanhood (18).

---

[5]   Brontë was accused, in particular, of coarseness, a charge discussed at some length in Miriam Allott's *The Brontës: The Critical Heritage*.

[6]   For more on the fluidity of gender, sex, and sexuality in a nineteenth-century context, see Ellen Rosenman's *Unauthorized Pleasures*, Helen Lefkowitz Horowitz's *Rereading Sex*, and Cathy Davidson and Jessamyn Hatcher, eds., *No More Separate Spheres!*

More significantly, inserting Brontë into such an attenuated gender category necessarily altered the terms of that category, if not fully reorganizing it then certainly inserting the thin end of the wedge into a diversified conceptual mold of gender that not only could, but must, expand to include celebrated genius, a process I call symbolic reappropriation. The logic goes something like this: if one has a limited category to which only an elite body might fit, then he or she must severely curtail the behaviors and expressions of any non-elite bodies to make them eligible for membership within the boundaries of acceptability. Gaskell thus constructs Brontë so that she might more fully fit within such a narrow category. And yet, Gaskell did not fully blunt all of Brontë's hard edges. While it is true that Gaskell domesticates Brontë to make her better fit conventional gender norms, in Gaskell's hands Brontë also retained her passion, her professionalism, and her fame. The characterization of Charlotte as the quintessence of Victorian femininity and womanhood thus requires that the gender/sex category itself must expand in order to include Brontë in its midst. Did Gaskell reformulate the original terms of the category intentionally? She may have, though I doubt it. I think, instead, that Gaskell's representation of Charlotte performed a cultural work far outside the parameters of her initial hagiographic designs. The symbolic reappropriation Gaskell employs in reconstructing Charlotte illustrates how representation carried a force capable of reformulating gender/sex paradigms.

Forfeiting the Society of Her Own Sex

To best see Gaskell's strategy in operation, consider how she answers Rigby's condemning critique of *Jane Eyre*. In a tone of righteous indignation, Gaskell demands to know if the reviewer could ever possibly have experienced events that would parallel Charlotte's. She asks:

> Who is he that should say of an unknown woman: "She must be one who for some sufficient reason has long forfeited the society of her sex." Is he one who has led a wild and struggling and isolated life – seeing few but plain and outspoken Northerns, unskilled in the euphuisms which assist the polite world to skim over the mention of vice? Has he striven through long weeping years to find excuses for the lapse of an only brother; and through daily contact with a poor lost profligate, been compelled into a certain familiarity with the vices that his soul abhors? Has he, through trials, close following in dread march through his household, sweeping the hearthstone bare of life and love, still striven hard for strength to say, "It is the Lord! let Him do what seemed to Him good" – and sometimes striven in vain, until the kindly Light returned? (260)

Given the confusion about sexed identity attached to the pseudonym Currer Bell, it is telling that Gaskell refers to the author of the *Quarterly* piece as "he," though she knew Rigby's sex when writing this response. In so gendering the attacking critic as a male bully and the defenseless writer as a female victim, she exploits gender stereotypes even as she explodes them.

In response to Gaskell's volley of questions to Eastlake, the reader is certainly meant to answer "no." This "mean-spirited" critic has not endured the terrible privations undergone by the misunderstood genius. He has not lived a life of isolation among rustics, he has not dealt with (or been embarrassed by) a drunken and opium-addicted brother; he has not undergone an existential crisis as six members of his immediate family died. Gaskell's rhetorical pitch compels consent from the reader—we are convinced of Charlotte Brontë's sad life and great virtue, or, as *Fraser's Magazine* challenged: "Hear, at last, Mrs. Gaskell's indignant protest, and then condemn if you dare" ("Shirley" 578). Indeed, if Gaskell's version of Charlotte strikes us as a bit over-determined, we need only look at other discursive constructions of Charlotte to see Gaskell's restraint. In an 1871 *Scribner's* article, for instance, Ellen Nussey described her friend as a "Christian heroine, who bore her cross with the firmness of a martyr saint!" (19). Although literary greatness has been referenced as the route to lasting fame since the age of Homer, Nussey's characterization of Brontë relied upon gendering the connection between literary celebrity and saintly immortality (a thought also voiced by such American authors as Emily Dickinson and Elizabeth Stuart Phelps and somewhat anticipating the celebrity studies work of Chris Rojek, who theorizes the cultural links between celebrities and deities).[7]

As I've noted, though Gaskell fiercely denounces Rigby's review, her references to the article simultaneously fix its gender critiques in the mind of the reader. In so doing, Gaskell might remind the reader that Brontë was considered coarse without threatening her own gender integrity through what might have been considered unseemly descriptions and explanations. Further, Gaskell localizes her defense of Brontë as a protection of Charlotte's femininity, corralling a multitude of complaints about the "lurid" writer into the more limited and controllable domain of gender appropriateness. Highlighting Rigby's review serves Gaskell in another crucial way: it allows her to fire a good number of her rhetorical rockets at once, employing an array of strategies that serve as "explanations of character" in full use throughout the *Life*. These include Brontë's Northern otherness, her sad life of pathos, her physical delicacy, her religious piety, her loss of siblings, and her unwilling exposure to debauchery out of devotion to her brother. Gaskell's insistence on these points underscores Rigby's—as depicted in the *Life*, Brontë did live a life largely bereft of the "society of her sex," and Gaskell emphasizes such absence over and over again in her attempt to offer the reader a "right understanding of the life of my dear friend, Charlotte Brontë" (6). According to Brontë biographer Juliet Barker, nineteenth-century Haworth was actually a fairly bustling market town, and while the Brontë children grew up without their mother, they did have nurturing female figures in their life. Represented isolation, then, performs an important end in that Brontë's purported dearth of female role models

---

[7]   See Jane Donahue Eberwein's "Is Immortality True?" in *A Historical Guide to Emily Dickinson*. See Elizabeth Stuart Phelps's "A Plea for Immmortality."

works as a powerful explanatory motif for Gaskell.[8] As with Gaskell's works of fiction, in which she encourages the reader to develop an empathetic regard for the central flawed female character, Gaskell here constructs the character Charlotte Brontë as a tragic and abandoned daughter of the moors, saddened by the successive losses of her mother and five siblings, dominated by a tyrannical father, and possessing precious few outlets for sanity, much less sensibility. Given this sad life, Gaskell argues, can we begrudge Charlotte the compensation of her writerly genius or fame?

Traces of Gaskell's line of reasoning are evident in transatlantic periodicals published soon after the *Life*. I look particularly at two American journals based in the U.S. Midwest, since I believe their interest in and references to Brontë attest to the overall intertextual workings of celebrity that is fostered through the pages of both esteemed literary journals and more obscure general-interest and trade periodicals.[9] Writing four months after the *Life*'s publication, the *Ohio Farmer*, primarily an agricultural journal established in 1848 in Cleveland, Ohio, noted, as does Gaskell, Brontë's poverty, "feeble frame," and lack of prettiness (it describes her as "destitute of personal beauty"), arguing that, "she was sent by God for better things" ("Charlotte" 4). Although this particular piece does not mention the standard narrative imparted by Gaskell—the death of Charlotte's siblings, a degenerate brother, an irascible father, or the remoteness of the moors—the logic here clearly indicates that Charlotte's tragic life compensated for her artistic passions and literary success. Moreover, since her fame was a consequence of these passions, and not something Charlotte sought through ambition or vanity, the *Ohio Farmer* extols this renowned genius as a model for every "true woman," who would gladly give up the "privilege of being an ornament to the gay world" and "suffer some of Charlotte Bronte's sufferings, that she might be what Charlotte Bronte was" ("Charlotte" 4). What Charlotte was, the periodical argues, was one of the foremost "sovereigns of thought, ruling us by a divine, unquestioned right" ("Charlotte" 4). The *Ohio Farmer* extends the image of the celebrity as royalty (and even deity) in a way that Gaskell did not dare, yet its message intimates the cultural work done by those deemed famous. In this regard, and quite ironically, the celebrated Charlotte is meant to stand for

---

[8]   One of Haworth's contemporary travel websites makes use of a similar myth of isolation in order to reinforce Brontë legend and influence. "More than a century ago, when the Reverend Patrick Bronte came to be a minister at Haworth Parish Church, the village was little more than a collection of stone-built weavers' cottages huddled together for protection from the harsh cold winds. Yet within a few decades, a series of books written by three of Patrick's daughters, Charlotte, Emily and Anne, caused this obscure Yorkshire village to become a major centre for literary pilgrimage" (Haworth online: http://www.haworthonline.co.uk/. Accessed July 29, 2011).

[9]   Due to the lax copyright laws in the nineteenth century, it is possible that the pieces referenced here did not originally or exclusively appear in either the *Ohio Farmer* or the *Democratic Standard*. A comprehensive historical periodical and newspaper search, however, revealed no duplication in any other paper.

the epitome of her sex, and in such position of exalted womanhood, she is credited for ridding the world of the effeminacies brought by "Byronism, Bulwerism, and Miss Nancyism" through her "clear vision" and artistic "rapture."[10] In the place of such "falsehoods," the paper argued, "men and women were ready to welcome the truthful humanity, the large love, the contempt for shame, and the merciless analysis that were daguerrotyped on the pages of Charlotte Bronte's work" (4). But since in many respects such displacements also overwrote the code of celebrity embodied so imperiously by the great but notorious Lord Byron himself, the paper here makes of Charlotte not only a new "sovereign of thought" but a feminized figure of fame.

Another indication of how American regional papers responded to and amplified Gaskell's construction of Charlotte comes from the pages of the *Democratic Standard*, a small weekly paper published in Janesville, Wisconsin. In an attempt to cheer its readers, the *Standard* exhorts any depressed citizen of Janesville to reflect on stories of "misfortune and sorrow": Milton's blindness and poverty, Cowper's struggle through madness, and Charlotte Bronte's "illness, loneliness, and grief." Following Gaskell's gendered cues and, indeed, quoting from the *Life*, the *Standard* notes that Charlotte's "literary pursuits were never allowed to interfere with household cares, or common duties." Significantly, however, the paper emphasizes, as does Gaskell, that Charlotte's genius, her "faculty of imagination," lifted her through the bad times and thus made it possible for her to fulfill her gendered duties of service to others by "cultivating the gift which God has bestowed upon us" and thus offering it "for the well-being of others" ("Sing" 1). Such articles demonstrate how Gaskell's version of Charlotte resonated for an Anglo-American readership. They also illustrate that the process of symbolic reappropriation had transatlantic purchase, for Gaskell's re-assembling of Charlotte through the component parts of perfect femininity—piety, obedience, patience, duty, modesty, humility, physical frailty—combined with new qualities of writerly passion, genius, vision, and fame—trickled into the very American heartland, naturalizing ideologies about femininity and fame through the trusted pages of small-town periodicals and newspapers.

Disputing the Charge of Coarseness

As I've noted above, coarseness was a particularly insistent criticism lobbed at Brontë and her novels. Responses to Gaskell's *Life* make these associations clear, particularly a letter Charles Kingsley wrote to Gaskell after the biography's publication and the series of libel suits it set off (claims filed in response to

---

[10]   Since *The Ohio Farmer*, along with *The Ohio Cultivator*, often included articles on women's suffrage, female higher education, and temperance in women-authored columns, they arguably had considerable stake in affirming Brontë's rightful claim to professional authorship and celebrated fame.

Gaskell's implied ill-treatment of several esteemed persons' reputations).[11] Kingsley's response, intended to reassure Gaskell of the biography's redeeming social value, tells us much about Charlotte's reputation and Gaskell's efficacy in "mending" it:

> Be sure that the book will do good. It will shame literary people into some stronger belief that a simple, virtuous, practical home-life is consistent with high imaginative genius; and it will shame, too, the prudery of a not overly-cleanly, though carefully whitewashed, age, into believing that purity is now (as in all ages till now) quite compatible with the knowledge of evil. I confess that the book has made me ashamed of myself. 'Jane Eyre' I hardly looked into, very seldome [sic] reading a work of fiction – yours, indeed, and Thackeray's are the only ones I care to open. 'Shirley' disgusted me at the opening, and I gave up the writer and her books with the notion that she was a person who liked coarseness. How I misjudged her! and how thankful I am that I never put a word of my misconceptions into print, or recorded my misjudgements of one who is a whole heaven above me. Well have you done your work, and given us a picture of a valiant woman made perfect by sufferings. I shall now read carefully and lovingly every word she has written. (qtd. in Lyall 121–2)

Kingsley must have represented the ideal reader to Gaskell: a formerly resistant and misinformed literary professional and influential taste maker who has turned away from Brontë's "coarse" works only to be persuaded by Gaskell of Charlotte's worth as a "valiant woman made perfect by sufferings." Further, the recalcitrant reader, now made sympathetic, pledges to re-consider the body of Brontë's literary outpouring so that he might examine it "carefully and lovingly." Though I think Kingsley's metaphor is meant to be more inspirational than sentimental, it is telling that his reformed sense of the formerly coarse Charlotte is now a woman who merits his care and love.

---

[11]   Three separate libel suits were charged against Gaskell upon the biography's appearance, March 25, 1857, with a second edition three weeks later. The three parties filing complaints were: Lady Scott, whom Gaskell obliquely identified as the seductress of Branwell Brontë and whom Gaskell somewhat cattily called a "showy woman for her age" (*Life* 195); Elizabeth Rigby, the *Quarterly Review* writer whom Gaskell had castigated in the *Life* for accusing Charlotte Brontë of having "long forfeited the society of her own sex" (Rigby 119–20); and William Newby, who had been involved in a publishing scam, billing Anne Brontë's *The Tenant of Wildfell Hall* as "by the author of *Jane Eyre*" when it went for sale in the United States. Friends, family and admirers supporting the Reverend W. Carus Wilson, the real-world counterpart to Lowood's tyrannical Reverend Brocklehurst in *Jane Eyre*, also caused a controversy, though no formal charges of slander were filed. In specific regard to Lady Scott, William Gaskell (and not Elizabeth, who was traveling on the Continent) issued public apologies in ads placed in the May 26, 1857, *Times* and the May 30, 1857, *Athenaeum*. The text of the *Life* was edited, and this expurgated third version, released August 22, 1857, remained the only version available for 50 years until copyright restrictions expired. The text reverted to its original content in 1907.

Kingsley is only a single, elite male witness, of course, yet other contemporary materials offer further evidence of Gaskell's successful makeover of Charlotte. In its review of Gaskell's *Life*, the *Saturday Evening Post*, for instance, noted that Brontë's writing had been censured "by some narrow critics" who did not appreciate the scope of Charlotte's Christian goodness. The *Post* credited Gaskell with proving that Brontë's novels contained spiritual truths, and further exclaimed, "No works ever written by a Saxon woman approach them in direct, Shakespearean insight. They have been called coarse. But the male and female prudes that fix that epithet on them would have fixed it on Dante or Shakespeare. They are no coarser than life and nature, which the greatest minds accept freely and reverently, and which only ninnies have the effrontery and the folly to call common and unclean" ("New Publications" 3). *The New York Daily Times* published a similar review, reminding their readers of the sex confusion that arose around the authorship of *Jane Eyre* and crediting Gaskell's biography for explaining the "sad secret" of the male pseudonym. "It is a cause of congratulation that the materials for the composition of this Life were placed in hands so perfectly competent to the execution of the work as those of the author of *Ruth* and *Mary Barton*" ("Mystery" 2). For both the *Saturday Evening Post* and the *New York Daily Times*, Charlotte's genius, celebrity, and femininity go unquestioned. Indeed, both periodicals not only congratulated Brontë's celebrated and feminine genius, they also attributed genius to Gaskell. The *Saturday Evening Post* noted that the biography "is the life of a woman of genius, written by another woman of genius" ("New Publications" 3); whereas the *New York Daily Times* contended that Gaskell's telling of the *The Life of Charlotte Brontë* exemplified Gaskell's own "natural genius" for which she was entitled the "gratitude of the literary world" ("Mystery" 2).

These examples suggest that Gaskell not only established the terms for how Charlotte might be remembered, but through her depiction of Charlotte she also recalibrated the terms for feminized genius.[12] Importantly, this new-and-improved Charlotte came with rich associations of writerly competence, creativity, and professionalism; she was an artist, Gaskell suggests, who wrote well because she was so feminine. Indeed, Gaskell presses on the symbiosis between Brontë's femininity, her deserved fame, and her literary genius throughout the *Life*. This is particularly evident in a long passage titled "Time and Mode of Composition" when Gaskell notes, "Any one who has studied her writings … must have noticed her singular felicity in the choice of words" (214). Gaskell contends that Brontë's syntax was a "truthful mirror of her thoughts," and because Brontë had a "strong practical regard for the simple holy truth of expression," she would wait patiently until just the right words came to her (214). Gaskell states that Brontë had the remarkable ability to drop each "component part" into place, never writing down "a sentence until she clearly understood what she wanted to say, had deliberately

---

[12] Dorothy Mermin call's Gaskell's *Life of Charlotte Brontë* "the greatest biography of the nineteenth century and the work that did the most to establish the ideal picture of a Victorian woman writer" (27).

chosen the words, and arranged them in the right order" (215). She describes Brontë's finished manuscripts as "clear, legible, delicate traced writing, almost as easy to read as print" (215). Gaskell here follows a model for depicting literary genius in accord with a common model of "the great man." Virginia Woolf reminds us, for instance, that Shakespeare was credited with never having blotted a line, thus indicating that the overworked text mars the overall value of the creative product (*A Room of One's Own* 66). In Gaskell's hands, it is not solely the never blotted page but patience and the ability to discern "fitness" that yields artistry, although as Figure 1.2 demonstrates, by 1890 a culture grown weary with talk of literary genius mocked a too-arrogant regard toward editing, suggesting that such slap-dash efforts often produced not literary genius and deserved fame but failure. In the particular case established by Gaskell at mid-century, it was Brontë's highly developed sensibility, evoked through the language of the tastefully decorated home, that merited her fame through a combination of artistic discipline and forbearance.

Modern-day critics have argued that Gaskell bifurcates Charlotte into domestic and private woman on one hand and professional and public writer on the other, a way of figuring fame that I also examine in relation to Fanny Fern in Chapter 2. Gaskell certainly characterizes Brontë's existence as "divided into two parallel currents – her life as Currer Bell, the author; her life as Charlotte Brontë, the woman" (237).[13] Indeed, arguing for the separation between woman and writer makes a kind of practical sense: as Suzann Bick notes, since so much of the *Life* is drawn from the over 350 letters Ellen Nussey provided to Gaskell, and since Brontë was less inclined to discuss literary matters with this non-intellectual friend, the text of the *Life* is necessarily skewed toward the domestic. The consequence, Bick suggests, is a representation of Brontë that exists as a "muted portrait" built on Gaskell's conviction "that the public, her old 'bugbear,' would honor Charlotte as a woman only if she emerged from the biography as traditionally docile and obedient" (45). Gabrielle Helms further argues that Gaskell eschews generic conventions of biography by not providing "detailed information about Brontë's works, nor critical exegesis of her novels, nor hardly any critical evaluation" (349). Ira Bruce Nadel notes in a similar vein that for writers of fiction, biography poses a trying genre, and in this particular case, "detail not fact was Mrs. Gaskell's principal concern. If she could concretely build the life of Charlotte, she could demonstrate her life as a moral woman. This took precedence over literary criticism of which there is little" (125).

As I've discussed above, Gaskell makes clear that the artistic integrity of Currer Bell's novels was enhanced through the long-suffering patience of the

---

[13]   In *The Brontë Myth*, Lucasta Miller argues that the split between Currer Bell and Charlotte Brontë is one that Charlotte herself constructed as a form of self-protection. For an extended and convincing argument about Gaskell's development of the parallel currents motif in her portait of Brontë, see chapter 3 of Linda H. Peterson's *Becoming a Woman of Letters*.

TOO MUCH GENIUS.

Poet. "OH--A—I ALWAYS WRITE MY POEMS RIGHT OFF, WITHOUT ANY COR-
RECTIONS, YOU KNOW, AND SEND THEM STRAIGHT TO THE PRINTER. I NEVER
LOOK AT 'EM A SECOND TIME."
Critic. "NO MORE DO YOUR READERS, MY BOY!"

Fig. 1.2   "Too Much Genius." *Punch*. October 11, 1890, 171.

woman Charlotte Brontë. Additionally, though there is virtual consensus that Gaskell worked to suppress aspects of Charlotte's career, and she did so by accentuating traditional feminine behavior while muting professional writerly activities, the *Life* contains a surprising wealth of concrete information on the profession of writing. Gaskell discusses writerly inspiration and blocks, adverse and positive reviews, negotiations with publishers, editing and re-editing, and financial arrangements. The *Life* also details the discipline required to write amidst the demands of domestic duties and fame. Indeed, in an 1881 essay called "Great Writers at Work" published in *Argosy*, H. Barton Baker credits Gaskell for leaving the world with important information about the Brontë sisters' mode of composition (381). Gaskell's bountiful description of the writer's daily discipline represents a glimpse into the world of the female literary professional, and her frequent depictions of Brontë as traditionally docile and obedient must be refracted through the competent, if sometimes obsessive, literary professional Gaskell creates in the text. By the time Charlotte Brontë's life and Elizabeth Gaskell's *Life* have run their course, then, the writer and woman are not two entirely separate entities at all but exist as one on the page.

Gaskell combines all of these factors—the obedient daughter, the disciplined artist, the neophyte learning the ropes of the publishing business—to form a portrait of Brontë that emphasizes how "quietly and modestly" (371) she deports herself in everyday life, while still maintaining a professional "self-reliant and independent character" (201). In this, as Hughes and Lund assert, Gaskell deploys a rhetorical strategy that "consistently bridges assertions of fiery passion, intellect, ambition, and fame to the domestic in Brontë's life," which, in turn, allowed Gaskell to celebrate Brontë's "rare talents" but to suggest that their link to "duty, piety, and selflessness" augured "no threat to feminine virtue" (136). Indeed, not only were the traditional tenets of feminine deportment allowed to remain unthreatened, Gaskell's reconstruction of Brontë made of her a woman who more fully possessed and expressed these virtues than others who were not famous and did not engage in the literary marketplace.

What we see, then, is an illusion: the professional woman seems a separate current from the domestic woman, but the two forces continually rely on, overlap with, and respond to one another. May Sinclair would describe the inter-relation between actual events and creation in *The Three Brontës* some five decades later: "Their lines may start from the same point in the actual, they may touch again and again, but they are not the same, and they cannot run exactly parallel" (*The Three Brontës* 165). At mid-century, Gaskell not only staked out the terms under which Charlotte will be celebrated and remembered but cemented her image in the public imagination as a representative figure whose story, and whose very body, is shaped to express the fascinations of Anglo-American Victorian culture through suffering, tragedy, death, desire, passion, resistance, sacrifice, and transcendence.

The Body of the Text and the Body of the Author

Given that Gaskell's portrait melds together the woman and the writer by showing their simultaneous existence in the famous body of Charlotte Brontë, that body, both physical and textual, has great significance. Throughout the *Life* Gaskell portrays Brontë's textual body in the form of her literary output as strong and robust. Indeed, the authorship controversy surrounding all of the Brontë works maintained that even if authored by a woman, the novels were too strong to be the product of a lady's pen. Though Gaskell gives some space in the biography to the debate that raged over the identity of Currer Bell—"the whole reading-world of England was in a ferment to discover the unknown author"—she never undercuts the idea that, whether male or female, Currer Bell wielded extraordinary writerly talent: "No one they knew had genius enough to be the author" (230). By the time of the biography's publication, everyone, of course, knew the identity and the sex of Currer Bell; the biography's task was not to ferret out the mystery, but to reconcile the robust text with the reclusive writer. Gaskell accomplishes this by emphasizing the delicacy of Brontë's physical body. Making repeated references to her "frail nerves" (287) and "failed health" (91), Gaskell haunts the vigorous text with the specter of the sickly Charlotte, a move that quite literally embodies the debate and turns corporeal liability (the masculinized coarseness of the robust textual body) into corporeal asset (the feminized and fetishized weakness of the fragile authorial body).

Gaskell reflects that in moments of stress, Brontë "would turn sick and trembling at any sudden noise, and could hardly repress her screams when startled" (110) and that she was often prone to recurrent bouts of a "deranged condition of the liver" (191), "bilious fever" (254), "racking headache and harassing sickness" (249). This was in addition to her weakened eyes (324), and a constitution Gaskell felt certain was biologically incapable of hope (77). With allowances for my subjective calculation as to what might qualify as a reference to Brontë's delicate constitution, I have counted upwards of 80 separate moments in the biography when these topics are mentioned by Gaskell: in a book of 402 pages, that's a reference roughly every five pages. Clearly, we know that much of the talk of illness was merited. The Brontës lived upon and drew their water from beneath a graveyard, which directly jeopardized the health of the parsonage. Each of the children and their mother died of what was vaguely termed an "internal wasting disease."[14] And certainly no history of the Brontë family could be told without frequent mention of illness and death.

---

[14] "Internal wasting disease" seems to cover the waterfront of ailments a body might experience, short of catastrophic accident. While there is debate over what actually caused the Brontës' respective deaths, the consensus seems to be that the mother, Maria, died in 1821 of cancer; the older sisters Elizabeth and Maria died in 1824 of consumption, the lone brother Branwell died in 1848 of drug and alcohol addiction, sister Emily died in 1848 of consumption (though she was reported to be anorexic), sister Anne died in 1849 of consumption, sister Charlotte died in 1855, most believe as a complication of pregnancy, and the father Patrick died of old age in 1861.

In this case, however, the pattern of references to Charlotte's weak body may be more telling than the percentage. If we divide the text and look at the *Life* before Charlotte achieved notoriety, there are only 32 references, or one every 8.3 pages. After Charlotte becomes a literary celebrity at age 31, Gaskell refers to her poor health 48 times, or an approximate average of once every two pages. The deaths of Charlotte's siblings come at roughly the mid-point of the narrative, and again, it makes sense that their demise would prefigure Charlotte's declining health and eventual death; yet the frequency of reminders serves a different end, for as the fame of Currer Bell grows, the body of Charlotte Brontë diminishes.

As I have noted, Gaskell's motivation for writing the *Life* has been hotly contested, in both her time and our own. A number of literary critics have suggested that Gaskell's representation of Charlotte in the *Life* served to diminish Brontë's legacy. So for instance, Deirdre D'Albertis has argued that Gaskell frequently employs a "logic of morbidity—the breakdown of mental and physical stability—tending towards disease and ultimately, death" as a means of establishing the "inferior" and "masculinized" mode in which Brontë worked (33). With its frequent allusions to death and illness, D'Albertis contends, "Gaskell's text attempts to show us how morbid, how self-absorbed, how culturally 'male' Charlotte Brontë was forced to become in her pursuit of an unattainable idea [for women] of [Romantic] genius" (35). Though I certainly agree that Gaskell encodes subtle and not-so-subtle gender criticisms of Brontë into her narrative, I am less persuaded that references to ill health are fueled by a rivalry bent on establishing Brontë's "inferior" and "masculinized" mode of production or even that there is a pejorative cast to those things read as sickly and "morbid."

As scholars from Bram Dijkstra to Miriam Bailin to Diane Price Herndl have persuasively argued, Anglo-American nineteenth-century iconography and ideology perceived the sickened female body as a powerful cultural signifier linking weakness in women with physical and mental purity. Anne E. Boyd has also noted that in the process of securing women's rightful position as both artists and literary producers in an American postbellum context, the author's body was often described in tropes that mirrored Romantic genius, particularly through an emphasis on a "tortured life" that, responding to forces beyond rational control, suffered greatly due to the exertions imposed by artistry (127). The domain of the sickroom is not exclusive to women, yet sickness connotes the weakened, passive, and culturally feminine. Dijkstra notes that in the mid-Victorian period, healthy and especially vigorous women were associated with dangerous or masculinizing attitudes (26); one way to quell the power of female strength was to idealize physical passivity, illness and even death, making images of beautiful women safely dead the equivalent to the transcendental spiritual value of passive female sacrifice (50). The dead and dying woman, then, was immediately recognized through iconographic and textual representations as the virtuous woman.

Kingsley's comments that Charlotte has been transformed in his mind from a woman who "liked coarseness" to a woman "made perfect by sufferings," and his avowal that he will now re-visit the textual body that he had formerly spurned, function as a clear marker of the virtue in perceived feminine weakness.[15] As the *Saturday Evening Post*'s review of Gaskell's *Life* further made evident, there is great representational power in sickness and death, "Life seems better worth living—truer, gentler, more august—when thought of over the closed leaves of a work that reminds us of Charlotte Brontë's grave" ("New Publications" 3).

Miriam Bailin has argued that sickroom scenes perform a therapeutic work in Victorian fiction, for they function as "registers of emotional tumult, as crucial stages in self-development, and as rather high-handed plot contrivances to bring events to their desired issue" (1). One might argue that as a biography, the *Life* does not conform to the same tropes of fiction Bailin references and in fact has its own formulaic model to adhere to.[16] Yet it seems to me that Gaskell's text crosses over a number of established generic boundaries, in this case blending fiction with biography and thus reconstituting the repertoire of imaginative possibility; or, as she might put it, her representation "insert[s] the small end of the wedge" into representation itself. I raise these questions of genre because they amplify possibilities for gleaning new cultural meaning from the *Life*. As Pamela K. Gilbert nicely argues, genre offers a "meta-reading, or a set of reading instructions, that coexists with a text and limits the range of its multiplicity. One productive way to expose both the imperatives of a genre and their roots in social values and concerns is to seek a different generic reading of the same text" (5–6). Following Gilbert's premise, scholars who read the *Life* as a factual accounting of Charlotte Brontë's life—which is to say, as a faithful and accurate rendition of a particular chronology and specific key events that culminated in both her celebrity and her death—can often miss the degree to which Gaskell organized the material of that text through her commitment to social action, the use of fictional devices (like her idea of what constituted an engaging story), and her own investments in how Brontë and famous female genius should be perceived.

Though I am in accord with Nadel, who argues that any biographer chooses his or her subject for what it might say about self, and thus "in her defense of Brontë's career, Gaskell supports her own" (123), I am more inclined to claim a cultural meaning in her representation than a psychological one. Such a choice makes Gaskell less a woman writing out of a personal need to redeem or renounce

---

[15] As authors, both Gaskell and Brontë were fond of the trope of illness. In *Ruth* alone, Gaskell depicts 12 separate sickbed scenes, and Miriam Bailin notes that though Brontë experienced many deaths in her immediate family, "illness in each of her novels nonetheless provides the sole access to a hallowed space of connection, of repletion, and of liberty" (7).

[16] For discussion on how Gaskell both conformed to and departed from conventional biography format, see Kershaw 11–24, D'Albertis "Bookmaking" 15–20, Nadel 121–30, and Altick *Lives and Letters* 206–8.

her maligned friend, and more a literary professional making insistent, though perhaps not always conscious, statements that markedly alter perceptions of gender and literary celebrity. I consider Gaskell's re-imagination of the cognitive terrain rather revolutionary, and here I follow Hilary Schor's determination to read against the grain of Gaskell scholarship, seeing her not as "the most conventional and soothing of the major novelists" (4), but as a perceptive and dedicated literary practitioner who was both aware and manipulative of oppressive systems.

We can see this most powerfully in a return to the scene of the sickroom. If the convention of sickroom moments in fiction is to advance the plot and establish a more complex characterological profile by provoking profound emotional epiphany, the many moments of illness portrayed in the *Life* do neither. Gaskell never depicts Brontë as achieving any form of altered state—save for a profound sadness—after the deaths of her five siblings. She rarely supplies the reader with details of suffering or with descriptions of the dying body. We see no blood or pus or tearing of the flesh; we hear few coughs, moans, or congestion-clogged breathing. Her representation is much more of a body dis-eased than diseased. Through her constant reminders of Haworth in its "unhealthy state, as usual" (362), she establishes a pattern in which normalcy is marked by illness; and importantly, that illness is not broken bones or cancerous lesions, but internalized complaints, restless feelings of dissatisfaction, nervousness, and fatigue—all the telling "female disorders" feminist scholars have identified as endemic to strong women in patriarchal systems (Showalter, Price Herndl, Smith-Rosenberg, Gilbert and Gubar). The many references to illness don't build cumulatively but provide a pale backwash against which all of the other events of the book take place.

In so doing, Gaskell alters a rather profound given—that the "normal" state of being is healthfulness—and by upsetting this supposition, she opens a potential space for re-examining other normative categories. In the particular case of the Brontë family, Gaskell makes it quite clear that what constitutes unmarked and marked categories, the normal and the abnormal, are radically reversed in the Brontë household. This device furthers the objective of reading Charlotte against a different set of others than a cultured London society might provide. So, for instance, if we read her as a wild rose amidst the tangled bracken of the moors, she appears more refined than if we read her as an errant bloom amidst the cultivated flowers of London. The remaking of the unmarked category highlights Gaskell's ability to take perceived absolutes and suggest a range of mitigating factors that make them not givens at all but malleable conditions in a complex web of perception and social interaction.

Embodying the Genius Charlotte

It is a fairly common narrative device to define by negation, particularly through the use of a foil character. Who is Charlotte Brontë? She is not like her sister Anne, who is patient and tractable and "would submit quietly to occasional oppression, even when she felt it keenly" (124); and she is not at all like her sister Emily, who possessed a "stubborn tenacity of will" that, according to her professor M. Heger, would have suited her well as a man (151). She is not like her brother Branwell, who is "utterly selfish" (123); nor is Charlotte like "the wretched woman" (188) who wickedly beguiled Branwell into his delusional demise. She is not like the common folk of Yorkshire, who possess a "remarkable degree of self-sufficiency … rather apt to repel a stranger" (6); and in particular, Charlotte Brontë, a good English lass, is not like Frenchwomen, with their "external morality more rigid than ours" (159) coupled with a "cold systematic sensuality" (177). These kinds of contrasts are at play throughout the text, leading Bick to comment, "Gaskell obviously felt that against a background of barely contained violence and overt eccentricity, Charlotte would appear as a rather normal young woman" (38).

Gaskell's strategy is a simple one, yet it serves a complex function, for in the depiction of Charlotte as "different from" a series of contrasts, there is also a rendering of her qualities, both physical and personal, in intimate detail. Consider, for instance, the first sight Gaskell has of Brontë, when they meet at the country home of the Kay-Shuttleworths. Gaskell notes that she could not see her at first "for the dazzle in the room" (310). Amidst the gaiety of high-society living, the dark and somber figure of the author was effaced, not distinct enough to be visible. Gaskell turns the readers' eyes to that shadowy spot in the bright room, increasing their visual acuity so that they can not only see but appreciate what was before indiscernible: the "little, quiet, resolute" (101) woman, "very quiet in manner and very quaint in dress" (61), with "soft, thick, brown, hair, and peculiar eyes" (60), and behavior and expressions "just befitting the occasion" (310).

As in the repeated mentioning of the dis-eased body, this effort to see genius embodies Charlotte Brontë, in effect offering the materiality of her body to the full gaze of the reader. Gaskell describes her with a minute attention to detail, savoring the constituent parts of Brontë and thus creating of her a catalog of parts. Gaskell's first description of Charlotte is exacting in its description:

> In 1831, she was a quiet, thoughtful girl, of nearly fifteen years of age, very small of figure – "stunted" was the word she applied to herself, – but as her limbs and head were in just proportion to the slight, fragile body, no word in ever so slight a degree suggestive of deformity could properly be applied to her; with soft, thick, brown hair, and peculiar eyes of which I find it difficult to give a description, as they appeared to me in her later life. They were large, and well shaped; their colour a reddish brown; but if the iris was closely examined, it appeared to be composed of a great variety of tints. The usual expression was of quiet, listening intelligence; but now and then on some just occasion for vivid interest or wholesome indignation, a light would shine out, as if some spiritual lamp had been kindled, which glowed behind those expressive orbs. I never saw the like in any other human creature. As for the rest of her features, they were plain, large, and ill set; but, unless you began to catalogue them, you were hardly aware of the fact, for the eyes and power of the countenance overbalanced every physical defect; the crooked mouth and the large nose were forgotten, and the

whole face arrested the attention, and presently attracted all those whom she herself would have cared to attract. Her hands and feet were the smallest I ever saw; when one of the former was placed in mine, it was like the soft touch of a bird in the middle of my palm. The delicate long fingers had a peculiar fineness of sensation, which was one reason why all her handiwork, of whatever kind – writing, sewing, knitting – was so clear in its minuteness. She was remarkably neat in her personal attire; but she was dainty as to the fit of her shoes and gloves. (60–61)

In this passage Gaskell evokes the body of the author—her soft hair, her glowing eyes, her crooked mouth, her large nose, her bird-like hands and diminutive feet. Importantly she does not celebrate the prettiness of Charlotte; indeed, she makes it quite clear in her description that Charlotte's face, like her writing, bore signs of coarseness and dissymmetry. In this close observation/articulation of the parts of Charlotte's body, Gaskell renders a "real" woman that can be laid over the imagined author, which in turn contributes to what Richard Dyer has identified in the construction of celebrity as the combination of ideal and typical forms (*Stars* 22). We see here Elizabeth Gaskell calling the body of Charlotte Brontë into being and then looking closely at that body (to the intimate level of noticing the changing variation of color in her irises) as she invites the reader to do the same. Dyer has suggested that the close-up in film led to the "discovery of the human face" (*Stars* 15), a discovery he and other theorists closely tie to the rise of celebrity and modernity in the twentieth century. Yet, Gaskell here reveals a discursive close-up, offering the spectator a magnified version of the star that the movies will re-create some 60 years later.

Gaskell's gesture also functions as a classic patriarchal trope—the appropriating and objectifying gaze that colonizes the captured subject through the power of a controlling vision—or does it? Gaze theory, as first articulated by scholars such as Laura Mulvey, contends that the act of the gaze is monologic and deeply gendered; the hypothetical seeing eye is figured as masculine, while the looked-at is feminized. Writing about film, Mulvey argues that "the mainstream, classical cinematic narrative constructs an Oedipal subject of desire engaged in the twin perversions of voyeurism and fetishism in order to master the potentially fragmenting and castrating threats of the body of the woman in the film" (7). Literary critics have taken up this hermeneutic aid and, often combining it with a Foucauldian method, have found the theory of the gaze particularly incisive in the analysis of realist texts that, like classic Hollywood film, organize information according to ostensibly mimetic codes. Gaze theory has thus provided a helpful language for feminists fighting representations that alienate and objectify women. Recent work on reader-response and gaze theory has complicated this model, however, by searching for a new paradigm in which gender does not represent the sole crucial site for identification or exclusion and in which heterosexist and essentialist logics do not predetermine the schema through which to read the gaze. One such critique of classical gaze theory by literary critic Belinda Budge asks for a "new vocabulary to describe the pleasurable associations for women of looking at images of other women" (104). Perhaps the road to this new theory runs through the nineteenth century, for as we can see in this portrait of the artist, the politics of the gaze function as a crucial dynamic in the Gaskell-Brontë relationship.

Gaskell's extended description of Charlotte serves an important objective, since it has the effect of personalizing and embodying the famous author, making her not a one-dimensional objectified commodity but a multi-faceted subject who is neither alienated from herself nor alienating to the reader. Gaskell's insistence that the reader stand as close to Charlotte as she herself has stood—in order to see the changing flecks of color in her eyes, perhaps even to feel her breath upon the reader's lips—suggests an intimacy among subject, biographer, and reader that breaks down fictions of distance. In this regard, Gaskell avoids what Richard Brodhead calls "spectatorial consumption," or the fan's capacity to disembody the celebrity through the voracious force of the gaze (52). Further, the power of the gaze, as described in Foucault's classic Panopticon metaphor, operates when the looked-at knows he or she is being observed, but not when or by whom; or as Foucault phrases it, "in the peripheric ring, one is totally seen without ever seeing; in the central tower, one sees everything without ever being seen" (*Discipline* 202). The viewer is not vulnerable because the act of seeing from a distance removes the body rather than insists upon it. Gaskell's representation, however, brings the spectator within feet, even inches, of the subject, making Charlotte more visible but also moving the reader out of a zone in which she is protected by her invisibility. Thus, Gaskell alters the terms of the gaze not only by giving Charlotte a body to be looked at, but by giving the reader a body to look. And to feel, since many reviewers commented that the *Life* "cannot be read without deep, even painful, emotion" that at times "pressed tears, as though they were drops of blood, out of the heart" ("Shirley" 577).

D.A. Miller makes a similar point about the reader's body in his discussion of the sensation novel, arguing that one of the fundamental suppositions behind the novel as a cultural institution is the implied sense of privacy promised through the reading process. "Novel readers," he writes, "take for granted the existence of a space in which the reading subject remains safe from the surveillance, suspicion, reading, and rape of others" (162). Miller argues that the sensation novel, as a genre, alters the terms of panoptic surveillance by evoking sensations from the reader's body—sweaty palms, sleepless nights, rapid heart rate—and this, in turn, implicates the reader's body, making it visible and violable (163). Clearly, we can see in Gaskell's representation of Charlotte a similar collapsing of removed reader into embodied reader simultaneously as she narrates a collapsing of the cultural signified—the coarse famous novelist— into the physical sign the worthy body of the woman. This is all accomplished through contrastive difference: Charlotte is not her sisters; Charlotte is not her environment; Charlotte is not like women of other nations. Gaskell invokes these conceptual binaries and plays upon them handily while blurring the interstitial matter between them. She makes Charlotte more sympathetic to the reader not by providing a "contrast to Charlotte's more temperate behavior" (Bick 38), but by moving the reader closer to the frail body of the woman, asking that reader to see the embodied version of Brontë that Gaskell presents.

In implicating the reader in gazing at Charlotte's diminutive body as a way of better appreciating her famed genius, Gaskell works according to a trope of modern celebrity whereby the star offers opportunities for intimacy as well as for idealization. Gaskell makes Charlotte both ordinary and extraordinary, both "like us" and beyond us. As I have noted, her frail body and weak constitution minimize the power of her genius, functioning as compensation for her feminized fame. And yet, Charlotte's small, slight, and sickly body also idealizes her, making the idea of Charlotte a powerful semiotic tool. Importantly, Gaskell's own (weakened) authorial persona is as critical in the construction of female celebrity as is Charlotte's.

The Persuasive Force of "poor and weaker words"

Downplaying her own agency and thus creating for herself a position of strategic powerlessness, Elizabeth Gaskell noted that she wrote in "poor and weaker words" and claimed, in particular, no great authority as a writer of biography. Refusing to interpret (or at least refusing to acknowledge interpretation), Gaskell justified her reliance on letters in the *Life*: "[T]he letters speak for themselves, to those who know how to listen, far better than I can interpret their meaning into my poorer and weaker words" (233). Indeed, her disclaimers are frequent and well-known, as when she wrote to her friend Harriet Anderson some months into composition about how difficult she found the process:

> And I never did write a biography, and I don't exactly know how to set about it; you see you have to be accurate and keep to facts; a most difficult thing for a writer of fiction. And then the style too! that is a bugbear. It must be grander and more correct I am afraid. But in all matters of style and accuracy I have a capital helper in my husband, who has an admirable knowledge of language, and an almost fastidious taste as to style. I sometimes tell him he does not read books for the subject but for the style. (*Stonehouse* 219)[17]

Some critics have argued that her frequent apologies, expressed both privately and in public, related to what they regard as her clumsiness with biography as a genre, and that her greater aptitude as a novelist led to a version of Charlotte

---

[17]   It may seem ironic that a woman credited with reclaiming silenced voices, to echo Schor's words, here subordinates her own voice to her husband's "proper style." William Gaskell did indeed peruse "Lily's" writings. He even pronounced several of her letters "slip-shod," which Gaskell italicized in her retelling (See L34). But Gaskell was a firm and often unbending author, particularly as exemplified by her disputes with Dickens over the length and direction of *North and South*.

Brontë heavy on stylistic metaphors and light on historical objectivity.[18] While I'm certain that Gaskell's expression of hesitancy and uncertainty vis-à-vis the writing of a biography was genuine, I'm equally inclined to believe that Gaskell's protests √ served her own gendered professionalism. By emphasizing a lack of certainty in her biographical abilities, Gaskell underscored her position as friend to Charlotte rather than as professional writer with a premeditated objective to exploit the great genius's celebrity. Gaskell's discursive humility allowed her to fill a role as sympathetic communicator of the Brontë story, responsive only to truth and, thus, not able to manage or influence the direction of the narrative. By implication, then, Gaskell was unable to *create* fame or genius; she was only able to *represent* them seemingly without bias.[19]

Working under the dual flags of self-criticism and "victim to the dictates of truth" allowed Gaskell to position herself as conduit rather than composer. As such, Gaskell performed a version of subtle gender deviancy of her own, one that allowed her to defend Charlotte without implicating herself as aggressive or defensive. So, for instance, Gaskell chastised "thoughtless critics, who spoke of the sad and gloomy views of life presented by the Brontës in their tales," assuring her readers that "such words were wrung out of them [the sisters Brontë] by the living recollection of the long agony they suffered" (238). Gaskell noted, as well, that all of the Brontë sisters, but in particular Charlotte, shrank from coarseness. Objectionable or unfeminine elements in their writings, Gaskell argued, were the consequence not of coarseness in the writers but rather of the facts of their existence, redeemed only through their craft. "The hard cruel facts, pressed down, by external life, upon their very senses, for long months and years together, did they write out what they saw, obeying the stern dictates of their consciences" (238–9). In this regard, Gaskell implores, all of the sisters must be declared exempt of gender crimes.

Importantly, in this defense Gaskell encapsulated a whole philosophy about the presumed role of the author that far superseded the generic obligation of the biographer: she is a seer of events, functioning best when observing most, writing with a commitment to truth and not venturing into the darker spaces of the mind. When Charlotte's text is unseemly, Gaskell assures us, it is not because Charlotte herself is vulgar but because her provincial Yorkshire and rural surroundings give her few options save the unrefined. Indeed, in its response to the *Life*, the *Saturday Evening Post* emphasized that the delicate Brontës grew

---

[18]   Uglow notes of Gaskell, "She was a clever child, but those warnings against displayed learning seem to have had their effect, since for many years, as an adult, she hid her cleverness, claiming not to have read economics, not to understand science, not to like sermons, not to be 'metaphysical'" (44).

[19]   It was not uncommon for Gaskell to assume a similar stance with her fictional writings. Uglow notes that though Gaskell always established elaborate writing outlines before beginning composition, she represented herself as at the whim of artistic caprice, not choosing what she would write, but channeling what "rose up and possessed her" (213).

up in a social context of Yorkshire boorism, since "the district [of Haworth and surrounding areas] was inhabited by a strange and savage race. Mrs. Gaskell describes them as sagacious, dogged, surly, quaint, insular, rough, harsh and brutal. They are, moreover, sleuth-hounds in the pursuit of money" ("New Publications" 3).[20] Gaskell used the roughness of the moors as a redemptive point of contrast, reassuring readers that Charlotte was so innocent that she was often unconscious of the coarseness of her texts. Indeed, Gaskell notes that Charlotte was naïve to such an extreme that she had to ask her publisher, George Smith, if her books were improper because she could not determine it herself. Gaskell argues that if Brontë "touched pitch," this exposure to the coarse things in life was only skin deep, and she was fast on the way to refinement—"if only she had but lived!" (375). Gaskell uses such reminders of Brontë's untimely death to apply yet another admonition to the reader to be compassionate, as she herself is being. "I do not deny for myself the existence of coarseness here and there in her works otherwise so entirely noble," Gaskell writes, implicitly acknowledging her own refinement linked here to gender legitimacy: "I only ask those who read them to consider her life, – which has been openly laid bare before them, – and to say how it could be otherwise" (375).

This appeal works according to a similar logic applied by Elizabeth Keckley and Eliza Potter, which I discuss in Chapter 4. The writer assures the reader that she possesses the knowledge of refined culture that her subject lacks; further, she suggests that in her role as writer and interpreter, she can offer a version of the white female subject that merits increased consideration. The writer admits that her subject is flawed, even suggesting ways that she, the writer, disagreed with the course of actions pursued by the subject. But we see a departure in rhetorical strategy as it concerns race. Where Potter and Keckley suggest, as I will later demonstrate, that skin color is an unreliable sign of virtue, Gaskell's depiction of Brontë's tiny white hand covered with pitch articulates a metaphorical equivalent between goodness and whiteness. In this regard, dark skin is the outward signifier of a dark soul. Gaskell makes clear that in Brontë this sign of darkness is misleading. Like the abolitionist images of white children covered with coal or blacking ink and mistakenly sold into slavery, Gaskell does not question the insidious logic of racism, but suggests it is misapplied in the case of Charlotte's pitch-covered hands.

---

[20]   In 1868, W.H. Cooke published a literary pilgrimage to Haworth, thus offering yet another discursive resurgence of the interest in all things Brontë. Leaning heavily on Gaskell's version of the Brontë myth, Cooke also dropped in several critiques of Gaskell, coming through the mouths of Haworth's townspeople who did not appreciate the way they were represented in the *Life*. "She were here," the sexton says about Gaskell, "but we do not like her nor yet her book. She says something about us folk that isn't true. We think her book's libelous" (166).

One Famed Genius Deserves Another

Gaskell's reconstruction of Charlotte also warranted a space for Gaskell in the pantheon of famed female genius. By the time of the biography's publication, Gaskell arguably needed this boost to her literary reputation. The *Life* marked Gaskell's fifth major work (*Mary Barton* [1848], *Ruth* [1853], *Cranford* [1853], and *North and South* [1855]) all of which, save for *Cranford*, had met with public opprobrium. *Mary Barton* was considered one-sided in its sympathetic regard to the proletariat as was *North and South*; *Ruth*, with its compassionate portrayal of a fallen heroine, was widely viewed as improper. Gaskell herself was hurt that "good kind people – and women infinitely more than men" criticized her and turned away from *Ruth* (Uglow 339). "I am in such scrapes about *Ruth*," she confessed to her friends Anna Jameson and Mary Rich, "I can't think how it is that I who am such an arrant coward, must always go headlong into people's black books; and good people's too" (Uglow 339). She had much experience in stirring the public's sense of propriety in the name of social justice, and in suffering the resulting stings of the "hornet's nest" brought on by critics. As Deborah Logan notes, "Gaskell's tenacity [in championing fallen women] was threatening because, for a woman of her reputation and social stature to align herself with so controversial an issue was to validate that issue, to acknowledge its credibility" (28). Alison Kershaw adds to this point, with specific reference to the *Life*, observing that "bringing such a life to public notice," in effect by feminizing the genius of Charlotte Brontë, Gaskell revealed "the 'boundless sphere of feelings and intellect' to which women were not commonly deemed to have access" (22). Both Logan's and Kershaw's reflections illuminate the difficulty that any woman invested in social standing and professional status would have faced in representing Brontë: how could a woman not only claim the authority to speak, but speak of things "coarse" without being tainted by them? Given this and Brontë's reputation, one wonders why Elizabeth Gaskell would so eagerly take up her defense.

The answer seems to lie in Brontë's increasing reputation for famed genius, for it was Brontë's celebrated genius that could shield Gaskell from charges of coarseness and Victorian culture's reverence for genius that might compel Gaskell to take on this challenging representation and assure an improvement of her own authorial reputation. But such exoneration through links to genius was hardly unproblematic. As Christine Battersby notes about codes of genius, it "was creativity, not reason or talent, that made man resemble a god …, made him more than an animal, and made some men superhuman and superior to others" (2). Battersby's use of the gender exclusive "man" is not accidental, for as David Higgins notes, the passion for understanding genius in the early nineteenth century was largely predicated on a desire to become familiar with the "characteristics and life histories of 'great men'" (1). Predominantly, though not exclusively, those characterized as geniuses were men, even if, as according to Andrew Elfenbein, such men were sometimes depicted as devious, anomalous, or queer.[21] The ties between men, masculinity, and genius are perhaps most obvious in discussions about female authorship. An anonymous 1835 *North American Review* piece about Lydia Sigourney, for instance, praised the author because she didn't claim "the very highest attributes of poetry," but showed an "unassuming" tone of "calm reflection" and "a pure and unostentatious faith" ("Mrs. Sigourney" 441). Literary talent for women was accordingly connected to ideological codes of middle-class femininity that positioned "proper" women as "unassuming," "calm," and "unostentatious" (not to mention devoutly Christian). To be "superhuman and superior to others" marked a woman not as a genius but as aberrant, excessive, masculine, even monstrous, a point Elizabeth Robins would make in her 1913 essay "Woman's Secret," which I consider more thoroughly in the conclusion to this book.

Battersby demonstrates that the connotation of genius praised the ability to create when it existed in men, but did not confer equal praise on women. "The creative woman was an anomaly .... A woman who created was faced with a double bind: either to surrender her sexuality (becoming not masculine, but a surrogate male), or to be feminine and female, and hence to fail to count as a genius" (3). This would likely account for why the *Dublin Review* in its article, "The Genius of George Eliot," commented that Eliot was more powerful an artist than the likes of Charlotte Brontë or Jane Austen precisely because there was "a certain affinity of [Eliot's] mind with the masculine" (380), whereas both Brontë and Austen, the journal claimed, created feminized domestic fictions relying on verisimilitude. Writing in 1908, May Sinclair countered the notion that genius could only be perceived as male or that Charlotte was somehow undeserving of the accolades accorded to genius due to perceptions of her coarseness. "It is high time that all this nonsense should be dropped," she declared in the introduction to Everyman's edition of *Jane Eyre* (xi). "Charlotte Brontë's genius, her heroic goodness and her sufferings should have placed her beyond its profanation" (xi). Sinclair noted, in keeping with Gaskell, that Charlotte's most significant quality of greatness was her passion. "Passion was Charlotte Brontë's secret" (viii). Yet Sinclair insisted that Charlotte Brontë's artistic fire not be perceived as "brutal animal passion" or the "sharp fever of the senses," but as the highly sentimental, if sometimes ignorant, expressions brought on by great feeling. Even here, however, Sinclair makes a tacit appeal, linking femininity with innocence and indicating that a woman who knows, or a "woman who did" (to paraphrase the title of Grant Allen's 1895 novel), could not easily lay claim to genius.

Alison Booth has reminded us that greatness has historically been conferred within a "male-dominated literary tradition" (*Greatness Engendered* 4).

---

[21] In *Writing for Immortality*, Anne E. Boyd persuasively demonstrates how four American authors—Louisa May Alcott, Elizabeth Stuart Phelps, Elizabeth Stoddard, and Constance Fenimore—worked to place themselves in a cadre of high-art literary producers, thus distinguishing themselves from mass-market "scribblers."

Even those women authors canonized into greatness, such George Eliot or Virginia Woolf, have had to contend with an aesthetic valuation of literary merit that relied upon a "model of the imperial masculine self" (*Greatness Engendered* 66).[22] As Battersby notes, the nineteenth-century gendered connotations of genius gave rise to a "sexual apartheid" in which women were moved to the peripheries of literary greatness, though not to the edges of literary production. Such a sexual apartheid had ramifications for how a work was assessed, since it required that a woman author be convincing in both her femininity and her artistry. Gaskell writes of Brontë: "She especially disliked the lowering of the criteria by which to judge a work of fiction, if it proceeded from a feminine pen; and praise mingled with pseudo-gallant allusions to her sex, mortified her far more than actual blame" (284). Brontë herself wrote to George Lewes on November 1, 1849:

> "I wish you did not think me a woman. I wish all reviewers believed 'Currer Bell' to be a man; they would be more just to him. You will, I know, keep measuring me by some standard of what you deem becoming to my sex; where I am not what you consider graceful, you will condemn me …. I cannot when I write, think always of myself and of what is elegant and charming in femininity; it is not on these terms, or with such ideas, I ever took pen in hand: and if it is only on such terms my writing will be tolerated, I shall pass away from the public and trouble it no more." (372)

All of Gaskell's work prior to the publication of the *Life* had been anonymously or pseudonymously published; this biography of Charlotte Brontë was the first of her works to carry the name Mrs. Gaskell.[23] Such a public and eponymous link with the subject increased Gaskell's potential for personal risk, but it also promised an exponential reward: she could be given full credit for the redemption of the worthy genius through the force of her own femininity, stature, and beliefs. Judging from the public response, Gaskell's gamble paid off. In both U.S. and British periodicals, critics reacted with relief that the job of representing genius fell to one so capable. *The New York Daily Times* proclaimed:

> It is a cause of congratulation that the materials for the composition of this Life were placed in hands so perfectly competent to the execution of the work as those of the author of *Ruth* and *Mary Barton*. No other living author could have done so well. Her affection for the subject, her personal knowledge, her previous experiences, and her natural genius, all fitted her for the work, and the manner in which it has been executed entitles her to the gratitude of the literary world. ("The Mystery of Jane Eyre" 2)

---

[22] For more on the gendered politics of canon formation, see Tricia Lootens, *Lost Saints*.

[23] Gaskell's novels were all listed as written by "anonymous;" earlier short stories were published either as being authored either by anonymous or by Cotton Mather Mills.

A brief biography of Gaskell written by Edna Lyall and published in 1899 as part of a compendium on the women writers of Queen Victoria's reign praised Gaskell's artistry 40 years after the fact:

> The enormous difficulties which attended the writing of a biography of the author of *Jane Eyre* would, we venture to think, have baffled any other writer of that time. It is easy now, years after Charlotte Brontë's death, to criticise the wisdom of this or that page, to hunt up slight mistakes, to maintain that in some details Mrs. Gaskell was wrong. To be wise too late is an easy and, to some apparently, a most grateful task; but it would, nevertheless, be hard to find a biography of more fascinating interest, or one which more successfully grappled with the great difficulty of the undertaking. (120)

This increase to Gaskell's literary fame was perhaps an equal if not a greater boon than the exoneration of her "dear friend." Though I do not believe that Gaskell's potential for personal and professional gain was her sole or even dominant motive for writing the *Life*, Gaskell's return in professional capital does suggest that the *Life* established for posterity two literary reputations—the misunderstood and much maligned novelist who, invested with genius, struggles against great physical adversity and therefore merits her fame; and the source of her redemption, the crusading and virtuous novelist of social conscience, who speaks through meek words to save, explain, and reconstruct the figure of the coarse and excessive author into a more sympathetic genius. Such a dyad makes Gaskell's presence in the text not only important but inescapable, for the biography becomes not about detached and objective accounting but the tale of two authors and hence, as much a rendering of Elizabeth's life, profession, and celebrity as of Charlotte's.

Re-membering Charlotte

I've argued here that Gaskell constructed the female genius by representing Charlotte as both brilliant and brittle, subject to the whims of a magnificent imagination and a delicate body. I've argued, too, that Gaskell created her own "arrant coward" persona as a way of claiming gender credibility through projected modesty and restraint. Doing so reconfigured the terms of both genius and literary celebrity, allowing a woman to be both conventionally feminine and deservedly famous. The combination seems to have yielded a brand of celebrity impossible to resist, since the heightening of Charlotte's artistic stature and gender credibility brought a frenzy of fan responses.

Juliet Barker notes that at the time of its original publication, the *Life* was "seized upon and avidly read by everyone, from London literati to provincial novel readers, all of whom were intrigued to discover how and why a woman as retiring as Charlotte Brontë could have produced some of the most passionate and explosive fiction the world had yet seen" (796). Writing in 1917, Alice Meynell noted that Gaskell's *Life* made a vivid and lasting impression on readers, particularly since it was so often "one of the first books of biography put into the hands of a child, to whom *Jane Eyre* is allowed only in passages" (80). It was the idea of Charlotte, rather than Charlotte's ideas, that the *Life* worked so assiduously to construct.

As soon as his daughter's biography was published, Patrick Brontë was deluged with requests for mementos of the author, particularly scraps of her handwriting, and he told Elizabeth Gaskell that he had been cutting Charlotte's letters into "strips of a line each" so that he might better meet the demand (Meta Gaskell 240). This must have come as a piece of rather disconcerting news to Gaskell, who by this time would have realized the material and historical value of keeping Brontë's letters intact. Two months after the biography appeared, Haworth experienced a deluge of visitors. The *Bradford Observer* wryly noted that the Brontë phenomenon had given rise to rampant capitalist tourism:

> Scarcely a day passes that a score of visitors do not make a pilgrimage to the spot where Charlotte Brontë lived and died. The quiet rural inns … have raised their tariff to an equality with the most noted hotels in the pathways of tourists…. The old proverb, 'make your hay while the sun shines,' is diligently obeyed by the bonifaces in this locality. (2 July 1857, in Barker 810)

Barker provides a vivid sense of the high-pitched desire for Brontë memorabilia soon after the appearance of the *Life*:

> Tourists walking up the main street were confronted with the first examples of Brontë souvenirs: even the chemist was cashing in on the trend, displaying photographs of Patrick Brontë, the church and the parsonage for sale in his windows. William Brown, who had taken his brother's place as sexton, was similarly milking the tourists for all they were worth, inviting them to see Charlotte's signature in the marriage register and then showing them his own collection of photographs "with an intimation that they were for sale." (811)

The trafficking in Charlotte held equal force across the Atlantic. As Barker notes, "The Americans appear to have been amongst Charlotte's greatest admirers, not only making their way to Haworth to visit her home but constantly importuning for her autograph" (814). In 1861 an American tourist bought the sash from the window of Charlotte's bedroom and the wire and crank of Mr. Brontë's bell-pull, announcing his purchases in a letter written to his mother on stationery sold by John Greenwood, which depicted an engraving of the Brontë vicarage and cemetery with the inscription, "The Home of Charlotte Brontë."[24]

The *Life* itself was a powerful tool in the commodification of Brontë and by itself constituted a transatlantic publishing phenomenon. Smith, Elder & Co., Gaskell's original British publisher (as well as Brontë's), brought out 27 printings between 1857 and 1900. D. Appleton in New York published the *Life* steadily between 1857 and 1895. J.M. Dent and Co., and E.P. Dutton joined forces

---

[24] "The Home of Charlotte Brontë," Sophia Smith Collection, Smith College.

in the twentieth century to publish the *Life* simultaneously in Britain and America, as augmented by several presses, large and small, including Penguin and Oxford. At this present moment, we can look back to more than 131 different dates for new releases of Gaskell's biography.

Throughout the nineteenth century and into the twentieth and twenty-first, a plethora of biographies and novels rose up in both Britain and the United States about Charlotte and the Brontë family. As both Lucasta Miller's *The Brontë Myth* and Patsy Stoneman's *Brontë Transformations* attest, in many ways, the Brontë legend has become the greatest story ever retold, with a new biography and/or fictionalized re-imagining of the Brontë life and work published every decade, continuing to the present time.[25] Indeed, George E. Woodberry, writing for *Harper's Bazaar* on the occasion of the 1899 re-issue of the collected Brontë sisters' novels, presciently observed, "Certainly the biographical interest shows as little indication of exhaustion as the literary interest itself, as such recent studies as Mr. Clement Shorter's have proved a generation after Mrs. Gaskell's first vivid presentation of the story" (979). Brontë came to represent the object of desire for talented (or just ambitious) young women who wanted to shake off the dust of their home soils and make their mark in the world, as evidenced in such writer-heroines as that in Charlotte Riddel's *A Struggle for Fame* (1883), who patterns her life and her writing on a model of authorship provided by Brontë, only to be left alone when fame and fortune find her. "To write! To be perhaps a second Charlotte Brontë! To spring a masterpiece upon my family!" daydreams the protagonist of Rhoda Broughton's *A Fool in Her Folly* (1920). To be like Charlotte Brontë was to hope for a form of professional success and public legitimacy, yet it was also to desire

---

[25]   These include: T. Wemyss Reid, *Charlotte Brontë: A Monograph* (1877); A. Birrell, *Life of Charlotte Brontë* (1887); C.K. Shorter, *Charlotte Brontë and her Circle*, 1896; Margaret Oliphant, "The Sisters Brontë" in *Women Novelists of Queen Victoria's Reign* (1897); Maurice Clare, *A Day with Charlotte Brontë* (1911); C.K. Shorter, *Charlotte Brontë and her Sisters* (1905); May Sinclair, *The Three Brontës* (1912); E. Dimnet, *The Brontë Sisters* (1924); I.C. Clarke, *Haworth Parsonage, a Picture of the Brontë Family* (1927); E. Romieu, *The Brontë Sisters* (1931); E.F. Benson, *Life of Charlotte Brontë* (1932); Irene Cooper Willis, *The Brontës* (1933); E.M. Delafield, *The Brontës: Their Lives Recorded by their Contemporaries* (1935); G.E. Harrison, *Haworth Parsonage, a Study in Wesley and the Brontës* (1932); F.E. Ratchford, *The Brontës' Web of Childhood* (1941); Laura L. Hinkley, *The Brontës: Charlotte and Emily* (1945); Phyllis Bentley, *The Brontës* (1947); L. and E.M. Hanson, *The Four Brontës* (1949); Phyllis Bentley, *The Brontë Sisters* (1950); Margaret Lane, *The Brontë Story* (1953); A.B. Hopkins, *The Father of the Brontës* (1958); Winifred Gerin, *Branwell Brontë* (1961); J. Lock, *Patrick Brontë* (1965); Winifred Gerin, *Charlotte Brontë—The Evolution of Genius* (1965); Elisabeth Kyle, *Girl with a Pen: The Story of Charlotte Brontë* (1967); Phyllis Bentley, *The Brontës and their World* (1969); Nancy Bryson Morrison, *Haworth Harvest* (1969); Winnifred Gerin, *Emily Brontë* (1971); Miriam Allot, *The Brontës: The Critical Heritage* (1974); John Cannon, *The Road to Haworth* (1980); Rebecca Fraser, *Charlotte Brontë* (1988); Lyndall Gordon, *Charlotte Brontë: A Passionate Life* (1994); Juliet Barker, *The Brontës* (1994); Lucasta Miller, *The Brontë Myth* (2004).

that one's labors be invisible and effortless, so that a newly successful author might astonish her family with her "overnight" accomplishments.

One of the primary authors considered in *Women and Literary Celebrity in the Nineteenth Century*, Elizabeth Robins, wrote her own testament to Gaskell's telling of Brontë's story. In her novel *White Violets, or, Great Powers* (1909), written soon after the *Life* was re-released in 1907, Robins constructed a humorous fictional world patterned on Gaskell's *Life* in which a parson's sickly daughter aims to write "the next *Jane Eyre*" and channels the ghost of Charlotte Brontë through a ouija board in order to do so.[26] The significance of the Brontë legend is something that Robins ironically underscores through mockery (and reverence) in *White Violets*. Unsympathetic characters outwardly scoff at Brontë, calling her writing naive and old-fashioned. Indeed in *White Violets*, the "contemptuous" love interest Michael Romford ridicules Brontë's celebrity, noting that the present rector of Haworth is constantly beset by fans incapable of realizing that the rectory is someone's actual home and not a "shrine of dead genius." It is a moment of great relief, he says, when the fans leave the rectory and go off to the museum in order to "apostrophize Charlotte's old shoes and prostrate themselves before the Brontë teapot" (263). Clearly Robins is a bit tongue-in-cheek when raising the Cult of Charlotte, but Robins also positions Brontë as a figure greatly revered by the women characters in the book, Selina and Barbara. For them, Brontë is a writer transcending time and condition who knew and understood the special trials of women.

Perhaps the oddest and most compelling example of the influence of the *Life* and the power of Brontë's celebrity came with the 1913 donation to the British Museum of Charlotte Brontë's letters written to Constantin Heger. Gaskell had simply glossed over the rumors of a relationship between Charlotte and her Belgian schoolmaster, Msr. Heger. Sue Lonoff notes, however, that these letters were "confessional narratives that make [Charlotte Brontë's] feelings for [Constantin Heger] disturbingly evident" (346). The letters had been kept a secret in the Heger family, guarded first by Louise Heger, Constantin and Zoe's daughter, and later by her brother Paul. Lonoff notes, "As late as 1913, there were relatives who worried that the family's good name might be dishonoured" (346). By the end of the century, the value of the letters was in jeopardy as a number of "tell-all" books were about to hit the marketplace speculating on the fictive relationship between Lucy Snowe and M. Paul Emanuel in *Villette* and its real-life parallel in Charlotte Brontë and Constantin Heger.[27] All four letters were consequently published on July 29, 1913, in the *Times*. Paul Heger wrote a particularly interesting letter to his family in which he makes no pretense about any connection between Brontë and his father but actually refers family members to her books as a way of substantiating family memories:

---

[26] For greater discussion of this novel, see Weber "Channeling Charlotte."

[27] Fredericka Macdonald, a former student of Heger's, published *The Secret of Charlotte Brontë* in 1914; Angus Mackay published *The Brontës: Fact and Fiction* in 1897. See Lonoff 346, as well as fn 9, 347–8.

> In Charlotte Brontë's novels, you can find a description of the big house where we grew up and of the garden…. Some partially accurate details have also been given by Mrs. Gaskell in her book, "The Life of Charlotte Brontë"…. In the portrait she has drawn of her hero [Paul Emanuel], Charlotte Brontë has caught many traits of my father's character. It is true that he sometimes had fits of anger, but they passed so quickly! – and were followed by effusions of kindness that revealed all the generosity of his heart. (qtd. in Lonoff 345)

As Paul Heger has written it, Charlotte Brontë becomes not the rift in the family fabric, a potential scandal that can hurt their good name, as would have been the case prior to the *Life*, but a gifted and well-known author who honored the patriarch by depicting him in her text. It works against posterity to believe M. Paul Emanuel can be anyone other than Constantin Heger, a radical reversal brought on by the cachet of Brontë's literary reputation and perceived gender purity.[28] The family's change in attitude suggests one way that gender-stains can be washed clean through public visibility.

In *Frenzy of Renown*, Leo Braudy distinguishes between celebrity as the unearned consequence of public attention and fame as the earned reward of merit. As I note in the introduction, although I often use the terms interchangeably in this book because I believe the separation between personality and merit is not so easily known or made, in this case I think Braudy's division is helpful. It was celebrity that made of Charlotte a commodity to be purchased in window sills, signatures, and bits of handwriting cut from her letters, all of which constituted a dismembering of the authorial body as it was appropriated and consumed by a mass-culture readership; it was fame that re-membered that body by gathering her papers at the British Museum and establishing various archival storehouses for the bits of paper ephemera that constituted her textual body. It was fame, as well, that Gaskell worked to construct in her making of the genius Charlotte one of the most highly recognized authors of all time. We see here, then, a process in which remembering simultaneously permits re-membering.

Devotionals

Throughout this chapter, I have attempted to demonstrate the very specific ideological agendas at play in Elizabeth Gaskell's representation of Charlotte Brontë and the manner in which Gaskell's *Life* has come to set the template

---

[28]   The Heger family was not alone in capitalizing on its brush with cultural capital through Charlotte's celebrity. In 1897, Anne E. Keeling published "The Real Charlotte Bronte" in the *Wesleyan-Methodist Magazine*, claiming that Mrs. Brontë had bestowed upon her daughter, Charlotte, a "delicate fragrancy of purity, piety, and sweet, refined affection," which, in turn, was "redolent of the atmosphere of early Methodism" (39). In the same year, Elsa D'Esterre-Keeling wrote in the *Dublin Review* of Charlotte's primary national allegiance (through her father) to Ireland. Indeed, there existed a widespread interest in Brontean Irish heritage, particularly in the last decade of the nineteenth century.

for crafting an understanding of femininity and female genius. As a point of contrast that reinforces the ends to which representation can be put, I end with the consideration of a 1946 Warner Brothers movie about the life of the Brontës called *Devotion*. From the outset, the film plays more as a rendition of *Little Women* than of the "tragedy of the Brontës." True, there is no smiling and patient Marmee always willing to curb her high-strung brood, and there is an irascible father akin to the moody and tyrannical Patrick Brontë of Gaskell's *Life* ever ready to strike fear into the hearts of his daughters, but we as viewers are constantly made witness to a life of zest and frivolity, led by three gay sisters and their naughty brother Branwell, replete even with a gratuitous scene of the girls in their under garments as they dress for the Christmas dance. The opening inter-title may announce that this story is the life of "three sisters and a brother, all of great talent—and two with genius" but it makes clear that the real genius in the Brontë family is the sensitive, passionate, and poetic Emily (Ida Lupino).[29] Charlotte (Olivia de Haviland) is the consummate flirt and busybody, too consumed by her own life and ambitions to be aware of the pain of others (eerily evoking the possibility of de Haviland's character, Melanie, from the 1939 *Gone With the Wind* if she had been playing Scarlett's part). Branwell is a drunk and a disappointment with a nasty mouth, but he has a prescient ability to read his sisters and their thoughts. Anne is a pleasant non-entity. Her books are never mentioned. (For that matter, no books are mentioned aside from *Jane Eyre* and *Wuthering Heights*.) The best that can be said for Anne is that in this happy Hollywood version, she doesn't have to die at the end.

The literary lives of these celluloid Brontës function as backdrop to the more pressing concerns of the love triangle involving Emily, Charlotte, and Arthur Nicholls (played here by French-accented Paul Henreid). Charlotte flits through an infatuation and heated kiss with Msr. Heger, confesses her love for him to Madame Heger, and is firmly rebuked. Immediately after, she decides to pursue Arthur Nicholls, whom Emily has admired and loved from the beginning. Nicholls leaves Haworth to save Emily's dignity, but he cannot forget Charlotte, who has become quite the toast of London in her striped top hat and matching silk gown, signing autographs like a natural celebrity. The authoress of *Jane Eyre* floats through literary London on the laurels of her success, arm in arm with the great, if fatherly, Thackeray. She returns to Haworth to discover Emily, pale and wasted, soon to draw her final breath. Emily dies bequeathing Nicholls to Charlotte; the movie ends with her death and Charlotte's final realization that fame is less important than romance.

---

[29]   Katherine Frank's 1990 biography, *A Chainless Soul*, hyperbolically contends that Emily Brontë was the greatest genius of the clan, albeit anorectic and miserable. In her introduction to the Longman edition of *Wuthering Heights*, Alison Booth credits poet Mary Robinson with turning the tide in 1883 toward a belief that Emily held the greater genius. Further, writes Booth, "In 1912, May Sinclair spoke for those who revered Emily Brontë as supreme poet and pagan visionary – infinitely Charlote Brontë's superior" ("Introduction" xvi).

The insistent heterosexual romance theme of this film makes it clear that the tale of the Brontës is really the story of Charlotte learning a necessary lesson in humility and domesticity. Significantly, she, the lesser genius, only learns this lesson when Emily, the genius par excellence, sacrifices her love for Nicholls. Charlotte is continually played as boisterous, egocentric, and unperceptive. Emily, on the other hand, knows Charlotte so well that even in her last moments of life, she is able to recognize Charlotte by the sound of her footsteps on the stairs. In neither case, as specifically contrasted with Gaskell's rendition, is literary production represented as labor, nor is fame or genius connected to the intrinsic quality of a literary product or feminine ethos (in Emily's case, genius is a by-product of her martyrdom and melancholy).

I find the representations in *Devotion* startling because they so strongly contrast with the version that has become normalized through repetitive telling—Elizabeth Gaskell's rendition of the delicate and demure Charlotte, a pure Victorian lady down to her bird-like fingers and toes, an unearthly bright light caught in the fragile frame of her weak body. *Devotion*'s Charlotte is cheeky, flirtatious, attractive, bold, and in desperate need of a lesson in deflecting her rampant sexual energy. This tale, ending with a moral of love and rapprochement, depicts Charlotte as needing to learn how to "really love" and to curb her flirty mannerisms. The cautionary tale is one that has restraint as its crux, a theme of particular relevance to the post-war period in American history when women were being coaxed back to the home after their lives in the workforce.

Interestingly, though, in its emphasis on heterosexual love as a domesticating device, this movie is much like the typical genre of nineteenth-century texts, both British and American, that take up consideration of the famous female author. Like Augusta Jane Evans Wilson's *St. Elmo* (1867), Rhoda Broughton's *A Beginner* (1894), Louisa May Alcott's *Little Women* (1868), or Margaret Oliphant's *The Athelings* (1856), *Devotion* maintains the theme of a woman committed to authorship throughout its narrative, only to drop her profession at the movie's end when she is published and famous but not fully happy. Full resolution for each of these stories requires dismissing the writerly aspect of the heroine's life altogether, so that she might be united with the man she has desired throughout the majority of the story and only earns through the sacrifice of her unwomanly hubris, marked here as famous authorship.

The marriage plot of this film and these other novels featuring famous author-character heroines, stand in marked contrast to Elizabeth Gaskell's rendering of Charlotte's marriage to Arthur Nicholls. Though historically Gaskell was compelled to inform the reader of Charlotte's marriage nine months before her death, she hardly romanticized the union. In fact, E.M. Delafield subtitles her section on the marriage between Brontë and Nicholls as drawn from Gaskell's *Life* as "The Pathetic Wedding" (232), emphasizing both its pathos and its futility.[30] Departing from a classic love/marriage plot and offering a successful literary career as replacement for the husband was in fact quite a bold bait and switch. Surely, *Devotion* was up to no such subversion. Yet Elizabeth Gaskell, whom Lord David Cecil dismissed in his *Early Victorian Novelists* as a "domestic, tactful, unintellectual ... typical Victorian woman," managed to reconfigure the very notion of what a writing woman might mean (qtd. in Schor 221). It was this idea of famous female genius that continued to circulate across the oceans and the decades, forming and influencing the enduring myth of Charlotte Brontë.

---

[30] A different gloss on the Nicholls/Brontë union comes through "Clever Married Women," published in *Chambers's Journal* in 1880. The author notes that Charlotte Brontë married Arthur Nicholls in the "zenith of her fame" and was pleased that Mr. Nicholls "would rather have preferred than otherwise that she had not written at all" since in this way Charlotte could be sure he was in love with her as a woman, not a famous authoress (285). When Arthur Nicholls died in 1906, *The New York Times* reinforced his paleness in contrast to the light of Charlotte's enduring fame. "This generation, and in fact, the one preceding it, has been accustomed to consider the author of 'Jane Eyre' and all those who belong to her as people of a bygone time, so that the news that her husband has been living all these years comes as a surprise to almost everybody" ("Romance" SM3).

Chapter 2
"A sort of monster":
Fanny Fern, Fame's Appetite, and the
Construction of the Multivalent
Famous Female Author

Literary fame! Alas – what is it to a loving woman's heart, save that it lifts her out of the miry pit of poverty and toil? To have one's glowing thoughts handled, twisted, and distorted by coarse fingers; to shed scalding tears over the gravest charge which can be untruthfully brought against a woman's pen; to bear it, writing in silence, and have that silence misconstrued, or speak in your own defense, and be called unwomanly; to be a target for slander, envy, misrepresentation, of those of both sexes who can not look upon a shining garment without a wish to defile it – all this, a man's shoulders may be broad enough to bear, but she must be a strong woman who does not stagger under it.
—Fanny Fern, "Charlotte Brontë," *Fanny Fern, A Memorial Volume*

Fanny Fern[1] wrote the above words in her enormously popular *New York Ledger* column soon after she had read Elizabeth Gaskell's *The Life of Charlotte Brontë*.[2] Fern's response was sympathetic and seemingly sincere, which would have come as somewhat of a surprise to her readers since she was widely enjoyed for both dripping sentimentality and snappy, sarcastic critiques of all manner of social injustices. "Poor Charlotte Brontë! ... Noble Charlotte Brontë!" Fern wrote of her fellow authoress, who, like a "little bird," tried "bravely with outspread wings to soar" but was "often beaten back by the gathering storm cloud" (Parton 433). Charlotte, Fern claimed in the manner of Gaskell, had been ill-used by her stern father, her weak body, and the rigid culture in which she lived, a culture unable to appreciate this "delicate" girl with the "blue veins on her transparent temples" until it was "Too late – too late!" (Parton 435). Fern's rendition of Brontë is an evocation of the author perfectly in keeping with Gaskell's—the delicate woman

---

[1]   Scholars refer to Fanny Fern by many names, the most common being her last name through marriage, Sarah Parton. I call her Fanny Fern, the name she used in both public and private.

[2]   Fern is unclear as to what she means by "the gravest charge which can be untruthfully brought against a woman's pen." It may well be that she was referring to the rumors that Charlotte Brontë and William Thackeray had more than a professional relationship, although this rumor never surfaced in Gaskell's *Life*, to which Fern is here responding. It is equally possible that her vague reference is a defense against Brontë's perceived "coarseness" and unwomanly character, a charge also brought against Fern's writing.

who suffers the eccentricities of a violent father, is ravaged by the deaths of those closest to her, and yet remains stalwart in her femininity and in her authorship—all reconstructed through the loving language of the sister author.

Fern's representation, however, departs from Gaskell's where marriage and fame are concerned. Fern reads the marriage between Arthur Nicholls and Charlotte Brontë not in the cursory manner in which Gaskell represents it, but as "the delirious draught of love" that could compel Charlotte's father to finally relinquish his "selfishness" and "relenting at last [give] the tender, shrinking flower to more appreciative keeping" (Parton 436). That Charlotte is doomed to die after she has found love (as distinct from dying after she has merely become married, as in Gaskell's version), constructs Charlotte Brontë as a tragic romantic character. This also makes Brontë more strongly resemble a host of sentimental heroines who suffer through life and only find happiness in the fleeting moments before death. As such, Fern takes Gaskell's public re-imagination of the author Brontë in a different direction than I outlined in Chapter 1, offering the reader a version of the famous female author built on the frame of the sentimental novel's heroine: she is weak, delicate, unappreciated, moral, and fulfilled less by fame than by romantic love and domestic activities. This portrait is ironic given Fern's representation of the famous authoress Ruth in *Ruth Hall* (1855), which depicts a young and physically delicate woman (cast largely in the mold of the Charlotte Brontë Fern portrays in this brief sketch), who, through necessity, shakes off her acculturated feminine passivity and begins to assert herself and her literary talents to become fully autonomous, financially independent, and, as an added boon, widely famous. Importantly, Fern's Ruth does not aspire to marriage but to writerly success, a detail that disrupts the normative frame of hetero-romance.

Another critical difference in Fern's re-interpretation of Brontë manifests in the above epigraph discussing fame. Though Gaskell is clear that Brontë did not write for attention and shrank from the notoriety she received, that she was a "solitary woman ... a little, motherless school-girl" (351), she imbues her subject Charlotte with qualities designed to make her not only a shrinking modest violet, but a case study in famous genius. In so doing, she constructs Brontë as a fascinating figure worthy of the public gaze, or, as I note in Chapter 1, a legitimately famous feminine and womanly artist. In response to Gaskell's *The Life of Charlotte Brontë*, Fern eschews notions of literary fame in images that underscore contamination, impurity, and the inadequacy of the female body to contend with the rough and tumble world of the masculinized public sphere. Her language evokes associations of the marketplace where "glowing thoughts" become commodities, like tomatoes on a fruit cart that can be "handled, twisted, and distorted by coarse fingers." The uncontrolled mauling of these "glowing thoughts" bruises their beauty, robs them of their assumed purity; in short, it transforms an idea from the sanctity of the mind to the heterogeneous mass of the social body where "coarse fingers" may mean Irish or black or working-class fingers as easily as it means ill-educated and unappreciative ones. It seems fitting, then, that Fern would underscore her author-character Ruth's distance from the celebrity machine by noting that after she has achieved success, Ruth argued most passionately "those articles were written for bread and butter, not fame" (*RH* 136).

Though fame is depicted as an undesired by-product of industry, *Ruth Hall* comes loaded with testaments to Ruth's great genius and the celebrity she, in the guise of her literary persona, Floy, deserves. For both Gaskell and Fern, the author as character (Charlotte and Ruth) does not actively seek fame but possesses a genius that can't help but make her famous. Fern takes this idea one step further in her version of professional authorship: in contrast to popular stereotypes, to be famous does not unsex a woman by putting her in a manly frame. She is not manly or "a sort of monster." By contrast, Fern contends that a woman can legitimately possess both female and feminine qualities and still have marketplace savvy and public visibility. These versions of the writing woman as both vulnerable to and triumphant over gender/sex codes accentuate Fern's multivalent construction of the famous woman. Indeed, due to a widely held belief that *Ruth Hall* was autobiographical, the multivalence in Fern's portraits of famous female authors extends not only to her characters but to herself, allowing her to capitalize on the "ambiguity of her identity" (Tonkovich 35). Fern thus leads her readers to the conclusion that the famous author (herself most pointedly) is not victimized by the marketplace; she thrives in it.

I argue here that this very form of mulitvalence functioned as a primary strategy Fern deployed to increase representative possibilities about women's place in a dynamic nineteenth century divided by changes in politics, industry, and social relations. Fern offered a transatlantic readership a broad range of woman writer personae through her frequent and popular columns and novels—from the delicate Ruth to the "monstrous" Gail Hamilton, from the tragic Charlotte Brontë to the "homely" Harriet Beecher Stowe, to more than twenty different (and conflicting) portraits of herself. In so doing, Fern widened the cultural sense of what the famous author could be and do. Accentuated in these increased liberties is the perceived threat that comes when denizens of the private sphere engage in public sphere concerns. Fern does not back down from these dangers; indeed, her marketplace metaphor that starts this chapter calls to mind scenes of sexual peril in which the protections a writer can rely on as a middle-class white woman are stripped from her. She references "one's glowing thoughts" as vulnerable to handling, twisting, and distortion; and as I have noted, images of "handling" and "twisting" connote tactile, concrete bodies in (unpoliced) physical spaces, thus suggesting a direct correlation between a woman's thoughts, her written text, and her body.

As part of the work of this chapter, I examine several portraits of Fern's famous women authors and then turn to a consideration of her author-character Ruth Hall. Within this analysis, I look specifically at the scenes of sexual peril depicted in *Ruth Hall*, since these are rife with information about the raced and classed body that illustrate how the weak woman's body (both physical and textual) becomes strong when made visible through and celebrated within the marketplace. These scenes, and the multiplicity of author figures Fern represents, suggest the degree of knowledge-power that a public woman must possess and the degree of control she must exert to both protect herself and project her public image. Looking closely at a number of Fern's portraits, I argue that she forms a plurality of author types. These, in addition to the many idioms she uses for her own self-representation, necessarily complicate easy gender/sex dichotomies that limit perceived agency and identity.

"Handled, twisted, and distorted by coarse fingers"

The passage that begins this chapter concerning Charlotte Brontë offers a helpful case in point of Fern's regard toward fame. Her ruminations indicate that Fern does not see the writing product as completely separate from the writer, as an entity entirely in and of itself. Rather, Fern expresses indignation that one's intellectual progeny might be mistreated and misjudged when put into public circulation, a metaphor that makes the text a form of child, the implications of which I discuss in Chapter 5. Fern's imagery thus assumes an inextricable bond between the assumed privilege of the author's body and the consequent treatment of the text.

One might argue that if there is a continuity among idea, text, and body, the circulation of a woman's thoughts makes the literary celebrity's body metaphorically vulnerable to the handling, twisting, and distorting Fern describes. Indeed, it became increasingly frequent for rising female celebrities appearing in public, such as Harriet Beecher Stowe, Jenny Lind, or Fanny Fern herself, to be besieged by mobs of people, eager to have a lock of hair or some other personal effect. Richard Brodhead has characterized this phenomenon as one in which "private, domestic women" moved into public entertainment roles, and in so doing "court[ed] an invasion of their privacy." Brodhead argues this new public identity exposed, even if it did not invite, "the public's vicarious consumption" of celebrated womens' private lives (70). But, of course, it was not quite so unidirectional as Brodhead's account presumes.

Louisa May Alcott's 1886 novel *Jo's Boys*, for instance, contains a chapter, "Jo's Last Scrape," that perfectly illustrates the porousness between domestic and public when fans invade the writer's home with a voracious appetite for autographs and memorabilia (and leave a mess from their muddy boots in their wake). In this final novel of the *Little Women* trilogy, "Mrs. Jo" has, at some point in the indeterminate past, returned to authorship after the family falls on hard times. As an author-character, Mrs. Jo is immediately successful and, as *Jo's Boys* opens, she professes both amazement and satisfaction that she possesses all she has ever desired: "Money, fame, and plenty of the work I love" (1). The fame, however, becomes increasingly problematic for her and, as Alcott reports, Jo soon tires of renown and begins to resent the loss of liberty fame brings:

> For suddenly the admiring public took possession of her and all her affairs, past, present, and to come. Strangers demanded to look at her, question, advise, warn, congratulate, and drive her out of her wits by well-meant but wearisome attentions. If she declined to open her heart to them, they reproached her; if

she refused to endow pet charities, relieve private wants, or sympathize with every ill and trial known to humanity, she was called hard-hearted, selfish, and haughty; if she found it impossible to answer the piles of letters sent her, she was neglectful of her duty to the admiring public; and if she preferred the privacy of home to the pedestal upon which she was requested to pose, "the airs of literary people" were freely criticized. (37–8)

Alcott's very punctuation here indicates her frustration, as she loads offense after offense into one very long sentence, strung together with semi-colons. These demands on the famous author, commonly read as an autobiographical statement on Alcott's life, soon begin to weigh on Jo's body. Her health suffers as the incessant demands for "More stories; more right away!" (38) come flooding into the "protected" domestic sphere. In these passages, we see Jo's body mirroring the distress and dis-ease that Gaskell attributed to Brontë. Alcott writes, in another string of semi-colons:

She felt that she had done all that could reasonably be required of her when autographs, photographs, and autobiographical sketches had been sown broadcast over the land; when artists had taken her home in all its aspects, and reporters had taken her in the grim one she always assumed on these trying occasions; when a series of enthusiastic boarding-schools had ravaged her grounds for trophies, and a steady stream of amiable pilgrims had worn her doorsteps with their respectful feet; when her husband was forced to guard her at meals, and the boys to cover her retreat out of back windows on occasion when enterprising guests walked in unannounced at unfortunate moments. (38–9)

Jo argues that these time-consuming and work-interrupting invasions do her bodily harm: "time is money, peace is health, and I lose both with no return but less respect for my fellow creatures" (39). What's more, she argues that she "shall have no time to eat or sleep" if she attempts to "satisfy these dear unreasonable children" (40).[3] Fanny Fern lodged a similar complaint, writing in her column in 1860, "Do you suppose I wouldn't read several MSS. a month, give my opinion, and find a publisher, were the days longer, and my head stronger?" (Warren *FF* 258).

In all of these renderings of invasion on the life of the author, the threat is more literary than literal; though Jo's carpets suffer, the reader never has a sense that the author's safety is seriously at risk, and Alcott's language connotes humorous frustration rather than bitter vitriol. Yet both Fern and Alcott suggest ways in which supposedly impervious barricades of home and hegemony, buttressed by class, race, and gender privilege, can be permeated by fame. This, in turn, depicts the

[3] *Jo's Boys* continues to demonstrate the complexities of literary celebrity when Mrs. Jo's domestic "sanctum" is penetrated by a mass of swarming invaders that include: a reporter, a celebrity-seeking sycophant, teenagers from a ladies' seminary, a "black throng" of boys in muddy boots, a sketch artist, and a "daffy old woman" hoping to catch a grasshopper that she might add to her collection of "grasshoppers from the grounds of several famous folks" (52).

professional author as radically different from how the public might commonly imagine her. She is not the rose-scented goddess who floats through the woods spouting poetry, a wild genius of the moors, or a gender/sex confused bluestocking, but a besieged and harried housewife who runs her writing business from her home and is frequently interrupted (and harassed) as a result. "Jo's Last Scrape" suggests several ways in which fame can intrude on the author's physical life (though interestingly, there are no further scenes of fans interrupting the narrative in the remainder of *Jo's Boys*, a seeming impossibility given the turmoil Alcott describes as quotidian). Fanny Fern's discussion of the famous author, by contrast, uses similar associations of invasion or, in her words, being "defiled," that put the famous woman in an irreparable double bind. If she writes on in silence, Fern contends, that silence can be easily misunderstood as arrogance; if she writes to protect her "glowing thoughts," as she says in defense of Charlotte Brontë, she is called "unwomanly." The female body, she says, must be unusually strong "not to stagger" under the weight of this contradictory public expectation.

It is fitting that Fern's article on Brontë ends in a pointed marker of sex difference and fame: "a man's shoulders may be broad enough to bear, but she must be a strong woman who does not stagger under it." The trope seems to resonate with Fern, since she made a similar comment about literary celebrity and the woman's body through the figure of Harriet Beecher Stowe, noting satirically, "Well, I hope your feminine shoulders are broad enough and strong enough to bear all the abuse your presumption [to fame] will call down upon you" ("Mrs. Stowe's Uncle Tom," *Olive Branch*, May 28, 1853). Through use of these metaphors, Fern seemingly resolves the fame debate at the level of physiognomy, arguing that broad male shoulders are better suited to shield the famous author from the injustices and personal attacks brought by celebrity, thus appearing to align herself with a biologically determined and male-dominated organization of gender and sex. But in her statement there is also a plausible argument for something quite different: any woman who is to exist as famous must be doubly strong in order to bear fame's weight. Hers is an argument not for female passivity and physical delicacy, but for a robustness of womanly character and frame, an argument she would make in her newspaper columns with repeated zeal throughout the course of her career.

In her columns for *The True Flag* and *The Olive Branch* and then later exclusively for *The New York Ledger*, for instance, Fern repeatedly criticized what she termed "fashionable invalidism" in women. She was a strong advocate of sensible clothing, physical exercise, and nourishing food and was fond of showing that men were often more vain than women.[4] Scoffing at the fad of female physical delicacy, she prophesied an equivalent to the Coming Man through her

---

[4]   See "Thoughts on Dress," *Olive Branch*, July 19, 1851; "A Law More Nice Than Just," *New York Ledger*, July 10, 1858; "A Law More Just Than Nice, Part II," July 17, 1858; "The 'Coming' Woman," *New York Ledger*, March 12, 1859; "Fashionable Invalidism," *New York Ledger*, July 27, 1867.

"'Coming' Woman" who, she maintained, "shall be no cold, angular, flat-chested, narrow-shouldered, skimpy sharp-visaged Betsey, but she shall be a bright-eyed, full-chested, broad-shouldered, large-souled, intellectual being; able to walk, able to eat, able to fulfill her maternal destiny, and able – if it so please God – to go to her grave happy, self-poised and serene, though unwedded" ("The 'Coming' Woman," *NYL*, February 12, 1859). Fern's strategy here is not to erase those ever-intruding coarse fingers brought by celebrity and the marketplace but to strengthen what they might touch—the woman's body. She does not eliminate the danger but fortifies the target, thus adding a new dimension to what the famous woman might be and mean and do. This is a rhetorical tactic similar to that employed by other authors examined in this book, specifically Margaret Oliphant, Elizabeth Robins, and Mary Cholmondeley. As a strategy for difference, Fern's representation heralds the power of the famous female author, who can marshal her imagination as the primary power in a cultural war of images.

Who is this "strong-minded horror"?

A crucial aspect of Fern's "Coming Woman" is that she be robust in mind as well as body. This differs markedly from Gaskell's Brontë, who is "made perfect by suffering" (Kingsley, qtd. in Lyall 121–2). Fern's portrait of the "Coming Woman" openly challenges the transatlantic Victorian ideal in terms that would most startle the power elite: Fern declares women shall be large of soul and body, with vigorous habits and demanding appetites.[5] In so doing, Fern offers an idealized portrait of womanhood that is almost a half-century ahead of itself. Indeed, Martha J. Cutter strings together a list of choice adjectives used to describe the New Woman of the 1890s that could easily apply to Fanny Fern's "Coming Woman" of the 1850s:

> Monstrous. Titanic. Hideous. Revolting. Rebellious. Screeching. Shrieking. Shrill. Extraneous. Odd. Queer. Mannish. Sexless. Oversexed. Undersexed. Indecent. Abnormal. Disobedient. Self-Centered. Self-Assertive. Self-Defined. Immoderate. Excessive. Wild. (14)

Perhaps it is not surprising that Cutter's list is itself internally incoherent and obsessed with categorizing and containing behavior through the idioms of sex and gender. Nor is it surprising that all of these adjectives were applied in one way or another to Fern. What may be surprising is the manner in which Fern, unlike Gaskell or Brontë, routinely turned the critics' barbs back at them, using the invective against strong and visible women to argue for their value.

To see evidence of Fern's talent in turning the discursive sword back into its sheath, consider a particularly vicious review of her work that ran without a byline

---

[5]   As Jaime Harker demonstrates, those appetites, for both Fern and her woman of the new age, included sexual desires. Harker contends that Fern's writings created "a public space for women's sexuality, which was both creative and redemptive" (52).

in the *New York Ledger* in October 1857, immediately preceding the publication of Fern's new anthology *Fresh Leaves*. (Though long, I include the review in full here because its substance perfectly illustrates Fern's critical reception).

This little volume has just been laid upon our table. The publishers have done all they could for it, with regard to outward adorning. No doubt it will be welcomed by those who admire this lady's style of writing: we confess ourselves not to be of that number. We have never seen Fanny Fern, nor do we desire to do so. We imagine her, from her writings, to be a muscular, black-browed, grenadier-looking female, who would be more at home in a boxing gallery than in a parlor, – a vociferous, demonstrative, strong-minded horror, – a woman only by virtue of her dress. Bah! the very thought sickens us. We have read, or, rather, tried to read, her halloo-there effusions. When we take up a woman's book we expect to find gentleness, timidity, and that lovely reliance on the patronage of our sex which constitutes a woman's greatest charm. We do not wish to be startled by bold expressions, or disgusted with exhibitions of masculine weaknesses. We do not desire to see a woman wielding the scimitar blade of sarcasm. If she be, unfortunately, endowed with a gift so dangerous, let her – as she values the approbation of our sex – fold it in a napkin. Fanny's strong-minded nose would probably turn up at this inducement. Thank heaven! there are still women who are women – who know the place Heaven assigned them, and keep it – who do not waste floods of ink and paper, brow-beating men and stirring up silly women; – who do not teach children that a game of romps is of as much importance as Blair's Philosophy; – who have not the presumption to advise clergymen on their duties, or lecture doctors, and savants; – who live for something else than to astonish a gaping, idiotic crowd. Thank heaven! there are women writers who do not disturb our complacence or serenity; whose books lull one to sleep like a strain of music; who excite no antagonism, or angry feeling. Woman never was intended for an irritant: she should be oil upon the troubled waters of manhood – soft and amalgamating, a necessary but unobtrusive ingredient; – never challenging attention – never throwing the gauntlet of defiance to a beard, but softly purring beside it lest it bristle and scratch.

The very fact that Fanny Fern has, in the language of her admirers, "elbowed her way through unheard of difficulties," shows that she is an antagonistic, pugilistic female. One must needs, forsooth, get out of her way, or be pushed to one side, or trampled down. How much more womanly to have allowed herself to be doubled up by adversity, and quietly laid away on the shelf of fate, than to have rolled up her sleeves, and gone to fisticuffs with it. Such a woman may conquer, it is true, but her victory will cost her dear; it will neither be forgotten nor forgiven – let her put that in her apron pocket.

As to Fanny Fern's grammar, rhetoric, and punctuation, they are beneath criticism. It is all very well for her to say, those who wish commas, semi-colons and periods, must look for them in the printer's case, or that she who finds ideas must not be expected to find rhetoric or grammar; for our part, we should be gratified if we had even found any ideas!

We regret to be obliged to speak thus of a lady's book: it gives us great pleasure, when we can do so conscientiously, to pat lady writers on the head; but we owe a duty to the public which will not permit us to recommend to

> their favorable notice an aspirant who has been unwomanly enough so boldly to
> contest every inch of ground in order to reach them – an aspirant at once so high-
> stepping and so ignorant, so plausible, yet so pernicious. We have a conservative
> horror of this pop-gun, torpedo female; we predict for Fanny Fern's "Leaves"
> only a fleeting autumnal flutter.

How surprised many readers would have been to discover this vicious attack of
Fanny Fern was written by none other than Fanny Fern. While the parody seems
obvious from our own vantage point, the tenor of this critique fits the tone of many
other reviews published in this periodical, and so few readers would have been
"tipped off" to the satire by Fern's hyperbole. It is perhaps a nineteenth-century
example that all publicity is good publicity, but it also evidences Fern's ability to
use her celebrity in order to gain power and alter stereotypes through mockery.

In her satiric review, she sets up a number of caricatured situations that expose
the biases of literary criticism. Her writer, who assumes the position of the male
critic, admits never having seen Fanny Fern but imagines her as "a muscular, black-
browed, grenadier-looking female … a vociferous, demonstrative, strong-minded
horror, – a woman only by virtue of her dress." The monster constructed out of
language does little to tarnish Fern's own reputation—she need not fear being
attacked by this black-browed horror—but her referencing of her own potential
monstrosity does suggest that one way for Fern to pretend to demonize herself is to
construct a male critic who relies (a bit too heavily) on the language and imagery
of gothic melodrama. In dismissing "his" exaggerated claims, the reader similarly
dismisses his critique.

The latter half of the first paragraph in praise of "appropriate" women fulfills
a similar function. By praising passive and docile women who are the pawns of
patriarchal demand, Fern again constructs a farcical situation where it is not the
women who "bristle and scratch" that the reader is encouraged to abhor, but the
weak men who need women to be yet weaker (and as a further bonus, Fern is
able to take a stab at lady novelists who are "not all that they should be" ["Male
Criticism on Ladies' Books," *NYL*, May 23, 1857]). Her parody is furthered by
the critic's suggestion in paragraph two that it would be much more womanly to
double up under adversity, or, as she says in another piece, "the majority would
consider it more 'feminine' would she unobtrusively gather up her thimble, and,
retiring into some out-of-the-way-place, gradually scoop out her coffin with it"
("A Bit of Injustice," *NYL*, June 8, 1861). Fern's constructed male critic doesn't
let her off the hook for unconventional stylistic choices, saying they are no
compensation for the dearth of ideas found in her piece. This attention to style,
however, might well have been a wave at the reader—for the piece is saturated
with the broken sentences, the play on words, the alliterative phrases, the dashes,
italics and odd usages of semi-colons that brand a piece of writing as Fanny Fern's.
Finally, the review concludes by reminding the reader that editors are often
patronizing to women writers: "[I]t gives us great pleasure, when we can do so
conscientiously, to pat lady writers on the head." It is appropriate that Fern makes

her ersatz critic rail against the "scimitar blade of sarcasm" since hers is so well sharpened and pointed in this piece.

Here and in other columns, Fern suggests to readers that they must adopt a level of critical detachment when reading reviews of literary materials, advising them to be aware that a bad review may be just as much due to the editor's too-tight boots or weak cup of coffee that morning as to a true flaw in the piece, noting that "critics are subject, like others, to envy, ambition, and little uncharitablenesses, which grow out of them" (*Ginger-Snaps* 24). If we were to put this into the lexicon of twenty-first-century literary theory, we would say that Fern is aware of the manner in which ideological and ontological conditions determine aesthetic assessments, that there is no such thing as a "pure" reception state, that our subject positions are in constant negotiation with, and sometimes reaction against, the text. By holding up her own work as the subject of critical analysis, Fern shows the reader the machinations of the magician's art; she teaches that reader how to perceive more critically, and in so doing, she openly challenges the idea, by turning it into farce, that famous women are monsters or that retiring women are the ideal. As such, she uses her celebrated platform to make a point that neither the hyper-feminine nor the hideously monstrous are categories sufficiently nuanced to represent the famous female author.

Rules, What Rules?

What, then, can we make of Fern's seeming capitulation to hegemonic demands for the delicate and passive invalid as the ideal woman, demonstrated at the opening of this chapter in her response to Gaskell's Brontë? How do we reconcile these versions of the famous woman that are both monstrous (in her representation of herself and, as I will discuss, of Gail Hamilton) and angelic (in her representation of Charlotte Brontë or Ruth Hall)? Was Fern's writing bifurcated into the journalistic and the novelistic, so that she could be more candid in the newspapers but conformed to what Joanne Dobson has called "strategies of reticence" in her fiction? What can we make of the Fanny Fern who calls forth a vigorous and vibrant woman, strong of body and mind, independent of masculinist paradigms, and yet also creates characters like Ruth Hall, who walks in moonbeams and sunshine, or "Our Hatty," who cries, "O, what is Fame to a woman? Like the 'apples of the Dead Sea,' fair to the sight, ashes to the touch! From the depths of her unsatisfied heart, cometh over a voice that will not be hushed, – Take it all back, only give me love!" (*Fern Leaves* 39). Did the famous Fanny Fern regard fame as a pollutant, a foul by-product that un-sexed a woman through visibility and the lack of modesty it conferred?

A closer look at Fern's representations shows that while she criticizes the ramifications of fame, she does not critique its terms. She does not re-imagine celebrity so that it can be cast in metaphors more pleasing and, one might argue, less powerful. Instead, she represents fame and the writer who contends with it through the trope of contagious agent and victim. This metaphor underscores the author's credibility by depicting her engaged in a contentious and dangerous physical struggle. The battle, if victorious, affords her greater physical fortitude. Indeed, such a context places her more firmly on the road where travels the "'Coming' Woman."

In the pantheon of characters who comprise Fern's author-characters, three very important elements are present: each woman is true to some sense of her artistic vision, regardless of the social, familial, or financial pressures with which she contends; each woman is given a body—some slim and white, others large and dark (unfortunately, none slim and dark)—rather than that body being effaced; and finally, whether delicate or demonic, each woman becomes known to the public and achieves some vindication through this fame.[6] Rather than weakening a popular sense of the role of women's authorship, these disparate representations disrupt prevailing codes governing gender/sex legitimacy by pluralizing the potential types of famous authoresses.

Fern accomplishes this empowerment by playing fast and loose with the "rules," not only by defying the gendered conventions of true womanhood (leading Lauren Berlant ironically to label Fern a "power transvestite" [435]), but also in deploying a non-conventional discursive style and expression in the production of her public identity. Fern's biographical sketch of Gail Hamilton (Mary Abigail Dodge) in *Eminent Women of the Age* (1872) is perhaps the most telling evidence of such strategies.[7] Almost all of the *Eminent Women* entries adhere to a rigid formula: a fairly straight detailing of the author's childhood and background, a description of her looks and carriage, some discussion on her critical reception and road to popularity, and whatever personal remarks the biographer feels are relevant about the subject. Fern's chapter on Gail Hamilton is immediately different. Fern arranges the beginning of the sketch in epistolary form, so the piece reads like a transcript of letters exchanged between herself and Hamilton. "My dear Miss Dodge, otherwise Gail Hamilton," she writes, "A book is in prospect. Many of our well-known literary people are to write for it. Its title is to be 'Eminent Women of the Time.' You and I are to be in it. I am to do you. Who is to serve me up,

---

[6]   Fern's writings are peppered with references to authorship and the business of literary production. When I speak of Fern's "pantheon of woman writers," I reference Ruth Hall as well as several author-characters in her newspaper columns, including "Tom Pax's Soliloquy," "The Soliloquy of Mr. Broadbrim," "Charlotte Brontë," "Our Hatty," "A Chapter on Literary Women," "Some Gossip About Myself," "The Women of 1867," "Bogus Intellect," "A Practical Blue Stocking," "The Widow's Trials," "Getting Up the Wrong Way," "Literary People," and her biographical sketch of Gail Hamilton in *Eminent Women of the Age*.

[7]   Covering many types of notable women including Rosa Bonheur, Florence Nightingale, Empress Eugenie, Queen Victoria, and Elizabeth Cady Stanton, *Eminent Women of the Age* was but one of many collective biographies edited by Fanny Fern's third husband, James Parton. Others included *Famous Americans of Recent Times* (1867), *The Peoples Book of Biography* (1868), and *Noted Women of Europe and America* (1883).

the gods only know" (202). After her own salutation, Fern includes Hamilton's responses, and so she seemingly authorizes her sketch of the famous Hamilton through that woman's own words. Indeed, it is possible to read this exchange of letters as historically valid, as Mary Kelley does when she notes, "The absurdity of one zealously private female pressing into print another equally private female was so apparent as to take on the trappings of farce, however unintentionally. 'I consider no crime more radically heinous than the violation of privacy,' Hamilton-Dodge wrote to Fern-Parton in response to the latter's request for information" (Kelley 136).

Since there is no archival record validating the exchange between these authors, I consider it likely that the Fern/Hamilton discourse was not an historical but a fictive conversation, created by Fern. As we have already seen, Fern had the talent and the wherewithal to mimic voices so that they might suit her own purposes. Though it may well be that Gail Hamilton wrote to Fanny Fern about her fiercely guarded private life, I doubt very seriously that the discussion in *Eminent Women* is a transcript of exchanged letters, particularly since they parallel, in style and content, Fern's own stance on the public woman and her private life. Let us look at a more extended excerpt from one of "Gail Hamilton's" letters:

> I shall have a lifelong quarrel even with you, if you spread before the public anything which I myself have not given to the public. I have really very strong opinions on that point; and, notwithstanding its commonness, I consider no crime more radically heinous than the violation of privacy. You must have suffered from it too severely yourself to be surprised at any abhorrence of it on my part. I most heartily wish you could find it in your plan to leave me out in the cold. Of course, if you judge from my writings that I am a woman, you can say what you please about that woman, that writer, and I have neither the wish nor the right to say you nay. So much of the woman as appears in an author's writings is public property by her own free will. All the rest belongs to her reserved rights. (204–5)

Whether this passage be authored by Fern or Hamilton, the choice for its inclusion, a choice Fern would have made, is telling, for in it she re-articulates her claim that no one has a right to tell the public anything about an author that the author herself has not willingly divulged. Fern took particular umbrage at critics who exposed a woman's "incognito-ship" (*Fresh Leaves* 300), suggesting that an author had the right to a protected privacy.

These arguments about celebrity and privacy are critical to the theoretical meanings of star culture. Those who write about celebrity in a post-Hollywood age have rightly noted the degree to which the commodification of the self through the brand label that is the celebrity constitutes one of the major dynamics of star culture. Jane M. Gaines's meticulous research in the area of legal rights and circulated images argues, for instance, that privacy doctrines in both the U.S. and the U.K. manifest differently for public figures since their status as "ordinary persons" is difficult to substantiate. Privacy laws, Gaines notes, are predicated on a norm of a singular being with rights to protection of a locatable self.

"Whose identity is signified," Gaines asks, when privacy issues are negotiated in the context of celebrity, "the identity of the person to whom the body belongs or the identity of the celebrity?" (87). Can the singular body, Gaines wonders, "stand for two identities at once?" (87). Gaines' analysis centers on the circulation of actual images, but Fern's epistolary discourse with Hamilton, and the verbal portraits that are so critical to such forms as the *Eminent Women* series, set up a similar set of questions about where the rights of the private subject become blurry in the context of public identity.[8] What constitutes the private, the degree to which it might extend into the domain of the public, and whether these are even stable and separate categories is, of course, not always easily discernible. Fern/Hamilton accounts for this slippage through a seeming clarification: what an author presents of herself in her writings "is public property by her own free will. All the rest belongs to her reserved rights." Such an idea is made highly problematic with a writer like Fanny Fern, who consistently wrote in persona, even when making reference to her husband, her daughters, her granddaughter, and her friends. She published in her columns discussions on "private" matters related to her clothing choices, her diet, her vacations, her moods, her sleeping habits, her illnesses (although in a somewhat veiled fashion), and her fame. And, ultimately, she divested herself of her patrilineal names through birth and marriage(s) and adopted in private and public the name she had given herself, the name linked to public celebrity. In this context, the celebrated Fanny Fern gives shape and form to Sarah Willis Parton; her celebrity is "natural," whereas what is constructed appears to be what is autobiographical. Accordingly, in the case of Fanny Fern private and public exist as discursive constructions that the author creates.[9]

Even if we allow that a separate spheres division was more ideological than actual and that social arrangements in the nineteenth century were far more complex than the separate spheres model suggests, Fern's division and consequent collapse

---

[8]   Shawn Michelle Smith notes that Fanny Fern was equally resistant to circulated images in daguerreotype form. "Fanny Fern was troubled by the craze for photographic portraits," writes Smith, largely due to a sense that "the mass circulation of the photographic portrait enabled by mechanical reproduction represents a kind of prostitution of the self" that paraded women in public showcases (93–4).

[9]   Mary Poovey's thoughts on the alienation of writers' from their work is illuminating in this context. She notes in *Uneven Developments* that the 1840s and 1850s first saw the emergence of both a mass reading public and the commodification of ideas as products for this mass market (101). While she argues that a male author like Charles Dickens is able to broker this conflict by speaking through the idioms of separate spheres, she notes the process was not so easy for women writers. "If the feminization of authorship derived its authority from an idealized representation of woman and the domestic sphere," she writes, "then for a woman to depart from that idealization by engaging in the commercial business of writing was to collapse the boundary between the spheres of alienated and nonalienated labor. A woman who wrote for publication threatened to collapse the ideal from which her authority was derived and to which her fidelity was necessary for so many other social institutions to work" (125).

of the private and the public allows her to stake out an important gendered claim. By protecting the private, she can be perceived as amplifying her feminine ethos. Further, her movement through what she herself terms the public also crosses over the very privacy boundaries she erects, thus lending her legitimate visibility by mobilizing the language of the private to speak publically. Fern's sketch of Gail Hamilton allows her to expand the range of what might constitute female celebrity by suggesting that the famous female author has the right to generate the domains of what can (and won't) be known, that there is a separation between who she is and who she purports to be, and that authors can both establish and violate these distinctions. In many ways, Fern is able to circumvent the binary oppositions inherent in (feminine) domestic and (masculine) public spheres, instead making the gendered nature of the literary celebrity dependent on representation. In so doing, Fern positions an author's "glowing thoughts" as only vulnerable to handling, twisting, and distorting if the author chooses for them to be.

Fern's sketch of Hamilton is also noteworthy for its refusal to conform to conventional biographical form. In particular, Fern's description of Hamilton is a non-description. The reader does learn that Hamilton's writing is strong enough to make stalwart men tremble, it displays a disregard for functionaries of authority, and it is mercilessly sharp. We also know that Hamilton herself has benefited financially from her wit and continues to write, though she has no economic need to do so. Yet, we learn little about the actual appearance of Gail Hamilton, a gap Fern continually reminds the reader she has not filled. Fern acknowledges that she disobeys biographical convention, as evidenced by her later comment in the piece:

> And now you will naturally say to me, – This is all very well; but tell us something about her personally. Where does she live; and how? Is she single or wedded? Is she tall or short? Plain or pretty? Has she made money as well as made mouths? In short, let us have a little gossip. That's what we are after.
>
> Don't I know it? I should think I had been laid on the gridiron time enough myself to understand your appetite. Well – here goes. "Gail Hamilton's" real name is Mary Abigail Dodge. Her birthplace is in Hamilton, Massachusetts. She is unmarried, a Calvinist, and an authoress from choice. (215)

Fern's seeming capitulation to the reader's demand for personal information and a physical description is anything but forthcoming. In this demand for the body— "Is she tall or short? Plain or pretty?"—Fern provides absence, turning the sketch to Mary Abigail Dodge's cat, who was accidentally left in the oven, and describing an idyllic life in New England that is everything but specific. She quotes several of her favorite "incendiary passages" from Hamilton's works and wonders how this "female monster came to exist" (206), but she never embodies this monster.

I have said earlier that Fern insists on a body in her representation of the author, yet here we see a sketch of Hamilton in which Fern refuses to provide details of the author's body. Her very evasions and her references to the reader's appetite for a visual image to consume, however, make the body inextricably present to the mind, even if invisible to the eye. Indeed, if the author's body is to be laid upon the gridiron for consumption by the public's voracious appetite, as Fanny Fern claims has happened to her, she makes of Gail Hamilton a bland dish. Although she has not described a body, Fern has made reference to its presence by cloaking its detail in a wrap of elaborate language that signifies the body, even when none is articulated. As such, Fanny Fern makes Gail Hamilton's "body-ness" present by evoking the blueprint of biography and blatantly refusing to conform to it. You ask for a physical description, she tells her audience. Well, here it is … but the description renders no body at all, merely the space where a body might be, a space filled by a physical presence that can make men tremble and that can impale on the point of a verbal lance, but it apparently cannot be described.

What I'm arguing here is remarkably (if surprisingly) comparable to the relation between the penis and the phallus. The penis by itself denotes male genitalia, yet its cultural power, in the form of the phallus, signifies more than a physical apparatus; the phallus evokes patriarchal values—dominance, muscularity, penetrating power. One need not see the penis in order to recognize the phallus; indeed, often the actual penis works against perceived phallic power. In a similar way, Fern erases the actual body of the famous author, yet the absence of the body signifies a greater presence of embodied power. To call it a phallic power would be a grave injustice, given that it is pointedly a female form Fern imbues with this power, yet we have insufficient options for naming a female equivalent of the phallus. In Fern's description of Hamilton, we see a woman's power that is both corporeal and not; it suggests a polymorphism rather than a dimorphism; it recognizes play and multiplicity; and, most significantly, it resists a conventional mode of representation that positions the woman's/heroine's body, to use Helena Michie's term, in "clichéd metaphors" (89).[10] Surely we see in Fern's handling of Gail Hamilton an overall treatment that allows, even compels, the famous woman to move outside the conventions of both the *Eminent Women* format and the "literary lady" stereotype.

Ruth Hall: Justifying Strength Through Weakness

As I have noted above, the rhetorical habit of tempering the "best" with images of the "worst," so that a more complex (and in some ways more ambiguous) middle ground might be achieved, seems ironic when we consider the character of Ruth Hall. It may also seem counter-intuitive that scenes of peril (sexual and otherwise) might actually allow for womanly power. To demonstrate just how Fern

---

[10] Michie writes, "The operation of cliché in Victorian heroine description has several important consequences. First, it defines and perpetuates an unceasingly iterable notion of 'woman;' all women are alike, all replaceable. Second, by reducing women's bodies to clichés, we deny the concept of individual or non-normative bodily experience and purge the deviant woman from representability. Third, cliché restricts sexual and intellectual arousal, making more possible a limited degree of enjoyment but erasing the potential for adventure" (89).

accomplishes these things, I offer in this section a close reading of Fern's literary protagonist Ruth Hall, suggesting that Fern's depiction of her author-character, particularly in the representation of fame and literary professionalism, provides both the need and the rationale for a newly constituted female power.

Ruth is a character cut from the cloth of the best of all sentimental heroines. She is lovely, lithe, and good-hearted, easily wounded, humble, and pious. Fern introduces the reader to her heroine on the night before her wedding, as Ruth ruminates on the coming changes in store for her in marriage. As many critics have noted, to begin with a wedding, rather than to end with it, immediately announces this book as contra-conventional in terms of its love plot; however, the depiction of Ruth at this point still adheres to the novelistic ideal, as expressed particularly through Ruth's body. Fern writes, "her lithe form had rounded into symmetry and grace, her slow step had become light and elastic, her eyes bright, her smile winning, and her voice soft and melodious" (15). This emergence into a woman's body has altered Ruth's relationship with the world. As a child she was bookish and clumsy; now she has grown into the sexual power that women of beauty possess, and she will use this power to her own ends, "that she might be loved" (13). But Ruth's appearance also makes of her a vulnerable figure. She is quickly on her way to the marriage market, an exchange of a woman's beauty and procreative power for a man's protection, "love," and financial support. This substitution is analogous to Ruth's later bartering of talents for financial sustenance in the literary marketplace.

The need for Ruth to exert financial autonomy emerges quickly in the novel with the death of her husband, Harry. Rejected by her natal family as well as by her in-laws, she moves from the cloistered setting of a rural resort to the working streets of a bustling city, a shift that represents the merging of her own body with the social body. After a series of failed money-making schemes, Fern depicts Ruth as wearily going from one publishing office to another. The editors, more "accustomed to dealing with hoydenish contributors" than with displaced ladies, fail to treat Ruth with the "respectful courtesy due to a dignified woman" (122). Fern underscores Ruth's class values (and privilege) by noting that the editors' remarks cause her to shrink back sensitively as "their free-and-easy tone fell upon her ear so painfully, as often to bring the tears to her eyes" (122). In this new working-class world, Ruth is treated as one of the great mass of the city, as indistinguishable from other dwellers in the working quarters in which she finds herself. Though now some months into her financial straits, Ruth is still wounded by the pointed absence of upper-class privilege, the "respectful courtesy" that used to be accorded her because she was a "dignified woman." Fern's representation conveys a sense that this treatment of Ruth is both unfair and unjust. Accordingly, the reader gleans that though Ruth lives *in* the Bowery, she is not *of* the Bowery. She is matter out of place, an enigma to her environment, which is equally enigmatic to her. Ruth is too naive to appreciate that she is no longer shielded by class or gender privilege (though one might argue she is still ontologically saturated with race privilege). Yet, the text makes clear the peril of her situation, and so the reader cannot be equally oblivious to Ruth's considerable risks.

Fern suggests that Ruth's safety is further imperiled by the way she is sexualized through the gazes of the Jims and Sams in the new neighborhood:

> "Jim, what do you think of her?" said a low-browed, pig-faced, thick-lipped fellow, with a flashy neck-tie and vest, over which several yards of gilt watch-chain were festooned ostentatiously; "prettyish, isn't she?"
>
> "Deuced nice form," said Jim, lighting a cheap cigar, and hitching his heels to the mantel, as he took the first whiff; "I shouldn't mind kissing her." (73)

It's hard to be a sympathetic character when you sport garish clothes and cheap cigars; it's downright impossible to be a romantic hero when you stand on street corners, leering after women, dreaming of pulling them to your pig-like face and kissing them with your thick lips. Jim and Sam haven't a chance. The threat they represent is potent and immediate: these men would violate Ruth's body as quickly as their eyes have violated her image.

In this scene, Fern builds the sympathy directed to her main character, and then imperils that character's safety by putting Ruth in situations both threatening and dangerous. Still naive, Ruth does not and cannot fully appreciate the dangers of her unprotected body, except to feel hurt by the harsh treatment she receives. Ruth's body is put on display, much like the literary celebrity's, largely due to the cityscape in which she circulates. It is not the heterogeneous environment that makes her body vulnerable to visual consumption, however. It is her ignorance. And, as I've noted, this is an ignorance the reader is not allowed to share. Because the reader overhears Jim and Sam's designs on Ruth, that reader is more aware of Ruth's peril than she is herself. This allows for a situation where the reader can see a clear need for an end to Ruth's lack of knowing. In effect, Fern constructs a scenario where Ruth's passive naïveté is not pleasing or "ideal" but a liability that threatens her very life. The only way for her to survive is to wise up.

Endangering Ruth's virtue and body, then, allows Fern to set up a condition that emphasizes weakness as a necessary call for power. She creates a motive for the Anglo-American Victorian woman to forcibly alter her circumstances by learning to perceive frailty, passivity, and ignorance as detriments rather than culturally approved gendered attributes. Indeed, it is soon after this scene that Ruth exerts herself. She perseveres against discouragement, outwits her unethical editor, becomes a widely famous author, and ultimately reclaims her children, thus indicating that determination and market savvy enable Ruth to fulfill her gendered and sexed roles more fully.

Fern employs a similar logic in her discussion of professional authorship: she emphasizes a seeming weakness, the inundation of demands brought on by fame, which, in turn, justifies the development of a new and unprecedented strength. As a fallen gentlewoman in a working-class world, Ruth must force herself to enter the fray, to walk past the Jims and the Sams who loiter at the front stoop, to take herself each day to the offices of the magazine for which she writes, because to refuse to engage with the public sphere will mean her death from neglect or starvation. After she becomes a celebrated author, she must also engage with a larger sphere through her readership, continuing to offer them a version of herself so that she might, in turn, receive what they give her—a public identity, financial security, and literary longevity.

Fanny Fern, as author, was all too aware of this delicate dance, writing in 1867, "Authors must expect the penalties as well as the rewards of their labors" (*Caper-Sauce* 86). One of the double-coded rewards/penalties to which Fern alludes is an abundance of letters from a transatlantic cadre of readers—in the form of commands, petitions, requisitions, and proposals—that constantly flood her desk. These demands from her fans are a burden, but they also provide indisputable evidence of her success. As documented in the novel, after Ruth in the guise of "Floy" has gained some fame, Fern similarly inundates her with fan mail. The letters, in their constant demands, requests, compliments, and complaints, suggest that Ruth/Floy has entered a market exchange, a bartering system that swaps her "glowing thoughts" for literary fame, financial solvency, and the demands of the public. Despite these connections, the operative word here is "suggest," for while the letters are represented by Fern as demanding something of Ruth, they also underscore Ruth's separation from those demands.

Several of the 18 fan letters in the novel underscore this point. For instance, the first letter of any length comes from a Reginald Danby who, after a two-page preamble, announces, "I wish to go through College; I have not the means. I wish you to help me" (155). Within the logic of the story, Danby's letter serves as an ironic juxtaposition. Ruth is still impoverished, separated from her older daughter, sustaining herself and her younger daughter, Nettie, on a diet of milk and bread, yet Danby feels quite certain that she will write his family history and sign the proceeds over to him. Fern does not comment on the letter, nor does she provide Ruth's response, instead cutting quickly to the next chapter. Such a demonstration of the author's narrative power suggests both victimization and strength. Ruth is embroiled in an exchange where there is a hungering public expecting, indeed demanding, that she satiate it at the same time as Fern mitigates the "motley crowd's" threat by forestalling any need for a direct response to the letters.

The rest of the fan mail furthers this sense. Marry me, says a slave-holding Southerner (152); send me your autograph, says a "Professor of some College" (152); I'm being sued and I'm in debt, says another, "I want you ... to assist me by writing out my story and giving me the book" (163–4); "My dog Fido is dead. I want you to write an epithalamium about him" (164–5); I am a "loving, but unloved wife" and believe I will soon die, 'Floy, will you be a mother to my babe?' (165); marry me, says an anonymous widower (181); I want a copy of your likeness to put in a Southern lady's rooms (181–2); I'm a bad editor, but I want to put your name on my masthead as Assistant Editress, and, "If, in addition to this little favor, you could also advance me the sum of one hundred dollars, it would be an immense relief to your admirer" (182). As Fern depicts it, each of these letters is capable of penetrating Ruth's private boundaries, putting her in a contact zone where she is subject to jostling and ill treatment, to the casual familiarity that her gender, race and class privilege has always insulated her from. Yet, the threat these letters represent is also fully containable, as they are dropped into wastebaskets, lost or forgotten in coat pockets, or made into toys for toddlers. Further, the power of her celebrity allows Fern (and one supposes Ruth) to describe through these moments how she is both much desired and fully able to snub her fan's demands.

As we saw early in this chapter in a discussion on Alcott's "Jo's Last Scrape" where autograph hounds and eager sycophants march into the author-character's home, the demands of fame are often represented as incessant and invasive. Rendering these scenes of violation in fictional form, however, shifts the balance of power. Alcott's biographer Madeleine B. Stern notes, for instance, that when Alcott's editor "objected to the indiscretions of describing 'Jo's Last Scrape,' Louisa reminded him that the success of *Little Women* had developed from precisely the same sort of experience and reality, adding that in no other way could the rising generation of autograph fiends be put to shame" (294). We see, then, that though her celebrity besets the famous author, that same celebrity allows her power in altering its conditions.[11]

Scholars who comment on the fan mail in *Ruth Hall* tend to group them into one of two categories: they are evidence of Ruth's and Fanny's personal connection with the audience and thus an indication of how closely Ruth/Fanny monitored the public pulse (Warren, Walker); or they provide incontrovertible evidence of Ruth's hard-won literary success (Brodhead, Harris). Susan Harris comes closest to my sense of the letters' function when she argues that letters communicate an indisputable sense of "Ruth's success as a writer" in ways that indicate, "All perceive Ruth as powerful," including Ruth herself (124). Indeed, the letters not only convince Ruth of her own power, they compel the reader to acknowledge the cultural authority that her celebrity wields. Similarly, in the same lengthy column in which Fern bemoans her own inundation by fan mail, she tells readers that she pockets their return postage, lets her granddaughter play with their postcards, and laughs at their ridiculous requests, clearly taking a position outside the scope of the letters' reach or her fans' opinions. The letters, both in *Ruth Hall* and in Fern's

---

[11]   By contrast, consider Augusta Jane Evans Wilson's management of fan mail for her author-character heroine Edna in *St. Elmo*, which does not participate in the form of ironic detachment or personal frustration evidenced in both Fern and Alcott: "The remaining eight letters were from persons unknown to her, and contained requests for autographs and photographs, for short sketches for papers in different sections of the country, and also various inquiries concerning the time when her new book would probably be ready for press. All were kind, friendly, gratifying, and one was eloquent with thanks for the good effect produced by a magazine article on a dissipated, irreligious husband and father, who, after its perusal, had resolved to reform, and wished her to know the beneficial influence which she exerted" (486). Even in the wake of harsh reviews, Edna's "avalanche of letters" offer her a protected "citadel, whence she could smilingly defy all assaults – in the warm hearts of her noble countrywomen" (520). See also Book III of *Aurora Leigh* in which Elizabeth Barrett Browning depicts Aurora contending with fan demands (129–99).

columns, suggest that the more the author receives, the more empowered she is to ignore "epistles which public persons receive" except from behind the mask of public persona in print (*Caper-Sauce* 84). As Figure 2.1 illustrates, Fanny Fern's coveted autograph may indeed be produced by the scribble of her pen, but it is just as likely a stamp fashioned in the shape of her signature.

Fern's elaborate representation here suggests a skillful ability to appear as if a part of her is vulnerable to the touch of coarse fingers, while evading their touch with relative ease. Further, just as in the case of Ruth's imperiled sexual well-being, Fern is able to position her character (and her own persona) so that the reader cheers at the acquisition and demonstration of both professional knowledge and cultural power. And so, though the celebrity must still cater to the public's appetite, Fern's styling allows the famous author-character some power in her discursive consumption. She does not just possess the power of Scheherezade to enchant or charm through narrative; she enjoys the power of the sultan to determine the terms under which storytelling takes place.

The Public that is "very much determined to look," and the Celebrity as Consumable Commodity

As we've already seen, Fern was particularly fond of a very vivid metaphor—the famous author on the gridiron being prepared for consumption by the hungry public. I've argued that Fern insistently embodied multiple representations of herself and her writer characters to confuse notions of "true" identity, and that such confusion, like a house of mirrors, led to a plurality of potential roles for women to occupy. By foregrounding the woman's beating heart, Fern appears to make it vulnerable to public appetites, a rather cannibalistic metaphor that speaks to some of the nineteenth century's greatest fears by evoking the dangers of dark peoples in savage lands. But Fern's gesture also allows for a slippage between the metaphoric and the literal, between the physical body and the discursive body, that affords her a considerable rhetorical power.

I do not mean to suggest that actual authors were not sometimes put in genuine physical peril by their celebrity and subjected to "visual consumption" (Brodhead 62). My argument here is that Fanny Fern was able to use her fame in order to mitigate victimization by discursively constructing her own and her author-characters' vulnerability on the page. Given her penchant for a good joke, it is fitting that Fern's method of dealing with potential threat brought by her fame was to retreat still further into it by finding refuge in the very thing that made her conspicuous, the many representations of Fanny Fern. Though Fern was certainly not the only female literary celebrity in the nineteenth century to devise a counter-strategy to offset the public's demands, she is, to my knowledge, the only woman who, as a widely syndicated columnist and novelist, could so frequently and so forcibly contribute to the discussion about gender, celebrity, and literary professionalism.

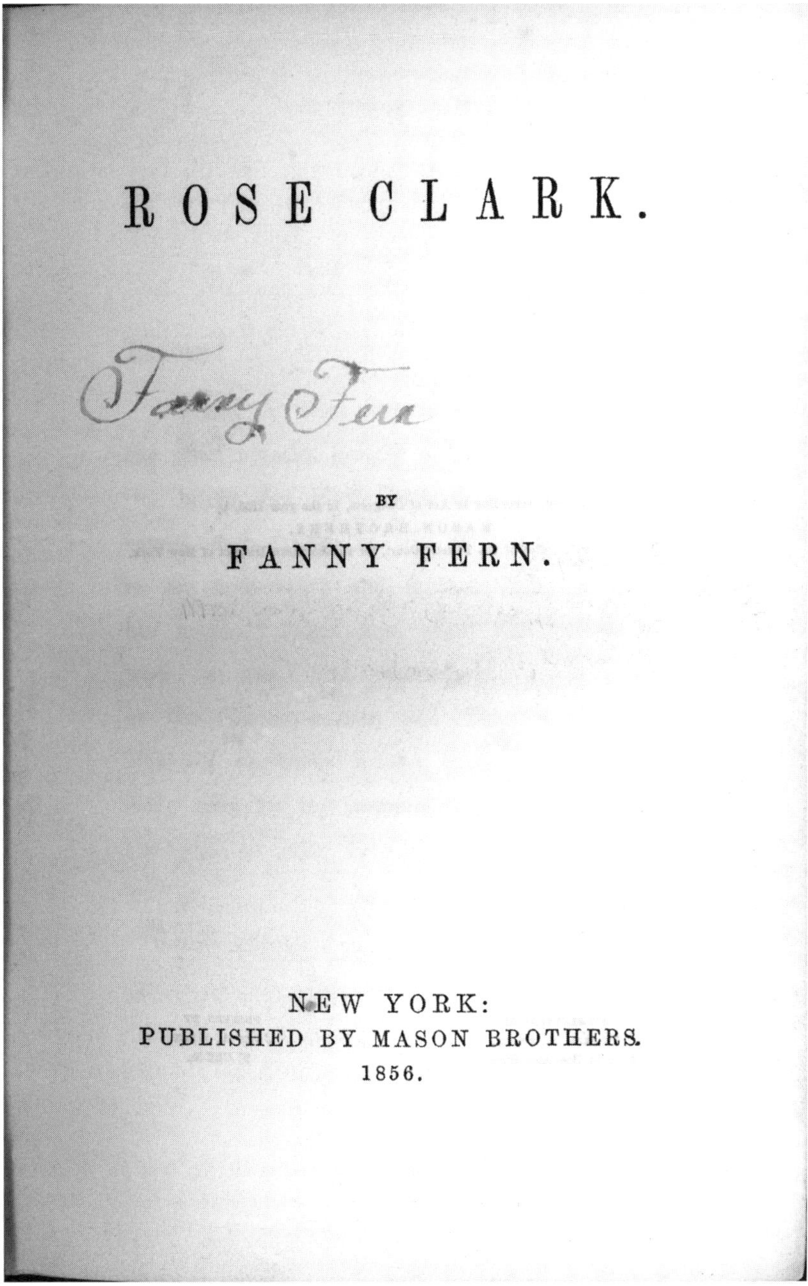

ROSE CLARK.

Fanny Fern

BY

FANNY FERN.

NEW YORK:
PUBLISHED BY MASON BROTHERS.
1856.

Fig. 2.1 Fanny Fern autograph. *Rose Clark*, 1856. Author's collection.

A bit of contrast with another celebrated author is helpful here. As I note in the introduction to this book, soon after the publication of *Uncle Tom's Cabin* (1852), Harriet Beecher Stowe experienced rather extraordinary transatlantic literary celebrity. According to the biography her son Charles would write about his mother, "Almost in a day the poor professor's wife had become the most talked-of woman in the world, her influence for good was spreading to its remotest corners, and henceforth she was to be a public character, whose every movement would be watched with interest, and whose every word would be quoted" (160). Stowe soon engaged in a publicity tour through Great Britain and Europe and was greeted along the way with a celebrity's welcome. Stowe's celebrity was in many ways a dividend of what Sarah Meer has described as "Uncle Tom mania," or the intense transatlantic response to and identification with the images of slavery and desires for freedom captured in Stowe's novel. When arriving in Glasgow, Harriet's brother, Charles Beecher, described her reception in his journal, saying: "they first clapped and stomped, then shouted, then waved their hands and handkerchiefs, then stood up – and to look down from above, it looked like waves rising and the foam dashing up in spray" (Hedrick 238). The architecture of this particular lecture hall, however, limited the public's visual and physical access to Stowe, since the "women's seating" confined her to the peripheries of the meeting hall, a social convention that kept her quiet like the "veils that covered women in Islamic cultures" (Hedrick 238). Although Stowe was the center of attention, it was her husband, Calvin, and her brother, Charles, who actually addressed the crowd. Richard Brodhead notes that the public's response to Stowe altered the terms of her relationship to that public: "The crowds that mobbed Stowe on her arrival in England were, in her words, 'very much determined to look' at her: on this tour Stowe became at once a figure of fame and an object of visual consumption" (62).[12]

In *Sunny Memories of Foreign Lands*, the travelogue/memoir that Stowe published in 1854 and that pulled together many of the letters she had written to friends and family during her post-*Uncle Tom's Cabin* journey to Great Britain and Europe, Stowe wrote with amazement at the crowds greeting them along their journey. In these letters, her response to her own celebrity is sometimes giddy, sometimes simply baffled, and sometimes convinced that the popular adoration she received spoke of the shared heritage and kindred parity between America and its "mother country" England and, in particular, Scotland. Writing to her sister, Stowe described the masses of fans waiting to see her as a gentle mob, noting, "The getting in to the hall is quite an affair, I assure you, the doorway is blocked up by such a dense crowd; yet there is something very touching about these crowds. They open very gently and quietly, and they do not look at you with a rude stare, but with faces full of feeling and intelligence" (*Sunny Memories*, I 84).[13]

---

[12]   Brodhead is quoting from Wilson, *Crusader in Crinoline*, 345.

[13]   As depicted in her published letters, Stowe did not consider the fan's frenzied appetite as a threat, either to her person or the fan him or herself. Instead, she saw communal fervor as an indication of something bigger than the self: "I do not regard it as

Throughout the 65 pages of introductory material that begins *Sunny Memories* —a section that was compiled and edited by Harriet's husband Calvin—the reader receives many pointed reminders that Stowe herself did not address these crowds. Accounts of her visits often include such statements as, "Professor Stowe then said, 'On behalf of Mrs. Stowe I will read from her pen the response to your generous offering ...'" (I xvii). According to these same introductory materials, such gestures of modesty were highly regarded amongst her Scottish and English "brethren," who applauded the famous author's, "still small voice which comes from the sanctuary of a woman's breast, and from the retirement of a woman's closet" (I xvi). Such retiring manners both affirmed and equaled a normative gender code whereby "the modesty of our English ladies ... shrinks instinctively from unnecessary publicity," thus requiring, in this case, that a male citizen stand up on behalf of the women of the town to offer the famous author, through the messenger of her husband, "a slight testimonial of their gratitude and respect" (I xvi).

We see, then, the self-conscious policing of femininity and silence. Yet, as I note in the introduction to this book, Hedrick describes Stowe as an agent in her separation, perpetuating her own silence since it afforded her an ability to move back and forth between different subject locations. Indeed, Sarah Robbins indicates that Stowe turned her celebrity and gender status to very specific economic and professional ends. On her travels throughout Great Britain and Europe, Robbins notes, Stowe cultivated a "careful self-presentation" that made of her a "humble, gentle, ladylike figure" as well as an assertive professional author (8). "While happily accepting gifts and accolades from enthusiastic fans," Robbins writes, "Stowe also followed through on her goal of negotiating copyrights" as well as securing financial remuneration and artistic material that furthered her authorial career (8–9). Stowe's recognition as a distinctly American yet wholly recognizable transatlantic celebrity allowed her to compensate for those gender-based restrictions that manifested through mobility and visibility. She was thus able to craft new options for what it meant to be a famous woman in the way she publicly displayed herself.

In May of 1853 Fanny Fern turned her particular form of scathing satire to the discussion surrounding Stowe's popularity and her writing. While not desiring to deflect the public's gaze from Stowe, she did alter its terms. Using a statement from *The Exchange* as a starting point, she soundly ridicules the argument that "Mrs. Stowe's Uncle Tom" is too graphic to be authored by a woman. In referencing the debate about the relative degree of indiscretion in the novel, Fern also offers some rich reflections on gender and literary celebrity. "'TOO GRAPHIC TO BE WRITTEN BY A WOMAN?' D'ye hear that, Mrs. Stowe? or has English thunder stopped your American ears? Oh, I can tell you, Mrs. 'Tom Cabin,' that you've

---

any thing against our American nation that we are capable, to a very great extent, of these sudden personal enthusiasms, because I think that, with an individual or a community, the capability of being exalted into a temporary enthusiasms of self-forgetfulness, so far from being a fault, has in it a quality of something divine" (*Sunny Memories*, I 54).

got to pay 'for the bridge that has carried you over.' Do you suppose that you can quietly take the wind out of everybody's sails, the way you have, without having harpoons, and lampoons, and all sorts of *miss*-iles thrown after you?" ("Mrs. Stowe's Uncle Tom," *Olive Branch*, May 28, 1853).[14]

Fern's letter to "Mrs. Tom Cabin," as we have seen in much of her other work, functions as a reminder to the reader to take advisedly published criticisms, but it also dances around the consequences of women's appearance, ambition, and fame. She tells this Mrs. Tom Cabin sardonically, "I'm sorry you have lost so much money by it, but it will go to show you, that women should have their ambition bounded by a gridiron, and a darning needle. If you had not meddled with your husband's divine inkstand for such a dark purpose, nobody would have said you was '40 years old and looked like an Irish woman.'" Riddled as it is with puns and double entendre, this is a good example of Fern's humor and satire. In this article, Fern purportedly attempts to come to Stowe's aid; yet, as so presented, the passage publicly emphasizes the criticisms directed at the famous author as a means of off-setting those criticisms. If you had not been ambitious, she tells Stowe tongue in cheek, you would not have been depicted as forty and "like an Irish woman," which is to say like a scullery maid or a washer woman.[15] Touching on the perks of celebrity, Fern pretends to chide Mrs. Tom, while reminding the reader of Stowe's significant prominence. What right, Fern asks Stowe rhetorically, did you have to be *paid* to go on a trip to Scotland, to enter the halls of English country homes, or to have "lords and ladies and dukes and duchesses paying homage to you." Ventriloquizing the gender regulation that was part of an Anglo-American popular press, Fern chastises Mrs. Tom Cabin for neglecting children, hearth, and home, only to "immortalize your name."

In this column, Fern creates a viable space for Stowe's fame through satire, yet to exonerate the author by reminding the reader of widespread public insults about her body and presence seems a somewhat enigmatic form of defense. And so we must ask what rhetorical function might be served by rearticulating in print that Stowe had been publicly maligned as appearing worn-out, middle-aged, and lower-classed, essentially as the white and Europeanized version of the "lowly" Stowe's book sought to redeem? It is clear that the juxtaposition is intended to strike the reader as particularly absurd, not to mention unjust and inappropriate. Reminding the reader of the petty criticisms directed at Stowe's body and appearance offers us another moment where Fern alters bias by turning it against itself. To memorialize Stowe as "like an Irish woman" is to knock the

---

[14]   http://www.iath.virginia.edu/utc/notices/noar34at.html. Accessed July 7, 2008. No page given.

[15]   Beth Lueck illustrates the degree to which Harriet Beecher Stowe was lambasted in the British papers for her appearance, including her "very curly hair, her diminutive stature, and her 'homely' face" (99).

exalted author off her sainted pedestal,[16] but more significantly, it is to use the terms of racial and class discourse to establish a revised system of value where celebrity can vie with domesticity to create a legitimate feminine/female self. It is only when the celebrated are deflated that the famous author can transform her features, that she can play with the shadows and light of her own celebrity in a way that allows her, to use Fern's metaphor again, to remove herself from the gridiron that roasts the celebrity's flesh. Instead of adopting through gender mimicry the dominant culture's notion of true womanhood, in these instances Fern champions the "pejorative" associations linked to age, ethnicity, class, and race as a way of claiming a powerful "other" voice and presence for the famous female author. Given this, Mrs. Tom's sturdy Irish body, coded as it is with working-class force, is precisely the body needed to do battle with fame's metaphoric appetites.

We can see this technique of aligning the narrator's approval with "discredited" social classes and bodies through much of Fern's writing but in particular it manifests in a piece retitled (by W.M. Moulton) "Mrs. Farrington on Matrimony." Fern's column begins, as do many of her essays, with a quotation to which she responds.

> 'Sambo, what am your 'pinion 'bout de married life? Don't you tink it de most happiest?'
>   'Well, I'll tell you 'bout dat ere—'pends altogether how dey enjoy themselves.' (Moulton 162)

Fern's response is one of playful chastising, "Sambo! Sambo! be quiet! You needn't always tell the truth. White folks don't. Just as sure as you do it, you'll lose every friend you have" (162). In the short article she cautions Sambo not to be fooled by appearances. "I hope you don't intend to insinuate that matrimony isn't paradise!" she cajoles him, for surely people standing up at the altar amidst "orange wreaths and bouquet de humbug" suggest perfect matrimonial bliss (163). As Lauren Berlant has noted, Moulton's retitling of Fern's work was intended to "undermine Fern's critical authority on marriage, since her own history scandalously includes divorce (from her second husband, 'Mr. Farrington')" (430). But it also allowed for a forum in which Fanny Fern's voice joins with, by commenting on, a dialogue between two black speakers conversing in a stereotypical "poor black" vernacular. It seems fairly obvious that Fern imports the voice of "Sambo" as a way of suggesting there is a truth that "the lowly" are better able to discern (and the implication here is that "marginalized" groups are automatically disqualified from the intoxications of 'bouquet de humbug'). Further, as Berlant argues, in

---

[16]   The pedestal is another metaphor of Fern's. "The writer does not like to descend from his pedastal [sic], and hear that he must begin at the foot of the ladder, and first of all, learn to spell correctly, before he can write" (*Folly as it Flies* 278). Though Fern is satirizing style, she also debunks the notion that the writer belongs on a pedestal at all, her self and her bad spelling particularly, though the pronouns in this piece conspicuously gender the arrogant author masculine.

the way Fern authorizes Sambo's voice, she "appears shamelessly to have chosen a degraded cross-margin alliance (with an African-American stereotype!) over the proper womanly marriage to white masculine authority, here embodied in her former editor [Moulton] acting in loco patriarchae" (430). Berlant argues that in so doing Fern's displacement of authority "redraws Fern in a kind of miscegenated moral blackface and makes her a kind of monster" (430). Berlant's implication here is that monstrosity results from a blending of incompatible idioms, the "vernacular speech," race, and class of Sambo and the rarefied domesticity built into Fern's speech, thus opening up "an ironic tap dance" that "reverberates far beyond the manifest frame in which marriage turns out to be a disappointment" (430). Berlant sees this tap dance headed to the "oft-used woman's rights analogy between white heterosexual women and enslaved African Americans" (430).[17]

The larger cannibalistic metaphor that imagines the literary celebrity as a virtual viand that can feed a ravenous public was thus matched for its vividness only by a trope whereby the celebrity's body operates in the same semiotic field as the slave's body. Michael Newbury argues, for instance, that famous antebellum authors, Fanny Fern included, experienced a form of bodily commodification on par with slavery. He claims, "The celebrity and slave were united through their shared cultural configuration as corporally consumable workers, laborers whose bodies rather than labor or production were available for consumption" (161). Newbury adds a crucial caveat that this analogy between the slave and the celebrity depends upon "select inclusions and exclusions, complex and ideologically charged constructions of property, and labor relations" (161).[18] The meanings of slavery and celebrity also vary in the mid-nineteenth-century according to location, since as a former slave-holding nation Britain looked with disdain on a United States that allowed and profited from slavery until 1865. While Newbury allows for a separation between "celebrity work" and "slave labor," he reads the bodies of both slave and celebrity as being comparably subjected to an "irrational non-economy" which, for the slave, was governed by "the master's pleasure, desire, and need to dismember, rape, or otherwise attack and consume the body of the slave at any cost" and, for the celebrity, was "defined not by the audience's desire for his cultural productions or by the possibility of economically profitable exchange between the celebrity and audience, but, rather, by the audience's irrational drive

---

[17]   Other scholars similarly stake a claim for Fern's significance by arguing that her writing evokes comparisons between the oppression experienced by white women and that endured by enslaved blacks. Joyce Warren, for instance, argues that "*Ruth Hall* is closer to the slave narrative of Harriet Jacobs', *Incidents in the Life of a Slave Girl* (1861), than to the novels written by middle-class white women of the period" because Fern refused to reproduce the "patriarchal preaching" that marked women "passive in the name of 'femininity,'" while Jacobs rebuked the "'patriarchal institution' that claimed that slavery was the ordinance of God" (*The (Other) American Traditions* 84).

[18]   For a contemporary reading of a racialized dynamics of celebrity that posits the star as slave, see Ramona Coleman-Bell "Droppin' it like it's hot: The Sporting Body of Serena Williams."

to see, touch, hold, possess, and consume the celebrity body itself" (161). Again, we see the invocation of the cannibal metaphor and the specter of race, as well as the suggestion that forms of social oppression in the nineteenth century are commensurate with slavery.

Certainly it is true that celebrities of the nineteenth century endured, even as they capitalized on, the public's fickle and incessant desire. Among the evidence I've already discussed of the public's hunger for celebrity, an account of Fanny Fern from the pseudonymous author "Sylvia" makes the public's fascination clear: "if Fanny Fern had been recognized at the Crystal Palace, she 'would have drawn the crowds to her like a magnet; there would have been more interest in her than in the president or all of the English lords and ladies'" (*Home Journal*, October 5, 1853, qtd. in Warren 222). "Sylvia" wrote this about Fern's celebrity before her best-selling novel *Ruth Hall* had even been started; after its publication, Fern was hounded by autograph seekers and fans demanding access to the famous Fanny. According to Warren, Fern felt extreme "impatience with celebrity hunters who pursued her" (Warren *FF* 274). She refused public lectures, went out disguised as a man or a working-class woman in order to hide from her fans as well as to circumvent class and gender-based injunctions that regulated white and middle- to upper-class women's bodies in public spaces. Fern repeatedly excoriated her over-eager fans, telling them in print that she had sent a piece of her poodle's hair to a fan seeking a sample of her own curly locks (see "Autograph Hunters," *Ginger-Snaps* 203).[19] All of this functions as support to the kind of celebrity Newbury elucidates, a celebrity that draws an audience eager to "see, touch, hold, possess, and consume" (161). Yet, drastically unlike the slave, Fern whetted the public's appetite, because, quite simply, though she was annoyed by its hunger, she, like all celebrities, relied upon sustained popular desire.

A Proliferation of Possibilities

Perhaps the best evidence of Fern's adroit handling of celebrity comes from "A Little Bunker Hill," written in 1853, about women's rights and suffrage:

> No sort of use to waste lungs and leather trotting to SIGH-ra-cuse about it. The instant the subject is mentioned, the lords of creation are up and dressed; guns and bayonets the order of the day; no surrender on every flag that floats! The only way left is to pursue the 'Uriah Heep' policy; look 'umble, and be almighty cunning. Bait 'em with submission, and then throw the noose over the will. Appear not to have any choice, and as true as gospel you'll get it. Ask their advice, and they'll be sure to follow yours. Look one way, and pull another! Make your reins out of silk, keep out of sight, and drive where you like!
> ("A Little Bunker Hill," *Olive Branch*, December 18, 1853)

---

[19]   Fern could also be more conversational with her readers, as demonstrated, as one example in "Chit-Chat with Readers and Correspondents," Forrester's *Boys' and Girls' Magazine*, and *Fireside Companion*. October 1, 1853: 124–8.

This advice drawn from Dickens, to "look 'umble, and be almighty cunning," is precisely the kind of counter-hegemonic move some feminist activists would advocate more than one hundred years later. Yet, in the middle of the nineteenth century, Fanny Fern was able to alter the signifying terms of the culture in which she resided largely by constructing various and contradictory figures of female literary celebrity. These representations covered a broad range—the misunderstood genius of Charlotte Brontë, the delicate and naive Ruth Hall, the "monstrous" and phallic Gail Hamilton, the "old and Irish" Mrs. Tom's Cabin, and, above all, the irascible independence of her own persona, Fanny Fern.

In her 1867 public call to all women to take up the pen as a way of saving their sanity, Fanny Fern remarks, "A woman who wrote used to be considered a sort of monster" ("The Women of 1867," *New York Ledger*, Aug. 10, 1867). Surely we can see how adeptly Fern herself depicts this monster, but she was equally adept at constructing a writer out of moonbeams and rose petals. All of this, I argue, was not merely to confuse her public or play an elaborate shell game designed to find the "real" author; it was a way of shattering stereotypes by revealing the ludicrously limited extent of their boundaries. It was a way of declaring in frustration and defiance that a professional woman who had earned a degree of fame was neither wholly monstrous nor completely angelic, or as Fern herself said, "although it is very shocking ... a woman who writes isn't always dressed in sky blue, and employed in smelling a violet" ("Bogus Intellect," *New York Ledger*, December 30, 1865). The construction of this "sort of monster" was Fern's way of giving voice and body to the author, allowing her to play outside and in between the circumscribed role of the "lady novelist" or the un-sexed and manly bluestocking. And thus, she provided a new way of working against prevailing Anglo-American cultural codes that imagined ideal women primarily in domestic roles.

Chapter 3
"Great genius breaks all bonds": Margaret Oliphant and the Female Literary Greats

Of our party that day was the authoress of Margaret Maitland, of Sunnyside – a fair Scotchwoman, not over twenty-two, a modest, quiet, lovable person, who seems far from having made up her mind to admit the fact of her own genius. Having wakened one morning to find herself famous, she believes the world to be laboring under some strange delusion, and accounts herself an immensely overrated little woman, after all.
> —Grace Greenwood, *Haps and Mishaps of a Tour in Europe*, 1853

Mrs. Oliphant was one of the most successful women writers of her time. She cared comparatively little for fame; what her heart longed for was human sympathy and love. She was oppressed with a sense of utter loneliness, which increased as she grew older and sorrow succeeded sorrow.
> —William Thomas Stead, "A Life Tragedy: Mrs. Oliphant's Autobiography," *The Review of Reviews*, 1899

By most reckonings, Margaret Oliphant Wilson Oliphant was one of the most prolific, influential, and widely known British writers of the nineteenth century. Over the course of her nearly half-century career, she garnered a substantial Anglo-American readership. Her first novel, *Passages in the Life of Mrs. Margaret Maitland* (1849), was published when she was 21 years old, followed two years later with another novel, *Caleb Field* (1851), and a third, *Adam Graeme* (1852), appeared a year subsequently. By the time that the American writer Grace Greenwood made her trip to England and the Continent as recounted in *Haps and Mishaps of a Tour in Europe* and would describe Oliphant as a "quiet, loveable person" who, perhaps disingenuously, "awoke to find herself famous," Margaret Oliphant was already a regular contributor to *Blackwood's Edinburgh Magazine*, writing for the prominent periodical so often over the second half of the nineteenth century that she termed herself a "general utility woman" on the magazine's behalf. Under *Blackwood's* auspices and through her stand-alone books, she became not only a household name but an important arbiter of aesthetic and intellectual standards—a veritable tastemaker—in both the United Kingdom and the United States.

At the time of her death in 1897, Oliphant could lay claim to a reputation as one of the most widely read and influential writers publishing in a transatlantic context. Oliphant's œuvre contained not only fiction, but also crossed into biography, literary history, and critique, thus situating her as one of the most featured and feared literary critics in the nation. Indeed, Oliphant's critical voice was at times so severe that her scathing reviews themselves occasionally contributed to her fame. Her denunciation of Thomas Hardy's *Jude the Obscure* was credited (or blamed) for Hardy's decision to stop writing fiction ("*Jude the Obscure*," *Blackwood's* 159 [January 1896]: 135–49).[1] Henry James famously complained of Oliphant that, "no woman had ever, for half a century, had her personal 'say' so publicly and irresponsibly" ("London Notes," *Harper's Weekly*, August 1897, reprinted in *Literary Criticism*, 1412). Yet, John Blackwood thought highly of Oliphant, considering her and George Eliot to be "probably the two cleverest women in the world" (qtd. in Finkelstein 32).

Given her stature and celebrity, it is thus more than ironic that Oliphant wrote about her own career as common rather than extraordinary. It is in particular in her posthumously published *The Autobiography* (1899) that Oliphant situated herself as a lesser literary producer who put the demands of family above career ambitions and thus would forever be relegated to a secondary tier of aesthetic regard. *The Autobiography* is itself a poignant and moving piece of writing that situates Oliphant at the aesthetic heights of her peers. It joins with the significant body of the rest of her published materials as a testament to a writer of great intelligence, fortitude, and talent. Indeed, I will argue in this chapter that rather than seeing Oliphant's rhetorical genuflection to an unworthy self as either a humble insecurity or an ironic modesty (both of which might have been quite sincere and "genuine" positions from which to write), the author-character that Oliphant crafts in *The Autobiography* performs a larger work, since she is able to link the "general utility woman" to greatness.

Although Oliphant was famously circumspect about personal divulgences and thus there is very little extant material from her life that might be considered a source of self-reflexivity about her own career, Oliphant's five decades of discourse on those she termed the "female literary greats" offered keen commentary on the multiple meanings of literary professionalism and fame. When these portraits of female genius are read in conjunction with *The Autobiography*, Oliphant's negotiations of her "self" and her career in relation to the larger ideological landscape of celebrity work not only to suture her life and writing to fame but to stretch the definition of gender roles for women. Much as with Elizabeth Gaskell's rendering of Charlotte Brontë's "great powers" through the dampening influences of normative femininity, Oliphant creates her character-as-self as strong on self-sacrifice and service and short on glory or achievement.

Such representation, of course, fits squarely within the Victorian idealization of womanhood. Although, as Alison Booth has noted, "Victorians were quite capable of admiring women who had nothing to do with that ability to be the font of selfless empathy," Oliphant's self-description reminds us that even in the context of nineteenth-century ideological heterogeneity, there was much to be

---

[1]   Dana J. Trela suggests that Oliphant's 1896 damning review in which she "lacerated Hardy's *Jude the Obscure*" actually hurt her reputation, since it suggested "prudish" and "squeamish" old-fashioned ideas out of tempo with the late 1890s (13).

gained by appealing to conventional scripts about gender propriety (Rosenman, "Gender Studies"). In contrast to those who had garnered the world's attention, Oliphant's literary career, as she renders it, accentuated her feminine sacrifice and her lack of fame; in effect, she fostered a notion of her uncertain claim to celebrity in a manner that reinforced her conventional articulation of gender, in the process establishing her own lasting significance as a woman of virtue, who also happened to be a formidable cultural producer.

Like Elizabeth Robins who uses a counter-intuitive writer heroine in the singularly unattractive George Mandeville—a point I will discuss in Chapter 5—in Oliphant's representation of the author-character who is herself, she reforms expectations of what the famous woman author should be through a construction of herself as of little consequence. This makes of her "failure" a moment that can be turned to her writerly account, even while offering a personal and poignant account of her life. Particularly in *The Autobiography*, Oliphant takes control of the representation of her literary life and professional celebrity by exercising the author's talent. She invents what Laurie Langbauer has termed the "Oliphant legend," the sense that she is a "hack" whose prolific output "blights a promise deserving better," and in so doing, Oliphant gains the artist's boon, posterity (*The Autobiography* vii). It seems somewhat fitting that the droll and clever Oliphant anticipated Daniel Boorstin's complaint that twentieth-century celebrity glorifies those who are famous for being famous since Oliphant heightened her fame in large part by publicly grieving its absence. In effect, Oliphant claimed fame for not being famous.

I thus argue in this chapter that although the invention of "herself" in *The Autobiography* suggests failure, Margaret Oliphant, "hack writer," affords Margaret Oliphant, professional writer, the possibility of pairing her name with England's literary greats, particularly Charlotte Brontë and George Eliot. In *The Autobiography*, the character she writes about is sympathetically steeped in self-doubt and mediocrity, thus affording this character—who remarkably possesses her own name, sex, and profession—an enduring reputation as a "modest, quiet, and loveable" woman, who would not assert her own prominence through more aggressive means. Like the retiring Harriet Beecher Stowe, who strategically accentuated her authority by performing the modesty expected of her, Margaret Oliphant created the terms for her own celebrity by constructing herself as undeserving of it. She accomplishes this, primarily, though a process of ever-finer comparisons: she establishes her own "diminished" writerly ability that she then puts in contrast to other great writing figures, only to reveal through means of this contrast that she is in many instances superior to these famous authors. Ultimately, whether the reader concedes Oliphant's greatness or sides with the likes of Eliot and Brontë, Oliphant succeeds in forever yoking her career to theirs, an achievement coming more fully into fruition now, more than a century after her death.

Oliphant was an accomplished and even searing literary critic who commented on every major and many minor literary works published within a 50-year period.

But it was particularly in the case of women where Oliphant's inclinations toward gender and celebrity are most evident. Through the processes of critical comparison, Oliphant constructs a portrait of female literary professionalism and fame that is compelled to accommodate both the quotidian writer and the transcendent genius, in the process uniting the culturally perceived male-ness of the paid writer and the culturally conferred female-ness of the domestic nurturant.

In effect, Oliphant lays out the rather startling proposition that the "exceptional woman" is not defined by *what* she writes but *that* she writes. And this leads to the necessary conclusion that a woman of talent is not "three-quarters male" by virtue of her ability or activities, as in Robins's *George Mandeville's Husband*, but that the signifying system itself must shift to accommodate her within its ideology. This is a representational device we also saw Elizabeth Gaskell deploy in her portraiture of Charlotte Brontë. In both cases Gaskell and Oliphant use the terms of a normative gender location that is saturated with information coding such an identity as middle-class, white, and conventionally feminine in that the author-character is moral, pure, and delicate. Gaskell and Oliphant each disassemble these differing parts so that they might engage in the work of critical exegesis. In the process of bringing the portrait back together again, the authors add new qualities previously anathema to the identity location, in the cases examined here, a newly heightened femininity "made pure through suffering" brings with it merited fame, perhaps even genius, garnered through professional authorship.

I do not mean to suggest that Oliphant was necessarily self-aware of these potential outcomes of her representations or, if deliberate, then only self-serving through them. But whether consciously or unconsciously performed, Oliphant contributed to a realignment of social codes that pertained to both gender and celebrity. Indeed, by juxtaposing her "self" as author-character against other famous author figures, both real and fictional, Oliphant expanded the register for what the category of female genius might mean and do. This may seem a rather audacious claim to attach to an author often remembered for her conservative stances on social issues, including suffrage and The Woman Question.[2] Yet, Oliphant was aware, as she wrote in a brief sketch of Elizabeth Barrett Browning, that there existed "many lines of limitation" promulgated by both convention and prejudice, which "prefer that a woman should not overstep" (*The Victorian Age*, Vol. II, 237–8). She noted such limitations had, in turn, led to an inferiority in female poets. "But great genius breaks all bonds, and these limitations are less and less respected as the world goes on," she argued, suggesting in one breath why a representational style that could imagine merited female genius might have resonance both to her own life and to posterity.

---

[2]   In her introduction to two centuries of critical responses to Mary Wollstonecraft, Harriet Devine Jump calls Oliphant "far from being a supporter of women's rights" (7).

"Rather a failure all around"

Dana J. Trela noted in 1995 that by the end of the nineteenth century Oliphant was called the "greatest living Scottish woman of letters," but she has been "largely overlooked in literary studies of the Victorian period" (12). Oliphant's significance to contemporary scholars is increasingly changing as the politics of canonicity more actively engage with discovering and discussing those female cultural producers who have been relegated to the canon's dusty peripheries. In the specific case of Oliphant, however, a common truism has held that it was her over-production rather than her sex or gender that laid the terms for her obscurity, since the bounty of her writing was perceived to have diluted its artistic value. As *The Contemporary Review* rather prosaicly put it, "Mrs. Oliphant is inexhaustible" (316). And while this reviewer considered most of her works to be "good," the author also seems to be somewhat overwhelmed by Oliphant's capacities to put ever more words on the page. Her voluminous production, like the drowning woman flailing in the ocean, seemed to speed her demise.

When Oliphant reflected on her own posterity, she often commented that her long career and massive output was detrimental to her literary legacy. In fact, she rather audaciously stated in *The Victorian Age of English Literature* that Charlotte Brontë's death at age 39 enhanced that author's long-term fame: "Miss Brontë had the great advantage with the public of ending there [at *Villette*], and leaving her fame to rest upon those three books" (Vol. I, 324). Oliphant's depiction of her own artistry as an activity hampered by material need and maternal sacrifice in many ways set the terms for describing her posterity that others have followed. As one of many examples, in his 1906 *Victorian Novelists*, Lewis Saul Benjamin (who also wrote under the name Lewis Melville) opined that Oliphant's fame diminished in direct proportion to her prodigious output. He noted that it was "highly improbable that there is any person living" who could have possibly read the entire works of Margaret Oliphant, seeing as they would cover "two hundred and twenty-one volumes [and] would occupy some nine yards of shelf-room, and would require the undivided attention of a diligent reader for at least a year" (259). Benjamin suggests that Oliphant was well aware "that her amazing literary fecundity was detrimental to her fame," but she voiced a hope that her writing would some day "get a little credit" (259). Writing in 1938, Virginia Woolf put the matter in starker terms: "Mrs. Oliphant sold her brain, her very admirable brain, prostituted her culture and enslaved her intellectual liberty in order that she might earn her living and educate her children" (*Three Guineas* 287). In her 1988 foreword to Oliphant's *The Autobiography*, Laurie Langbauer describes Oliphant's work as a "drug on the literary marketplace" that came about by "making herself a household name" and thus "an ultimately and appropriately forgotten one" (i). As so framed, it was pressing economic need and maternal duty that led to Oliphant's voluminous output, her artistry and claim to posterity forever marred by her obligations as breadwinner and mother.[3]

In a helpful article that details the discursive construction of Oliphant's productivity, John Stock Clarke has argued that we should be skeptical about the "over-production myth" that stands as a founding truth to her reputation. Clarke does not dispute the idea that Oliphant wrote much or that her popularity seriously waned in the twentieth century, but he argues that there were other factors, such as the decline of the triple-decker novel, Oliphant's attack on Hardy's *Jude the Obscure*, her popularity as a Mudie's lending library author, considered, claims Clarke, as "the haven for the mediocre," and her "deep distaste of publicity" that isolated her from the literary world and led to her posthumous obscurity (46). Like Clarke, I believe we must question the causality between hyper-production and prestige, but I believe that Oliphant was a more adroit manager of literary reputation than others have noted. The primary work of this chapter will thus be to ascertain how Oliphant managed to create the terms for the credit that so many felt she was owed, largely by exploiting the idea that the bounty of her writing marred its genius.

Publicly announcing that her works did not equal, and so could not rival, the female literary greats—George Eliot, George Sand, Charlotte Brontë—seems a somewhat ironic manner to go about achieving a literary legacy. In many ways, however, Oliphant fought against her own erasure by writing about it. This discursive awareness of her failure to excel had a bittersweet flavor, for Oliphant's writings coupled with her "modest career" only served to enhance her overwhelming confidence that she held the *potential* for greatness. In *The Autobiography* Oliphant writes of herself and her literary work in terms of unrealized possibility—that she didn't achieve genius was a matter of circumstance rather than of constitution. Had she no children to care for, had she not been the primary breadwinner, had she not been so willing to sacrifice quality for quantity, had she been given the intellectual time and space, the "mental greenhouses" she attributes to Georges Eliot and Sand, she could have risen to great heights of genius rather than being a "general utility woman." Sadness, melancholy, and a regret verging on bitterness are the affective themes that govern the pages of *The Autobiography*. As Mary Jean Corbett notes, these saddened emotions speak of personal and professional experience, since "Oliphant's resignation is linked not only to family trouble, but also to her estimate of how little her extensive literary production will weigh in the balance of literary history" (104).

An interesting contradiction is embedded in Oliphant's remarks about her legacy if we examine them through the combined lenses of gender and celebrity. Though Oliphant describes her long career in terms that depict it as a failure, she simultaneously underscores her sacrifices for God and family and thus her marked success at living in accord with the prevailing Victorian ideals for how

---

[3] For a discussion on *The Autobiography* that "takes seriously" Oliphant's equation of maternal duty and writerly ambition, see Laura Green's "Long, Long Disappointment."

white middle-class women might enact their gender. Statements that Oliphant did not achieve significant fame, that she could make no claim to "greatness," that she believed to "bring up the boys for the service of God was better than to write a fine novel," all function discursively to establish her congruence with gender codes that glorified womanly sacrifice in the name of piety, humility, and other-orientation (*The Autobiography* 6). For the famous literary Woolf family, these sacrifices of art and career in the name of family made of Oliphant a courageous soul. Virginia Woolf called Oliphant's *The Autobiography* a "genuine and indeed moving piece of work" that demanded the reader's admiration and indignation. Writing in 1899 for the *National Review*, Woolf's father, Leslie Stephen, praised Oliphant for the way she had refused to lay "parental duty" at the sacrificial altar of "'art' or the demands of posterity" (*Studies of a Biographer* 741).[4] In effect, Oliphant's good mothering mattered more than her celebrity, a clear statement of value that positioned femininity and fame as mutually exclusive.[5] How, then, to bring them to the same side of the ledger sheet?

One way to see how conventional gender codes and notions of celebrity might coexist was to show the degree to which posterity was subject to the whims of time and place. Oliphant would say at mid-century in "Modern Novelists" (1855), "Greatness is always comparative: there are few things so hard to adjust as the sliding-scale of fame" (554). Her statement here implies that, though greatness itself may be universally desired, notions of genius, ability, and talent are culturally constructed and situationally contingent. This position contradicts a more conventional standard for conceptualizing the "great man," which upholds the idea of a timeless touchstone that regulates who might enter the rarified ranks of glory. Fame in this regard is not a shifting category but a stable ontology, rewarding those whose genius qualifies for greatness. Oliphant asks the reader to accept this idea but in modified form: fame marks the meritorious, yes, but what constitutes one's worthiness for fame is relative. Just as Eliza Potter critiques individual ladies but exonerates and reinforces the validity of The Lady as I will discuss in Chapter 5, Oliphant disputes the constituent factors that lead to greatness even as she idealizes Greatness itself. In so doing she allows for a new conceptual possibility that there may be worthy (female) claimants to the ranks of the literary greats. If Oliphant could not overtly adjust the sliding-scale of fame, she could perhaps influence its balance.

---

[4]   Dorothy Mermin relates another account of the "subordination of art to womanliness" in the case of Charlotte M. Yonge, "whose best-selling novels ... inculcate a high-minded pious ideal of family life" (18).

[5]   In *Greatness Engendered*, which examines the life and careers of George Eliot and Virginia Woolf, Alison Booth addresses the complications for women in claiming greatness. Booth writes, "plausibility dictates that female greatness be of a circumscribed sort, always tied to 'life.'" For most women, "the domestic or private story *is* their only story" (106).

"She shrank from publicity"

As I have noted, Oliphant's fame was in many ways built on a scaffolding of self-abnegation, a public persona fostered and upheld by a proclaimed distaste for personal disclosure or publicity. When William Thomas Stead thus declared in 1899 that Mrs. Oliphant "cared comparatively little for fame" and that she instead was a lonely woman desiring only love, he was following a prototype that Oliphant herself had established (498). Throughout her career, Oliphant's public image was grounded in her reputation for eschewing the spotlight of literary celebrity, her modesty thus indicating that what portion of fame she garnered came to her as a consequence of talent and popular approval rather than as the calculations of hubris. She commented little on her writerly process and was fiercely protective of her privacy, noting, "I am a writer very little given to explanation or to any personal appearance," a statement Annie Coghill uses in the first sentence of her preface to *The Autobiography* (v). This declaration about Oliphant's personal reticence and reluctance to be crowned with the glories of fame has been frequently reprinted in discussions of Oliphant's career as evidence to support her modesty, all while perpetuating the very public favor she claimed not to seek. Indeed, as if to cement this connection between modesty and merit, a column called "The Outlook" in the *Zion's Herald* (of Portland, Oregon) conceded that Oliphant's massive output might have diluted her artistry, but her humility in the public eye redeemed both her professionalism and her gendered ethos: "One may feel that she wrote too much and yet marvel at the fine level of solid excellence maintained in it all. She was to the last the warm-hearted helpful friend of scores of struggling young women and the eager champion of good causes wherever to be found; yet she shrank from publicity as keenly as if her name had never been mentioned in print, instead adorning more than one hundred title pages" (1).

Given that Oliphant was known in a transatlantic context as a somewhat reclusive author who did not trumpet her literary achievements or divulge unseemly details about her own or her biographical subjects' personal lives, the decision to write an autobiography is somewhat enigmatic, particularly since any faithful accounting of Oliphant's life would have threatened the codes of propriety for which she was known. Indeed, Margaret Oliphant lived a life of significant emotional and pecuniary hardship, even in the context of the nineteenth century. If part of Charlotte Brontë's claim to fame was the life of domestic sacrifice she lived steeped in the teas of death and loss, Margaret Oliphant could surely make claim to a life of similar hardship. Oliphant's early life seemed quite charmed, so that by age 24 she was married and a famous authoress. In the span of seven years, she would birth six children, three of whom died in infancy, lose her husband to consumption, and begin to function as the only wage earner for herself and her extended family, a financial obligation she would uphold for the rest of her life. In the 1860s Oliphant's only daughter, 11-year-old Maggie, died while the family was on an extended trip to Rome. In this same decade, she also took on the support of her brother's son, Frank, after that brother, also named Frank, experienced financial ruin and expatriated to Canada. Her brother would undergo a nervous breakdown and become completely dependent on her by 1870, while her nephew would die in India in 1879. Though two of her sons lived to adulthood, both would struggle financially and ultimately pre-decease her, Cyril "Tiddy" in 1890 and Frances "Cecco" in 1894, making Oliphant in her seventies the only surviving member of her nuclear family. By most accounts as well as by her own, Oliphant's life was one touched by "incessant work, incessant anxiety," but it was also a life filled with purpose, optimism, and moments of happiness all filtered through what she termed her "obstinate elasticity" (*The Autobiography* 4, 119). Her career was both an escape from these anxieties and the financial lifeline that kept an extended family afloat, and thus her public representation of her own writing life as a necessary labor undertaken purely in service to her children has to be understood as a discursive masquerade. Why and for whom she created this masquerade is critical.

In her preface to *The Autobiography*, Annie Coghill (Oliphant's niece, editor, and personal secretary) notes that on her deathbed Oliphant extracted a promise that no biography would be written. She also instructed Coghill and her niece Denny to "deal with" the scraps of autobiography Oliphant had written, "as we thought best, believing that it would serve for all that was necessary" (ix). Coghill here indicates that such a gesture on Oliphant's part spoke to the author's natural feminine modesty, a point rather tellingly made since two paragraphs prior to this moment Coghill offers an elaborate description of Oliphant's body and demeanor that includes her "lovely hands," "wonderful eyes," and "exquisite daintiness," all of which combined to create the "very atmosphere about her which was 'pure womanly'" (viii). In her introduction to the 1990 edition of *The Autobiography*, Elisabeth Jay argues that Coghill's description distorted the ordering and editing of the "autobiographical impulse" begun by Oliphant, turning her manuscript into a blueprint for "decorum and restraint" modeled on hegemonic femininity (*The Autobiography of Margaret Oliphant* ix). Jay contends that editing of the text included "small excisions of barbed comments ... that seemed at odds with the qualities of charm and grace" accentuated in Coghill's introduction (*The Autobiography of Margaret Oliphant* ix–x). Primary amendments were of Oliphant's "outpourings of grief," passages of extraordinary tenderness and poignant heartache, but also, potential contenders in the "literature of bereavement" (*The Autobiography of Margaret Oliphant* x).[6]

---

[6]   As I have already indicated, the intent behind the generation of the manuscript and the very order of its contents is a matter of some debate, as evidenced in our own time by two fairly recent versions of *The Autobiography*, one edited in 1988 by Laurie Langbauer, who follows Coghill's arrangement, and the other edited in 1990 by Elisabeth Jay, who works according to an unedited version roughly put together by Oliphant and containing 20 percent more information. (For ease of reference, I indicate quotations from Langbauer's edition with *The Autobiography* and from Jay's edition with *The Autobiography of Margaret Oliphant*. When citing from Coghill's preface, I use the American printing from 1899.) The Langbauer/Coghill manuscript is more highly edited, but it is also the text that readers

Coghill asks readers to believe that Oliphant intended these bits of memory as private reflections on a grief-filled life, intended only for Oliphant's sons as readers. She writes of Oliphant, "Many years ago she had begun in a time of great trial and loneliness to write down scraps more or less autobiographical, and later had added more cheerful pictures of her early life. Later still, to please her last surviving child, she continued this memoir, bringing it up to the time when her two sons went to Oxford" (ix). Oliphant remarks early in the text that she had initially intended *The Autobiography* as a memoir for her sons, but mid-way through it is clear, both because of her sons' deaths and due to her increasing financial need, that she will seek a wider readership.

In her biography of Oliphant, Elisabeth Jay makes a compelling case for believing that Oliphant turned her hand to "a little try at autobiography" in 1885, when she was beset with her brother Willie's alcoholism and increasing demands to support her extended family through her writing. Jay notes, "Burying the faults of their lives with them, Mrs. Oliphant was able to persuade herself that she had written 'for my boys, for Cecco in particular,' but the fact remains that she had shown none of it to them" (27). Jay further observes that a letter of 11 March, 1890, written by Oliphant when both of her sons were still alive, made offers to publish "'various fragments of autobiography which may make a publication of a little personal interest' to the publishing firm of Macmillan as one of a number of securities against advances already received" (27), thus suggesting that Oliphant may have intended to sell the autobiography some ten years before it appeared. This would mean, then, that the entire autobiographical text—both that drawn from personal notes and that composed—was compiled with a public audience in mind.

It's worth pausing to consider that Oliphant, a biographer of some note, essentially blocked the possibility that anyone aside from herself would lay down the authorized interpretive framework, if not the full content, of her life. Since Oliphant did not ask that her "scraps" be destroyed but that they be dealt with, Coghill and others interpreted Oliphant's instructions as permission, even a request, to assemble the scraps into a manuscript. What I'm suggesting here is that Oliphant's packaging of her life and her career through her autobiography was in many ways driven by the need for a paying reader. Her self-portrait is, thus, both a "deliberate creation," as Laurie Langbauer terms it, which can sustain narrative interest, promote ideological objectives, and motivate purchase as well as what Langbauer terms an "authentic" and "truthful" bid to tell her own story (*The Autobiography* xi). To "interpret" herself publicly, in effect giving herself the right to self-determination in what Sidonie Smith has termed an "androcentric genre

would have seen in 1899 and through subsequent editions. The Jay edition relies on a revised approach to the manuscript, culled from new research conducted at the National Library of Scotland (see Jay's forward, xix). Though authorial intent is always a sticky matter in literary criticism, in this case the situation is all the more vexed due to *The Autobiography*'s posthumous publication and, as Jay notes, Oliphant's barely indecipherable handwriting and somewhat erratic punctuation. In the matter of these two different, but overlapping, texts, I cull evidence from both.

that ha[d] written stories of woman for her, thereby fictionalizing and effectively silencing her" (45), required that she tell her own story through a seemingly counter-intuitive model, whereby the "pitiful little record of my life" makes of her a sympathetic failure (*The Autobiography* 41). In such guise she is able both to influence interpretation through her authorial role and to allow for the possibility that an ordinary and self-described homely woman can have a career as a writer, perhaps even as a famous genius.

"I wonder if I am a little envious of her"

Early in *The Autobiography*, Oliphant credits George Eliot's influence, "I have been tempted to begin writing by George Eliot's life … I wonder if I am a little envious of her" (*The Autobiography* 4). Yet, Oliphant reflects that writing for her is not about intellectualizing and formal consideration, which she suggests is the soul and substance of Eliot's occupation.[7] According to Oliphant, writing for her (author-character) is a matter of personal satisfaction and natural proclivity. Oliphant wrote, she says, "because it gave me pleasure, because it came natural to me, because it was like talking or breathing" (*The Autobiography* 4). In a matter of a few pages, Oliphant lifts the curtain on the comparative trope that structures her analysis. She begins with affirmations of George Eliot's genius, indicating her own potential envy and lesser status. She then critiques Eliot's stature by indicating that the great author's writing sounded only the notes of formal intellectualism—high praise compared to Oliphant's dismissive statement in *The Victorian Age* that Miss Evans is "unremarkable" and "mediocre" as an essayist, though genius at fiction (Vol. II, 167). Oliphant concludes her discussion on George Eliot in *The Autobiography* by offering her reader another possibility of what an artist might look like, "herself" as author—a writer who wrote not for fame or money, she says, but out of "natural" inclination and for personal pleasure.

In the process of creating the terms for the author-character who is herself, Oliphant, inadvertently perhaps, poses a necessary question that gets at the very heart of celebrity: can one merit fame for doing what comes naturally? If writing is like breathing, would we be inclined to praise, or even notice, a famous breather? Though the question may seem a bit absurd, in many ways it anticipates a feature of celebrity culture typically tied to twentieth and twenty-first century image production, specifically through the motion picture industry. Joshua Gamson, for instance, notes factors that constitutes fame and celebrity were put at odds in a twentieth-century context where fame was considered to be the "natural result of irrepressible greatness" and thus a reward for talent and virtuosity, whereas celebrity stood for the fleeting results of the "publicity apparatus," an "assembly line of greatness" that substituted charisma for talent ("Assembly Line" 259–61).

---

[7] David Finkelstein notes that Oliphant never matched Eliot's success or profitability, "a point that rankled with her" (33). She was, by contrast, consistent, if not spectacular, in the sales her writings generated.

In a somewhat similar vein, Oliphant deflates the heights of fame, obliquely suggesting that Eliot's intellectual writings were deliberately constructed as an edifice on which to perch her literary celebrity, and so her stature is the result not of natural fame but of premeditated celebrity.

Oliphant observes that, by contrast, her own career, which evolved not through deliberation but as the consequence of her "natural"—and even involuntary—need to write, exempts her from the charge of unwomanly ambition or deliberate self-promotion. Although Oliphant's gloss is subtle, it is also deft. If readers buy the terms of her description, they must offer the kind of author she stands for greater worth because she did not premeditate or construe the terms of her own visibility. Indeed, Harriet Prescott Spofford seemed inclined to consider Oliphant's stature humbly won, even before Oliphant's *The Autobiography* was published. Writing for *Harper's Bazaar* at Oliphant's death, Spofford felt that it was precisely because Oliphant "made no attempt to display a literary technique, to dazzle with satire or with word-painting" that "the future will accord her an artistic eminence that the hyper-critical reader of to-day has sometimes hesitated to grant" (571). *The Chautaquan* strengthened such associations, noting with approval, "Though she is so widely known through her books Mrs. Oliphant has permitted the public to find out very little of her personality, preferring quiet seclusion to all visitors except press reporters" ("Mrs. Margaret O. Oliphant" 569). The paper did remark, however, that Oliphant was on good terms with Queen Victoria, who "read her manuscripts before they went to the publishers," thus sealing Oliphant's ties to the elite, even while giving her credit for avoiding the limelight (569). An anonymous writer for *Blackwood's Edinburgh Magazine* equally praised the career and fame possessed by Margaret Oliphant in an essay begun weeks before her death and published three months after her passing. Noting that Oliphant had averted the "endless round of self-advertisement and vanity" that came from "blow[ing] your own trumpet" that had so lately become a part of the "'profession' of literature," this writer praised Oliphant for her self-respect and self-restraint, suggesting that refusal to divulge details of her private life had garnered her "the legacy of an untarnished name" ("Mrs. Oliphant as a Novelist" 319).

In her *The Autobiography*, Oliphant's perpetuation of this idea—that merited fame can only come passively, a reward for self-sacrifice and natural labors but not as the object of desire—suggests the currency associated with unsought fame, while reinforcing the stigma attached to avarice and overt ambitions to be famous. Lord Byron could have joked about awaking one morning to find himself famous, but the metaphor was far more useful to women, for whom the passive acceptance of fame was critical. As Leo Braudy observes in his comprehensive study *The Frenzy of Renown*, the ambition for fame has long carried a pejorative cast, requiring that "great men" hide their desire for such laurels. However, codes of masculinity often praised the man who desired greatness, precisely because such ambition accorded with values of domination, competition, and success built into a Western framework for conceptualizing masculinity. As I have noted, fame studies have infrequently considered how women grappled with these competing desires for distinction and gender conformance. For Oliphant, as with all of the authors considered in this book, it is only when fame comes without the woman's bidding that she merits the glory it brings. She must write with no desire for fame, waking one morning, as Grace Greenwood described Oliphant, surprised to find herself famous.

Oliphant's passive stance is underscored in her evasive responses to why she wrote. Though biographical accounts suggest otherwise, Oliphant claims to not have needed the money that writing brought. Instead, she only hints at what might be her primary objective for writing, an evasiveness which she foregrounds for the reader, "When I laugh inquiries off and say that it is my trade, I do it only by way of eluding the question which I have neither time nor wish to enter into" (*The Autobiography* 4). She concedes that she admires and is envious of George Eliot, and that other great George, George Sand, but she claims no desire to exchange her literary career for theirs, primarily because, she argues, they lived privileged and protected lives that nurtured fame and genius but put them out of touch with the realities of most people's lives. This thought about the protected artifice of fame extends from the biographical sketch she wrote about George Eliot in *The Victorian Age of English Literature* (1892), where she described the author as living in a "close circle where nothing was heard but adoration of the divine figure in the midst, where strangers were charily admitted to gaze with awe over the shoulders of the initiated, and await in reverence the possibility of a word: where never jarring sound was permitted, nor breath of criticism, nor even a suggestion that the standard of perfect excellence was not always there" (Vol. II, 174). We can almost hear the crackle of Oliphant's cynicism.

Despite such critique, when speaking of the Georges, Oliphant invokes the terms of celebrity as the epitome of the love-object, a position of consummated appreciation and affection that she feels has eluded her:

> George Eliot and George Sand make me half inclined to cry over my poor little unappreciated self – "Many love me (i.e., in a sort of way), but by none am I enough beloved." These two bigger women did things which I have never felt the least temptation to do – but how very much more enjoyment they seem to have got out of their life, how much more praise and homage and honour! I would not buy their fame with these disadvantages, but I do feel very small, very obscure, beside them, rather a failure all round, never securing any strong affection, and throughout my life, though I have had all the usual experiences of woman, never impressing anybody, – what a droll little complaint!
>
> – why should I? I acknowledge frankly that there is nothing in me – a fat, little commonplace woman, rather tongue-tied – to impress any one; and yet there is a sort of whimsical injury in it which makes me sorry for myself. (*The Autobiography* 8)

Here again Oliphant engages in a series of ever-finer contrasts. Eliot and Sand are famous writers whom she admires, yet she is not in the least tempted to do what they have done, although we've already seen her more than a bit covetous of the privilege of mental greenhouses. She acknowledges their vast fame and literary stature, and denigrates her writing, her sadness, and her very body, yet she claims normalcy, a position as a "commonplace woman" who has "had all the usual experiences of woman" and by doing so reminds the reader that these are culturally approved locations that neither of the scandalous Georges could occupy.

Oliphant is particularly insistent that Eliot's personal life marred her resultant fame, for she argues the great author could lay claim to an unparalleled genius, yet she lived life "under a cloud, which it is unfortunately impossible to dissipate" (*The Victorian Age*, Vol. II, 165). Oliphant begins her discussion of Eliot with an awkward introduction: "There is perhaps no name so influential and important in the imaginative literature of the half-century as that of George Eliot, 1819–80 (Marian Evans, Mrs. Lewes, Mrs. Cross, however the reader chooses to call her)" (*The Victorian Age*, Vol. II, 163). In reminding the reader of Eliot's many names, she also calls to mind Eliot's breaches of convention, particularly her common law marriage to George Henry Lewes and her ultimate marriage to a much younger man, John Cross. Though, as I've noted, she calls "Miss Evans's" work as an essayist "mediocre," Oliphant is more kindly predisposed to Eliot's fiction. Even here, however, Oliphant reminds the reader that the power of Eliot's prose always existed in tension with the scandals of her personal life (specifically, living with Lewes, who was married to another woman). Oliphant writes that society "instead of finding in her another example of the wickedness of genius, as was done in such cases as those of Byron and Shelley, condoned the offence which strikes at the root of all law, and relaxed its standards for the sake of that genius which was too great to be doubted" (*The Victorian Age*, Vol. II, 166). This passage tacitly grants the author-character that is Oliphant a discursive advantage: She gains credit for affirming the value of Eliot's talent and genius, but her disapproval of Eliot affirms a higher moral authority than fame confers. Oliphant may not be renowned as a literary genius, but she can make a claim for lasting value as the epitome of feminine deportment, whose "code of ethics," was termed by the writer of "Mrs. Oliphant as a Novelist," as being "as old-fashioned as the Ten Commandments" (306).

There is considerable evidence to suggest that Oliphant's fame in the Victorian period was largely earned both through the volume of her publications and by the perceived moral tone of her writing. In its obituary, for example, *The New York Times* argued that Oliphant should be remembered not just for the amount she wrote but for the "wholesome" quality of her books. "Their influence has been as wide as it has been beneficial." They added that "no writer in her time … deserves greater honor" for such things as avoiding "sensational themes" particularly those based on crimes. "There are no figures at hand to indicate what has been the extent of her popularity, but it is known to have been enormous" ("Death of Mrs. Oliphant" 13). Long before her death, *The Washington Post* wished Oliphant a happy 61st birthday in its "People in General" column, noting that she was a morally pure and "tireless producer of novels, biographies, histories, and editions of foreign classics" (4). Oliphant herself considered it part of her professional duty to create published writings that were "pure from all noxious topics," which included such things as bigamy, seduction, and forms of "forbidden knowledge" ("Novels" 261).

In Oliphant's handling, a professional writer can be an independent genius, but she can also be a commonplace woman. To say this in terms of contrast, Oliphant considers her writing, not as a "solemn profession" or a divine calling, but, as literary scholar Margarete Rubik terms it, "as a profession to be adapted to the demands of the market, as an activity that may provide personal satisfaction, but which does not raise any claims to artistic perfection" (47). Ironically, however, by positioning herself as the avatar of mediocrity rather than as an extraordinary genius, she makes a place for herself and others like her (though, of course, no one else is like her) in the pantheon of famous women.

Oliphant's representation of herself through self-deprecating remarks, in which she highlights (even as she bemoans) her lack of extraordinary qualities in either talent or appearance, serve to underscore value in terms of socially constructed notions of gender. The result of this representation yields a portrait of Oliphant that encompasses seemingly mutually exclusive characteristics: she is intellectually modest, yet sharp enough to detect errors of thinking in the greatest minds of the period; she is humble and commonplace, yet of a decided rank and reputation that she can call Charlotte and the Georges peers; she is a hack writer, yet she can specifically lay out why brilliant writing is flawed; she is an unappreciated professional author, yet she is unmarred by the personal scandal that stains the lives of greater genius, or at least she appears unmarred since she declines to elaborate publicly on her familial troubles.[8]

For such a portrait to gain traction, it is important that the reader not be completely persuaded by Oliphant's claim to "extraordinary normalcy." The reader must see her as both commonplace and rather extraordinary, two qualities that fuse together to magnify the fascination invested in the figure of the celebrity. Indeed, the ordinary/extraordinary paradox stands at the heart of stardom, since in Su Holmes's words, the paradox "is used to capture the cultural 'essence' of stardom and, as such, it is posed as a transhistorical 'myth'" (119). Richard Dyer notes that the ordinary/extraordinary paradox narrates and naturalizes the success story, balancing contradictory elements such as a star's unique qualities that might mark him or her as special with the "just like us" characteristics that code the celebrity as a plausible role model and aspirational figure (43). The ordinary/extraordinary paradox thus constitutes a balance of the elite and the egalitarian of particular importance to an American sensibility but also equally appealing within a British context where celebrity might trump class.[9]

---

[8] Jay notes the extra burdens, financial and otherwise, Oliphant bore due to her brother and son's public drunkenness and the efforts she took to suppress public knowledge of their dissipations.

[9] Bestselling British author Marie Corelli offers the perfect example for the manner in which celebrity could serve as a leverage tool for modifying notions of the intractibility of class, since Corelli started her life in very humble circumstances and wrote her way

Oliphant adroitly uses the ordinary/extraordinary combination to good advantage. She is a person who can say, "I acknowledge frankly that there is nothing in me – a fat, little, commonplace woman, rather tongue-tied – to impress any one." But she can also boast, "[I]t may perhaps be suspected that I don't always think such small beer of myself as I say" (qtd. in Jay 35). Like Fanny Fern, who had a great proclivity for representing herself as both scatterbrained and sharply intelligent, Oliphant strategically positions herself as a bit pitiful, yet formidable. Both versions of herself—the modest author, and the imperious and sometimes intimidating intellect—are equally "authentic," and both play into, and work against, a gender code that posits womanhood as obsequious and only passive. We need only look more closely at Oliphant's discussion of Charlotte Brontë, both in *The Autobiography* and in biographical sketches of Charlotte, as well as Oliphant's further regard toward George Eliot, to see greater evidence of such stretching of the boundaries of femininity through fame.

Depicting Female Genius

In the 1890's Oliphant authored two brief biographical sketches of Charlotte Brontë, the first, a six-page treatment of Brontë's life and career that appeared in *The Victorian Age of English Literature* (1892)[10] and the second, a 60-page chapter called "The Sisters Brontë," included in an 1897 anthology, *Women Novelists of Queen Victoria's Reign: A Book of Appreciation*. Joan Bellamy has noted, Oliphant demonstrated a career-long fascination with Charlotte, considering in print the famous author's writing on at least seven occasions "over a period of forty-two years" in which she endeavored to "evaluate and re-examine the power and influence of Charlotte Brontë's work" (39). As evidenced from the previous chapters in this book, such an attraction to Brontë is not a unique, since her life and career functioned as a litmus test for women's fame in the nineteenth century. Yet, even given the century-long fascination with all things Charlotte, Oliphant's attachment to Brontë merits attention.

As a reminder, Margaret Oliphant is both the historical author-agent under consideration in this chapter and the fictive author-character built and referenced in her work, a character called "I." This "I" marked a type of professional female authorship in which femininity was heightened due to the author-character's passive relation to fame. To help make the representation of herself more evident, throughout this section when I mean to indicate the author-character (rather than the author-agent), I put Oliphant's name in quotation marks so as to underscore

---

to fame and fortune. See Teresa Ransom's *The Mysterious Miss Marie Corelli: Queen of Victorian Bestsellers* and Annette R. Frederico's *Idols of Suburbia: Marie Corelli and Late Victorian Literary Culture*.

[10] Oliphant authored this survey of Victorian writers and periodicals with her son Frances, but I follow other literary scholars in attributing the attitudes reflected therein primarily to her.

the discursive construction of her identity. Charlotte Brontë and George Eliot are also discursive constructions, of course, but I do not put their names in quotation marks since their creation as the subjects under discussion are more discernable than is Oliphant's as the agent of representation.

It is particularly Oliphant's extended treatment of Brontë through the sketches I examine here that evidence her regard for the genius Charlotte as residing in an uneasy balance between experience and imagination. "Oliphant" contends that Brontë's life gave her no extra assistance; she had no pre-established contacts in the literary world, and she did not circulate among people who helped her career. Brontë had "no artificial means to heighten [her literary triumph], nothing but the genius on the part of a writer possessing little experience or knowledge of the world, and no sort of social training or adventitious aid" ("The Sisters Brontë" 4). Despite the fact that Oliphant accords to Brontë a version of innate genius rather than nurtured ability, she does not regard her books as great. "Their philosophy of life is that of a schoolgirl, their knowledge of the world almost nil, their conclusions confused by the haste and passion of a mind self-centered and working in the narrowest orbit" ("The Sisters Brontë" 6). The kind of genius that Oliphant ascribes to Brontë, then, produces a lack-luster text built on the ability to represent, though she concedes Brontë did so masterfully.

In this micro-portrait, Oliphant approaches the great writer, acceding to her genius, though also redefining the terms of that genius. In this case, Oliphant makes clear that Brontë is not great in any widely transcendent sense of the term; there are glaring and serious flaws in her work, she avers. Charlotte's genius lies in her ability to overcome the limits of her circumscribed life. In effect, it is Charlotte's perseverance, rather than her innate talents, that lift her to genius and also to fame. Of course, by this point, the critic has so redefined genius that it merely means enduring hardship. Brontë's masterful ability to represent is acknowledged, but this in itself is a kind of backhanded compliment, since, as I discussed more thoroughly in Chapter 1, to paint from life was considered derivative rather than artistic, mimicry rather than creativity. To represent is to write from experience—essentially to be a faithful scribe to a worldly script. To imagine is to call forth ideas and images that have never before existed. The latter invokes tensions between the gendered components of creation and procreation, grounded in governing cultural investments in sex-dictated behaviors. Early phrenological theories, for instance, espoused that, "Certain mental powers are stronger, and others weaker in men than in women, and vice versa. … [W]omen do not extend their reasoning beyond the range of the visible world. Nor do they make any great or daring excursions into the region of fancy" (qtd. in Russett 18). To make an excursion into the imagination, then, is to violate cultural gender/sex boundaries, and yet it is the only way to demarcate the terrain of famed genius.

As critic and reviewer, "Oliphant" claims the primary vantage point from which to assess Charlotte's ability (and lack of it) as well as her consequent fame. This rhetorical placement interjects "Oliphant" into the discursive frame of famed genius, making her not only a peer and colleague to Brontë and thus potentially equal in both talent and stature, but also theoretically a greater authority than Brontë on matters of literary style and composition. "Oliphant" contrasts her own work to Brontë's by noting, "I don't suppose my powers are equal to hers – my work to myself looks perfectly pale and colourless beside hers – but yet I have had far more experience and, I think, a fuller conception of life" (*The Autobiography* 67). Here we see a compliment that is anything but complimentary, for through her praise of Brontë's work, she is able to evoke Charlotte's bleak and empty life. This reminder, unlike in Gaskell's usage, does not seem intended to evoke pathos. Indeed, the adjectives "pale and colourless," which the critic uses to describe her own work, become interestingly associated with the genius writer, so that it is Charlotte's bland life that diminishes in comparison to "Oliphant's" greater experience and fuller living. The result of this juxtaposition between herself-as-character and Brontë is not so much to diminish Charlotte's writerly ability or literary celebrity, but to enhance "Oliphant's" career and reputation by suggesting that her fuller life clearly compensates for "working too fast and producing too much" (*The Autobiography* 44). In effect, her prodigious output redeems her from gender role conflicts: as a failed author she is a more successful woman. This comparative strategy works by locating herself-as-character in the same register as writers of genius, but it subtly places "Oliphant" in an advantaged position where she can be a culturally idealized widow and mother.

On the subject of her own potential for genius, and thus her comparative career in relation to Brontë's or Eliot's, "Oliphant" admits that she does not know with certainty that different circumstances would have indeed allowed her greater access to genius. She acknowledges that she possessed little of the interest, opportunity, or self-discipline necessary to live the self-restrained life of the great artist, conceding that her critique of female genius in many ways is a pose to make herself appear superior to that genius:

> What casuists we are on our own behalf! – this is altogether self-defense. And I know I am giving myself the air of being *au fond* a finer sort of character than the others. I may as well take the little satisfaction to myself, for nobody will give it to me. No one even will mention me in the same breath with George Eliot. And that is just. It is a little justification to myself to think how much better off she was, – no trouble in all her life as far as appears, but the natural one of her father's death – and perhaps coolnesses with her brothers and sisters, though that is not said. And though her marriage, so called, is not one that most of us would have ventured on, still it seems to have secured her a caretaker and worshipper unrivalled – little nasty body though he looked, and hideous in nastiness as his previous story was. (*The Autobiography of Margaret Oliphant* 16–17)[11]

---

[11] Here is a particularly telling moment of difference in the two versions of *The Autobiography* that makes the editorial hand of Annie Coghill evident, since the 1899 prototype did not include the critique of Eliot's "so called" marriage to Lewes or the comments on his "hideous" and "nasty" character.

Here "Oliphant" makes explicit her contrastive rhetorical maneuver, which positions the character she has created of herself as simultaneously superior and inferior to the women she discusses. In Eliot's particular case, "Oliphant" reminds the reader of the author's sexual and domestic pairing with a man, George Lewes, whom she had implied, in her *Edinburgh Review* article on J.S. Cross's *George Eliot's Life as Related in Her Letters and Journals*, was well experienced with "all the lowest scenes of London life" (534). That "Oliphant" is aware of this tendency for comparative rumination in herself, and even points it out to the reader, makes it all the more effective.

It also links her portrait of famous authorship to other modes of celebrity in the nineteenth century. Indeed, Joshua Gamson identifies a knowledge/mystery tension as the telling feature of celebrity culture perfected by such impresarios as P.T. Barnum, who would let his customers in on a secret (offering them knowledge) only enough to ease them into a less critical mode of reception (and thus perpetuating more mystery) ("Assembly" 262–3). In confessing she has a tendency to compare herself unfavorably to others, "Oliphant" emerges as refreshingly candid and disingenuous, with nothing to hide or obfuscate. Despite laughing at herself for her foibles, and so perhaps easing the reader into a less critical frame of mind, her use of the knowledge–mystery tension allows "Oliphant" to be justified in claiming greater credit for her lesser fame. Since everyone is convinced of her lower status anyway, she argues, what harm does it do that she adapts representation to her greater satisfaction? She says by way of rationale that no one would ever pair her name with George Eliot's. Yet, her very complaint constitutes the mention she predicts would never happen, a rather adroit method of coupling herself with the genius George Eliot even as she earns the greater sympathy evoked by positioning herself as the lesser author. "Oliphant's" self-depiction of her merited, but refuted, fame operates to implicitly ask the reader to make arguments on her behalf, to fight for her earned place next to George Eliot's.

In light of the emphatic assurance that she would never be thought of as a talent on par with Eliot, it is somewhat surprising to discover that there is a good degree of historical evidence that indicates Margaret Oliphant's works were received by publishers and newspaper critics in ways that fully acceded her great ability. As I've already mentioned, John Blackwood considered Eliot and Oliphant to be peers in talent and intelligence. A number of American periodicals not only favorably compared Oliphant to such female literary geniuses as Jane Austen and George Eliot but found her the superior artist, indicating the degree to which her protestations of mediocrity bespoke if not a false then certainly an overly modest representation of her career. Although these statements attesting to Oliphant's genius largely appeared in obituaries for her—meaning, obviously, she would not have read them—the praise for her does not strike me as anomalous. No columnist suggests, for instance, that Oliphant's death has caused him or her to re-evaluate the merits of her person or work, as was the case with Charles Kingsley's response to Charlotte Brontë through Gaskell's *Life*, which I discussed in Chapter 1. The *Providence* (Rhode Island) *Journal*, noted for instance: "Of all the names that mark Victorian literature, that of Margaret Oliphant Wilson Oliphant will not be the first to be forgotten. Her name is as secure, we feel confident, as that of Jane Austen or George Eliot; and in some respects she was more a finished artist than either" ("Mrs. Margaret O. Oliphant" 569). *The New York Times* declared there was "no writer in her time who deserves greater honor" ("Death of Mrs. Oliphant" 13). *Chicago Daily* observed, "It is difficult to say in which department of literature Mrs. Oliphant will survive longest, but it is a notable fact that her novels have been a recognized feature of the best English literature for years. Yet, though she has been one of Queen Victoria's favorite authors, she cannot be said to have attained the sweeping popularity that has attended some more sensational writers. But the highest critics have come to regard Mrs. Oliphant's fiction as standing high in permanent literature – some say only next below George Eliot" ("Death of Mrs. Oliphant" 10).

Ranking Oliphant with the greats of Victorian literature also had some purchase in twentieth-century literary criticism. In her introduction to the 1966 edition of Oliphant's *The Autobiography*, Q.D. Leavis reminded her readers that as a "massive contributor to the novel of several kinds, the short story, the biography, to the reviewing and the critical essays in many Victorian periodicals, as well as a maker of solid books of non-fiction," Oliphant could stand as a "case-history of the woman of letters in the nineteenth century" in a category that pointedly included Charlotte Brontë, George Sand, and George Eliot, "with all of whom she may be profitably compared" (10). Leavis considered Oliphant's *Miss Marjoribanks* a "long-sought missing link between *Emma* and *Middlemarch*," which not only equated Oliphant with Eliot and Austen but gave Oliphant a "completely new status" that eclipsed Charlotte Brontë ("Introduction to Margaret Oliphant's *Miss Marjoribanks*" 14).[12] But, as we have seen, Oliphant herself was not so quick to dismiss Charlotte, who she reckoned "influen[ed] the entire generation, at least of female writers, after her" (*The Victorian Age*, Vol. I, 321).

Oliphant's reading of and sometimes resistance to all of the Brontë sisters' work was predicated on their seeming predilection for absolutism over concession. She was bothered that, "Branwell could not be seen as an 'ordinary ne'er-do-well' or Patrick as a high-spirited eccentric: they had to be transformed in their fiction to Byronic heroes or capricious tyrants" ("The Sisters Brontë" 6).[13] Jay notes that Oliphant's work is "supplied by an ironic perception of the discrepancy between the idealized vision of life, which occupies a portion of most peoples' thinking,

---

[12]   In *Virginia Woolf and the Nineteenth-Century Domestic Novel*, Emily Blair makes a compelling case for Oliphant's influence on Virginia Woolf.

[13]   This strikes me as a criticism of Gaskell rather than of the Brontës, as the hyperbolic portraits Oliphant resists come from Gaskell's *Life* rather than from any of the Brontë sisters' novels. It could well be that Gaskell cut her male characters in the *Life* from the same Byronic cloth of which Rochester and Heathcliff are made, but there is no evidence, as Oliphant assumes here, that the Brontës based their heroes on exaggerated models of their brother and father.

and the compromises, accommodations, and failures that characterize awkward reality" (220). Oliphant found fault in texts that did not portray a "sudden breaking in of the ordinary and common-place" (Jay 220).

This may be why Oliphant's telling of Charlotte Brontë's life, limited as it is in length, contains few of the hyperbolic conflations of the author Charlotte and culturally popular notions of pure womanhood that we see in Gaskell's rendition. Though Oliphant possessed a similar ideological stance to Gaskell's as to what might constitute the virtuous woman, Oliphant allowed for a difference between fantasized ideal and lived ordinariness in her representation of Brontë. Further, she—as a famous author representing this famous author—takes a different stance from Gaskell's portraiture, in that Oliphant expresses a far greater investment in publicly meeting Brontë at the intellectual level of the text. With Gaskell, praise and stature emerge through the tricky task of representing coarseness while remaining untouched by it; for Oliphant, genius shows itself through her interpretation and critique of the great Brontë's ideas. And again, it is Charlotte, rather than Anne, Emily, or Branwell, who merits the philological gaze.[14] Oliphant admires Charlotte's "independence of mind," and she considers her resistance to conventional tropes of the period as expressed through a "vivid individuality" and an uncanny talent for detail "evidently taken from life" as the foremost factors of her genius (*The Victorian Age*, Vol. I, 306). She claims that Brontë is capable of conveying a "universal impression which scarcely anything in the story of recent literature has equaled" (*The Victorian Age*, Vol. I, 306).

Looking to Brontë's heroines as the primary example of her ground-breaking vision, Oliphant notes that at the time of *Jane Eyre*'s publication, a typical heroine would be arrayed in "white muslin, the immaculate creature who was of sweetness and goodness all compact" ("The Sisters Brontë" 17). Jane, she notes, is far from this submissive and muslin-cloaked bit of feminine ephemera, functioning throughout the novel with an independence of mind and dressed in dark clothes that exaggerate her plain visage.[15] Yet, Oliphant resists Jane's depiction, saying, "I am not sure, indeed, that anybody believed Miss Brontë when she said her

---

[14]   Though Oliphant's piece is titled "The Sisters Brontë," she makes short work of Emily and Anne, dismissing them after only cursory examination. In fact, after a limited discussion suggesting her lack of patience with the siblings, in which she calls *Wuthering Heights* "strange, chaotic and weird" and *Agnes Grey* and *The Tenant of Wildfell Hall* "disagreeable novels of a much commoner order" (6), Oliphant kills off Branwell, Emily, and Anne in one fell paragraph. Branwell is "unwept yet not without leaving a pathetic note in the record" and Emily dies in foolish resistance "for the sake of pride and self-will alone," an act that is not to be viewed with "reverential sympathy" (30). Anne dies in "all sweetness and calmness" ("The Sisters Brontë" 30).

[15]   In "Modern Novelists," Oliphant describes Jane as "something of a genius, something of a vixen – a dangerous little person, inimical to the peace of society" (557). Hughes and Lund cite Oliphant's characterization of Jane as "incendiary, a self-declared feminist, an aggressive warrior locked in hand-to-hand combat with men – or rather with men's outworn chivalric notions" (127).

heroine was plain. It is very clear from the story that Jane was never unnoticed, never failed to please, except among the women, whom it is the instinctive act of the novelist to rouse in arms against the central figure, thus demonstrating the jealousy, spite, and rancour native to their minds in respect to the women who please men" ("The Sisters Brontë" 18).[16] This is an incisive bit of textual analysis that effectively articulates "Oliphant's" intellectual powers, for she at once establishes Brontë as a genius, capable of rethinking conventional tropes of the period, and demonstrates her own ability to think herself outside of and beyond Brontë's characterization.

"Oliphant's" sagacity is perhaps even more evident in her handling of Elizabeth Rigby's *Quarterly Review* critique, which, as I showed in Chapter 1, constituted a significant assault on Brontë's perceived womanhood and thus a way for Gaskell to raise concerns about Charlotte's gender without fully explaining them herself. We've seen that nine years after the critique appeared, Gaskell recalls this most "scandalous" of reviews to establish the necessity of defending Brontë's gender. Oliphant, now nearly 50 years later, also reminds the reader of Rigby and, similarly, uses Rigby to invoke gender codes. But again we can see Oliphant resisting the conventional mode of interpretation, this time by laying a firm emphasis on social class. Brontë was not unwomanly or "vulgar," Oliphant claims, but naive and out of her element. "Miss Brontë did not know fine ladies, and therefore, in spite of herself and a mind the reverse of vulgar, she made the competitors for Mr. Rochester's favour rather brutal and essentially vulgar persons, an error, curiously enough, which seems to have been followed by George Eliot in the corresponding scenes in 'Mr. Gilfil's Love Story'" ("The Sisters Brontë" 18–19). Here Oliphant establishes the famed reputation of Brontë (instantiating her as genius, "the reverse of vulgar," the possessor of an independent mind), but she equivocates on Brontë's brilliance by calling her naive and in error (while lumping George Eliot into Oliphant's flattening ruminations.)

Oliphant furthers her resistance by arguing that the chief concern about the authorship of *Jane Eyre* should not have been the sex of the author but the representation of Rochester's indiscretions, including his egregious confessions to Jane.[17] Oliphant finds fault not with his character but with his conversation. His past amours and mistresses would be "a subject so abhorrent to a young woman" ("The Sisters Brontë" 20), Oliphant feels, that a gentleman would never have erred to this level of indiscretion. The fact that Brontë does err in imagining her gentleman hero underscores a glaring lack of class knowledge in

---

[16]   Oliphant offered her slant on the *Jane Eyre* story in 1891 with *Janet*, where a governess is astounded to find not a long-lost wife in the attic but a long-bearded husband.

[17]   Indeed, Oliphant was rather consistent in her response to *Jane Eyre*, since in 1855 she called the "furious love-making" in the novel a "wild declaration of the 'Rights of Woman' in a new aspect." Sarcastic in her appraisal of the book, Oliphant suggests that its "ferocious appropriation" is "very much unlike the noble and grand sentiment which we used to call love" ("Modern Novelists" 558, 559).

the novelist. Oliphant remarks, "In this was a point of honour which [Brontë] did not understand …. The woman less enlightened in practical evil considers less the risks of actual vice; but her imagination is free in other ways, and she innocently permits her hero to do and say things so completely against the code which is binding on gentlemen whether vicious or otherwise that her want of perception becomes conspicuous" ("The Sisters Brontë" 20).[18] In so saying, Oliphant manages to point out a glaring gap in Brontë's writerly ability, a conspicuous want of perception, and she makes particular note that, to her mind, Elizabeth Gaskell's attempt to account for Brontë's omissions are singularly unsuccessful. Oliphant writes, "When Mrs. Gaskell made her disastrous statements about Branwell Brontë and other associates of Charlotte's youth, it was with the hope of proving that the speech and manners of the men to whom she had been accustomed were of a nature to justify her in any such misapprehension of the usual manners of gentlemen. It was on the contrary, as I think, only the bold and unfettered imagination of a woman quite ignorant on all such subjects which could have suggested this special error" ("The Sisters Brontë" 20–21).

Oliphant notes, as a form of tribute, that Brontë's writing flew in the face of Victorian feminine emotional discipline and allowed for a passionate expression that had no precedent. She contends that in *Shirley*, Brontë's representation of her eponymous character was "revolutionary to the highest degree, casting aside that discreet veil of the heroine which almost all previous novelists had respected" (*The Victorian Age*, Vol. I, 307). As such, she contends Brontë was "daring and extraordinary" ("The Sisters Brontë" 14) in her attempts to overthrow the superstition that "the woman should be no more than responsive, maintaining a reserve in respect to her feelings, subduing the expression, unless in the 'once, and only once, and to One only' of the poet" ("The Sisters Brontë" 23). Yet, praise of this sort is obviously double-coded, a point Oliphant makes less subtly in her discussion on sensationalism and the relative degree of an author's genius. In "Novels" (1867), Oliphant contends, "Writers who have no genius and little talent, make up for it by displaying their acquaintance with the accessories and surroundings of vice, with means of seduction, and with what they set forth as the secret tendencies of the heart" (259). Without segue or paragraph break, Oliphant immediately moves to a discussion of Brontë's *Shirley*, saying it introduced a "new sensation to the world in general" (259). Though she only obliquely critiques Brontë in this passage, she suggests that the "passionate lamentation" contained in Brontë's novels opened a Pandora's box that influenced minor novelists, who

---

[18] Rochester's indiscretion is also one of Rigby's major lines of attack. She dislikes the manner in which Rochester "purrs into [Jane's] ear disgraceful tales of his past life connected with the birth of little Adele, which any man with common respect for a woman, and that a mere girl of eighteen, would have spared her; but which eighteen in this case listens to as if it were nothing new, and certainly nothing distasteful" (104). Rigby also takes particular umbrage at the representation of Blanche Ingram and her mother, the cold and cruel society ladies made perfect for ridicule by their heartless class snobbery.

willfully depict "burning kisses and frantic embraces" for heroines who wait in a "voluptuous dream" for a man's "flesh and muscles, for strong arms that seize her, and warm breath that thrills her through" (259). Oliphant indignantly argues, "[T]his new and disgusting picture of what professes to be the female heart, comes from the hands of women, and is tacitly accepted by them as real" and is "not in any way to be laughed at" (260).[19] As is evident from her clear castigation, Oliphant rejects Brontë's radical ideas about publicly exposed desire. Oliphant instead espouses an ardent regard for traditions of feminine reserve and decorum, what she calls "superstitions." She notes, "Personally I am disposed to stand for the superstition, and dislike all transgression of it" ("The Sisters Brontë" 24).[20] In one review, Oliphant thus topples two women of famed genius from their exalted pedestals and rattles the base of a third. Though Oliphant praises these female geniuses, her emphasis on Eliot's, Gaskell's, and Brontë's errors presumes a category of famed author who knows better—and is better—than these literary greats.

A Turn to Fiction—*The Athelings*

One of the best ways to see the possibilities for difference built into Oliphant's author-characters is to examine briefly a third portrait, the character of Agnes Atheling in Oliphant's *The Athelings, or, The Three Gifts* (1857). Agnes is a young girl of seventeen, the eldest child in a family of seven, existing on the father's meager salary of £200 a year. (We are told of his income at least seven times in the early stages of the novel.) Agnes is the clever one, gifted not with beauty, like her sister Marian, or shrewdness, like her brother, the "big boy" Charlie, but with a talent for putting pretty words upon the page. Agnes is amused rather than insulted when told to "read some of your nonsense" (6) during quiet evenings at home. As an author, she is more drawn to the "pretty sentences" and the "admirable orderliness of her manuscript" than she is to intellectual profundity or any potential for authorial fame. "After all," Oliphant writes, "she was only a girl" (7).

Given what we've already seen in Oliphant, that she can deftly twist a representation so that praise functions more precisely as critique, one might expect her to show the world that Agnes neither writes nonsense nor is "only a

---

[19]	Oliphant reserves particular invective for Mary Elizabeth Braddon, who, she felt, suffused her novels with sensationalisms, and exploited her celebrity to compel readers to accept shoddy merchandise. Oliphant writes, "To have made upon your contemporaries that the whole civilized world thus acknowledges your sway, is a thing rarely achieved even by the greatest. But it has been achieved by Miss Braddon; and in sight of such a climax of fame and success, what can any one say?" ("Novels" 263).

[20]	Since Oliphant writes "The Sisters Brontë" in 1897, exactly 50 years after *Jane Eyre*'s publication, Oliphant's advocacy of terse-lipped traditionalism strikes me as a way to deflect fin-de-siècle "New Woman" associations rather than to specifically distance herself from Brontë, thus endearing herself to a readership that is still sympathetic to the economy of emotions, "the superstitions," she discusses.

girl," but neither possibility emerges. Agnes does write a book and it is published and received with some early acclaim and her literary life is enough to fuel the momentum of the plot in the beginning of *The Athelings*, yet Agnes as novelist soon takes second seat to a heterosexual romance narrative in which her lovely, white-handed sister Marian wins love, riches, a title, and a handsome husband. Agnes may indeed be "only a girl" who is an author, but when it comes to femininity, Oliphant's book suggests that real power is in beauty and attracting male attention, not in cleverness.

Throughout *The Athelings*, writing is always secondary to conventional gender appeal. One's literary output and success are pre-determined by the worth of its producer; the authoress who possesses no artifice will produce a text that is simple and sweet, and we should think higher of the writing because of the moral worth of the writer. Oliphant does not seem sympathetic to the claim, as voiced by a male author-character in the book, Lionel Rivers, that ladies should not write. Indeed, she deeply upholds the notion in this novel that writing belongs in the domain of appropriate domestic tasks for women, or, as the omniscient narrator notes, writing is not "unfeminine" but the "prettiest kind of fancy-work a woman can do" (127). Such an idea is borne out by Agnes, who wins over Lionel through the very prettiness of her book, for it is not the ideas encapsulated in it, but the mellifluous flow of the lovely words on the pages themselves that hold his attention. In fact, though Agnes has encoded a special message in her book for Lionel, he is oblivious to it because he finds himself distracted by its form. "He read the book over again when he went home, to make it [the mystery of his inheritance] out if he could, but fell so soon into thought of the writer, and consideration of that sweet youthful voice of hers, that there was no coming to any light in the matter" (171). This puts Agnes Atheling in marked contrast to the "free thinking" and scandal-indifferent geniuses, Charlotte Brontë and George Eliot, for the goodness of Agnes' text is meant to be a direct index of the goodness of her person. The genius writers' texts may be great, but Oliphant raises the distinct possibility that their non-conventional lives lessen the possibility for their writings to be good.

Oliphant wrote *The Athelings* at mid-century, and it is roughly contemporary with Brontë's novels and with Gaskell's biography. Though Oliphant makes clear in her autobiography and in "The Sisters Brontë," published at century's end, that much has changed in the way of social conventions, she never publicly alters her opinion that certain topics—and by this she generally means deeply emotional or scandal-related issues—are beyond the proper bounds of the text. Indeed, she termed Gaskell's *The Life of Charlotte Brontë*, the "dreadful art of confidential revelation" (*The Victorian Age*, Vol. I, 324). Oliphant is strongly derisive of the notion that all should be told in the name of verisimilitude, as evidenced in *The Athelings* through her caricature of a "bona fide" writer, Mr. Foggo A. Endicott, a pretentious American journalist and poet, who has come to England to gather material. He's also a great blatherer, and Oliphant lets him spew to his heart's content. In particular, Endicott advocates the idea that "a literary man, belongs to the world" and thus has no right to privacy. "Unenlightened people have complained of me, in vulgar phrase," Endicott notes, "that I 'put them in the newspapers.' How strange a misconception! for you must perceive at once that it was not with any consideration of them, but simply that my readers might see every scene I passed through, and in reality feel themselves traveling with me!" (35). The egotism of the American writer is clear, but also evident is a sense that a public platform does not free one to depict scenes and people without respect to circumstance or decency.

The caricature of Endicott underscores the precise grounds on which Oliphant takes exception to Gaskell's portrait of Charlotte Brontë in *The Life*. It was not so much Charlotte's intrigue with M. Heger that Oliphant considered too scandalous to reveal (though Gaskell took great pains to efface this connection in her text), but the revelation of Branwell Brontë's drunkenness and debauchery that Oliphant found unseemly. Though Oliphant doesn't think much of Branwell and disputes the idea that he was the lost genius of the family, she suggests that his masculine shame is all the greater for having been outdone by his sisters. Oliphant also expresses a feeling that Gaskell erred in her representation by providing gratuitous scenes of Branwell's drunken demise, noting, "The unhappy attempt of Mrs. Gaskell in writing the lives of the sisters to make this melancholy young man accountable for the almost brutal element of Emily Brontë's conception of life, and the strange view of Charlotte as to what men were capable of, has made him far too important in their history; where, indeed, he had no need to have appeared at all, had the family pride consisted, as the pride of so many families does, in veiling rather than exhibiting the faults of its members" ("The Sisters Brontë" 9). Such a claim gets to the heart of issues of verisimilitude, and hence, as we have seen, of genius. What constitutes appropriate material for one's writing also engages matters of the hazy terrain of public–private boundaries, and hence, of celebrity. It is clear that Oliphant views family honor as a higher priority than faithful description, particularly when that description yields lurid scenes evoking debauchery and drunkenness. Though Oliphant praises the power to see and represent, she clearly draws a boundary line demarcating what is suitable for representation. Indeed, Corbett notes that Oliphant followed a strict code of conduct, such that, "If the autobiographer writes about her peers, she should do so with restraint and diplomacy; if she writes of her intimates and relatives, she must be careful not to disclose anything the least bit uncomplimentary, and certainly nothing downright personal or private" (94).[21] In this particular case, Branwell's travails merit his blotting from the public account

---

[21]   *Christian Observer* praised Oliphant's code, specifying her satisfactory role *in locus parentis*, "Throughout her long career as a writer, she held consistently to one principle in the character of her word. She believed that fiction was lowered when the writer dealt with subjects or with characters that 'would not be admitted into any family in the empire.' The result was that she never wrote anything about the criminal classes, avoiding immortality as a subject as she would have avoided a contagion, and she came well into that classification of British authors who wrote for young men and women as their fathers or mothers might have done" ("Mrs. Margaret Oliphant" 18).

of the Brontë sisters' careers because Oliphant considers it unconscionable to contribute to the bitter fruit of scandal.

In *The Athelings*, Oliphant's open critique of Endicott, and its probable meta-textual link to Grace Greenwood,[22] as well as the representation of Agnes Atheling, establishes a code of literary practices that Oliphant positions herself as resisting. Her opposition to authorial excess thus makes her portraits of authorship, both within *The Athelings* and in her biographical sketches, interestingly subversive, even though ideologically they seem to conform to dominant values. So, for instance, in taking Gaskell to task for her portrayals of Branwell, Oliphant seems to reinforce a cultural logic in support of feminine decorum, yet she equally disrupts a sexist paradigm that prevents the public criticism of women (particularly a criticism launched by other women). Likewise, by constructing an author-character, Agnes, as sweet, plain, and ultimately invested in marriage, Oliphant undercuts the notion of the unsexed bluestocking at the same time as she positions professional writing as a wholly womanly task. In each case, she plays with a restricting logic that suggests the only two locations one might occupy are either the private/female or the public/male, again demonstrating how the nineteenth century grappled with gender issues through practical and ideological means.[23]

"I have said all that is in me to say"

Olphant's comparative representational strategy offers a means of both acknowledging another's fame and inserting the importance of a different sort of literary career. As such, her "self" description allows two versions of the famous female author to occupy the space occupied by the writerly ideal, a genius who writes of grand passions, and the quotidian scribbler, the author who

[22] Jay argues that the characterization of Endicott is a piece of literary revenge against American writer Grace Greenwood (*Mrs. Oliphant* 35). Her assessment seems quite likely given that Oliphant's reminiscence of her encounter with Grace Greenwood recounted in *The Autobiography* suggests that she did not enjoy either the woman or being spoken of in *Haps and Mishaps* in a way that discredited Oliphant's rightful stature as a published author. Oliphant writes that she and her husband encountered "a dark, dashing person, an American lady," headed to the same house party as they. After some conversation in which Greenwood struck Oliphant as "patronizing," Oliphant observes somewhat indignantly: "She thought me, I supposed, the poor little shy wife of some artist, whom the Halls were being kind to, or something of that humble kind. She turned out to be a literary person of great pretensions, calling herself Grace Greenwood, though that was not her real name, – and I was amused to find a paragraph about myself, as 'a little homely Scotchwoman,' in the book she wrote when she got back" (*The Autobiography of Margaret Oliphant* 41).

[23] In *Novels of Everyday Life*, Langbauer makes a complementary point about Oliphant's treatment of the everyday and the exceptional in her serialized fiction particularly *Phoebe Junior* (1876) and *Salem Chapel* (1863). Langbauer argues that in merging the quotidian with the extraordinary, Oliphant reconceptualizes her own role and status as a cultural producer.

by dint of circumstances or choice aspires not to lofty genius but grapples with the "compromises, accommodations, and failures that characterize awkward reality" (Jay 220). That Oliphant can be inserted into a newly diversified pantheon of eminent women writers and that she can underscore her own accordance with ideological gender prescriptions, even as her behavior suggests a defiance of those codes, indicates that something in the ideological framework has to give. In this case, that "give" comes in the signifying system that makes fame and gender intelligible. The public contestation of the meanings of gender, fame, and genius ultimately work to expand their applicability.

I'm suggesting here that Oliphant performs the same sort of symbolic re-appropriation that Gaskell enacted through her representation of Charlotte Brontë and that Fanny Fern created through her multiple portraits of "herself" and her famous peers. Oliphant's depiction of the professional female author at work in the figure of Charlotte Brontë evokes a writer who resists prevailing, and limited, stereotypes of authorship: she is flawed, she is often coarse, she is naive. She has genius, yes, but just exactly what does one mean by genius? Under what terms do we ascribe her lasting fame? Oliphant's use of femininity as a topic of central relevance to famed genius also allows for a repositioning of other concepts: legitimacy, artistry, transgression. By juxtaposing "herself" as "failed author/successful woman" against the perceived "successful author/ failed woman" of Charlotte, Oliphant interrogates the founding concepts on which those categories are presumed. Oliphant's depiction of herself as a professional writer who always stood outside of literary fame due to her sacrifices as wife and mother destabilizes a binary arrangement of idealized masculine/male and feminine/female, thus making space for paid and famous authorship in the single body of the woman. Significantly, these ideas about the value of her own life and the severity of her personal and professional pain serve as an effective springboard and framing device for a discussion on literary celebrity and gender.

Oliphant furthers her bid for change by crafting the terms of her fame:

> When I die I know what people will say of me: they will give me credit for courage (which I almost think is not courage but insensibility), and for honesty and honourable dealing; they will say I did my duty with a kind of steadiness, not knowing how I have rebelled and groaned under the rod. (67)

Even if we take these words as the utterances of a persona and therefore not necessarily the "authentic" reflections of Margaret Oliphant, we still must acknowledge their power. For through them, Oliphant directly challenges a status quo ideology that positions middle-class women as willing, even jubilant, martyrs to self-sacrifice. Though Oliphant could have clearly adopted the culturally valued position of bereaved widow and mother, she does not do so. Instead she points to the doubleness of her condition, suggesting that a woman who appears to have "done her duty" may not have been invested in the ideological mandate undergirding that duty. In effect, she severs the sign— the woman's female embodied identity—from the signified—the essentialized cultural sense of what that body/self will do. Like an elaborate game of dominos, the separation of sign from signified allows for an ideological chain reaction of similar imperatives, including the "tyranny of binary sex opposition" (Epstein and Straub 21). The disruption of this chain of naturalized signifiers as they relate to women's identity and as they are enacted through the process of writing and dynamics of literary celebrity in turn allows for an expanded set of options through which to conceptualize gender. As Oliphant noted, "great genius breaks all bonds," thus the impediments fostered by restrictive gender codes can be powerfully rewritten through the representation of a woman's famed genius, even if she be a general utility woman.

Chapter 4

Correcting the Record, Creating a New One: Elizabeth Keckley's *Behind the Scenes* and Eliza Potter's *A Hair-dresser's Experience in High Life*

Thousands of persons followed me to the ferry-boat, which was to convey me across the Ohio River – some in sorrow and some in joy; all, believing I had made my final exit from Cincinnati – which, however, as the reader will see, was a mistake.

—Eliza Potter, *A Hair-dresser's Experience in High Life*, 1859

Messrs. G. W. Carleton & Co have in press *Behind the Scenes*, by Mrs. Elizabeth Keckley, who is described as "for forty years a household slave in the best Southern families," "and during the plotting of the rebellion a confidential servant of Mrs. Jefferson Davis," and "since the commencement of the rebellion, and up to date, Mrs. Abraham Lincoln's *modiste* (dressmaker), confidential friend, and business woman generally." This work the publishers expect, probably with reason, to "produce a great sensation;" but when they go on to assert, with an hyperbole to which we have become pretty well accustomed, that it will "be read by every man and woman in the land with the deepest interest," it is well they should be reminded of a circumstance they have often seemed to be unaware of – that there *are* men and women in the land to whom the literature of the kitchen does not appeal, and to whom neither the act of receiving nor of retailing the confidence of servants comments itself as creditable. Still – and this, no doubt, is with them the chief point – the conception of the book being essentially vulgar, its success will probably be complete.

"Table-Talk," *A Saturday Review of Politics, Finance, Literature, Society*, 1868

The above epigraphs function as a fitting curtain raiser for this chapter, since they highlight the experience of public visibility experienced by two women of color in the nineteenth century, Eliza Potter, a free black hairdresser, who catered to a high-society clientele, and Elizabeth Keckley, a former slave, who bought her own freedom and became the dressmaker to women of style and status such as Mrs. Jefferson Davis and Mrs. Abraham Lincoln. In the first passage, Potter vividly narrates her own celebrity, describing the crowds of people who have congregated in order to track her comings and goings. Sharon Dean calls this scene of celebrity, "worthy of film director King Vidor" (xxxvi). In the second passage, Keckley does not speak for herself, but is spoken of, in terms both derisive and dismissive. The writer for *A Saturday Review of Politics* takes issue both with what is characterized as the tell-all nature of Keckley's *Behind the Scenes* and Carleton & Co's hyperbolic advertising campaign. The paper deems both the author and the publishing house to be vulgar and thus sure to appeal to baser tastes, which none-too-subtly references the word's dual meanings as both coarse and of the people. It was perhaps in response to such critique that the *American Literary Gazette* made note of Carleton & Co's willingness to "produce, if necessary, unimpeachable references in regard to the character, ability, and standing of Mrs. Keckley" ("Notes on Books" 314).[1]

These scenes may strike us as radically different, since one allows the woman of color to claim her visibility jubilantly while the other scene silences her voice before she is ever heard. Yet, these two moments are particularly illustrative for this study, since they establish the continuum on which celebrity and gender find their meaning. For just as we have seen in other discussions of literary professionalism, celebrity, and gender, the perks and punishments afforded to a public woman required that she manage her image with deliberation and care. Throughout this book thus far, I have examined how women authors altered the cultural terms for understanding both sex and gender by using representations of literary celebrity to introduce new possibilities that allowed a woman to earn her living, appear in public, and claim her legitimate place as fully female and feminine. In this chapter I turn very specifically to a greater consideration of race, gender, and celebrity through two African American authors, Elizabeth Keckley[2] and Eliza Potter, who fought for gender, race, and class legitimacy through representation.

There are, of course, other women of color who experienced widespread celebrity in the nineteenth century. I rely on Keckley and Potter because, like the other authors examined here, they emerged as public figures intelligible in a transatlantic context who used writing to shape their public images. As I have noted, by trade Keckley was a dressmaker and Potter a hairdresser, and thus, both depart from the other authors considered in this book in that neither functioned in primary roles as professional authors committed to establishing the profession itself. At some level, then, it could be argued that Keckley and Potter may have come to their writings and their fame accidentally, rather than through the deliberate work that I have outlined in past chapters. Indeed, the fact of their professional work outside of literary production might seem grounds to dismiss Keckley and Potter from my study. In *A Portrait of the Artist as a Young Woman*, for example, Linda Huf

---

[1]   Potter was also charged with vulgarity in reviews of her memoir. *The Cincinnati Daily Commercial* vehemently attacked Potter for the "innate vulgarity," of her memoir, which they described as a "prying curiosity," and an "offensive coarseness of the class to which [she] belongs" ("Reviewer Reviewed" 2). Another article deemed Potter a "vulgar and incompetent person" who had undertaken "to criticise things utterly beyond her capacities" and chided *The Cincinnati Gazette* for its more liberal reception of Potter's book ("The Gazette on Hairdressing" n.p.).

[2]   In *Mrs. Lincoln and Mrs. Keckly*, Jennifer Fleischner argues for spelling Keckley as Keckly based on a persuasive argument about the spelling of her name in legal documents. I, however, keep the more typical spelling as a means of consistency with other scholarship.

explains her decision to exclude black women from a study of women-generated *Künstlerroman* on the grounds that, "none ... depict, in fictional form, their efforts to become artists. The black woman is even less eager than the white woman to strike the grandiose pose which since the Romantic period has been expected of the Artist .... If the white heroine sees herself as presumptuous in her aspiration to become an artist, the black heroine must see herself as preposterous" (13–14).[3]

I believe we need to take such comments advisedly. P. Gabrielle Foreman argues, for instance, that the so-called invisibility of the actual black woman writer is more a function of a forgetful history than of any fear on the part of black women that they were being either presumptuous or preposterous (*Activist Sentiments* 175). In terms of black women's representation through *Künstlerroman*, Foreman reminds us that the recent "discoveries" of such books as *The Bondswoman's Narrative* indicate, as Henry Louis Gates, Jr. has surmised, that "black reading culture was likely to have produced many more creative works [and inventive characterizations] by men and women than we had ever imagined" (Foreman "Introduction" xxvii). The black woman artist may well, as Huf determines, be a "missing character in fiction" (14), but the famous black woman writer is not. As Frances Smith Foster makes clear, author Anna Julia Cooper's contention that the African American woman had been "voiceless" is "more rhetorical than factual" (*Written* 2). In addition to Cooper herself, nineteenth-century African American female professional authors who had some public presence included Maria Stewart, Harriet Jacobs, Ann Plato, Mary Jane Patterson, Frances Harper, Mary Church Terrell, Charlotte Forten Grimké, Fannie Barrie Williams, Ida B. Wells, Josephine St. Pierre Ruffin, and Victoria Earle Matthews (*Written* 2).[4]

We should not be too easily persuaded, then, that a black woman author-character would see her self-representation as unbelievable. Indeed, the public profile that a career in professional literary production afforded could be an important way to gain cultural power for many women of color. In popular magazines and journals, many writers, such as Mrs. N.R. Mossell (Gertrude E.H. Bustill Mossell), exhorted younger black women to consider journalism as a viable career alternative to "domestic work, teaching, or dressmaking." Mossell not only publicly endorsed professional authorship, she argued for a new zone of superiority and suitability made intelligible by celebrity, saying women were "often more popular if not as scholarly" as men (qtd. in Shockley 118).

---

[3]   Other books that examine the representation of the woman as artist, such as Deborah Heller's *Literary Sisterhoods*, Anne Boyd's *Writing for Immortality*, Suzanne Jones, ed. *Writing the Woman Artist*, and Paula Bennett's *Poets in the Public Sphere*, make no argument for the exclusion of women of color.

[4]   Foster's "Testing and Testifying" in *Written by Herself* provides a comprehensive overview of the African-American woman's literary tradition. For a larger historical consideration see Barbara Christian's *Black Women Novelists*. Ann Allen Shockley's *Afro-American Women Writers, 1746–1933*, is a useful anthology of black women's voices.

I select Keckley and Potter for study in this chapter, rather than these other black writers of note, because their particular representational strategies are consistent with a tactical position manifested by the other authors examined in this book. Indeed, Keckley's and Potter's trades as dressmaker and hairdresser, respectively, make them ideally suited to my study, since their social strategies set to narrative focus on similar tactics of self-representation and self-promotion that required a careful negotiation within the embodied bounds of respectable womanhood. Their work therefore not only accords with, but in many ways expands, the governing paradigms of gender and celebrity we have seen emerge through discussions in earlier chapters, in that both discursively created mediated images that allow for a version of female subjectivity otherwise not widely imagined in other cultural contexts. Together they function as powerful hermeneutic agents, who are able to offer decisive commentary on, and alteration of, what the metaphor of the famous female author instantiates and disrupts. Indeed, both Keckley and Potter make of themselves figures worth noticing and capable of seeing, authorities who claim governance of a narrative domain, subjects who uphold their rights to self-determination. And thus, both Keckley and Potter make significant contributions to the figures of fame examined in this book.

In both texts under consideration in this chapter, Elizabeth Keckley's *Behind the Scenes, or, Thirty Years a Slave, and Four Years in the White House* (1868), and Eliza Potter's *A Hair-dresser's Experience in High Life* (1859), not only do their author-character-selves fulfill intimate domestic functions for white women of considerable means, both books establish their writers as the final arbiter in what constitutes refinement and gentility, reinforcing Rafia Zafar's contention that African American writers of both sexes often "adopted many of the ideas and genres of the white dominant culture in order to declare themselves part of it" (7). Yet, both Potter and Keckley claim an insider status that alters the terms of what the inside might mean. The promise of each memoir, therefore, is not overt racial commentary or autobiographical romance, though these themes are present in Potter's and Keckley's writings, nor is it access to the (whitened) figure of the author. Instead both memoirs promise an inside look at a celebrated elite white culture that is depicted and governed by the black woman, thus providing a unique glimpse into and reorganization of the dynamics of power that are inherent in labor and race relations, gender assignments, and public visibility.

As Witness and Testifier

Elizabeth Keckley was born in Virginia in 1818, the daughter of her white slave-holding father, Armistead Burwell, and her enslaved mother, Agnes Hobbs. Moving as a slave of the household to St. Louis in 1847, she was able, after considerable negotiation and effort, to buy freedom for herself and her son, George, in 1855 at the cost of $1200. Keckley moved to Baltimore and then to Washington, DC, and used her formidable skills as a needlewoman to develop a client base that began with Mrs. Robert E. Lee and by the 1860's reached the first lady, Mary Todd Lincoln. Beginning in 1861 and extending past Lincoln's assassination, Keckley took on the role of Mrs. Lincoln's personal modiste. Mary Todd Lincoln was a woman famous, in lore and perhaps actual demeanor, for her sometimes outrageous behavior and appearance. Jennifer Fleischner credits Lincoln with wearing daring formal attire, including off-the-shoulder and low-cut gowns, that made her the focus of Washington gossip circles as well as national press commentary. She notes that Lincoln's clothes were often the subject of commentary in both lighter periodicals like *Frank Leslie's Illustrated* and more "serious-minded" newspapers such as the *Herald* or *Tribune* (*Mrs. Lincoln* 197). Though we do not know this for certain, Fleischner argues that Lincoln enjoyed the attention and courted the press's public fawning on her, which, in turn, soured the public to Mary Todd Lincoln's coarse western (read as unrefined) ways. We do know, however, that Mrs. Lincoln held considerable celebrity—even notoriety— in a transatlantic, even global, context. Keckley's role as Lincoln's dressmaker made her both the handmaid to transatlantic celebrity and a co-conspirator in multi-national infamy.

Like Mrs. Lincoln, Keckley's fame turned to infamy soon after the assassination of Abraham Lincoln. Since Lincoln died intestate, Mary Todd Lincoln was compelled to appeal to the Congress for an annuity that would support her. Due to their delayed deliberations, she claimed that she felt forced to secretly sell items from her extensive wardrobe, an act that was exposed by the press as the "Old Clothes Scandal," creating much public ire. It was at the moment of the scandal and in effort to explain to the public Mrs. Lincoln's choices that Keckley authored *Behind the Scenes*. But just as Mary Lincoln's choice to sell some of her clothes backfired, so did Keckley's purported attempt to exonerate herself and Mrs. Lincoln. *Behind the Scenes* generated what Xiomara Santamarina has termed a "scandal of publicity" due to the fact that Keckley was perceived as "promoting a crisis" that should be protected by "bourgeois norms of privacy" ("Behind" 529). Carolyn Sorisio equally contends that Keckley exposed the "delicate self-construction of the white American middle class," thus indicating that a black servant women could see beneath the masks and behind the scenes of a façade that was not supposed to exist (20). Incensed by the publication of his mother's letters in the back of *Behind the Scenes*, Robert Todd Lincoln called in favors from Keckley's publishing house, G.W. Carlton & Co., to suppress the book and destroy all extant copies, so that Keckley ultimately earned very little in the way of royalties. Several accounts exist of Robert Lincoln snubbing Keckley when she attempted to explain her motivations. And while very few people were actually able to read Keckley's book, news of its publication was rampant. Going public with the Lincoln scandal jeopardized Keckley's position with her rich white clients, while also alienating her from a black community fearing reprisals. Keckley, like the other authors considered here, thus experienced a contested relationship to both visibility and celebrity.

Much like Elizabeth Keckley, it was Eliza Potter's proximity to a white elite that afforded her vantage point on privilege as well as her own portion of fame. Believed to have been born around 1820 in Cincinnati but raised in New York state, by her own account Eliza Potter earned for herself a degree of prominence as a hairdresser to the wealthy in the tonier areas of the United States, England, and Europe (France and London, in particular), before returning to Cincinnati in 1856 and staying until at least 1861. (No extant records indicate a Cincinnati residence after this date.)[5] Potter published *A Hair-dresser's Experience in High Life* in 1859, and it caused a considerable publicity storm in Cincinnati, as evidenced by the local papers, *The Cincinnati Daily Gazette* and the *Cincinnati Daily Commercial*, which ran several columns on her revelations of the "upper ten of Cincinnati" (*Gazette*). Both *Behind the Scenes* and *A Hair-dresser's Experience in High Life* have earned a degree of posthumous cultural currency for their respective authors, particularly since they are part of the Schomburg Series of Nineteenth Century Black Women Writers, edited by Henry Louis Gates, Jr. Both memoirs thus enjoy a form of transatlantic recognition likely unimaginable to either author at the time of her respective texts' composition.

There is much that marks Keckley and Potter's works as distinctive in both aim and content, but particularly noteworthy is their difference from the bulk of material published by other African American writers in the nineteenth century. Neither classic slave narratives nor romance novels, *Behind the Scenes* and *A Hair-dresser's Experience* seem particularly uninterested in, as Sharon G. Dean puts it, "explaining black folks to white folks" (lvii). Both take up a different task of gazing critically at the white woman to, as Zafar words it, provide "a fashionable and fashioned sense of the white world in order to reveal its failings," a composite critique that is offered to a primarily white middle-class readership (153). This, of course, puts Keckley's and Potter's narrating and focalizing presences in the superior positions of both witness and testifier, of arbiter and rule maker. Though each author acknowledges herself as a black woman who must work to earn her living, both claim a position superior in knowledge, morality, and refinement to the white upper-class women (and often men) they describe, thus offering the possibility that the black woman who works for her bread may know quite a lot more about enacting hegemonic codes than do the white people for whom Keckley and Potter work.[6] As such, these authors demonstrate Nancy Hartsock's original version of the feminist standpoint theory, that women's insider/outsider position(s) in society afford them a vantage point from which to examine and

---

[5]   See Susan P. Graber, "*A Hair-dresser's Experience in High Life*, by Mrs. Eliza Potter: Cincinnati in the Mid-Nineteenth Century," *Bulletin of the Historical and Philosophical Society of Ohio* 25.3 (1967): 215–24.

[6]   It's worth noting that one of the criticisms of Charlotte Brontë's *Jane Eyre* was Jane's point of view as governess and a consequent focalized critique of the behaviors of a higher class of people, a critique that was inappropriate for the governess to make about her employers and social "betters."

evaluate truth claims as well as providing them with a method through which to analyze epistemology.[7] As Patricia Hill Collins applies this theory to black collective experience, standpoint theory becomes an "interpretive framework dedicated to explicating how knowledge remains central to maintaining and changing unjust systems of power" (375). The standpoint of Potter and Keckley allows them a critical power in determining the lens through which upper-class white women (which is to say, the ideal "true woman") will be read, and in so doing, they contribute to a mode of looking that, as Elizabeth Gaskell espoused, "inserts the thin end of the wedge," allowing for a recalibrated ideology of blackness, class, womanhood and, not incidentally, celebrity.

It seems to me this claim for Keckley and Potter's importance holds up even when issues of ghostwriting are factored in. Though both are known to have been literate, no evidence exists to support the possibility that either Keckley or Potter had any formal education.[8] This, of course, does not preclude their authorship, as slave/literacy narratives such as those by Frederick Douglass or Harriet Jacobs attest, but many scholars consider *Behind the Scenes* to be ghostwritten by a white author, whereas very little ancillary or academic analyses of Potter's work exists to speculate whether Potter was its actual writer or not.[9] The unclear circumstances of these texts' generation thus proposes an important set of questions: Can authorship practices be examined when the texts under consideration are not necessarily generated by a single voice? Can the famous subject be interpellated through a mediating, and unnamed, third party?

In some ways I agree with James Olney, who argues that "Whether Elizabeth Keckley was assisted in writing … is quite beside the point" (xxxi). Regardless of its mode of production, Keckley should be considered the primary author of *Behind the Scenes*, not due to historical accuracy, or because the book "authentically" reproduces Keckley's subjectivity (though it may), but because the text establishes

---

[7] As Susan Hekman notes in "Truth and Method." Hartsock's theory has grown increasingly out of vogue among contemporary feminist scholars due to its reliance on Marxist theory, its seeming essentialism of women, and its apparent opposition to postmodernism and poststructuralism (341–2). Hekman's analysis (as well as responses from Hartsock, Patricia Hill Collins, and Sandra Harding) complicates the theory, suggesting ways in which standpoint theory is still applicable. In addition to Nancy Hartsock's rethinking of standpoint theory (see *The Feminist Standpoint Theory Revisited*), special topic editions of both *Signs* and *Women & Politics* have contributed to the ongoing conversation about feminist standpoint theory and its present application. See *Signs* 22:2 (Winter 1997) and *Women & Politics* 18:3 (November 1997).

[8] It is probably helpful to be reminded that Abraham Lincoln had only one year of formal education and that an absence of schooling doesn't necessitate an absence of intelligence or authorial ability.

[9] See Foster's *Written by Herself* for a discussion of *Behind the Scenes*' production (126–30). See also Sylvia D. Hoffert's "Jane Grey Swisshelm, Elizabeth Keckley, and the Significance of Race Consciousness in American Women's History." John Washington disagrees with the ghostwriting charge. See *They Knew Lincoln* (226–41).

a speaking/writing subject the reader thinks of as "Elizabeth Keckley." Still, the questions exist: Were these women real? Did they actually write these books?[10] If the answer is yes, that they did indeed author these texts in the conventional sense of that verb, Keckley and Potter must be ascribed a degree of literary agency not normally associated with working women of color in the nineteenth century. But if the answer is no, do they lose agency? Do they become silenced? Not necessarily. For in many ways, the mere presence of the texts themselves testifies to the culture's ability to imagine a black woman in the role of speaking subject. As Richard Brodhead phrases it, "the literary sphere is the subject of plural and changing cultural organizations, determining what forms of writing are in cultural operations at any time or place" and thus any authorial profile emerges from what the culture is able to produce (113). These narratives, then, may not "authentically" inform the reader about Keckley and Potter's "real" lives and circumstances, but they are rhetorical artifacts that attest to the very precise historical and cultural organizations from which both women emerged.

"[L]adies could be guilty of almost any species of folly"

Both *Behind the Scenes* and *A Hair-dresser's Experience* develop the premise that their authors possess a great ability to read situations and people accurately and to react to them with better judgment than do the upper-class white men and women who are in supposed superior positions. Indeed, simply by assuming the role of (black) narrator/subjects who describe (white) characters/others, Potter and Keckley claim a power to define knowledge systems that reorganizes social hierarchies. In Potter's text, the degree to which she knows more than the "vapid" people for whom she works becomes laughable. Incident after incident allows Potter free range of representation, and her text often seems like a long line of, if not stupid, then certainly naive, rich white people, too dense to leave a burning building, too immoral to resist an adulterous affair, too lazy to dress themselves, too insecure to venture into public without the advice and counsel of their lady's maid, too flighty to sustain the image of their own precarious social images, too patronizing to recognize the intelligence and talents of the woman under their employ.

Keckley includes shades of this same commentary in her work. Instead of a parade of the mindless wealthy, however, Keckley takes on a more delicate rhetorical task in her depiction of the famous Mary Todd Lincoln. Whereas Potter makes no great pretense of actually liking the people for whom she works, even calling them "the veriest toadies for the sake of society" (230), Keckley attests to a strong feeling of sympathy and friendship for her clients, in particular the renowned, if not infamous, Mrs. Lincoln. Yet her apology for the First Lady contains

---

[10] For more on these debates about authenticity and accuracy, see Fleischner's *Mastering Slavery* (202, fn 6) and Henry Louis Gates, Jr.'s foreword to the Schomburg series on the complexity of authenticating slave narratives. See also Paula Giddings's *When and Where I Enter* and Joanne Braxton's *Black Women Writing Autobiography*.

many criticisms, both overt and covert, and the reader is left to wonder how fully committed Keckley really is to the project of exonerating Mary Todd Lincoln's tattered reputation.[11] At the end of both books, it may be the white woman who has served as the central figure— she has been examined and discussed, explained and vilified, criticized and praised—but it is the black author who profits, for she unequivocally establishes her own gendered worth on the public scale of merit where the white woman fails to excel.

This notion—that a person of a "demeaned and lesser race" might actually be shrewder and even more moral than a white master/employer, and that she might be more ladylike and decorous than her own mistress/client—turns the whole ideology of nineteenth-century class and race stratification on its head, an outcome, I would argue, totally in keeping with the overall rhetorical efforts of these two memoirs. Surely, both books repeat a refrain of mistakes, misjudgment, and ill-conceived actions performed by white women of the "fashionable set," as Potter would say. In different ways, we see both texts offering the possibility that their narrators might actually be superior to their white counterparts— better equipped to perceive and discern both value and hypocrisy, better adjusted to condition and circumstance, better attuned to the important movements of the age, better suited to empathize and direct awareness toward injustice, particularly injustice in stereotypes against black people.

Portraying the black female servant as more morally pure and intelligent than her white mistress is not entirely a new device. One can see the trope played out in several slave narratives and novels of domestic indenture, including Harriet Wilson's *Our Nig* (1859) and Harriet Jacobs' *Incidents in the Life of a Slave Girl* (1861), to name but two examples. Harriet Wilson, through her heroine Frado, regards the white mistress, Mrs. Belmont, as a vindictive tyrant, writing "[Frado] was under [Mrs. Belmont] in every sense of the word. What an opportunity to indulge her vixen nature! No matter what occurred to ruffle her, or from what source provocation came, real or fancied, a few blows on Nig seemed to relieve her of a portion of ill-will" (41). Harriet Jacobs openly critiques her mistress, saying, "Mrs. Flint, like many southern women, was totally deficient in energy. She had not strength to superintend her household affairs, but her nerves were so strong, that she could sit in her easy chair and see a woman whipped, till the blood trickled from every stroke of the lash. She was a member of the church; but partaking of the Lord's supper did not seem to put her in a Christian frame of mind" (10).

---

[11]   *Mr. Lincoln's Wife*, Anne Colver's 1943 novelization of Mary Todd Lincoln's life, imagines her response to *Behind the Scenes*, saying, "Bitterest of all had been Mrs. Keckley's book. Her memoirs of the White House and the Lincolns. Mary remembered how Robert had tried to hide the book from her when it was first published. But she had found it in a shop .... The false sympathy, the patronizing kindness. The lies she had twisted out of things Mary had told her in confidence ..." (390–91). Apparently, by this point in American history, there was some sense that Keckley's "defense" had been anything but sincere.

In his 1984 introduction to *Our Nig*, Henry Louis Gates, Jr., calls Wilson a groundbreaking writer in the use of this sort of rhetorical strategy, and P. Gabrielle Foreman reinforces Wilson's narratological inventiveness in her 2009 introduction, both introductions underscoring the association between artistic mastery and deserved literary celebrity. Gates describes Wilson as "subject who writes her own thinly veiled fictional account of her life in which she transforms her tormentors into objects, the stock, stereotypical objects of the sentimental novel." Gates calls Wilson's representation here, "the most brilliant rhetorical strategy in black fiction before Charles Chesnutt's considerable talent manifests itself at the turn of the century.... Harriet Wilson's employment of this device is unparalleled in representations of self-development in Afro-American fiction" (li–lii). Foreman references Patricia Wald's reading of *Our Nig* as a "sociopolitical allegory" that functions as a "narrative *about* autobiography" (Foreman "Introduction" xxxiii, Wald 169).

I wholly agree that Wilson's book deploys an insightful representational strategy in its objectifying of the white master in the context of the heightened subjectivity of the black author/narrator. But I would argue that both Potter and Keckley exert a similarly "brilliant rhetorical strategy" in their texts. Like Wilson and Jacobs they turn the powerful into the pitiful, often by employing sentimental tropes, a device, as Lori Merish notes, that "could provide African American writers with a significant vocabulary of political expression" (229). Remarkably, Keckley and Potter employ the power of sentimentalism while resisting simple binaries of self/other or tormentor/victim, instead laying out a complicated hierarchical structure in keeping with the cultural codes of the societies in which they are apart. The significance of this finely nuanced ideological arrangement is that as black women, they are nowhere near the bottom of the re-constituted social strata, the place assigned to them by the conventional white hierarchy.

Eliza Potter provides a telling illustration. "Society is made up of varieties," she notes, "but it is easy for the humblest servant to distinguish the well-born and highly bred lady, under the plainest garb, from the parvenu woman, whose sudden good luck and well-filled purse dresses her in lace, seats her in a carriage, and places her in circles where she is more endured that courted" (13). Potter here provides the reader with a nice series of contrasts between the humble servant, the parvenu pretender, and the high-bred lady. Interestingly, Potter occupies none of these identity locations. She is clearly neither humble nor a servant, a point she emphasizes at length through repeated reminders to the reader that she controls her own destiny and can come and go (and work) as she pleases. Although Sylvia D. Hoffert notes that "one of the privileges of having white skin ... was that a person had freedom of movement that was unavailable to either slaves or free blacks," Potter's representational author-character-self refutes those limitations (21). Potter is also not well-bred or high-class, though she knows how to construct the illusion of such things on the bodies of her clientele as well as on her own body, for she boasts of having "a suit that cost me one hundred and fifty dollars" (100) in addition to many other fine items.[12]

She is not nouveau riche, either in wealth or in social pretension. We might call her, then, a not-so-humble and not-so-dependent working woman who counts among her "friends" people of the highest social class. She can look down on newly wealthy white people, partially because they betray their lack of sophistication in their gaudy appearance and garish appurtenances, but also because people of the higher class also look down on them. Thus, we can read Potter's gesturing toward her extensive and expensive wardrobe, as well as her lack of need to be affirmed by the vast majority of white people, as a most effective thumbing of her nose at operative power arrangements that would put her lower on the social hierarchy than she places herself. As I have argued about contemporary makeover television, Potter here makes good use of style savvy to support the scaffolding of selfhood. I am a valuable person, she declares in her memoir, because I can lay claim to the knowledge capital necessary to support celebratory selfhood, the celebrity and the self here fused into one well-dressed subject.

Potter depicts herself as well liked and widely accepted by the elite and, because she is often compelled to offer them advice, simultaneously on par with and equal to them. In the scene above she has just been accepted by "well-bred people" to dine with them aboard ship; the parvenu women, by contrast, are snubbed. Wealthy women court Potter; they endure parvenu women, thus suggesting that the working black woman can not only exist but flourish in an elite white social enclave, desired, petted, appreciated, admired, even adored. She can rank above other women who are wealthy, white, and famous. She can play to the logic of a social hierarchy and insert a few new rungs on the ladder for herself to climb. And what this really indicates is that the person who counts most in terms of a social hierarchy is she who defines the rungs of the ladder. By taking on the power of observer and author, then, both Potter and Keckley play a formative role in publicly (re)conceiving the working woman of color in a way that problematizes conventional notions of race, class, and gender. Precisely through their depictions, Keckley and Potter are able to point to a re-formed version of black, working-class female subjectivity that contrasts with major stereotypes operative in the culture at this moment: they are not debased; they are not sexualized or animalized; they are not chattel; they are not unwomanly.[13] Even more significantly, they are not inarticulate or like children, two stereotypes, which Carla L. Peterson notes,

---

[12]   This link to fashion as an index of class is a point Merish makes through nineteenth-century historian Henry W. Ravenel, observing that "modes of freedwomen's dress – specifically, their access to the material signs of gentility (veils, parasols) – signified a dangerous departure from codes of racial deference; such practices comprised endlessly proliferating evidence of black insubordination" (236).

[13]   On the topic of sexual identity and appetites, Claudia Tate notes, "[R]acist ideology had characterized black men and women as the possessors of overactive libidos; thus the dominant society held the viewpoint that black women were wanton and black men had insatiable sexual appetites" (167).

dominated public opinion of both male and female African Americans in the nineteenth century (x). Potter and Keckley claim for themselves full capability and credibility in the generation of their mediated self-representations.

The relation between cultural stereotype and celebrity is critical, in this regard, since both gain their saliency and recognizability through similar cultural axes and signifying systems, which have a direct relation to race. As E. Nathaniel Gates notes in his introduction to *Cultural and Literary Critiques of the Concepts of "Race,"* organizing metaphors can be powerful tools to "reproduce or reinforce a racialized order of dominion," and the result of representation is often to produce a "virtual archive of information detailing what it means to be normative, as well as what it means to embody social and cultural alterity" (vii). Gates observes that the power of representation has often been in the hands of the dominant culture, which could depict "racialized others" as marginalized and devalued. Representation, he argues, "wield[s] enormous epistemological power" due to its capacity to "designate, identify, and in an important sense, (re)constitute" locations of the subject (vii).

This epistemological power to shape understanding, imagination, and forms of identity, as well as the very codes that define dominant/normal and deviant/marginalized, are also central to what makes celebrity such a compelling and contested force. As we have seen, often the study of fame implicitly privileges the "great (white) Man," whose class and race status is marked as invisible through the purviews of normativity. In the emerging field of celebrity studies, race and gender still go largely unexamined, particularly in an historical context. This is precisely why Keckley and Potter's respective work in *Behind the Scenes* and *A Hair-dresser's Experience in High Life* offers us much to consider about the constituent relationship between race, gender, and celebrity. Jacqueline Jones Royster's contemplation on the genesis of public authority, specifically narrative authority, is germane here. Royster develops the idea that the postbellum woman's "positive and productive self-concept" is a composite developed over a long trajectory, not a brief one (78). She identifies two Swahili terms for time: sasa, the individual's life, and zamani, collective memory, terms that bear remarkable similarity to Leo Braudy's distinction between celebrity and fame. "Sasa," Royster explains, "becomes personal time, the time during which individual people exist physically in the world and also the time during which they are remembered, even after physical death, by the living.... [S]asa is the present, the immediate past, the immediate future" (79). Through sasa and zamani, Royster suggests that African American women writers succeeded at circumventing the limits of the personal to achieve historical prominence. In effect, they yoked their stories to zamani, or memory over time, in order to claim a perpetuity and prominence of long-term relevance that has specific relevance to both race and gender.

We can see this link to posterity demonstrated in a return to Keckley. Though her narrative is ostensibly a "behind the scenes" account of the Lincoln White House and thus centered around the President and his wife, a statement she makes about her life in slavery speaks of her desire to reformulate options for black female subjectivity. Early in the narrative, Keckley confides, "I was repeatedly told, when even fourteen years old, that I would never be worth my salt" (21). The resulting text, replete as it is with ethos-enhancing moments, can largely be read as evidence to her former mistress that she is, indeed, worth not only her own salt but her bread and butter as well. Keckley makes this clear both in the telling of her early life and in her narration of time with the Lincolns. We are meant to understand her as someone resilient, reasonable, and hard working. She is able to quickly gain a reputation as a quality dressmaker so that the "best ladies" wherever she lives become her patrons. When her owners fall on hard times, she is astoundingly able to keep "bread in the mouths of seventeen persons for two years and five months" (45). She buys herself and her son out of slavery, refusing to run away when given the option (48), is trusted with expensive merchandise (79), angrily turns down bribes (94), gives advice on state dinners (96), attends to the bedsides of the sick and dying Lincoln family (103, 189, 193), and still manages to operate a thriving business. "Orders came in more rapidly than I could fill them," she notes, after returning from Chicago to see Mrs. Lincoln (222). For her to end the narrative destitute and publicly maligned because she attempted to help Mary Todd Lincoln suggests why Keckley may be bitter toward her.

It also suggests how cripplingly difficult it is for any subaltern individual to work against dominant cultural dictates, particularly those ideas about self-worth that have been internalized. Dana Nelson's analysis of this dynamic is helpful here. In *The Word in Black and White*, she references a 1987 article by Abdul JanMohamed that outlines "how the dominant culture attempts to school members of subordinate cultures to accept their own less-than human status—in fact, to acquiesce to their own negation as social subjects" (133). He observes, Nelson notes, "that 'the most crucial aspect of resisting hegemony consists in struggling against its attempt to form one's subjectivity, for it is through the construction of the minority subject that the dominant culture can elicit the individual's own help in his/her oppression'" (Nelson 133, JanMohammed 247). For slavery to operate efficiently, Nelson continues, "the slaves must to some extent agree with their degraded status" (133). What we see in the case of Keckley, however, is that even when a former slave emphatically does not agree with her degraded status, she is not always able to overturn fully the material conditions of her life imposed by a culture of white privilege.

One example of this concerns the principal reason Keckley was widely criticized after the publication of *Behind the Scenes*. As I have noted, included in an appendix were letters addressed to her from Mary Todd Lincoln. These letters, largely unedited, gave the public a former first lady who was petulant, paranoid, and excessive. Keckley argued later that she never meant for Mrs. Lincoln's letters to be published, that she had only provided them to the publisher to attest to the facts. "He was not to print anything very private or personal," reminisces Anna E. Williams (J.E. Washington 222). The letters, however, transformed Keckley's memoir from something interesting to something salacious (and thus more publicly desirable), and it is a sign of the powers of class and race privilege that Keckley was made to pay for the resulting intrigue associated with the book.

Indeed, though Keckley's preface suggests her public image had already sustained a substantial blow through participation in the Old-Clothes scandal, it was the memoir itself that most materially hindered Keckley's reputation and finances. Soon after publication of *Behind the Scenes*, the National News published a ten-cent parody called *Behind the Seams: By a Nigger Woman Who Took in Work from Mrs. Lincoln and Mrs. Davis by "Betsey Kickley."* The parody decimates any sense of ambiguity in Keckley's motivations and attitudes: the Kickley persona writes as a "hard up 'extraordinary nigger'" (i), who "puts on airs" (10) and exaggerates the representation of her "bosom friend" in order to sell books (14). Jennifer Fleischner reports that the "*The New York Citizen* listed Keckley's book as the latest in a series of scandalous exposes, and called it 'grossly and shamelessly indecent … an offense of the same grade as the opening of other people's letters, the listening at keyholes, or the mean system of espionage which unearths family secrets with a view to blackmailing the unfortunate victim'" (*Mastering* 95). These are similar issues linked to biography and privacy that we saw Oliphant, Fern, and Gaskell managing through their portraits of the famous woman. In the case of Keckley, however, the injustice of "telling tales" was perceived to be all the more scandalous since she was deemed not just an employee but a servant. As the epigraph starting this chapter attests, class and race biases discredited Keckley's memoir as vulgar, labeling it sensationalist "kitchen literature." Yet, the victory Keckley won in writing the text may not have been entirely Pyrrhic.

Equal Blame, Equal Credit

Believing that no one is guilty of a crime if she or he has committed an act with good intentions, Keckley argues in her preface that "Mrs. Lincoln may have been imprudent, but since her intentions were good, she should be judged more kindly than she has been" (xii–xiv). Since the world has only "been acquainted with her acts" and not the emotional motivations behind them, Keckley argues, it is her obligation and her duty to set the record straight, to give a country that has been exposed to countless caricatures of the excessive Mary Todd Lincoln the real Mrs. President. Keckley's assertion that she can explain this controversial public figure to the reading public allows her early on to claim a rhetorical edge in the presentation of celebrity. Not only is she a White House confidante and insider, but she can also rectify distortion and injustice. Keckley thus resolves to explain and make sympathetic the behavior of a woman thought by turns elegant, refined, and charming, or coarse, masculine, excessive, hyper-emotional, shrill, and unwomanly. This is no easy task, for Keckley's role as apologist makes her vulnerable to charges that she is either "uppity" for championing someone of the wealthy classes or that she is "degraded" for associating with an unwomanly "haridan." Much like Elizabeth Gaskell's retooling of Charlotte Brontë, to succeed at the redefinition of Mrs. Lincoln offered Keckley an unprecedented opportunity—for surely an interpreter who can make the former First Lady appear misunderstood rather than insane, or ill-treated rather than ill-mannered, must possess a formidable power of her own. In choosing the redemption of Mary Todd Lincoln as her narrative assignment, Keckley claims her own powerful agency, a personal efficacy made possible through the public platform of the Lincolns' lives.

Keckley proceeds in the memoir through the risky strategy of linking her personal reputation to that of Mrs. Lincoln, suggesting that any injustice done to one is also done to the other:

> My own character, as well as the character of Mrs. Lincoln, is at stake, since I have been intimately associated with that lady in the most eventful periods of her life. I have been her confidante, and if evil charges are laid at her door, they also must be laid at mine, since I have been a party to all her movements. (xiv)

By claiming equal blame for the "evil charges," Keckley also demands equal credit, thus establishing parity between herself and Mary Lincoln, a point reinforced when she takes Washington's social networks to task for their unkind gossip about the First Lady:

> I do not forget, before the public journals vilified Mrs. Lincoln, that ladies who moved in the Washington circle in which she moved, freely canvassed her character among themselves. They gloated over many a tale of scandal that grew out of gossip in their own circle. If these ladies could say everything bad of the wife of the President, why should I not be permitted to lay her secret history bare, especially when that history plainly shows that her life, like all lives, has its good side as well as its bad side! (xv)

Keckley's point is clear: if one group of women can spread malicious rumors, why can't another woman, in this case a very dear friend of the maligned party, work to counteract that slander? In phrasing the question as she does, Keckley posits an equal status between herself and those who populate Washington's social circles. She is free to think, act, and speak at the same level as white women of means and stature. She lays out for herself the same degree of social credibility and moral legitimacy as women who, in most other contexts at this time, would be considered her superiors.

The ensuing credibility the reader gives Keckley as storyteller and "truth shaper" rests on a founding premise that her right to speak is as firm and valid as the most refined of white women. Hers is a gesture of parity: I belong on the same page with the President's wife. This is an important subversive sign, for as Jennifer Fleischner observes, "When Keckley rhetorically positions herself alongside Mary Todd Lincoln as the subject with whom she shares narrative center stage, she openly alters one of the working assumptions ordering antebellum narratives—the subordinate position, relative to the white woman, of the female slave" (*Mastering* 123–4). Saidiya V. Hartman similarly notes that under slavery, the "close contact of master and slave and the character of slavery as a civil and public institution had necessitated an annihilation of public right and private choice" making "all blacks not visibly servants ... 'an assault upon the purity of private society'" (167–8).[14] Given Keckley's status as both former slave and friend, as an independent black business owner and confidante to the First Lady, it is clear why her representation is so potentially disruptive to the newly postbellum America. In her co-equal and public pairing of a white and a black woman, race and class relations become both visible and untenable. This point builds on Michele Birnbaum's contention that through a "logic of intimacy," familiarity allows the authorial agent to create the depicted object as a "site of both desire and discipline" over which the author has mastery (15).[15] So Keckley, in her role as dear friend to and chronicler of Mrs. Lincoln, exerts a critical form of control over her.

We can see this "logic of intimacy" working in Keckley's depictions of many of the white women for whom she sews. After the preface the reader observes a shifting of status positions—not to the detriment of the former slave Keckley, but to the disadvantage of the "women of refinement" she describes. Repeatedly, we see these women making faulty assumptions about their circumstances, only to be better led by Keckley's sound advice and counsel. One example occurs early on, before Keckley has ever met Mary Todd Lincoln, when she sews for Mrs. Senator Davis (wife of Jefferson Davis). Mrs. Davis warns Keckley that a civil war is coming and admonishes her to come south with them, where Keckley will be well taken care of for the few months of the unrest. Keckley ruminates and tells the reader:

> I thought over the question much, and the more I thought the less inclined I felt to accept the proposition so kindly made by Mrs. Davis. I knew the North to be strong, and believed that the people would fight for the flag that they pretended to venerate so highly. The Republican party had just emerged from a heated campaign, flushed with victory, and I could not think that the hosts composing the party would quietly yield all they had gained in the Presidential canvass. A show of war from the South, I felt, would lead to actual war in the North; and with the two sections bitterly arrayed against each other, I preferred to cast my lot among the people of the North. (72)

Keckley here reasons through the debate as well as might any Secretary of War advising the President. She astutely assesses nationalistic fervor, military preparedness, and recent political events and lays her loyalties with the winning side. Of course, she is aided by hindsight in telling her story. And so the important point here is not whether Keckley judged correctly in picking the North over the South (and thus Mrs. Lincoln over Mrs. Davis), but that she represents herself

---

[14]   Hartman is quoting George Washington Cable, "The Freedman's Case in Equity," in *The Silent South* (New York: Charles Scribner and Sons, 1907), 145.

[15]   For discussion on the bonds of intimacy, both homosocial and homoerotic, inherent in black/white female relationships under slavery, see Elizabeth Fox Genovese *Within the Plantation Household*. See also Hortense Spillers "Mama's Baby, Papa's Maybe."

as fully able to make reasoned deductions about political events and outcomes in ways that elude the people for whom she works (including a good many male politicians). By depicting herself calculating the outcomes of the North/South debate, she suggests that her loyalties are not a foregone conclusion determined by her race. Additionally, Keckley claims here a significantly superior position to the southern Mrs. Davis, for as Louise L. Stevenson notes about the postbellum period, "Unlike southern white men, white women had not surrendered on the battlefield." Thus "ideal womanhood … had the power to lead white southerners back to their idealized past and to protect them from the radical changes the war had brought" (169). This scene with Mrs. Davis, then, shatters "an ideal past" by positioning Keckley as both a superior true woman and a more "rational" person.

Keckley's reason shows itself best when contrasted with Mary Todd Lincoln's "impulsive ways." Keckley's stalwart sense of judgment is evident in the first four chapters of the text that are given over to a hasty overview of her life as a slave. Her good sense is also evident when she works at the White House and can provide another perspective on Abraham Lincoln and his inner circle. But it is really in the last half of the book, after Lincoln's death, that Keckley's judgment edges ahead of Mrs. Lincoln's. Their infamous rendezvous in New York City to place Mary Lincoln's expensive wardrobe in the hands of second-hand clothing dealers provides an excellent contrast between the sensible 'Lizabeth and the excitable Mrs. Lincoln. Up to this moment, Keckley has made a point of informing the reader that the First Lady thought of clothing as a hedge against the future, considering her dresses and jewels as objects of material value, like gold bricks in a safe that could stand between her and destitution. Though Keckley does not dispute that Mrs. Lincoln has lovely things, she does make it clear that she is not always sure Mary can differentiate between what is valuable and what is worthless. When Mary Lincoln packs to leave the White House, for instance, Keckley tells the reader that Mrs. Lincoln's "boxes were loosely packed and many of them with articles not worth carrying away. Mrs. Lincoln had a passion for hoarding old things, believing, with Toodles, that they were 'handy to have about the house'" (204).

In the annals of Mary Todd Lincolniana, this scene of leaving the White House stands near the top of the more contentious scandals. While she lay for weeks, overwrought in her West Wing bedroom after Lincoln's assassination, several thousand dollars worth of damage was done to the White House by vandals and souvenir hunters. Jean H. Baker reports that White House artifacts, including china and silver, were spotted in secondhand shops and saloons up and down the Eastern seaboard and "neither the state china with its distinctive seal of the Republic nor the nanny goats … were safe" (249). Mary Todd Lincoln was publicly criticized for allowing the vandalism to happen in the first place (by firing the steward who oversaw the house) or, alternately, for stealing the articles herself (hence the contention surrounding the multiple boxes packed at her departure). Though Keckley does not consider Mrs. Lincoln responsible for "stealing" the goods, she admits "to put the case very plainly, Mrs. Lincoln was 'penny wise and pound foolish'" (206). To dismiss the steward was imprudently to invite vandalism. To be in New York, then, with Mary Todd Lincoln's bulging bags of "plunder," as Lincoln's son Robert called the materials she took away from the White House, is to remind the reader of the recent scandal associated with her hoarding.

Although the entire trip constitutes an opportunity to demonstrate Keckley's good judgment in contrast to Lincoln's erratic behavior, their initial encounter at a New York hotel provides conclusive evidence of their differences. Keckley notes that Mrs. Lincoln desires to travel incognito and to stay at an obscure hotel. "I had never heard of the St. Denis," Keckley reports, "and therefore presumed that it could not be a first-class house. And I could not understand why Mrs. Lincoln should travel, without protection, under an assumed name" (271). When Keckley arrives at the hotel she is shocked to "see the widow of President Lincoln in such dingy, humble quarters," thus signaling to the reader Keckley's discerning eye and refined sensibilities (276). Mary Lincoln, by contrast, seems far from shocked by her seedy surroundings; indeed, she revels in the intrigue of the pseudonym and her quarters. After several failed attempts to get dinner for Elizabeth, Mrs. Lincoln resolves to take to the street to find something to eat, a proposition that frightens Keckley. She confides to the reader, "Her impulsiveness alarmed me," then cautioning Mrs. Lincoln, "You are here as Mrs. Clarke and not as Mrs. Lincoln. You came alone, and the people already suspect that everything is not right. If you go outside of the hotel to-night, they will accept the fact as evidence against you" (282–3). Unfazed, Mary Lincoln resolves to go where she pleases; Keckley refuses to accompany her, "No, Mrs. Lincoln, I shall not go outside of the hotel to-night, for I realize your situation, if you do not" (283). As reported in the memoir, the former First Lady is impulsive and reckless, whereas the former slave is prudent and rational. It is Keckley, moreover, who clearly possesses the upper hand.

Many scholars have read the dynamics of this dyad as evidence of a counter-balance between the two women. Fleischner, for instance, perceives Mary Todd Lincoln as the constructed Other to Keckley. As such, Lincoln is a straw woman figure who can be represented in a way that allows Keckley to work through racial oppression. Fleischner writes:

> Keckley tries to manage her anxiety-producing confrontations with her own "otherness" in her dealings with the family in the White House by utilizing the figure of Mrs. Lincoln as Other, placing her in the imaginary role of social and economic outcast. This strategy constitutes a dramatic inversion of the positioning of the mulatta/black woman as outcast "other" by white anti-slavery women writers; as such Keckley's narrative can be read as resisting the images of black slave women that were codified by [Lydia Maria] Child and [Harriet Beecher] Stowe and integrated into [Harriet] Jacobs' self-perception. (*Mastering* 7)

Fleischner's reading of Mary Todd Lincoln as Keckley's Other makes clear the many ways Keckley both works through and works out the systematic oppression she herself has experienced as slave and free working woman. These two sides of her experience provide interchangeable parts in an integrated whole, forming, as Fleischner calls it, "narrative inversions" in which "Mrs. Lincoln 'substitutes' for Mrs. Keckley in the imaginary role of social and economic outcast, becoming for her a mechanism of defense on behalf of her self-esteem, in the face of the social and economic reality of her subjugation to the President's widow" (102). Keckley thus employs the representation of Mary Todd Lincoln as an important contrast against herself. However, I would argue that, just as in the case of Elizabeth Robins in her depiction of uneven role reversals in *George Mandeville's Husband*, Keckley's depiction of Mary Lincoln suggests not their interchangeability, but Mary Todd Lincoln's complete incapacity to be Keckley's equal other.

By the end of the book, for instance, not only does Keckley claim most of the credit for better judgment and perception, but she exerts a power over Mary Lincoln that clearly asserts Keckley's dominance. In the section of *Behind the Scenes* that includes Mary Todd Lincoln's letters, we see Mrs. Lincoln repeatedly cajoling, begging, pleading, or demanding some kind of response from Keckley. "Write me often, as you promised" (301), she urges, and three days later again reminds Keckley, "Write me everyday" (335). A week later, she has begun to be imperious: "I am greatly disappointed, having only received one letter from you since we parted …. After your promise of writing to me every other day, I can scarcely understand it …. How much I miss you cannot be expressed" (336). And then there is an edge of desperation to her appeals: "Write me, my dear friend" (338), "Write me, dear Lizzie, if only a line; I cannot understand your silence …. I am always so anxious to hear from you, I am feeling so friendless in the world" (339). "Do write me every other day at least, I am so nervous and miserable" (345); "Write me, if only a few lines, and that very frequently" (345); "Write me, do, when you receive this. Your silence pains me" (346). Clearly, Keckley's lack of response signifies a form of power in this exchange regulated not by the white mistress's wishes but by the black seamstress's withholding of attention. Merish suggests that "Mary Lincoln seems to feel herself entitled to the labor as well as affection of Elizabeth Keckley—suggesting that forms of cross-racial sympathy between white women and 'free' black domestic workers are … structured by sentimental proprietorship and continuous with the proprietary relations of slavery" (252). Yet, Keckley's deft rhetorical move quashes Lincoln's overtures for sentimental proprietorship. Like Fanny Fern with her fan mail, through her memoir Keckley can record the pleas for a response and publicly refuse to answer, thus using the exchange as a means of heightening her advantage. Indeed, Keckley's position of influence was ratified some 75 years later with John E. Washington's account of "colored folk" who knew the Lincolns. He writes, "Mrs. Keckley's power over Mrs. Lincoln was uncanny, and just a kind word, or a pleasant smile from her would bring the desired result" (224).

By withholding those kind words or even any mediating commentary as context to Lincoln's letters, Keckley focuses the bulk of Mary Todd Lincoln's considerable nervous energy on that which is longed for, on Keckley herself. Like all of the people in her life for whom Mary Todd Lincoln has loved and pined—

her assassinated husband, her two dead sons, her father, her mother—Elizabeth Keckley becomes elevated to a pantheon of what Mary Todd Lincoln desperately wants but cannot have. It's not entirely incidental that the appendix of letters puts Keckley as love-object in the same category as "The Great Emancipator" Abraham Lincoln, a man whom editorial cartoons posthumously depicted as sitting on the left hand of God. Such a connection allows Keckley a good bit of virtue by association and allows for a different possibility than that offered by Frances Smith Foster that Keckley profoundly misjudged her readers, who could not tolerate and "routinely resented and resisted any African American volunteering any opinion on any matter that did not focus upon slavery or racial discrimination" (128).

Mid-way through the appendix, Mrs. Lincoln finally acknowledges receipt of a letter from her "dear Lizzie." Though we cannot know what that letter contains, it seems telling that Lincoln alters her salutation in her next letter from "My dear Lizzie" to "My dear Keckley" and switches her frequently repeated refrain from a desire to hear from Keckley to a determination to pay her for past services. Following this, Mary Lincoln's promises turn again to pleas, "Why are you so silent?" she begs to know (366). "Write when you receive this" (369). Whether Keckley did write in response or not, we cannot say. *Behind the Scenes* ends not in Keckley's voice but with one of Mary's letters, and the reader, like Mrs. Lincoln, is left to fill in the blanks of the missing Lizzie.

Whether she realized it or not, by ending the book as such, Keckley subtly plays out a trope of independence for black Americans: when freedom beckons, the free woman is off in the night, her higher obligation not to her mistress but to herself. A parallel of this dynamic is narrativized in Frances Ellen Watkins Harper's now iconic novel of racial uplift *Iola Leroy* through the figure of Robert Johnson, Iola's uncle. Robert propitiously flees the plantation where he is raised and purportedly loved by his white mistress, Mrs. Johnson, in order to fight for the Union. Aunt Linda, also a former slave, asks Robert:

> 'But warn's ole Miss hoppin' wen she foun' out you war goin' to de war! I thought she'd go almos' wile. Now, own up, Robby, didn't you feel kine ob mean to go off widout eben biddin' her good bye? An' I rarely think ole Miss war fon' ob yer. Now, own up, honey, didn't yer feel a little down in de mouf wen yer lef her.'
> 'Not much,' responded Robert. 'I only thought she was getting paid back for selling my mother.' (175–6)

Behind the Scenes' appendix of letters and their showcase of the uneven exchange between Keckley and Lincoln mirrors this same imbalance of affective debts incurred and owed. The abrupt cessation as conclusion to the book, produces a parallel moment where a character "go[es] off widout eben biddin' her goodbye." When Keckley abruptly closes the text on the pleading Mary Todd Lincoln, the terms of sentimental proprietorship discursively interrupt a Reconstruction trope of intimacy and dependency.

Read in this way, *Behind the Scenes* is not a text that ruins Keckley's reputation and career but functions instead as an important tool for public image construction and racial uplift. As represented by Keckley, Mary Todd Lincoln functions as the perfect celebrated vehicle, allowing, as Merish notes, the intimacy between Keckley and Mary Lincoln to operate "as a means both to register the entitlement of black women to the privileges of 'femininity,' and to disrupt the privileged, domestic enclosure of white womanhood" (252). In Keckley's construction of the public image of Mary Todd Lincoln, she both writes a story and rights a story. Fixing the scales of justice means adjusting the public perception of a former first lady, but it also requires righting/writing a different kind of injustice, that done not only to Keckley but to thousands of black Americans. "A wrong was inflicted upon me," Keckley states, "a cruel custom deprived me of my liberty, and since I was robbed of my dearest right, I would not have been human had I not rebelled against the robbery" (xii). In so saying, Keckley identifies resistance to slavery as an important signifier of her humanity and a motivation for her text. Joanne Braxton similarly argues that there is a critical link between the desire for freedom and the production of the text: "[T]he early autobiographical writings of black Americans linked the quest for freedom with the quest for literacy. To be able to write, to develop a public voice, and to assert a literary self represented significant aspects of freedom" (15). As such, it is evident that *Behind the Scenes* functions as a form of rebellion predicated on social justice. The memoir allows Keckley to assert her rights publicly and textually and to reclaim her humanity through the auspices of her construction of a visible literary self.

"In writing as I have done," Keckley acknowledges in the foreward to *Behind the Scenes*, "I am well aware that I have invited criticism; but before the critic judges harshly, let my explanation be carefully read and weighed. If I have portrayed the dark side of slavery, I also have painted the bright side" (xi). A present-day reader might be incredulous that a "bright side" of slavery could have indeed existed, just as many nineteenth-century readers would have been incredulous that a "bright side" existed to the "most lied about woman in the world," Mary Todd Lincoln (Morrow 12). Indeed, Keckley's statements here play with an overall sense of credibility in what strikes me as their purposeful ambiguity. Though slavery is the wrong inflicted on her by a "cruel custom," her words suggest she is referencing the social ostracism she experienced by association with Mary Todd Lincoln; Keckley acknowledges inviting criticism for her candid assessments, yet she turns the sentence so that her judgment is of slavery, not Mrs. Lincoln. In this sense, it is not herself so much as slavery that she places in diametrical opposition to the First Lady, an inversion that allows her to escape the self/other dialectic. As narrator, she sidesteps race and class stereotypes; as embodied character in her own narrative, she occupies roles such as lady, social critic, and famous author not commonly inhabited by working black women.

Ultimately, Keckley is able to accomplish some rather extraordinary tasks with *Behind the Scenes*. Though she (perhaps purposefully) doesn't completely succeed in her stated goal to exonerate the First Lady and pays a material price for the publication of the book, she publicly demonstrates unquestionable power over a very famous white woman. Perhaps more remarkably, she links herself perpetually to the Lincoln story, so that now, some 150 years later, to tell the story of Lincoln's private life is necessarily to consult Keckley as an important witness and teller of events. Among many other fictionalized accounts of Mary Todd Lincoln's exploits, for example, two twentieth-century stage plays, *Mrs. Lincoln* (1969) and *The Last of Mrs. Lincoln* (1974) attest to Keckley's importance. Though each play tells a different story of the much-contested life of Mary Lincoln, both feature Keckley as a critical character, even 30 years before Keckley is "rediscovered" through Oxford's publication of the Schomburg Series.[16]

"Permitted to go free ever afterward, in both free and slave states"

Much as Elizabeth Keckley positions herself as a moral authority to the infamous Mary Todd Lincoln, Eliza Potter shows herself to be a cut above the celebrated white women she depicts, not by representing a particular personality, but by making the daughters and wives of rich men an unholy amalgam of biting antagonisms, petty jealousies, fickle fidelities, and rampant vanities, only rarely encountering rich white women who are kind, noble, or gracious (and this usually as contrast to someone else's coarseness or injustice). The white men in her narrative scarcely do any better, and she continually takes them to task for their indifference to her personal freedoms. She says of one of her employers, "He never seemed to recognize that I had any right to amuse myself or to be happy upon any occasion;" the turn in this statement comes after her semicolon, "but for this I invariably cared precious little, though I never permitted myself to behave toward him as perhaps he deserved, in consequence of the high regard and esteem I bore my lady, who possessed a noble, unselfish disposition, and always treated me with the greatest kindness" (23). In suggesting there is a disconnect between the way a white man is treated and the way he deserves to be treated, Potter introduces a gap between the way things are and the way they ought to be.

Into that gap she immediately inserts herself as arbiter and interpreter, a role that allows her, as Sharon G. Dean has noted, to "violate boundaries at the same time she defines them" (1). In this particular scene of the unjust employer, Potter offers the reader a situation in which a white male behaves in a way that denies Potter what she considers to be an intrinsic aspect of her personality—the pursuit of happiness, here instantiated as freedom to enjoy the sights of Europe. Writing as she does in 1859 (with this episode set much earlier in the past), Potter is clearly playing with a U.S. racial politics that denied the black slave not only her freedom and liberty, but her very personhood. Even for free blacks in the North, injustice was rampant. Potter's blithe disregard of restrictions imposed on

---

[16] Fleischner's *Mrs. Lincoln and Mrs. Keckly: The Remarkable Story of the Friendship Between a First Lady and a Former Slave* further cements this claim in a twenty-first-century context.

persons of color allows her an amazing public authority, for Potter reports that she can simply disregard her white male employer's restrictions, that she "invariably cared precious little." Such a characterization speaks volumes. She is a woman whose identity is not dictated by the codes and conventions of the dominant white culture; indeed, the very notion of dominance needs re-evaluating given Potter's blasé indifference. For surely, according to the logic Potter lays out, if a black working-class woman can casually dismiss the orders of her white employer and not be punished in any way, how much power can that white man actually hold?

Throughout the text, Potter magnifies this representation of herself as a potent personality who can shrug off insults and bring the callous to their knees. She has frequent opportunities to upbraid white men and women, and though she takes several oaths to keep her temper in check, she often succumbs to the temptation to "give a good lecture." On one such occasion, she tells the reader, "I went and fastened the door, took my chair, and sat down right before her [a white employer], and told her … never to treat any person with contempt before another because she was rich and highly educated, for there were many simple looking people, and poor people, who understood more than those who were speaking of them" (163). Potter's bid for social justice is evident here; it is unfair and unjust, she declares, to assume that those who are poor in wealth or education are also contemptible. But she makes an equally strong bid for social justice through the manner of representation, here depicting a black woman barring the door of a white woman's boudoir and scolding her. In effect, Potter sets up a physical barricade and demands both to speak and to be heard. The lady, she tells the reader, responds to her forced lecture by becoming "very much agitated" and offers money for silence. Potter refuses to be bought (or to be quieted)—a clear commentary on the state of slavery and her extraordinary ability to supersede its pervasive dominance through the force of her will and moral superiority. Potter suggests that if she gives her word not to speak, she need not be degraded by the hint of hush money.[17] But she makes the larger point that, at least in her own particular case, it is quite possible for a black woman to refuse to internalize the shackles of oppression.

Potter makes this point early in the book when she is arrested in her home in Cincinnati, under the aegis of the Fugitive Slave Act, for aiding a slave she had spoken to on a visit to Louisville. He seems to know nothing of the North, and so Potter tells him of Canada, thus making herself liable to imprisonment. When the officers come to arrest her, she is alone, tending a baby, and unwilling to leave until the mother's return (17). She notes, "I also refused riding to the place of

---

[17]   On another occasion, she helps a male employer deceive her mistress in an extra-marital dalliance. In return, he offers her ten dollars in gold and an ivory cameo, which she refuses. Potter is livid, rhetorically asking the readers, "Did this satisfy me? No, nor would anything else till I had given him a good lecture. I told him it was a good lesson for me as I never would be caught in a like manner again. I gave him such a talking to, I am sure he remembered some of my words to his dying day" (167). Interestingly, though her efforts have aided adultery, she wins morality points for refusing a bribe.

justice in a carriage which they had provided for the purpose, which very much disconcerted plans on foot in my behalf, as they intended, doubtless, conveying me to Kentucky, where I should, probably, in the excitement of the moment, have been severely handled" (17–18). Potter's resistance is here depicted as a sign of her moral fortitude. As a point of comparison, in 1959 James A. Rhodes and Dean Jauchius describe Mary Todd Lincoln's unfair seizure and arrest for insanity as follows:

> Mary Lincoln decided stubbornly that she would not go with Swett to the courtroom. Swett said she had no choice in the matter. She had two alternatives, as concerned how she was to be taken to court. She could either go peaceably with him, or be handcuffed and taken forcibly by two officers now waiting downstairs. (11)

Though Rhodes and Jauchius's book does not present itself as an historical document (they endeavor to tell the trial of Mary Todd Lincoln as it *should* have happened), their depiction here shows that represented resistance works toward the positive perception of the woman depicted. That she is powerless in the face of the legal system, a system the authors consider wholly corrupt, makes Mary Todd Lincoln a sympathetic figure. Potter similarly depicts herself as resisting unjust police agents, which makes her sympathetic. Unlike Mrs. Lincoln, however, Potter's resistance works. She is taken to jail but seemingly on her own terms. That anyone could have the audacity to dictate the conditions of her arrest is rather startling. But Potter's experience with the law becomes all the more audacious when, after three months in jail, she succeeds in giving a speech on her own behalf that convinces the court to acquit her. The result of her acquittal? She is "permitted to go free ever afterward, in both free and slave states" (19).

This free-and-open-access-to-mobility pass awarded to her early on in the narrative has ramifications through to the end of the book, for Potter is incredibly well-traveled. Never constrained by place or position, she is able to journey to France and England, New York City, Saratoga, and New Orleans, as just a few examples, staying in the finest homes, learning French, and enjoying many of the amusements offered in these places, including Parisian "concerts, balls, hippodromes, theaters, operas and fetes champetre, without number" (26).[18] She brags of her cosmopolitanism to the reader, "I saw more in France than Americans of the highest position see generally" (27), and when that "old desire for traveling" (44) hits again, she simply "wandered away" (37) to a new watering hole. Cheryl Fish argues that Victorian women's travel writing, whether for the black or white author, required that a woman "carefully negotiate with her reader in order to claim public space" (68). Yet, Potter seems little interested in discursive negotiations.

---

[18] For a reading of Eliza Potter's New Orleans, see Lisa Ze Winters, "'More desultory and unconnected than any other': Geography, Desire, and Freedom in Eliza Potter's *A Hairdresser's Experience in High Life.*"

Her emphasis on unrestricted transatlantic mobility suggests that life as a hairdresser actually heightens Potter's ability to see and go, and this freedom of movement puts her in a culturally superior position to both the ladies she serves and any of the other black characters represented in the text. Further, as Fish notes, travel for women in the nineteenth century, whether depicted in fiction or lived in everyday experience, was often "limited unless initiated by husbands, imposed by national policies, or related to family obligations" (134). That Potter's travels are instigated by her own desires and fed by the transatlantic demand for her professional services lifts *A Hair-dresser's Experience* to a wholly different sort of ideological meaning. Through the image of her geographical freedom, Potter establishes a form of her own race/class privilege, as distinct from those who might be perceived as "above" or "below" her, by constructing a hierarchy where neither a white nor black complexion signifies value. This new structure privileges mobility, exposure to cultural artifacts, consumption of spectacle, and self-determination—one might argue, the very constituent qualities of Modern experience—and Potter has access to them all. So, again, the hierarchical structure that reinforces status inequity is not undone, but what qualifies as valuable within the hierarchy changes so that cultural capital factors over race and class.

Sharon Dean makes a similar observation about Potter's redefinition of marriage, which Potter introduces on the first page of her tale as a "sort of ceremony called matrimony" (11) and dismisses on the second when the "desire for roving again took possession of me" (12).[19] Dean notes that Potter's "initial identity is as a woman who, like many of her hairdressing clients, has been victimized by the institution of marriage. But this point of 'equality' with white women only serves to underscore her superiority to them. In refusing to be a victim, she also claims for herself a heretical freedom of movement and identity" (xxxvii). Though I do not entirely agree that Potter's depiction of her own marriage suggests she was victimized by the institution, I do agree that Potter's rhetorical strategy establishes a common ground between herself and the white women she observes, a ground that she occupies and then vacates, thus suggesting her own superior position and, like Keckley, articulating her right to speak on the same terms as not only a "white," "true" woman but as a famous woman of color.[20]

---

[19]   Hannah Crafts's *The Bondwoman's Narrative* (1857) dismisses marriage as "especially designed for the free" and thus "something that all the victims of slavery should avoid as tending essentially to perpetuate that system" (Kirkpatrick A20).

[20]   Adopting the values of the dominant culture, it should be noted, was not just a tactic employed in fiction, but a fairly common assimilationist tool during Reconstruction. In the introduction to *The Journals of Charlotte Forten Grimké*, for example, Brenda Stevenson observes, "early on, many Northerners hoped to begin to 'reconstruct' the South by instilling in these [contraband] blacks Northern cultural values and practices. Charlotte, who was an avid assimilationist, was no different in this respect from her white peers and adamantly believed that blacks would never be accepted as equals to whites in society if they remained culturally distinct .... [S]he was greatly relieved that the contraband were conforming to Northern mores, such as solemnizing their relationships through legal marriage" (40).

Like the ship that must steer to the east in order to sail a straight course against a strong westerly wind, Keckley and Potter's representations of themselves and their employers tend finally to establish not equality or parity but clear superiority on the part of the supposed subaltern, for in every portrait that either Keckley or Potter renders of white women, the authors not only stand side-by-side with these white women, but in most ways surpass them.[21] It's as if the portrait painter has inserted herself in a family tableau, and she stands just a little taller, just a bit more luminescent, than the rest of the assembled forms. In both of these glimpses into high society, it is Keckley and Potter who become the benchmarks against which to measure famous stature and ideal femininity.

Telling Secrets

When scholars consider *Behind the Scenes* or *A Hair-dresser's Experience*, they frequently comment on the "lack" in both texts, specifically, the lack of a fully developed narrating presence.[22] Most critics read such omissions as a subjectivity gap, due to a lack of either ability or confidence to narrate classic norms of the coherent subject.[23] I see this "gap" as no failure at all, but as a refusal to narrate that signifies resistance to coherent embodiments of the white bourgeois literary subject. Commonly, the reader is jolted into an awareness of a biographical omission when either Keckley or Potter make reference to a scene but refuse to play it out, say, for instance, Potter's two-sentence marriage, or Keckley's oblique comment after the death of Willie Lincoln that "Previous to this I had lost my son" (105). Fleischner has concluded that, "Keckley's narrative identity is marked by striking suppressions or repressions, ruptures, substitutions, splittings, and inversions. It is in these moments that Keckley's narrative suggests the hidden presence of a cluster of more primary scenes, associated with feelings of sorrow, rage, and longing for her (by now) dead black slave family; these scenes exist 'behind the scenes' of the liberated (white) world, represented in the White House, in which—as a mulatta woman—she necessarily serves" (*Mastering* 7).

---

[21]   This is likely due to the idea, as William Wells Brown phrases it in *Clotel*, that "The necessities of the case [for black Americans] require not only that you should behave as well as the whites, but better than the whites; and for this reason: if you behave no better than they, your example will lose a great portion of its influence" (190).

[22]   James Olney notes in his introduction to *Behind the Scenes*, "we hear much of Mrs. Lincoln's opinions and emotions and much of Lincoln's weariness and his teasing humor but little of Elizabeth Keckley's feelings or attitudes" (xxxiii–iv). Likewise, Sharon G. Dean comments, "*A Hair-dresser's Experience in High Life* [is] a narrative more about the absurd and tragic secrets of upper-class white women than about [Potter's] own private self, [and] seems itself a secret book" (xxxiii).

[23]   In *We Wear the Mask*, Rafia Zafar's readings of Keckley and Potter's powers of autobiography are substantially different than those I've broadly characterized here.

Fleischner helpfully encourages us to consider Keckley's title a clue to look behind the scenes of the tale she tells. Yet, I'm not entirely sure, as Fleischner suggests, that doing so reveals "repressions, ruptures, substitutions, splittings, and inversions" or, for that matter, an unmitigated sorrow and longing for her dead black slave family. Keckley's text is complicated; while she longs for the family of her blood, she also longs for the family of her past, the white family that benefited from her enslavement.[24] Similarly, while Keckley expresses much antipathy toward her primary subject, Mary Lincoln, she also conveys a deep regard and compassion for her, which problematizes the conventionally conceived power dynamics of an upstairs/downstairs or white woman/black woman arrangement. In the same way, Potter is by turns sympathetic and spiteful toward the women for whom she works. Yet, in a text that, as Dean puts it, denies the reader a "private self," Potter's version of telling tales on high-society folk allows her to assert her self-determination while inserting reconstituted race and class hierarchies.

It strikes me that both texts contain "secrets" that reveal very specific information about the narrating "I" but that "I" is not necessarily aligned with white and Western rationalism, an idea that mirrors my discussion of Fanny Fern in Chapter 2. In both contexts, through a fracturing of conventional (and restrictive) subject positions, the implied author is able to challenge regimes of knowledge and forge new possibilities that work against reductive categories. This a point Trinh T. Minh-ha discusses in relation to Asian and African texts, noting that a "challenge is taken up everytime a positioning occurs: for just as one must situate oneself (in terms of ethnicity, class, gender, difference), one also refuses to be confined to that location" (229–30). For Minh-ha, an additional "third scenario" involves the amplification of difference, of finding a "shifting multi-place of resistance" to the restricted options offered through polarized positions (229). It is this "third scenario," I would argue, that stands as the master trope of both *Behind the Scenes* and *A Hair-dresser's Experience*, for while both books are predicated on the promise of secrets told— Keckley's that she will reveal the goings on "behind the scenes" at the White House, Potter's that she will give a first-person account of the lifestyles of the rich and famous—each text ultimately succeeds in demystifying a far vaster secret, namely that black women are not silent, submissive, and sexualized. Or, as Daphne Brooks describes it in her powerful reading of the meanings of bodies marked by race, these black female bodies refuse their containment in "powerful stillness" (5). Rather, each author instantiates a black woman's right to occupy a culturally coherent subject position—to be situated in gender, class, and race locations—at the same time as she resists those very categories, signaling a "third scenario" here coded as racial uplift. In so doing, she invents strategies that "maintain the integrity of black female bodies as sites of intellectual knowledge, philosophical vision, and aesthetic worth" (Brooks 8).

---

[24] For a discussion of former slaves returning to the site of subjugation, see William L. Andrews, "Reunion in the Postbellum Slave Narrative: Frederick Douglass and Elizabeth Keckley."

How is this racial uplift achieved? Largely through a double-coded technique, remarkably similar for both Keckley and Potter, based on gender critique and the concomitant suppression/revelation of secrets. Both authors are skillful in pointing the reader's gaze to scenes and situations from their lives that pique the imagination but are not fully narrated; both authors juxtapose these elements with meticulously rendered details of the lives and bodies of the white women whom they assiduously observe. In so doing, they reverse a tacit precept of racial oppression that the black woman's body conforms to the desires of the white ruling classes. Rather than her (in)visibility being a factor of white custom and comforts, Keckley and Potter each show the black woman controlling the representation and the material reality of her own body. This does not, to use Carla L. Peterson's terms, "decorporealize" the black woman; it instead allows her to become "normalized" (xiii), a rather radical notion for the time. So, merely by giving the reader a good look at the bodies of white women and keeping their own bodies safely out of sight, Keckley and Potter contribute to a counter-ideology that allows them the possibility of directing the terms of their own public image by controlling the deployment of their (dis) embodied representations, a strategy that puts a high premium on the body itself.[25] In many ways this strategy links directly both to the workings of celebrity and to W.E.B. DuBois's famous contention in *The Souls of Black Folks*, which maintains that self-consciousness is cloaked "behind a veil" where one always perceives self-hood as reflected back through others. If, however, we consider that this feeling of remove from the site of one's subjectivity might also create a zone of protection or privacy from which to self-consciously manipulate notions and images connoting identity, then we can see how Keckley and Potter manage to use the body in order to exploit the currency of celebrity. This, in turn, enables them to capitalize on the dividends of gender and identity.

Sometimes overtly and at other times covertly, both Keckley and Potter reveal a rather damning secret: in her body and in her behavior, the white woman has

---

[25] The importance of embodiment speaks not only to representation but also to epistemology. Katherine Fishburn's observations in *The Problem of Embodiment in Early African Narrative* are particularly illuminating in this context. Building on the work of critics such as Trudier Harris, Ann duCille, Karen Sanchez-Eppler, and Laura Doyle, Fishburn's work contends that "early African narrative ... depends upon ... the fundamental dependence of human be-ing on human embodiment – a dependence that ... has been denied in Western culture" (2). For Fishburn, it is not enough to read the African American narrative as the product of a people "identified with and by their bodies" (xii), nor is it sufficient to limit one's analysis to working through a need for improved material conditions that arise out of physical and psychological oppression. The fuller picture comes, Fishburn argues, in re-thinking the terms of what it means to occupy a body, whether erased or observed, particularly if we note that the "body-self," as exemplified in the African American text, is not one necessarily conceived and born of the Western conflict between mind and body, but one that offers a new form of body-knowledge free of Cartesian dualism. Fishburn notes, "ex-slaves were not trying to write themselves into Western metaphysics as equal to white, but were instead more radically and daringly, rethinking metaphysics itself" (xii).

trouble living up to the cultural ideal of The White Lady. Indeed, all women in the public eye require assistance to uphold what Carolyn Sorisio, referencing the work of Karen Halttunen, calls the "genteel performance" that masks social identity. As Rynetta Davis rightly observes in the case of Potter, her strategy of representation often plays up the degree to which a white elite relies upon a "slave and servant labor to sustain their fashionable appearance" (49). Potter speaks of knowing scores of "gentlemen and ladies who would not put on a suit of clothes without the servants say it is suitable," all the while acknowledging that such powers of discernment only extend so far since "if the same servants chance to offend them, they will sell them to go as far as cars and boats will carry them" (158). Potter's description makes a key distinction here, for she doesn't suggest that gentlemen and ladies need the servant's help to get dressed in the first place but that they need their black hairdresser or dressmaker's style savvy and consequent approval to be dressed fashionably. Rather than such codes of distinction, as Pierre Bourdieu might put it, offering the style expert unquestioned higher status, there are multiple ways in which the power dynamics between the style-savvy guru and the style-needy subject can be reversed, reified, and re-organized, a point I discuss at greater length in *Makeover TV*. In the context of these memoirs, narration functions as critical to upholding the knowledge-capital possessed by both Keckley and Potter.

Here is where the "hodgepodge" of genres in both texts comes into play. Although it is clear that Keckley and Potter are writing about "real" women and events, both resort more than once to tropes of sentimental fiction, causing the subjects of their works, including themselves, to oscillate between fictional and fact-based registers. The poly-generic nature of the text consequently allows for the figures represented to be simultaneously inside and outside of expected roles; it allows them to be perceived as idealized characters, who can and should live up to ideologies of appropriateness; at the same time, the historical placement of the people and situations suggests that the romanticized ideal of fiction does not apply. That Keckley and Potter are the most heroine-worthy and fictionally ideal women of their texts, and yet also the most historically specific representations, sets up a field of interpretation in which black women dominate in both fictional and non-fictional forms.

As I note above, *Behind the Scenes* and *A Hair-dresser's Experience* construct author/narrators who are triply "marginalized": they are women, they are black, and they work for their living. As Michele Birnbaum explains, "black women's work was historically considered a mark both of their race and against their femininity" (53). In the case of Keckley and Potter, their race, class, and gender are ontologically loaded onto their speaking selves, representing a baseline that can never be equivocated or mitigated against. One might argue that there could be no other alternative—that a black working woman must always announce herself as such. But both Potter and Keckley are of mixed race, a fact they do not raise. So here, both authors refuse the trope and the discursive advantage of the tragic mulatta that we see used to sentimental effect in other mid-century literatures such as Harper's *Iola Leroy*, Harriet Beecher Stowe's *Uncle Tom's Cabin*, or William Wells

Brown's *Clotel*.[26] They equally deny the terms and privileges of passing, which Harryette Mullen defines as "active denial of black identity … while the chosen white identity is strengthened in each successive generation by the presumption that white identities are racially pure" (72).[27] In their racing of the author-characters' bodies, Potter and Keckley make a point of their identification as "black" women, refusing to pass as white (or whitened) and suggesting that whiteness, as a socially generated category, is not pure, either genetically or morally.[28]

Just as they reorganize the governing tropes for conceptualizing race, *A Hair-dresser's Experience* and *Behind the Scenes* similarly destabilize "givens" about the black working-class woman's body and mind by allowing their physical labor to factor as a key component of their right to ladyhood. Neither author deflects

---

[26] Deborah E. McDowell notes about Emma Kelley-Hawkins' *Four Girls at Cottage City* that "in choosing to create heroines who are physically indistinguishable from white women, Kelley was no different from Frances Harper and Pauline Hopkins, both of whom wrote novels featuring heroines who could pass for white" (xxix). Dana D. Nelson notes through Susan Koppelman that Lydia Maria Child was the first to devise the "tragic quadroon" theme and to make "it a successful vehicle that could at once reveal the sexual plight of women and slaves and satisfy the refined tastes of white middle-class readers" (*Romance* viii). Significantly, William Wells Brown's 1853 *Clotel, or, The President's Daughter* also employs the trope, which allows Brown to articulate the concept of a "hierarchy of color" and to note that one's whiteness does not necessarily afford a greater degree of protection. Whiteness does seem for both Brown and Child, and later for Harper, to heighten the sense of injustice attached to slavery and thus to heighten the sentimental appeal of the respective works. See Hortense Spillers for a resistant reading of the conceptual trope of the tragic mulatta.

[27] Harper's *Iola Leroy* offers a rich text about the politics of passing, particularly through the character of Latimer. Michele A. Birnbaum calls Latimer "quite dark" (76). But Harper describes Latimer differently: "His complexion was blonde, his eyes bright and piercing, his lips firm and well moulded; his manner very affable; his intellect alive and well stored with information" (239). Latimer is a key figure in demonstrating the buffoonery of Dr. Latrobe who says he can detect "nigger blood," even in the absence of any external identifying factor. "Dr. Latrobe's Mistake," the chapter detailing Latrobe's ignorance, is that he confuses Dr. Latimer for a white man. This is an important point, for it shows that though Latimer (and Iola) could both pass for white and thus enjoy the spoils of white privilege, they actively choose to acknowledge and fight for their black identities. Harper makes this clear saying, "Dr. Latimer had doors open to him as a white man which are forever closed to a colored man. To be born white in this country is to be born to an inheritance of privileges, to hold in your hands the keys that open before you the doors of every occupation, advantage, opportunity, and achievement" (265–6).

[28] Interestingly, both Keckley and Potter were described by their contemporaries in ways that emphasized their elegance, using terms that heightened their "white" features. As Susan Graber notes, a February 5, 1850, *Cincinnati Daily Commercial* personal ad described Potter as having "brunette skin, auburn hair and black eyes" as well as a "good form" and "looks equal to an average" (217). Mrs. Eva N. Wright, a companion of Keckley's when she taught at Wilberforce University described her, "Mrs. Keckley was light mulatto, tall and graceful in bearing. In profile she suggested the Grecian type, thin lips and an aquiline nose, high cheeks, twinkling eyes and a keen sense of humor" (J.E. Washington 216).

or euphemizes the sheer amount of work she regularly performs—labor engaged in not for pleasure but to earn a living. Both suggest their own physical deportment conforms to a refined standard, but neither shrinks from reporting the physical demands in sitting up late to finish a dress or getting up early to accommodate more hair appointments. Clearly, both authors possess a degree of physical fortitude, but their bodily strength is also undermined, and their congruence with conventional gender codes affirmed, by fainting spells and fevers, details that underscore a marked difference between the lady's body and the slave's body.[29]

We can assume that Keckley and Potter had choices within a fairly circumscribed range of how they might represent themselves. Had they written wholly in the sentimental heroine mode of the novels cited above, the "purity" of their character-selves would be announced through their paleness, their passivity, and their submissiveness. Had they chosen the slave narrative mode exemplified by Harriet Jacobs, they would likely have worked to underscore their equal femininity and/or humanity rather than asserting their superior manifestation of womanly virtues. Had they adopted the middle-class black woman's or the spiritual autobiography modes of writing, like that of Mary Church Terrell or Charlotte Forten Grimké, they would have undoubtedly emphasized the religious and social obligations a black woman has to the race. But Keckley and Potter depict themselves as highly competent, moderately religious, exceedingly ambitious, resourceful, reasonable, and refined—all in marked contrast to the prevailing stereotype of the black woman as "immoral and ignorant" (M.H. Washington xxx). Though Keckley and Potter were both free black women at the time of their books' writing, they confronted pervasive stereotypes about the character of the black woman that were necessarily influenced by the bleakest images generated during slavery and could only be rectified in the public imagination through counter imagery. In working against this racist mythology, Keckley and Potter underscored their respective superior qualities as ladies—not through the norm of white womanhood, but through a reconstituted mode of the black lady who can work, bring in an income, have an opinion, speak her mind, and negotiate the public sphere as a figure of fame.

Paula Giddings explains this strategy of using public images to redefine the class and race-based terms of womanhood so that the black woman might prevail:

> In the racial struggle—in slavery and freedom—they fought every way that men did. In the feminist battle they demanded the same protection and properties that the "best" White women enjoyed, but at the same time redefined the meaning of what was called "true womanhood." For the Black woman argued that her experience under slavery, her participation in the work force, and her sense of independence made her more of a woman, not less of one. (7)

---

[29] See Jacqueline Jones's *Labor of Love, Labor of Sorrow* for a gripping account of "women's work" under slavery and through Reconstruction.

As we see with Keckley and Potter, their experiences as black women beauty-workers not only improve their chances of being "more of a woman," they legitimate their ability to determine what constitutes a lady in the first place.

Evidence of a challenge to the logic of racial difference comes in a rather rousing speech Eliza Potter gives near the end of her narrative. Putting down her work and rising to her feet, like an orator preparing to take the lectern, Potter defines those qualities that make up a lady:

> I do not think all those are ladies who sit in high places, or those who drive round in fine carriages, but those only are worthy the name who can trace back their generations without stain, honest and respectable, that love and fear God, and treat all creatures as they merit, regardless of nations, stations or wealth. These are what I say constitute a lady, not those who would move out of one neighborhood into another for the sake of society, crowding into high circles, making themselves the veriest toadies for the sake of society; they merely put themselves out of society trying to get into it, for their old friends will have nothing to do with them, and the new circle they try to get into are disgusted with them. I do not call those ladies who drive around, call on ladies, and invite them to their parties without knowing them …. I do not appreciate those ladies who employ me simply because other ladies employ me. I like to work for a lady who puts confidence in me, and treats me accordingly as I merit …. I remember a time when a lady would never for a moment think of speaking despairingly of another in any way; but now the ladies have got a habit of talking about others to make themselves grand; they pick to pieces and talk to their hair-dresser, and some to their milliner or dressmaker, about Mrs. or Miss This-or-That, and pick her to pieces. (280–81)

Potter here authoritatively demonstrates a very detailed accounting of the necessary behavior required to deserve the name *lady*. Given all of this, and the unabashed gossip she includes in her own narrative, as well as the way in which the historical experience of slavery complicates tracing one's generations "without stain," it is striking that she claims, "I can defy any individual, North, South, East or West, to say I ever did or said anything but was ladylike or courteous" (201). By changing the idiom from *lady* to *ladylike*, Potter here allows herself entrance into an ideal that she pointedly denies her clients (a clientele that seems without exception white). Her lecture on what makes the lady also succeeds in pressing home a very important point: appearances are deceiving, and she who looks the lady rarely acts it. This point is made by both Potter and Keckley, most specifically, through the telling of the greatest secret of all: what white ladies look like in private.

Behind the Veil of White Privilege

Keckley and Potter's positions allow for proximity to and closeness with the white woman's body, allowing for what Santamarina terms an "intimately gendered labor" (*Belabored* 154). As hairdresser and dressmaker, they know their subject's hair type, her measurements, her dress size, what she looks like in her underwear, the gossip that goes on in her boudoir, how she gets along with her husband and children, the temper tantrums and nerve-calming narcotics, the secret liaisons, the woman beneath the facade. In short, the dressmaker and hairdresser are privy to every intimate function of their white subjects' embodied experience, and the white woman's body is laid open to the black author's gaze, a sort of turning of the tables on the physical oppressions of slavery. Though clearly the analogy is unequal—neither Keckley nor Potter can exactly whip the white woman's body— the symbolic reversal constructs a space in which the white woman plays as court jester and/or histrionic shrew to the black narrator's good taste and sound reason. Indeed, seemingly without irony, Susan Graber writes, "many a Cincinnati *grande dame* felt the lash of [Potter's] tongue" (216).

In *A Hair-dresser's Experience*, the contrast between flawed white-bodied employer and the superior black-bodied servant is frequently set up in moments of the absurd that allow Potter to both laugh at "her ladies" and separate herself from their folly. Her critique is especially caustic when directed at the very beauty service she performs. Two scenes in particular demonstrate this nicely. In Saratoga, Potter describes a hotel fire that turns into a vignette on dentures and bad hair:

> Ladies in every variety of dishabille rushed into the halls like so many scared ghosts and witches; and I was then particularly struck with the transformation made by dress in the fair habitues of Saratoga. One of the most beautiful, for example, among the day promenaders, was certainly the ugliest woman I ever saw, in undress. In her fright she had hastily gathered up some valuables, among which was a full set of false teeth, with which she rushed into the hall; but when the alarm was over, and she returned to her room, she found, alas! that, among other things, she had dropped her false teeth, and what on earth should she do? (65–6)

A companion moment in New Orleans repeats this trope of the horrors that lurk under the whitened facades of beauty:

> [W]hen I had first seen her, she had jet black hair, a profusion of curls, clear red and white complexion, and magnificent teeth; her eyes shone like diamonds; she was tall, slender, and apparently a magnificent form. On entering the room, ... I did not know [her].... Her hair was white, and her beautiful curls were all false; her complexion was eau de beaute, blond de pearl, and rouge; her teeth were the most perfect deception that ever was made, and her beautiful form was a perfect skeleton; and to hear her swear, I will acknowledge I was frightened for once by a woman. (150)

Aside from showing herself a first-rate humorist on par with Mark Twain, Fanny Fern, or Gail Hamilton, Potter accomplishes the more serious work of publicly humiliating the woman of refinement by revealing the bare face (and gums) behind the facade. Rynetta Davis has observed that in such moments Potter not only illustrates the degree to which "beauty is a performance, but she disrupts this performance by figuratively undressing these women and uncovering their disguises" (37). This representation of elite beauty's lack is heightened by the fact that Potter need do little other than depict the toothless hags. The images themselves tell the secret: fashionable ladies are the product of smoke and mirrors (and French cosmetics). By this logic, doesn't it make more sense to admire the magician—she who can perpetuate the illusion of beauty through hair and dress—than to idealize the elaborate masquerade itself? In case the reader might be tempted to sustain an allegiance to the image, Potter stresses how easily her "amused spectator" (103) vantage point puts the looked-at in the fool's position. "[I]t was amusing to see the airs they put on," she recalls, "I thought I should die with laughing at some of them" (37).

Similarly, Keckley engages in telling her secret by tinkering with the constituent parts of the true womanhood ideology without dismantling the overall ideological structure. In her case, she does so not by portraying her white female subject as a buffoon, but by playing up Mary Todd Lincoln's eccentricities in ways that write her as a woman of excess. In short, Mrs. Lincoln is conceived of as an emotional hurricane, waiting to strike havoc in the otherwise placid world of the domestic home front. This prefigures other great moments of women out of control, notably Charlotte Perkins Gilman's representation of a woman come undone in "The Yellow Wallpaper." Elizabeth Ammons describes the Gilman persona as "violent, wild, physical," in short, "the narrator is the complete antithesis of the inhibited 'lady' that Victorian America so carefully nurtured as a symbol of male power" (39). Surely, there is a similar baring of the ideology in Keckley's treatment of Mary Todd Lincoln.

When Keckley initially meets the First Lady, she notes, "Mrs. Lincoln was in a state bordering on excitement" (77); the emotional intensity linked to Mary Lincoln never abates. Keckley tells the reader at various points through the narrative that her mistress is temperamental (87), "inconsolable" and in "convulsions" (104), "completely overwhelmed with sorrow" (105), "extremely jealous" of her husband (124), "jealous of the popularity of others" (128), suspicious and paranoid (131), governed by fits of hysterics (200), and alarmingly impulsive (282). Keckley recalls, "I never in my life saw a more peculiarly constituted woman. Search the world over, and you will not find her counterpart" (182). While the ambiguity of this assessment might incline the reader to feel that Keckley had complimented Mrs. Lincoln, her "peculiar constitution" takes on rather monstrous proportions when filtered through the sheer excessiveness of representation. For again, Keckley tells the reader, "I found her in a new paroxysm of grief …. I shall never forget the scene – the wails of a broken heart, the unearthly shrieks, the terrible convulsions, the wild, tempestuous outbursts of grief from the soul" (191). Though surely Mary has much to cry over, having lost two sons and her husband, Keckley's frequent reminders of the high hysterics in the White House ultimately inure the reader to Mary's pain, and we are soon echoing Keckley's viewpoint, "I had listened to her sobbing for eight weeks, therefore I was never surprised to find her in tears" (213). Mary Todd Lincoln emerges from *Behind the Scenes* like a Victorian Cruella de Vil: we are as fascinated by her exaggerations as we are repelled (and callused) by her excesses.

Keckley's representation of her own emotional state, by contrast, seems sparse. What would arguably be the most emotionally wrought moments for her—the death of her son, her mother being sold away, her own rape and whippings—pass by calmly and quickly. Such seeming glosses have led Fleischner to speculate that "Keckley's critique of slavery custom and law issues from an analytic position that disavows emotional or cognitive entanglements with the situation itself.... [I]n her apparently guilt-free break from the conflicts intrinsic to surviving the assaults of slavery (conflicts arising out of the need to adapt oneself to a hostile environment), Keckley must suppress at least this one 'black' familial attachment" (*Mastering* 96–7). Indeed, hiding the emotional register functions much as does obscuring the black woman's body: it becomes the unrepresented and thus that which cannot be appropriated. As contrasted with Mary Lincoln's excessiveness, Keckley's controlled emotional response allows her to utter a secret without whispering a word: the black woman's intrinsic value can topple social injustice. We see this demonstrated when Keckley's resistance, manifested as an ability to endure suffering, ultimately brings her violent oppressor, Mr. Bingham, to his knees: "My suffering subdued his hard heart; he asked my forgiveness, and afterwards was an altered man" (37). Though Keckley is not blind to Bingham's injustice, she narrates herself as attempting to rise above it, as trying to "smother my anger and to forgive those who had been so cruel to me" (35). Andrews calls Keckley's attitude a "progressive, forgiving spirit" and suggests it was a useful strategy to bolster a positive public image ("Reunion" 6). Additionally, I would argue that the forgiving and silent posture allows Keckley not just to assume the role of a dispassionate white observer, but to construct the role of the black observer. This is true particularly since part of the cultural indictment against Mary Todd Lincoln, both in the mid-nineteenth century and today, is a criticism of her over-the-top emotionalism, which was presumed to lead to madness.[30] Keckley's narrating perspective mirrors the rational (also read as male) perspective and serves as a corrective to the "excessive emotionalism" written onto the hysterical and hyper-feminized Mary Lincoln. So, here we see a character/narrator whose ontological identity as working-class, black, and female cannot be denied, yet she occupies the narratological position that is almost exclusively the purview of the learned white male. In so doing, Keckley powerfully turns culturally compelling stereotypes that blackness and neurasthenia are intricately linked, or as Frantz Fanon has described it, that the black subject must always be thought of as experiencing a nervous condition.[31]

---

[30]   Most literature on Mary Todd Lincoln takes a stand on whether she was insane or not—few being willing to account for sanity as a non-stable category. Recently, two texts in particular foreclose on the ambiguity of her insanity. A 2001 *American Experience* documentary for PBS advertised their six-hour film by noting Mary Lincoln's "heartbreaking descent into madness." Lloyd Ostendorf's foreword to the 1995 *Lincoln's Unknown Private Life* describes Mary Lincoln's "temper tantrums and anger" in terms of a sin to be forgiven. "To her credit," he notes, "she later regretted her outbursts and tried to make amends" (19).

[31]   For a helpful contextualization of black hysteria, see Birnbaum, 75–80.

Keckley offers up the white woman's excessive body—from her coffee-stained bodice to her ample bust line. Similarly, Potter offers the reader a surfeit of (flawed) white women's bodies—from her bunioned toes to her dandruffed hair. These representations put the focus squarely on the white woman but also communicate a rather telling and insidious secret: the black woman standing in the periphery and narrating the tale is the legitimate subject. While both narrators succeed in suggesting themselves as living the more appealing lives to be narrated, however, they also deny the reader a satisfying access to their bodies or their stories. In effect, they hold out the possibility of their bodies as desirable commodities but then remove them from the figurative auction block, instead putting the excesses of fashionable ladies, quite literally, up for sale. Since, as Merish notes, the display of the slave woman's body on the auction block is a consequence of the complete power of the slave master over the slave body, and thus of "the corollary negation of the black woman's desire and self-possession" (244), the inversion afforded by white women on display and for sale (even if only through the pages of the book) disallows conventional truisms. As such, through their discursive deployment of the white woman's body, Keckley and Potter reclaim their rights for self-determination and self-possession.

Whether through austere silences or a forceful tongue, Keckley and Potter disarm an important function of the code of whiteness by inverting tropes of "the gazer" and "the looked-at" and by appropriating the terms of material exchange. Does this happen merely because, as authors, they can represent themselves as having more power than they might actually hold in the culture? Perhaps yes, perhaps no. But one thing is certain, by claiming authorship, they necessarily grasp the two-headed tool writing offers: a power to direct actions by both language and silence. In so doing, they also draw attention to the possibility that norms of privacy, secrecy, and celebrity differ according to racialized experience.

No Ordinary Women: Iconoclasts, Lunatics, and the Audacious

Many scholars have successfully demonstrated that a woman's right to speak, particularly in public, was tremendously circumscribed in the nineteenth century, even for women who held societal privileges through race and class that gave their thoughts and ideas public credibility. Consequently, to aspire, as a black woman, to the stature of the white woman was not necessarily to aim toward an egalitarian ideal or to topple patriarchal power. Surely, the larger objective of this book demonstrates how professional authors, even those firmly entrenched in the white middle class, necessarily worked to establish a legitimate public voice for themselves as well as a persona for the typology of the famous author. Doing so often required subversive strategies, or a guerrilla warfare as Caird called it, in order to incite ideological change.

Frances Smith Foster affirms the subversiveness of the politics of visibility for black women, noting, "It was an audacious act for a nineteenth-century woman to presume to address any audience outside of her own family and female friends. There was definitely a woman's sphere, and those who wrote for publication were dangerously close to exceeding its bounds" (xxxii). Foster points out that the politics of gender were particularly problematic for the black woman, and specifically for the "Afro-American middle class, which so strongly desired the social approval and respect of their fellow Americans and so consistently received neither. For a black woman to address an audience of mixed race and sex, to accuse her readers of having sinned by commission or omission, and to urge their active involvement in social and political reform was to risk being totally rejected as an iconoclast or lunatic" (xxxiii).

These issues of race, class, gender, and celebrity, still nascent for black women in the 1850s and 1860s when Potter and Keckley authored their memoirs, were raging concerns by the end of the century. M.H. Washington observes, for example, that Anna Julia Cooper, a noted author and scholar, who had been born in slavery in 1858 and earned a PhD from the Sorbonne in 1924, had grave concerns about her public image that affected the sorts of material on which she published. Washington writes:

> As a middle-class black woman, Cooper, like all of her contemporaries—Fannie Jackson Coppin, Frances Harper, Mary Church Terrell, Ida B.Wells, Josephine St. Pierre Ruffin—had a great stake in the prestige, the respectability, and the gentility guaranteed by the politics of true womanhood. To identify with the issues and interests of poor and uneducated black women entailed a great risk. Cooper and her intellectual contemporaries would have to deal with their own class privilege and would undoubtedly alienate the very white women they felt they needed as allies. Burdened by the race's morality, black women could not be as free as white women or black men to think outside of these boundaries of "uplift"; every choice they made had tremendous repercussions for an entire race of women already under the stigma of inferiority and immorality. (xlvii)

A literary generation earlier, Keckley and Potter were also participating in the invention of a what it meant to write about racial uplift while appealing to a primarily white audience; they were helping to establish a new way of thinking about women who worked for their bread by allowing for the possibility that the dressmaker or the hairdresser could be refined and decorous, possessing tact, discretion, and integrity. Potter and Keckley's portrait of themselves as working "ladies" offered a significant contrast to both the public stereotype of the black woman and the material reality of most women of color, particularly in the South. Jacqueline Jones reports that in 1870, roughly eight out of ten Southern blacks were illiterate and "for most women, the rigors of childbearing and rearing, household chores and outside employment, represented a continuum from slavery to freedom, unbroken by schooling or other opportunities to expand their horizons beyond the cabin in the cotton field" (77). Keckley and Potter's version of black womanhood—as self-reliant, unfettered by domestic obligations, empowered, refined, and financially successful—functions as a considerable challenge to the social order. Rather than automatically devaluing the knowledge they draw from socioeconomic locations, they suggest that hairdressing and dressmaking, so-called menial work that might be perceived as underscoring woman's oppressed status in a patriarchal culture, actually heighten a woman's ability to develop the traits the culture praises. As I've noted with the other writers considered in this book, they do not attempt to topple the ideological code that imagines what ideal behavior might look like, but they manage to problematize the raced and classed bodies who can occupy and project the celebrated ideal, and this, in itself, is an audacious re-imagination that allows for difference.

And so perhaps more than any of the other depictions of celebrity and gender considered in this book, Keckley and Potter are able affect change through representation. They do this less through detailing their own embodiment and more through the detached observer role they assume toward the white women they help primp and prepare for the public gaze. What's remarkable about *Behind the Scenes* and *A Hair-dresser's Experience* is that the same attention that makes the services of a top-notch seamstress and hairdresser necessary actually authorizes Potter and Keckley's private-gaze-turned-public. Because public women are looked at and because Keckley and Potter can equip ladies of wealth to bear the weight of public scrutiny, the dressmaker and hairdresser gain access to an intimate life that in turn creates a market for the public re-telling of their observations of these white women (and the white men they are involved with). In both of these texts, the figures, who possess the single greatest power of looking (and critiquing), are the two figures who should ostensibly hold the least power, the hired help. That both of these women are black and working-class, and also wholly in command of their texts as well as fully versed in the rigors of ladylike deportment, automatically allows for a reconstituted notion of not just the terms of womanhood but of celebrity itself. Significantly, in this new mode of seeing and telling, both texts advocate an active knowledge over a passive receivership. Ammons explains that, "To be written is to be passive. To write is to be active, to take action, to be the actor—to own and create one's self" (38). Keckley and Potter both claim active roles in the construction of their public identities, a form of empowered agency that puts them in diametric opposition to entrenched patriarchal norms. Merish affirms such an idea as it relates to Keckley, noting, "Whereas slave codes had institutionalized white men's effort to control the appearance of blacks and the meaning(s) of the racial body, Keckley's narrative appropriates that authority, emphasizing a black woman's power to fashion the public identities of whites while registering the centrality of black female labor to Anglo-American culture" (242). That the writers can make a dress, design a hairstyle, set up a relief fund for contraband slaves, rescue invalids from a hotel fire, set the convoluted record straight, and dictate decorum—rather than having it all done for and to them—articulates a level of agency and independence rarely expressed in representations of white women writers of the nineteenth century. That both women exert such agency free of heterosexual bonds—as married women who have divested themselves of worthless husbands—suggests an even greater degree of agency than that we saw illustrated in *Ruth Hall* or that we will see in *Red Pottage*. As such, both *Behind the Scenes* and *A Hair-dresser's Experience* are able, in their manner of telling details, to heighten the respective role of the narrator/author as observer and critic rather than as powerless functionaries in the white women's world of wealth and beauty regimes.

Behind these scenes, is a very clear sense that Potter and Keckley claim (and deserve to claim) the full credit for their perspicacity, shrewd acumen, and visible prominence. Not only can they dictate the terms of middle-class womanhood to the ladies whose bodies they serve, as stage managers in the artifice involved in achieving the illusion of the ideal, they have the discursive power to move beyond that ideal because they are able to de-naturalize its component parts and manifest them in a way that appears genuine rather than artificial. One might argue that in eschewing superficial markers (cosmetics, false teeth, and wigs) and relishing other signifiers (silk dresses, fine living quarters, simple decorous behavior), Keckley and Potter demonstrate an achievement of the authentically famous, one whose intrinsic qualities lift her to visibility, rather than the constructed celebrity, who stage manages publicity. In so doing, they also work to reclaim the figure of fame as a legitimately female and feminine cultural iteration.

Chapter 5
The Text as Child:
Gender/Sex and Metaphors of Maternity at the Fin de Siècle

> Today I snap the fetters of your literary bondage. There shall be no more books written! No more study, no more toil, no more anxiety, no more heart-aches! And that dear public you love so well, must even help itself, and whistle for a new pet. You belong solely to me now, and I shall take care of the life you have nearly destroyed, in your inordinate ambition.
> —Augusta Jane Evans Wilson, *St. Elmo*, 1886

The above speech from St. Elmo Murray to Edna Earl caps the competing plot lines of famous authorship and romantic love running through Augusta Jane Evans Wilson's *St. Elmo* (1866). Although the novel devotes extensive narrative space to detailing Edna's intellectual and professional growth as she "tackles the whole of knowledge," Wilson assures her reader that Edna's bookishness has not supplanted her feminine attractions (Garrison 77). Indeed, in the rather bold commandeering of Edna's body and identity demonstrated in the above epigraph, the fact that she can "solely" belong to St. Elmo, comes only after Edna has been proposed to on eight separate occasions thus reinforcing her heterosexual attractiveness (her eight proposals of marriage include two each by an English nobleman and a well-respected member of the literary establishment, as well as a previous unsuccessful venture by St. Elmo himself). Throughout the novel, Edna contends with fainting spells and neurasthenia brought on by over work. And like Gaskell's rendition of Charlotte Brontë, though Edna is depicted as a talented, intelligent, and famous writer, her abilities are housed in (and reinforced by) a woman's weak body.

As she nears the completion of her book, for instance, Edna falls into a dangerous illness, diagnosed as hypertrophy of the heart. Her doctor orders rest and demands that she, "Refrain from study, avoid all excitement ... above all things, do not tax your brain" (337). Edna denies his patriarchal authority, exerting her own "masculine" aggression, and finishes her book, so that finally she recognizes her "own heart ... throbbing in its pages" (443). St. Elmo's masculinist agency does her one better, however, as his rather violent promise to "snap" her "literary bondage" and remove her from a world of study, toil, and anxiety (and, not incidentally, intellectual fulfillment and public adoration) wins her over at the same time as it equates her with a commodity to be owned. Though Edna is willing to imperil her health and well-being for the sake of her literary progeny, once her book is birthed, she agrees to a more conventional life of private and domestic tasks. This new life puts Edna out of the glaring lights of celebrity, but the ıestic Edna is also out of the scope of the narrative's interest, for it is Edna's ascent toward intellect and fame, rather than her domestic contentedness, that fascinates in this novel. *St. Elmo* thus suggests that the separation between literary celebrity and conventional domesticity remains stable, and a woman's fulfillment comes not through a successful career and celebrity but through a husband and children.[1] The novel's logic sustains the idea that Edna's authorship and ensuing fame can only flourish as a precursor to marriage and motherhood, not as a substitute for them.

In this chapter I examine the presumed mutual exclusivity between fame and femininity as suggested here by *St. Elmo*. Looking less at the discursive production of celebrity itself than at ideas celebrity makes salient through the artistic product, I use three novels authored in the 1890s—Mary Cholmondeley's *Red Pottage* (1899), Rhoda Broughton's *A Beginner* (1894), and Elizabeth Robins's *George Mandeville's Husband* (1894)—to analyze a recurrent trope in late nineteenth-century fiction: the author who mothers a textual baby. I demonstrate how these particular writers imbued their author characters with the signifiers of motherhood in a way that modified the dialectical dilemma between literary celebrity and gender/sex. Though Wilson describes Edna as laboring over her literary children, Edna is ultimately tamed through her commitments to God and family, her fame and genius contained by conventional manifestations of gender and motherhood. By the turn of the century some 30 years later, Cholmondeley, Broughton, and Robins would offer a more nuanced text-as-child metaphor.

New Women, New Threats, New Mothers

By the 1890s, the representation of female authorship and public fame had become increasingly complicated since women's literary success and visibility also made them susceptible to a growing public backlash, exacerbated by anxieties about female professionalism and autonomy, sexual degeneracy, social decay, and imperial weakness. Public fears cultivated a notion that strong women made men weak, a scare rhetoric that expressed itself in both words and images (see Figure 5.1). It was particularly in the decade of the 1890s that educated and New Women were charged with having become "unsexed" for seeking professional and public lives that put them in the hurly-burly of the masculinized marketplace. Though we understand from our present critical vantage point that the metaphor of separate spheres does not accurately map onto actual lived experience in the nineteenth

---

[1] *St. Elmo* itself was one of the most celebrated books of the nineteenth century. Within four months of its publication, it had sold a million copies and remained in print into the early twentieth century. *St. Elmo* fostered an 1867 parody, *St. Tw'elmo, or the Cuneiform Cyclopedist of Chattanooga*, and almost one hundred years later, Edna served as the model for Eudora Welty's protagonist in her 1954 novel, *The Ponder Heart*. Much like the real Fanny Fern, the fictional Edna Earl was immensely famous and became the inspiration for baby names, plantations, railway carriages, steamboats, a punch, and cigars.

WHAT OUR FIN-DE-SIECLISTS ARE GROWING TO.
"OH, OH, OH ! CONFOUND IT !"   " WHAT *IS* THE MATTER, ALGY ?"
"I JUST LET MY FOOT OUT OF THE STIRRUP, AND THIS BEAST OF A PONY'S TROD ON MY TOE !"

Fig. 5.1   "What Our Fin-de-Sièclists Are Growing To." *Punch*. May 2, 1891, 210.

century or that, as Ellen Rosenman and Claudia Klaver argue, "private life was not so private after all, nor was the public world exclusively populated by men" (3), the ideology of private and public realms itself held a particular coercive appeal, even if not exactly manifest in every aspect of social relations. As the conservative cultural critic and novelist Eliza Lynn Linton would say in her tract against women's suffrage, in an ideal arrangement of home, "the man has the outside work to do, from governing the country to tilling the soil; the woman takes the inside, managing the family and regulating society" ("The Wild Women: As Politicians" 81). Never mind that regulating society is already a task outside of the home.

As I discuss at greater length in the conclusion, in a deterministic order where intellectual work stems from "male faculties," a biological woman who crosses into masculinist behavior violates ideological gender symmetry, interrupting social prescriptions by announcing a third man-woman category. The rigid polarization between ideal iterations of male and female presumed that biology ordered social arrangements, a logic evident, in particular, through the cult of motherhood. The mother, already a figure of some mythic proportion, became the critical signifier of sex/gender appropriateness, a sign that was read as domestic, nurturing, and other-oriented. Again Linton solidifies this ideology, when she declares, "an absolute truth – the *raison d'être* of a woman is maternity. For this and this alone nature has differentiated her from man, and built her up cell by cell and organ by organ" ("The Wild Women: As Politicians" 80). Of course, the point here is not that Victorian women needed telling about the ideology of motherhood but that enough of them in sufficient proportion were defying prescriptive codes that the rhetorical fervor heightened. By century's end, as Bram Dijkstra notes, the Victorian male establishment had become "obsessed" with women's degeneration, which they attributed to excessive stimulation, both sexual and intellectual. Indeed, Canadian-born Grant Allen, author of *The Woman Who Did* (1895), a book that scandalized readers on both sides of the Atlantic, published a piece in 1890 in which he claimed that if the "girl of the future" did not produce children and renounce emancipation, she would soon be as "flat as a pancake and as dry as a broomstick" (Allen 50). The corrective was clear: "Only complete absorption in the practice of motherhood was considered a fit activity for women" (Dijkstra 74).

This indexical link between sex/gender and motherhood came with its own dilemmas. Obviously, not all women were mothers, some by choice and others by circumstance. For professional women, motherhood was often not an option sought or desired, and their very resistance to "maternal instinct" unsexed them. The sort of semiotic power afforded to women through the trope of the mother was, consequently, not equally available to all women. Yet, women's engagement in professional authorship and status as literary celebrities in many ways offered a means to breach the tensions between gendered and sexed behaviors, precisely because writers could turn maternal sex imperatives to their advantage by birthing texts rather than children. And authors had particular need of gender/sex redemption. In both Britain and America, the 1890s marked a period of immense visibility and commercial success for women writers. Indeed, as Susan Coultrap-McQuin has noted about famous American authors such as E.D.E.N Southworth and Harriet Beecher Stowe, professional authorship functioned as a viable career choice for a very particular sort of woman precisely because she could integrate "female" values with career aspirations. Yet, women's success was insistently coded with sex/gender meaning since, as Coultrap-McQuin equally observes, "almost no one in the nineteenth century was entirely able to separate the evaluation of literary work from the sex of the author" (18).

In the transatlantic fin de siècle, a time described by Sally Ledger and Roger Luckhurst as having "limitless generative power" as well as a haunting sense of "decay and degeneration," cultural ambiguity reigned (xi). The professional woman, primarily associated with the New Woman, was a double-coded signifier that underscored this ambiguity: she symbolized "an image of sexual freedom and assertions of female independence, promising a bright democratic future," while also signifying an "apocalyptic warning of the dangers of sexual degeneracy, the abandonment of motherhood, and consequent risk to the racial future of England" (Ledger and Luckhurst xvii). Though authors such as Charlotte Brontë, George Eliot, Margaret Oliphant, Ellen Wood, and Mary Elizabeth Braddon, among others, had made for themselves viable and visible (if not uniformly celebrated) careers from mid-century forward, the increasing number of women who claimed identities as professional and famous authors at century's end, combined with the double-coding of the New Woman herself, increased the sense of potential threat.

As a consequence, the writer and her work were often vilified through a public smear campaign that denigrated them through a series of metaphors that equated women and their literary production as pestilence, trash, narcotics, and diseases. Women literary professionals responded in multiple ways to this coercion through representation. Some acquiesced to traditional values, continuing to write but undermining the power of female characters; some rebelled and were branded bluestockings and New Women; some played a bit of both games, seeming to adhere to the dominant ideology but offering opportunities for subversion within their texts. It is this third category that interests me in this chapter, for the professional writer was at once able to offer through her characters a "docile body," as Foucault terms it, perfectly in keeping with the cultural imperatives of feminine appropriateness, while also depicting a discursive deviant body, which was too fluid, too plural, too different to be fully restrained by patriarchal representation (*Discipline* 136).

In this chapter, I examine how Cholmondeley, Broughton, and Robins turned what might have been a symbolic deficit to their advantage. They did this by creating women author-characters who flourish in literary careers by conceiving and birthing textual children. In so doing, they used literary celebrity and professionalism as a leveraging tool for difference by fusing idealized Victorian womanhood (expressed through the trope of the mother) to the fin-de-siècle professional writer. The text-as-child trope was not by any means exclusive to these three texts or to the fin de siècle, nor is it a metaphor only employed by or about women. Indeed, it was quite common for male Romantic and Transcendentalist poets, in particular, to talk of their fathering vis-à-vis the text, a move that allowed them to claim roles as both creators and procreators. However, given the widespread cultural pressure for women to mother, the use of the text-as-child trope is an adroit strategy, particularly when its use gave professional women greater agency.

Indeed, in the small, but insistent, body of Victorian literature in which women writers created characters who were also women writers, the cultural mandate that good women be good mothers underwent multiple displacements and relocations. As with most abstractions, the mothering metaphor was slippery, particularly since the textual progeny were viewed by the larger culture as not only a writer's children, but often as a societal pollutant requiring regulation and elimination. The text-as-child metaphor, therefore, could often work against women, functioning as a complicated disciplinary trope to pull them more tightly into hegemonically sanctioned roles. Since, as Cynthia Eagle Russett notes, Victorian women were never "permitted to forget that their essence was reproductive," the text-as-child metaphor participated in a critical form of didactic instruction (43). Rhetorics about the "natural obligation" of the woman's womb placed Victorian women writers in a discursive straitjacket, disciplining the possibilities of the mind by restricting the representations of the physical body.

Yet this imperative connection between a woman's reproductive body and her imagined offspring when portrayed in fiction could be conveyed with great complexity (and ambiguity). Indeed, the text-as-child offered a sort of cultural legibility turned askew, what Judith Butler has described as a subversive repetition that "challenge[s] conventions of reading" and "demand[s] new possibilities of reading" (Osborne and Segal 38). In Mary Cholmondeley's *Red Pottage*, for example, Hester Gresley's text is embodied as the "child of her brain," which is then "murdered" at the hands of her bad-reader brother. In Rhoda Broughton's *A Beginner*, if the text is child, we can see the novel authorizing nothing short of infanticide. In Elizabeth Robins's *George Mandeville's Husband*, tropes of the mother's body and her "natural" responsibilities to both daughter and text are interrupted by a volley of referents that refute the naturalness of sex/gender categories, coding male bodies feminine and female bodies masculine while leaving pubescent bodies dead in a pool of their own (menstrual?) blood. In these books, the representation of mothering requires a significant alteration of the overriding sense of what mothering might mean, and hence, of a woman's "natural" role, a move in line with other late-Victorian intellectual projects, from regenerative motherhood through eugenics.

As such, these three novels perform an important counter-cultural work in their re-imagination of sex/gender differences, which, in turn, had implications for women's participation and legitimacy in public commercial spaces. They do so in a way markedly different from many New Women texts, which frequently deployed a more standard trope of failure at literary professionalism. Indeed, in her introductory essay to *Red Pottage*, Elaine Showalter contends that it required "a great deal of self-esteem to allow one's writer-heroine to succeed in the 1890s, and Cholmondeley could not quite bring herself to be so optimistic" (xiii). Penny Boumelha has further argued that to make the woman writer fail is the only way to assert her artistry. And though each of the novels I consider here could in many ways be considered evidence for professional failure, I contend that Cholmondelely, Broughton, and Robins primarily recalibrated the meaning of women's failure through the trope of the mother. It should be noted that none of the authors depicted here is a "successful" mother, each losing her textual (and sometimes biological) children through negligence or murder. And yet the subversive repetition depicted in these novels authorizes, as Wendy Parkins notes, "new forms of knowledge and new subject positions for women" (48). My examination thus seeks to reveal the ways in which Cholmondeley, Broughton, and Robins used the trope of the famous author who mothers her book in ways that both enclosed their author-characters in a cultural straitjacket yet enabled them to wiggle free of confinement.

Pregnant With Meaning: Issues of Sex and Gender in Birthing the Text

Before thinking specifically about each of the novels I consider, it's helpful to map out some of the nuances of the text-as-child metaphor. Though produced at mid-century, Charles Dickens's *David Copperfield* vividly illuminates the intricacies inherent in sex/gender and writing. "I was," David Copperfield says, "born with a caul, which was advertised for sale, in the newspapers, at the low price of fifteen guineas" (9–10). A caul is the fetal membrane that in rare cases still covers the head of the infant at birth. It grew to have talismanic significance as a good-luck charm and is offered for sale in young Davy's case for its ability to guard against death by drowning. With no suitable bidders, the caul is stored away until ten years later it is "put up in a raffle." Copperfield recalls, "I was present myself, and I remember to have felt quite uncomfortable and confused, at a part of myself being disposed of in that way" (10).

The fetal membrane wrapped around the author's infant skull and later offered for sale indexically links to the text itself, the issue of his brain, packaged and sent into the world in exchange for money. Though David refers to the caul as "a part of myself," it is more accurately a part of his mother.[2] By itself, the caul symbolizes female procreative power, specifically the woman's ability to produce within herself the fluids, membranes, and nutrients necessary to sustain life. Wrapped around the head of the author-character David, the caul signifies his creative power, for it allows the male author to appropriate the womb by draping it around, and thus conflating it with, his mind. He is, at once, creator and procreator. The membrane lends him female generative powers that he can confer on his male womb, the brain, yet it underscores his own absence, or lack, of the biological apparatus for creation. Dickens's metaphor indicates that the penis may be the male organ of procreation, but the brain is his womb for creation, and any concretizing of the metaphor necessitates the displacement of woman's membrane onto man's mind. This underscores the rightness of ontological separation—of women being linked to the body and to nature, of men being linked to the mind and to culture. It also reifies a perceived rightness of sex/gender sameness since, within the logic of the metaphor, it is impossible for male/masculinity to enact female/femininity except through appropriation and performance.

Such a division has implications for women's authorship, for as Gaye Tuchman observes, the "authority of the woman [as author] is based on her feelings, her intuitions, her connection with the earth and nature, in short, on her reproductive body; the authority of man is based on his will, his reason, his name which both identifies him with the patriarchal good and distinguishes him from other men in

---

[2]   In this particular instance, the image of the caul also allows the abandoned David Copperfield a form of symbiosis with his idealized, though largely incompetent, mother Clara. As critics of the novel have noted, a central preoccupation of the text is its working through of mother issues. Mary Poovey notes that the idealized mother figure "takes the form of a series of substitutions that exposes and punishes the mother's guilt without jeopardizing the idealized woman she retrospectively becomes" (*Uneven* 92).

short, his productive mind" (25). David Copperfield, and through him Charles Dickens, can here claim access to the procreative powers of the female womb without problematizing male/intellectual gender identity.

As this suggests, the "creation as birth" metaphor is rife with hermeneutic complexity. Many literary-historical scholars have engaged with and critiqued the metaphor, suggesting that it can be both elucidating (for the discursive empowerment it allows) and essentialist (for the way it forever links the woman to the procreative body).[3] It is a metaphor deeply vexed, internally incoherent, occasionally essentialist, and potentially empowering: in short, a metaphor of considerable richness and complexity. In particular reference to the sex/gender overlap in the construction of the late-Victorian writer, the metaphor evokes other questions. These include: Does the body function as a reliable source of self-knowledge? Does female sexuality exist prior to social construction? Do women experience their bodies outside of acculturation? And to draw on questions of eugenics dominating at the end of the nineteenth century: Can women use their maternal roles as important safeguards against social decay? Can rational reproduction, whether of textual or physical child, result in a stronger race and nation?[4]

My particular task is not to resolve the debate about whether it is appropriate to invoke the body and mothering as metaphors for describing the writing process, nor is it necessarily to sort out how fully these images presuppose a biological essence. As a trope about nineteenth-century transatlantic literary production, the metaphor functions as a political concept that shapes cultural norms. The use of the childbirth metaphor compels imaginative conformity to an economy of sameness that represents all women as heterosexual, able-bodied, and pre-menopausal. It is hegemonic in that it appears to command consent "naturally." In short, it normalizes the body and the sexuality of a woman so that she is in all circumstances able and willing to function as a mother, and the metaphor pushes

---

[3]   See Nina Auerbach, "Artists and Mothers: A False Alliance," *Women and Literature* 6 (Spring 1978): 1–17; Margaret Homans, *Bearing the Word: Language and Female Experience in Nineteenth-Century Women's Writing* (Chicago: University of Chicago Press, 1986); Sandra M. Gilbert and Susan Gubar, *The Madwoman in the Attic: The Woman Writer and the Nineteenth-Century Literary Imagination* (New Haven: Yale University Press, 1979); Elaine Showalter, *A Literature of Their Own: British Women Novelists from Brontë to Lessing* (Princeton: Princeton University Press, 1977); Susan Stanford Friedman, "Creativity and the Childbirth Metaphor: Gender Difference in Literary Discourse" in *Speaking of Gender*, ed. Elaine Showalter (New York: Routledge, 1989); and Margaret Wise Petrochenkov, *Pregnancy and Birth as a Metaphor for Literary Creativity.* (PhD Diss., Indiana University, 1992).

[4]   See Chris Waters, "New Women and Eugenic Fictions," *History Workshop Journal* 60:1 (2005): 232–8; Angelique Richardson, *Love and Eugenics in the Late Nineteenth Century: Rational Reproduction and the New Woman* (Oxford: Oxford University Press, 2003); and George Robb, "Race Motherhood: Moral Eugenics vs. Progressive Eugenics, 1880–1920" in *Maternal Instincts: Visions of Motherhood and Sexuality in Britain, 1875–1925*, ed. Claudia Nelson and Ann Sumner Holmes (New York: St. Martin's Press, 1997).

to the margins the "odd women" who risk "physical and emotional" disease and a "shorter life-span," not to mention social ostracism, by refusing the natural call of their maternal "destiny" (Smith-Rosenberg 336).

The gendered and sexed implications for writing and celebrity are profound. Given the prevailing Victorian stance that both public identity and artistry are male and masculine, we see a cultural imperative for the male writer to appropriate (female) procreative powers, while the woman who writes must appropriate (male) intellectual ability. Though, as illustrated in the case of Dickens's *David Copperfield*, it is possible for the man to wrap the procreative membranes of the woman's body around his brain without compromising his gendered and sexed identity, a similar reversal is not allowed the woman. The woman who writes is "unsexed"; she is "three quarters male" as a character in Robins's *George Mandeville's Husband* says about George Eliot. To perpetuate her gendered identity, the woman who writes must undergo several contortions in order to reconcile her behavior with her body. Like a woman pretending to be a drag queen, she must be a woman acting like a man, borrowing from a woman—all of which underscores a belief in simple sex and gender binaries at the same time as it explodes these polarities and allows for transgressive modes of performativity.

When sex identity exists in such simultaneous overlap and contradistinction to gender roles—in this case, when behavior (artistic creation) is taken to be identical with biology (physical procreation)—the stability of both concepts is potentially at risk. We can see some evidence of that imbalance in the cultural anxiety operative at the end of the century as demonstrated through Cholmondeley, Broughton, and Robins.

Red Pottage: The Author as (Masculinized) Mother

Red Pottage is a novel with interlocking narratives, each guided by a separate heroine: Hester Gresley, an unmarried woman writer, highly committed to her artistry, and Rachel Ward, a more "conventional" female character whose primary work seems to be securing a husband. Hester and Rachel offer important succor and support to one another: Hester is always on hand to soothe Rachel's poor choices in potential husbands, and Rachel is ever present to encourage and sustain Hester's authorial ambitions. They share bonds of friendship and affection to such a degree that it is only their union at story's end that allows either a future.

Because it is the author-character's maternal coding that concerns me here, I necessarily skew my analysis toward Hester, though I will revisit the relationship between her and Rachel at the end of this section. Mary Cholmondeley codes Hester in cultural signifiers (such as thinness, frailty, and obedience) that underscore her conventional femininity. At the level of the body, she is most pointedly not a threat. Yet, Hester possesses access to "imagination" and thus to an artistry that borders on genius, and this marks her as deviant for the way she embodies masculine expression. Hester's first book, *An Idyll of East London*, is moderately well received but, to many characters in the book, troubling for its unfeminine commentary on poverty and urbanization. As Cholmondeley depicts it, the manner in which Hester tackles pressing social issues devolves for those who discuss her work into tedious debates of autobiography versus imagination, a larger cultural and historical criticism lobbed at other Victorian authors, in particular the Brontë sisters. Essentially, the question is: how can a "protected" woman possibly imagine degradation? The answer suggests that any woman capable of imagining vice is no (true) woman at all.

Cholmondeley deploys Hester's body as a sort of corrective, her frailty standing in feminine compensation to the masculine aggression of her mind. The novel's early pages work to emphasize Hester's diminutive stature. Contrasting Hester with Rachel, Chomondeley writes, "Rachel was physically strong. Hester was weak. The one was calm, patient, practical, equable, the other imaginative, unbalanced, excitable" (36). Subsequent scenes reinforce Hester's slight body and impetuous nature, by calling the reader's critical gaze to Hester's "white exhausted face" (36), her "small slight figure" (52), her "innocent, childlike face" (77), her "slight graceful figure" (155), her "thin hands" (320), all of which, in terms of artistic output, follow the dictates of "blind instinct" (335). The narrator notes, "Her irregular profile, her delicate pointed speech and fingers, her manner of picking up her slender feet as she walked, her quick alert movements, everything about her was neat, adjusted, perfect in its way" (54).

This sense of Hester's "perfection" (or rather, her perfect alignment with white, heterosexual, upper-class femininity) makes of Hester a polyvalent signifier of hegemonic femininity. The hyper-articulation of idealized femininity is particularly pronounced in the novel's mothering tropes. Though Hester challenges convention by being neither married nor a biological mother, she is given the primary maternal role in the novel as articulated through her status as the mother of books. When her brother James discovers, surreptitiously reads, and then destroys the manuscript for her second novel, *Husks*, Hester responds with what is coded as a mother's fury. When her nephew, Regie, was ill, she tells her brother, "I did not let your child die. Why have you killed mine?" (276). The young Regie immediately enters this scene of confrontation, carrying a potato he has baked in the dying embers of the bonfire made of her manuscript, and Hester "turn[s] on him like some blinded infuriated animal at bay, and thrust[s] him violently from her." (277). Her capitulation to a more bestial form is justified, we are led to believe, by the murder of her own child. She later tells the bishop:

> "If I had a child … and it died, I might have ten more, beautiful and clever and affectionate, but they would not replace the one I had lost. Only if it were a child," a little tremor broke the dead level of the passionless voice, "I should meet it again in heaven. There is the resurrection of the body for the children of the body, but there is no resurrection that I ever heard of for the children of the brain." (344)

Here Cholmondeley turns the text-as-child metaphor so that the textual child possesses greater value than a physical son or daughter. The loss of the issue of the brain is represented as irreparable, beyond a mother's grieving. Hester has been told that the "pang of motherhood is that even your children don't seem your very own.... [but] spiritual children, the books, are really ours" (334–5). Because Hester has gone a step further than the maternal ideology allows, because she has claimed and sustained a belief that the text is her "very own" (and autogenously conceived) child, Cholmondeley's characterization of Hester pushes against a dominant and limiting trope, reconfiguring the value conferred on women through motherhood. As a consequence, the author Hester not only has the right to wear the mantle of mother, it is gendered creation rather than sexed procreation that makes her worthy of that honor.

Even so, Hester's relationship to her art plays out largely according to the terms of Victorian motherhood, for she sacrifices her well-being, her presence of mind, and her good health so that the textual more-than-child might prosper. She says of her text:

> "I loved it for itself, not for anything it was to bring me …. It was part of myself.
> But it was the better part. The side of me which loves success … had no hand in
> it. My one prayer was that I might be worthy to write it, that it might not suffer
> by contact with me. I spent myself upon it." Hester's voice sank. "I knew what
> I was doing. I joyfully spent my health, my eyesight, my very life upon it. I was
> impelled to do it by what you perhaps call a blind instinct, what I, poor simpleton
> and dupe, believed at the time to be nothing less than the will of God." (335)

In language that mirrors the cult of motherhood, Hester suggests that her call to artistry supersedes all. This is an interesting use of the self-sacrificing ideology, for it displaces the body of the child with the body of the text, yet it underscores the same values—womanly sacrifice to a duty that is greater than oneself. Importantly, as we have seen in other treatments of literary celebrity, the side of Hester that "loves success" had no part in the birthing of her novel. Cholmondeley's (per)version of the mother ideology allows for repetition, alteration, and difference. In this case, the written work moves to center stage in a woman's motherly responsibility. Hester is allowed to fulfill the dictates of a culture hungry for motherly devotion, but she does so by spending her fragile body so that her writing might live. Her frail, delicate, and slender body—all of which underscore her situatedness in patriarchal codes—refuses the signifying system it is placed within. Giving birth to a text rather than to a child, Hester alters the code of expectation, so that professional determination overrides biological determinism. This model, in which (woman's) will exerts more power than genetics, is an important reorganization of the prevailing ideological order, allowing possibilities for change in both ideology and social arrangements through rational reproduction.

Allowing Hester to claim maternal validity through her text correlates to another significant reorganization—that of pairing the heroines to one another at novels' ending, thus disrupting heternormative family arrangements.[5] The doubling of heroines, although a common trope in many literary forms, reproduces a typology of the New Woman genre. Ann Heilmann notes about New Woman fiction more broadly, that such a doubling of characters offers a "reflection of multiple female subjectivities," and thus, "the texts may challenge modern readers to engage in a diversity of perspectives" (*New Woman Fiction* 9). As I've already noted, Cholmondeley's first description of Hester contrasts her with Rachel, thus making them separate but co-determinant characters. Their seemingly distinct story lines play out in a contrapuntal fashion that ultimately requires their union in order to secure their happiness (and narratological coherence). It could be argued that the dual plots function as a narrative mirror; Rachel struggles to be happy in love, while Hester strives to be successful and recognized in her career. Thus, Cholmondeley's conflation of the two female characters legitimates literary professionalism and celebrity for women by equating it with the more normative objective of romance. Indeed, the narrator describes Hester's relationship to her book as a love object: "Eagerly, shyly, enthusiastically, she talked to her friend about the book, as a young girl talks of her lover. Everything else was forgotten. Hester's eyes burned. Her colour came and went. She was transfigured" (80). In this description we can clearly see that Hester's body responds as a lover to her text, allowing for an interesting collapse of eros and maternal duty through a text that is ambiguously sexed and infantilized.

But to see Hester's relationship to the page as the center of her romance plot doesn't pay sufficient attention to the symbiosis between her and Rachel. Cholmondeley characterizes Hester and Rachel's friendship as "very deep, very tender" (29), and she makes it clear that Hester's inspiration to become a writer is conceived through her connection to Rachel:

> And as Hester leaned against Rachel the yearning of her soul toward her
> suddenly lit up something which had long lain colossal but inapprehended in
> the depths of her mind. Her paroxysm of despair at her own powerlessness was
> followed by a lightning flash of self-revelation. She saw, as in a dream, terrible,
> beautiful, inaccessible, but distinct, where her power lay, of which restless
> bewildering hints had so often mocked her. She had but to touch the houses and
> they would fall down. She held her hands tightly together lest she should do it.
> The strength as of an infinite ocean swept in beneath her weakness, and bore it
> upon its surface like a leaf. (37)

---

[5]   One indication of the transgressions represented in both the bond of friendship between Rachel and Hester as well as their independence appears in Rhoda Broughton's *A Fool in Her Folly* (1921). Reflecting back on her own experience in the "old" days of the Victorian period from her vantage point in 1921, Broughton observes, "That a couple of girls should find an affinity in each other which their own family circle did not provide, and 'forsaking all others' betake themselves to a joint flat, to maintain which their own industries should furnish the means, was an idea that would have consigned the holder of it to Bedlam" (8–9).

Penny Boumelha reads this scene as indicative of Hester's passivity and so as a reification of cultural norms, arguing, "There is here nothing of choice, will, ambition, but only surrender to a greater power, so that the language and moral configuration of orthodox femininity are retained even while they are unquestionably put to new uses." (173). But "surrender," which would seem to bespeak orthodox femininity, is in many ways double-coded in this passage.[6]

Cholmondeley's usage makes clear that "higher power" is configured not as something bigger than or outside of Hester but as something deep within her. In effect, Hester's bond to Rachel allows her access to an ability that has always been immanent. The "yearning" of Hester's soul toward Rachel allows her to become increasingly aware of a power that lies in the "depths of her mind," the ability to write. In other words, the union between Hester and Rachel conceives the textual child. Subtly coding Hester's actualization as an artist/ mother with the threat of women's (homo)sexuality heightens the sense of its potency, as measured by Nicholas Francis Cooke's warning on female sexual desire in *Satan in Society* (1876) that, "The most intimate liaisons are formed under this specious pretext [of the 'guise of friendship']; the same bed often receives the two friends" (107). For Cooke, and a large majority of middle-class Anglo-American Victorian culture, the desires of women, between themselves and even with themselves, threatened to deteriorate the cornerstone of a healthy (heterosexual) society. "What remains of the family," he announces, "is only held together by the graces and virtue of woman" (87). The connection between Hester and Rachel works to establish an extra-normative gender/sex practice by creating a context where the erotic love between women can produce superior children. By contrast, Rhoda Broughton's *A Beginner*, though constructing its writer heroine in much the same way as Cholmondeley's *Red Pottage*, offers curtailed possibilities for change.

---

[6]   Some present-day scholars have characterized *Red Pottage*'s ending in a way that allows for a particular meaning not seemingly suggested by the text. For instance, Boumelha contends, "Cholmondeley's Hester Gresley is an artist of ennui, but when her pompous brother destroys the only manuscript of her second novel, in a combination of envy and moral outrage, she knocks down his child with an intent to kill him, and thereafter lapses into a fatal brain-fever" (173). Certainly, Hester is debilitated by the fever, but it is far from fatal. Similarly, Wendy Parkins argues, "On discovering the fate of her manuscript, Hester suffers a complete physical and mental breakdown and by the close of *Red Pottage* it is clear that she will never write again" (52–3). Yet, Cholmondeley writes in a postscript that in a future peopled by Hester, Rachel, and children clustered about, "the old light rekindled in Hester's eyes" (375). Judging from the body of the text, that light could mean nothing other than her artistic fire. In both cases, critics have read for and established a failure that is not clearly indicated by the text.

A Beginner: Cautionary Tale to the Lady Novelist and Would-be Mothers

Emma Jocelyn is *A Beginner*'s literary protagonist, and the title of Broughton's novel points to both Emma's status and identity, for she is a beginner when it comes to textual production and she adopts the name "a beginner" as the *nom de plume* for her book *Miching Mallecho*. Broughton's novel about naïve authorship can be read as a cautionary tale for all would-be upper-class women who believe they can join in the fad of authorship. Through multiple clashes—between upper and working-class sensibilities, between old-fashioned values and progressive liberalism, between vicious critics and earnest writers—we are made to understand that a woman like Emma is better off living according to normative conventions. Yet, her limited foray into authorship opens an imagined space for the reader to glimpse difference, even if Emma cannot ultimately live in that alterity.

Like Hester in *Red Pottage*, Emma's body bears the signs of upper-class white femininity, though with little hint of same-sex affection save through a cousin character named Lesbia. Emma is described as a "charming white nymph, who looks at once so fresh and so high bred" (69); characters are continually asked, "Why can't you sit and stand and walk as Miss Jocelyn does?" (58), and her physical form, her "bow and gait" (255), unlike her literary offspring, are beyond criticism. Though Broughton offers unfailing praise of Emma's physically feminine and whitened features, particularly those parts of Emma's body responsible for touching the text—her "affectionate white hand" (120), her "pink palm" (63), her "long white hands like lilies" (243)—Broughton is relentless in demonstrating the utter worthlessness of Emma's book, the "offspring of her brain" (122). *Miching Mallecho* may well be the child of Emma's white, delicate and upper-class body as fashioned by her lily-like hands, and she may indeed watch over that "beloved offspring" with "gnawing anxiety," but Broughton makes clear that Emma's ambition is misplaced and her book is ill-developed and irrelevant; as a particularly sadistic review of Emma's book notes, echoing Samuel Johnson, *Miching Mallecho* is "ill-fed, ill-killed, ill-kept, ill-dressed, and ill-carved" (20, 126). Already we can see the body metaphors piling up, as the text becomes both child of the lady novelist's mind and animal for slaughter and consumption.

Emma seeks to defend her child/text throughout the course of Broughton's novel, arguing that she writes in order to be a "teacher and a benefactor to her kind!" (79). Yet, the stronger evidence of the novel's content comes through the response of its greatest advocate, Lesbia Heathcote, a second cousin to Emma. Lesbia finds the novel enchanting, and when reading, she becomes so absorbed that she is "unconscious of [her children's] clamour or even of their presence" (105). Further, Lesbia uses the novel to justify dalliances in extra-marital romantic adventures. So we see that Emma's efforts to "benefit her kind" actually encourage her cousin to abandon her joint roles of mother and wife, a consequence completely unintended by the naive author. "How frightfully you have misunderstood me!" Emma says to Lesbia (112). Indeed, though Emma's novel is defended throughout the course of Broughton's novel, it is never quoted. Readers never gain access to

Emma's ideas; the ray of light never shines upon our brains.[7] Instead, the novel receives the response it purportedly merits: it is ridiculed and castigated, tossed on the floor, figuratively killed (the critic's hand is "red with her infant's blood"), pulled from circulation, and ultimately destroyed (166).

Through it all, Emma is both conflated with and distanced from the text. As "mother" of the novel, it is an extension of her body.[8] And though "perfect prosperity" is written on "every detail of her appearance," Emma's own body cannot be separated from the public scorn accorded to her text (252). When Lesbia's husband throws Emma's book to the floor in disgust, for instance, Emma feels as if "some degrading physical indignity had been inflicted on herself" (114). Though *A Beginner* makes insistent references to *Miching Mallecho* as the "offspring of her brain" (122), Emma's "beloved offspring" (20), her "literary infant" (122), it so castigates Emma's novel for unfeminizing Victorian women, for making a "good, if rather foolish, woman neglect her duties to God and man" (115), that the novel ends with Emma becoming persuaded of its dangers and mournfully agreeing to burn the entire printing, save five copies lost in the circulating libraries.

Lest we think that the metaphor of child has receded at this point, Broughton depicts Emma as in "tragic dejection as she stands motionless" and watches as the "whole little family" is dumped upon the bonfire (390, 391). The fire then "assert[s] its supremacy, and is licking and shriveling and crackling the gaily coloured boards, and tossing up the exultant brutality of its flames above their crumbling paper and vanishing type" (390–91). As a final act of "expiation," Emma steps forward with her original manuscript in hand, "the beloved, the much-treasured, the sole" and she "tosses" this as well into the "funeral pyre" (391). The act is described as sad for Emma, and as she walks away from the burning mass of her literary children, Lesbia endeavors to cheer her up, "'Do not cry,' says Lesbia soothingly. 'At least, cry as much as you please, for there is no one near – no one, that is, except George!'" (393).

---

[7]   The absence of evidence of the novel itself was, in fact, was one of the criticisms raised by an 1894 *Athenaeum* review: "We are told little about the volume (Miching Mallecho) except that it is concerned with 'passion.' Yet it is the principal feature of 'A Beginner'" (574).

[8]   See Pamela Gilbert, *Disease, Desire, and the Body in Victorian Women's Popular Novels* (Cambridge: Cambridge University Press, 1997). While I have argued here for Emma's book being a textual child, Gilbert sees Emma Jocelyn's novel as "the woman's body entering the realm of exchange—although 'innocent' and 'virginal' in its purposes, to the extent it succeeds in the market, it becomes dangerous, contagious, and seductive" (114). In either reading Broughton incorporates the text as an extension of the female body that must be contained through death by fire. Mary Poovey offers a compelling reading of a different infanticide metaphor in her contention that mid-Victorian rationales for colonization and capitalism are expressed in Dickens's *Our Mutual Friend* as the narrator's "offspring" that must be killed or sacrificed for the good of material exchange. See Mary Poovey, *Making a Social Body: British Cultural Formation, 1830–1864* (Chicago: University of Chicago Press, 1995), 163–4.

And who, pray tell, is George? None other than a tertiary character who, we are told in the afterword, emerges to marry Emma. This is an important development, as it must surely be deduced that one of the problems inherent in positing the text as child and the lady novelist as its mother is the absence of the father. Without a "father" to assist in the creation of the baby/text, that offspring is illegitimate and must be discarded in order to protect reputations. The textual baby is even more troubling to a patriarchal society than would be a biological "bastard child," moreover, because no man, whether husband, lover, or even rapist, is needed for its conception, and in this case, unlike in *Red Pottage*, no woman stands in as partner either. The textual baby, then, is not only illegitimate, it is somehow monstrous, the offspring of a woman who can reproduce alone. This rendering of a child without a father (and so without sex) is clearly akin to religious lore and virgin birth. The woman's textual progeny, however, is not born immaculately, for it is her unsexed position, her crossing over from feminine practices to masculine behaviors that "fertilizes" the seed that will become her book. As such, the female author can fuck herself: she is not a virgin, waiting for divine seed, but a monster, neither man nor woman, able to displace and replace both the phallus and the penis. She does not blur categorical boundaries but refutes the categories altogether.

What we see in *A Beginner*, then, is a story of a professional author, depicted as physically delicate and intellectually naive, unable to control the destructive power of her own creation repetitively referred to as her monstrous child (an interesting echo of Mary Shelley's claim that *Frankenstein*, like Victor Frankenstein's monster itself, is her "hideous progeny," 173). In *A Beginner*, the text functions as an elaborate testing ground for the woman's literary product, and it eventually depicts her as saddened, humiliated, and recommitted to the values of middle-class Victorian culture through the contract of marriage and the promise of "real" (legitimate) rather than textual (illegitimate) children. But there is one redeeming moment, for though Emma's baby-text has been destroyed by fire, it was not possible to retrieve all of the copies, lost as they were to Mudie's circulating library. Infused into the general book population, Emma's rarified text has some hope of survival. It is a meager consolation, but better than complete genocide. And too, there is poetic justice in the fact that though the fictional text-child *Miching Mallecho* is destroyed, its material counterpart, *A Beginner*, survives intact.

George Mandeville's Husband: Refusing the Mother, Refusing to Mother

In Elizabeth Robins's *George Mandeville's Husband*, a novel that might well be considered a horror story about female authorship and fame, we are presented with a startling departure from the delicate and chastened author characters constructed by Cholmondeley and Broughton. Robins's novel, which she wrote under the pseudonym C.E. Raimond, seemingly castigates the professional woman author for the way in which her over-large presence diminishes and emasculates men. Much like George Eliot's attack on silly women who write silly novels, Robins's novel excoriates the trend for women to adopt male pen names (particularly those of George!) only to suffuse the literary marketplace with textual trash (in this case Lois Wilbraham changes her name to George Mandeville, thus creating a celebrated author figure).[9] *George Mandeville's Husband* has been little studied, largely because it poses such a dilemma: how could the feminist activist and pro-suffrage Elizabeth Robins create a text in which she damns female authorship? We can tease out an answer by looking closely at how motherhood and authorship are written onto George Mandeville.

According to her effeminate husband, for whom the novel is named and through whom most perspective is focalized, George Mandeville is vulgar and unwomanly, her body is overlarge and unappealing, and her novelistic output (perhaps as a consequence of her physical excesses) is meaningless tripe. In this sense, Elizabeth Robins's George Mandeville is no true woman at all, her deviance announced by a body completely opposite to Hester's or Emma's. Scene after scene portrays Lois Wilbraham—to the public, George Mandeville—increasingly obsessed with her persona as famous author. Gorged on food and flattery, George Mandeville becomes a spectacle of excess, not even the death of her daughter calling her back to her "womanly duties."

Plumpness may well be an articulation of maternal characteristics—an accentuation of breasts, hips, and the body fat needed to sustain pregnancy—but on the body of George Mandeville, plumpness turns to obesity, maternal ability to dysfunction, ambition to aggression. As such, Robins effectively converts what might be read as feminine and maternal into that which is monstrous, masculine, and terrifying. George/Lois is further "de-sexed" in that that her maternal obligation is expressed in only the remotest forms of distracted interest. Though she is the only "real" mother of the three author characters considered here, George Mandeville is pointedly a bad mother whose child has "few illusions as to her place in her mother's life" (8).

George/Lois's life is consumed not with producing children but with the production of text—hack novels and bad plays. What little biological maternal investment she possesses takes the form of talking to her slender, docile, and fragile daughter, Rosina, about "sordid" topics such as (we can only assume) menstruation and coming womanhood. This topic between Rosina and her mother, which both is and is not narrated, is precisely Rosina's maturation into puberty, a fact that biologically links Rosina's girl's body to the woman's body of the mother. Rosina is deeply insulted that her mother takes great liberties by asking her invasive questions about her health. She complains, "It might do if you've always told your mother every blessed thing from the time you were a baby. But if she's left you to yourself till you're fourteen, she can't suddenly – suddenly – tell you things – without a girl's feeling like murdering her" (138). These "things" her mother tells her are "facts of existence" that Rosina finds "so ugly, so ugly" (136).

---

[9]   For ease of classification, I call the "real" woman in this novel Lois, the author-character persona she adopts George, and the inevitable collapse between them Lois/George.

In Rosina's repulsion from her mother and the coming womanhood of her own body, we see the results of her gender-skewed parenting, for the brusque and disinterested masculinized mother frightens the child from a body that the overly fastidious and effeminate father cannot fathom.

Though it is surely not unusual to make the rites of menstruation so secretive that they become taboo, Robins points to the presence of Rosina's blood, and her telling death marked by a large hemorrhage which stains her white sheets "bright with new-spilt blood," through euphemisms that signify nothing at all (211). This functions as an effective sleight of hand that compels the reader to fill in the gap, much as we saw in the case of Fanny Fern's narration of Gail Hamilton or Elizabeth Keckley and Eliza Potter's refusal to describe their own bodies. In this case there is a hermeneutic fissure between ideology and embodied practice. George Mandeville is physiologically capable of having a child, but she does not possess maternal instinct, a contradiction that erodes a prevailing ideological belief connecting female bodies and motherly love. Likewise, her more tractable and seemingly "natural" daughter, who should theoretically flourish due to her congruence with the dominant bodily ideal, ultimately recoils at the realities of her own body and dies. The gap suggests, then, that biological sexed capacity does not necessarily determine embodied gendered behavior.

This disconnect between sex and gender is announced most pointedly in the figure of Ralph Wilbraham, Rosina's father and Lois's husband, a male character who is decidedly unmasculine. One significant result of depicting George Mandeville in such graphic and extreme terms is that the mother's excessiveness cements the "dysfunctional" bond between father and daughter. Rosina goes to Ralph for comfort, compassion, and commiseration. Thus, to play out the cultural logic, she turns to her father for a mother's support. If this were merely a novel of role reversal, Rosina would find succor in the mothering she receives from her father. Yet the kind of haven Ralph offers Rosina is rife with peril, precisely due to Ralph's belief that men work and have public identities and women sacrifice themselves to families.

Rosina's anxiety about what she shall "do" manifests itself repeatedly through the latter half of the novel: "'Suppose, father,' she asks, 'nobody ever loved me but you, and suppose I lived the longest – I might, you know – and suppose I was very poor – what then?'" (85). With this Rosina asks Wilbraham the question of the age: If a woman does not or cannot compete in the marriage market, and if she is not trained or prepared to earn a living for herself, and if her father is not in a position to support her, what kinds of options are open to her? Ralph assures her that "a dozen womanly things" await her, like tending to small children or keeping house or sewing, but he is adamant that she shall never be an artist or a writer. As she approaches death, Rosina hits on a vocation that will support her. She tells her father in a sort of dazed elation, "There's something I could do for my living, that even you would say was quite 'seemly' – that is, of course, if I live to be very old and very poor, and you aren't here to take care of me" (196). Her brainstorm? "[M]ending's my great accomplishment" (201). It's a rather pitiful prospect, even to Ralph.

As Rosina's awareness of the uncertainties of her future grows, Ralph's anxiety that Rosina will become another George Mandeville increases. "Rosina! Good God,' he reflects to himself in some panic, 'if she should turn out a woman-dabbler in some art or craze! No, that should not be.' He had been very weak and poor-spirited in giving up his own pursuits and predilections, but, by Heaven! he would fight for Rosina" (39–40). Ralph cautions Rosina to avoid her mother's slovenly habits: don't breakfast in bed (56), don't wear your dressing-gown out of your room (58), and the most important of all, don't even think about being a writer or an artist. "I'd rather my daughter scrubbed floors than wrote books," he exclaims with some venom (59). Ralph refuses the possibility that Rosina could learn to paint. "No woman ever learns," he says derisively. "Rosina," he chastens, "nothing on earth would be so disappointing to me as to see you trying to paint – nothing, that is, except seeing you try to write" (79). The obedient and docile Rosina agrees to never attempt either writing or painting, yet she cannot fully assuage her fears about what will become of her in the future. The only answer seems to be a passive-suicide, to do away with fears of the future by eliminating the future itself.

Through Rosina's struggles, Robins depicts the consequences that befall a young girl, who is denied self-making and self-supporting autonomy, a topic I will take up again in the conclusion with "Revolt of the Daughters." With professions that might feed her creativity barred to her and virtually no other viable path open, Rosina undergoes a transformation from embodied character to idealized image, dying upon her invalid's couch in a death scene worthy of any consumptive Victorian heroine. Consider the language Robins uses to describe Rosina on her deathbed, "What tiny little hands she had! Her face, with the small, regular features, was even unusually pretty to-day. Her creamy skin had that look common to her type, as though a soft light shone behind it – that pale, luminous quality which is the peculiar compensation of complexions that are very fine, and yet not fair or ruddy. No one ever saw that light in a face of 'lilies and roses,' but these for whom it shines are not bereft of beauty" (196).

The resulting death scene is the quintessence of high-Victorian sensibility, a response underscored by a review in the *Chronicle* that described Rosina's life and death as filled with "painful pathos."[10] Yet, this scene depicting Rosina's death is also the most subversive moment in Robins's novel, for she turns the code of the passive consumptive askew so that it registers less as an illustration of peaceful apotheosis and more as proof of the failure of patriarchy. This repetition of a

[10] The longer excerpt reads: "Rosina, the daughter of 'George Mandeville' and her husband, is a beautifully drawn and touching figure, both in childhood and girlhood. The defensive alliance that springs up between her and her father is admirably imagined, and several of the scenes between them – notably the episode of the nigger doll and Rosina's discovery of the secret of the box-room – are touched with a restrained yet almost painful pathos. So vivid indeed is our sympathy with Rosina that we cannot but wish that the author had found some means of letting her live, though her death is doubtless the artistic culmination of the tragi-comedy" (*Chronicle*, July 24, 1894).

literary trope in a way that refuses to conform to familiar ideological registers nicely engages Judith Butler's concept of subversive repetition. Nancy Cervetti notes that similarity offers a form of recognizability; at the same time "a subversive repetition disrupts old ways through differences in tone, in recontextualization and location, and in deviant endings. A repetition with a difference displaces the old through ambiguity, irony, hyperbole, parody, and dissonance" (4). Robins's ending to *George Mandeville's Husband* operates in just this manner.

I've already noted that Rosina dies in a pool of blood, and given the undercurrent of whispered conversations, the scarlet stain on Rosina's white bed sheets resonates with sexual meaning. It is not particularly innovative to imbue a death scene with sexual implications, particularly for the Victorians. It is innovative, however, to undercut the erotics of such a scene by averting the reader's gaze from the death itself. When Rosina dies, both Ralph and the reader are in George Mandeville's parlour, entertaining her "insufferable" literary throng. Rosina's death is narrated not by the sometimes-present narrator or through the more common focalization of Ralph, but by the great lady of popular rubbish herself, George Mandeville.

In her hands, Rosina becomes nothing other than representation, her image adjusted to fit her novelist mother's purposes. In essence, Rosina transforms from biological child to textual child, a move depicted in the novel as unjust and dehumanizing, although, ironically, Lois confers upon Rosina the iconicity of celebrity. George Mandeville's idealized stories erase the conflicted relationship between Lois and Rosina and create, instead, an account of perfect love between mother and daughter (as well as a daughter whose unruly brown hair has suddenly become flaxen and ringletted). Though whitewashing through memory is surely common as human experience, Robins emphasizes that George Mandeville's fictionalization of her daughter tragically erases the "real" Rosina. Unlike a character in a book who can live in "a thousand homes" where there is "still some sign of them" in the material reality of the book itself, Robins notes, Rosina is truly gone in both body and memory, particularly since George Mandeville's evocation of Rosina is discursive and never fixed in a published characterization (219).

In these final images, Robins offers a different, and more insidious, version of the death of the innocent, for this girl's end figures as a tragic waste, built upon the sandy foundation of vanity and weakness. Her legacy in memory is unstable, and her life is overshadowed by her mother's textual children. We also see a different orientation of the text as child than that suggested by Cholmondeley or Broughton. Whereas Hester and Emma consider the "child of the brain" more real (and thus more tragically dead) than a child of the body might be, Robins suggests that the dead child of the body experiences a finality in mortality that a textual character, who can live on in the material reality of books, never quite possesses (though, of course, the irony here is that Rosina comes to us as fiction in Robins's own textual child). As it is depicted in the novel, however, Rosina's complete erasure—both in being misunderstood during life and in her reappropriation as a heroine after death—is her true tragedy. It's a tragedy made all the more poignant by the self-awareness, the ability to read her own suffocation, that Rosina possesses. To finally die not because she is too sweet, good, and pure for this world—the standard fate of the Victorian heroine—but because she has been ill-prepared and disallowed from any kind of meaningful activity, must strike the reader as an injustice most foul.

So not only does Robins engage in subversive repetition through this death of the consumptive, which works against Victorian idealizations of illness, she participates in a subversive repetition by seeming to revere motherhood, only to finally undercut it. We see the character of George Mandeville/Lois Wilbraham failing as both artist and mother, and we also witness her daughter failing to mature into adolescence. In effect, by refusing her mother, Rosina refuses to mother, and her impending puberty—signified by the menstrual blood that marks her as ready to uphold the symbolic weight of a fecund female body—gives way to physical collapse and a final hemorrhage into death. Though it is significant that Robins both points to and effaces Rosina's development into a body capable of bearing children, it is, ultimately, more significant that, in killing the character, Robins refuses to represent Rosina's life.[11] She kills her off rather than let her be co-opted by Ralph Wilbraham's beliefs, which disallow meaningful work for women, or a larger social order that idealizes and disempowers women, in effect, depriving then of personhood and turning them into text.

Deviant Endings: Economies of Difference

The novels I examine here offer a range of representations of the professional and famous woman writer, what she looks like and how her work should be valued, all conveyed through the "cult of motherhood." As I have noted, each novel differently imagines author-characters who conceive and birth their child texts, only to see those children die (whether through murder, neglect, or outright infanticide). For *Red Pottage*'s Hester the author is represented as physically feminine but intellectually masculine. Her textual child is misunderstood and ultimately murdered, leaving the author/mother shaken and mourning, consolable only by same-sex friendship. For *A Beginner*'s Emma, her own body is refined, whitened, and elite, but her

---

[11]   I borrow this concept from Catherine Wiley, who notes Robins's refusal of representation in her 1893 play *Alan's Wife* (co-written with Florence Bell, though produced and published anonymously). Indeed, across the Robins canon, it is a common device for her to refuse to represent a controversial topic or theme, even as she insists that the reader acknowledge its presence. In Robins's 1894 unpublished play *The Mirkwater*, for instance, Robins leads us to believe that Felicia Vincent may well be responsible for her never-represented sister's disappearance, but ultimately, though obliquely, we learn that the sister weighted herself with stones and threw herself into a river when she discovered she had breast cancer. We see this same technique at work in *The Convert* (1907), Robins's novelized version of the stage play *Votes for Women* (1907). In both, Vida Levering crusades for suffrage, but only after Robins has made clear that she carries some mysterious secret from the past. We discover in elliptical references that she was seduced, impregnated, and lost the child, whether through miscarriage, stillbirth, or abortion we don't know.

textual baby is hideous. Emma must be coerced into offering her deformed baby to a funeral pyre in a public rite of symbolic cleansing. Her "reward" for doing so is realignment with heteronormative codes through promises of a "real" husband and "real" children. In *George Mandeville's Husband*, the characterization of George/Lois heightens the tension between author and mother roles. She is the only biological mother of the three characters considered here, yet she is also the least sympathetic character. Her yellowed fingers, her over-large body, her loudness and indiscreet behavior all signify excess. Her appropriation of a male pseudonym, primary role as breadwinner, consequent emasculation of her husband, and "unearned" celebrity equally suggest a mannish "unnaturalness," underscored by her complete lack of what all women are supposed to instinctively know: how to mother. George Mandeville's self-absorption leads to her biological daughter's death, a death she exploits by turning her daughter's memory into idealized fiction.

So, given this range in which none of the author-characters here ultimately come off well or produce literary or biological children who are allowed to remain alive, how can I argue that these representations are ultimately salutary? I do so because whether the author/mother characters be murderess, monster, or naïf, the sheer range of possibility problematizes a seemingly monologic sign system. The representations here redefine both motherhood and womanhood, two roles intertwined at this time, and supposedly so natural that no clear articulation of their meaning is necessary. In so doing, these representations interrogate unmarked categories, ultimately giving the power for definition to the author behind the author, to Cholmondeley, Broughton, and Robins.

In these novels, the representation of mothering alters who mothers (and by extension women) are, what they look like, and what they do. Since, as E. Ann Kaplan notes, mothers are everywhere in filmic and literary texts, yet are rarely discussed and so comprise an absent presence, the mother figure, much like the celebrity, carries meaning that often operates free of cultural scrutiny. My objective in this chapter has been to show how three fin-de-siècle authors exploited this familiar yet often unexamined sign of the mother by joining it with the author, extending it through the child/text, and contesting the naturalness of "natural" categories. As such, these books perform a subversive repetition that expands (and explodes) binaried sex/gender categories, undermining monologic narratives and laying the ground for pluralistic identities and outcomes. These outcomes are not actualized in the conclusions of the texts themselves but, I believe, in the minds of the readers who are invited to interrupt "naturalized" presumptions about gender and sex differences as guided by a new multivalent form of "natural woman," the famous professional author. Ultimately, analysis of the text-as-child trope offers information on how these three often over-looked authors configured new agency for women, joining their texts with other late-Victorian conversations aimed at establishing new options and ideologies.

Conclusion:
Doing Her Level Best
to Play the Man's Game:
Literary Hermaphrodites
and the Exceptional Woman

Amongst our most renowned women, are some who say with their whole heart, "I would rather have been the wife of a great man, or the mother of a hero, than what I am, famous in my own person." A woman's own fame is barren. It begins and ends with herself whilst when reflected from her husband or her son, it has in it the glory of immortality – of continuance.

—Eliza Lynn Linton, "Wild Women: As Politicians," 1891

Let men, above all, ask themselves with regard to women – to wives – this question – and answer it in a manly, honest manner, whether it is condemnatory of their own "line of conduct" or the contrary: Should I be willing to endure what I expect my wife to bear, were I a woman and a wife? If not – is it just, or right, or manly, then, for me to expect if of her?

It is needless to say that this is the last question asked; and this is the root of all the evil. This making by men a broad easy road of license for themselves, while women are clogged, fettered, penned in, worried, harassed and unjustly treated, till even they – "become dangerous."

—Fanny Fern, "English Notions About Women"
(Ginger-Snaps 92–3, italics in the original)

On March 11, 1911, *The New York Times* announced a new play, staged to support women's suffrage, that would co-star "Miss Jane Austen, distinguished for her years, character, and social position." Another starring actress, Mrs. John Winters Brannan, confided to the paper that, "it was only the comforting presence of the sedate and conservative Miss Austen that is sustaining her [through stage fright]." The paper continued, "Miss Austen spends her life quietly in the country, but will be brought to town for her debut." Miss Austen, the paper soon revealed, was a 15-year-old black and tan terrier, with "an aristocratic little head, a funny little tail, and now, in her mature years, a comfortable broad back like that of a circus horse" ("Dog" 9). The paper's joke, then, was that the literary fame represented by the august Jane Austen could so easily, and amusingly, be appropriated by a little dog.

I use this anecdote to illustrate a different point, made evident through the feature's title: "Dog to be a Star in Suffrage Play: Miss Jane Austen to Show How to Gather Contributions at Benefit Matinee." It is not just an American dog named for a great English author of the past, but the star power of Jane Austen's name linked to suffrage that strikes me as relevant to how celebrity can act as a transatlantic political tool to effect change. In this case, once the headline has done its work and the purple, green, and white suffrage league decorations of the performance hall have been duly described, the piece turns to a thoughtful commentary on votes for women. The paper quotes a patron, John Bigelow, who as a veteran diplomat, former Ambassador to France, and long-term advocate of women's suffrage, was himself a bit of a celebrity.[1] Bigelow had written to Mrs. Brannan, saying:

> I never saw any good reason why I was permitted to vote and my mother was not, if she cared to.
>
>   Neither do I see any reason why the ballot box should be withheld from your sex under any government which has espoused the doctrine of popular sovereignty. That was the position I maintained in our last State Constitutional Convention, and I voted both in the committee and in the convention to strike out the word "man" from the constitutional provision which confers the elective franchise.

Including this passage from Bigelow's letter to Brannan allowed the *Times*, even if unintentionally, to further the cause of women's suffrage under the auspices of women's news (published here, some nine pages into the Sports section). But I would argue that leading the article with the terrier, Miss Austen, also accomplished political work, since her name alone—even when attached to a dog—drew a popular attention that conflated woman's fame with political change.

      Throughout *Women and Literary Celebrity in the Nineteenth Century*, I have argued that the public visibility that coalesces into literary celebrity could often pose a gender problem, since celebrity threatened to code Anglo-American women who undertook careers in literary production as aggressive, ambitious, and, worst of all, un-sexed. As the Victorian best-selling author Marie Corelli would say with exasperation in the introductory note to *The Murder of Delicia* (1896):

> The woman who paints a great picture is 'unsexed'; the woman who writes a great book is 'unsexed'; in fact, whatever woman does that is higher and more ambitious than the mere act of flinging herself down at the feet of man and allowing him to walk over her, makes her in man's opinion unworthy of his consideration as a woman; and he fits the appellation of 'unsexed' to her with an easy callousness, which is as unmanly as it is despicable. (viii)

In examining the gendered dynamics of literary celebrity, I have also aimed to show that literary fame could offer a resource for change. As the above epigraph indicates, authors such as Fanny Fern, Elizabeth Gaskell, Margaret Oliphant, Elizabeth Keckley, Eliza Potter, Elizabeth Robins, and Mary Cholmondeley were deeply, if differently, invested in awakening their transatlantic readers to the need

---

[1]   See "Woman Suffrage Advocates; John Bigelow's Plea for the Women – Discussion Goes on To-night." *The New York Times*, August 15, 1894: 8.

for revised opportunities for women, and the representation of fame offered them a prime tool for doing so. The professional authors I have examined in *Women and Literary Celebrity in the Nineteenth Century* each undertook in separate ways to rewrite women's options by using the unlikely catalyst of literary celebrity. In doing so, they waged war with a broad range of cultural stereotypes that positioned the famous female author in a metaphorical straitjacket, bound by images of angelic purity on one side or monstrous and masculine excess on the other, or, as Figure C.1 suggests, as hopelessly foolish even in the context of her ability to earn money. In this conclusion to *Women and Literary Celebrity in the Nineteenth Century*, then, I want to turn my attention more fully to the metaphoric battle of gender waged through the figure of the famous woman, suggesting, in turn, how celebrity keyed into a larger transatlantic warfare of politics and language, each feeding a complicated campaign for women's emancipation and enfranchisement.

Gender Masquerade: Is the Famous Authoress "Three parts man" or is She Merely Cross Dressing?

Although an old-guard establishment might have been reassured by the palliative that women could never possess genius and so would forfeit whatever public attention they might have acquired to the quicksands of time and memory, many cultural critics were deeply unsettled by female fame and sought to pull it out by its roots rather than allow it to spread like kudzu across the marketplace of ideas. One strategy for doing so was to position ambitious and visible women as unsexed monstrosities. Eliza Lynn Linton, for instance, published several anti-suffrage articles in *The Nineteenth Century* in which she decried those publicity-seeking "wild women" who were a travesty to their sex. They are, she wrote, "political firebrands" and "moral insurgents," who violate the "sweetest qualities of their sex" and thus must be thought of not as errant women but as "unnatural creatures," who have not "'bred true'" ("The Wild Women: As Politicians" 79). "There is in them," Linton cautioned, "a curious inversion of sex, which does not necessarily appear in the body but is evident enough in the mind." Wild women were "quite as disagreeable as the bearded chin, the bass voice, flat chest and lean hips of a woman who has physically failed in her rightful development" (79). In fact, claimed Linton, not only were they as disagreeable as these "inverts" of sex, they were morally and physically worse because their otherwise feminine looking bodies made their masculinized minds all the more subversive.

Literary critics used a similar strategy to undermine the gender/sex legitimacy of women-authored fiction. As just one of many examples, in 1895 the British literary critic George Saintsbury questioned the legitimacy of Charlotte Brontë's genius and fame, arguing that it was precisely her feminine powers of representation that barred her from the halls of greatness. "I do not think that she was exactly what can be called a great genius," he wrote, "or that she would ever

Fig. C.1   "Husband of Popular Author." *Life*. February 18, 1904, 169.

have given us anything much better than she did give; and I do not think that with critical reading Jane Eyre improves, or even holds its ground very well …. [I]t is to me a very suspicious point that quite the best parts of Charlotte Brontë's work are admittedly something like transcripts of her personal experience" (159–60).[2] Despite holding *Shirley* and *Villette* in higher esteem than *Jane Eyre*, Saintsbury could not help but grimace at the "rather fatal note of the presence and apparent necessity of the personal experience" (161). This "fatal note" diminishes Brontë's texts, Saintsbury argues, and makes her writing a portrait of her own experience rather than a creative artifact (and just for good measure, Saintsbury contends, George Eliot does the same). To this Saintsbury adds his most damning and gender-essentialist blow: "Neither of them [Charlotte Brontë nor George Eliot] seems to have had in any great degree the male faculties of creation and judgment" (164).

Coming late in the century, Saintsbury's opinions continue to reinforce the biases about literary genius and fame I articulated in Chapter 1: women artists were largely thought blocked from the sacred and masculine realm of genius because they seemingly did not possess the faculty, always coded male, for creation and judgment. Were either Brontë or Eliot to possess such an ability, Saintsbury suggests, they would not be geniuses, but freakish man-women, or literary hermaphrodites, in that they would be biological women who possess what were considered to be biological male qualities. To Saintsbury and many others, such hybridity of form and ability created a species too monstrous to consider. Surely, the charge that educated and New Women had become "unsexed" was in large part attributable to new social opportunities for women that arose in a nineteenth-century transatlantic context and that put them in some contested position to conventional gender/sex designations. This would explain why M. Eastwood describes the New Woman in 1894 as masculinized for the way she "cultivates man's pet vices, drives four-in-hand to the races and snaps her fingers in the face of respectable Mrs. Grundy" (qtd. in Ledger *Fin de Siècle* 91). It would also explain charges that the professional and famous female author is often perceived as "three-quarters man," as Fanny Fern complained in the 1860s (qtd. in Warren *RH* 371).

George Eliot's infamous article "Silly Novels by Lady Novelists" complicates this idea of writing as a transgression that speaks of a larger gender/sex crime. Eliot derides the "feeble" language of women's writing, saying it is an "absurd exaggeration of the masculine style, like the swaggering gait of a bad actress in male attire" (328–9). She points to this imperfect masquerade not to argue that women should stop writing, but to make clear that their work will always be "insipid" if they are deprived the education and experience that make literary production significant. If women are allowed the privileges accorded to men, and if they "exercise patient diligence, a sense of the responsibility involved in

---

[2] See Loeffelholz's "Mapping the Cultural Field" for a discussion on female genius at mid-century that conflated female artistic talent with the daily chores of household maintenance (141).

publication, and an appreciation of the sacredness of the writer's art" (319), they can, she argues, "produce novels not only fine, but among the finest" (320). She maintains, however, that "incompetent" women, who do not uphold sufficiently "rigid requirements" of style and substance, will never produce anything other than silliness. Eliot thus argues that the "incompetent" practitioner can never authentically produce the "masculine style." She equally reifies the notion, moreover, that quality artistry will resolutely be coded masculine, suggesting in this case that the literary hermaphrodite must also be a drag king who can go about the world, as Elizabeth Robins would say, playing the manly part.[3] In all, the contortions mapped onto gender/sex identity may well have provided what Daphne Brooks has theorized as a nineteenth-century transatlantic fascination with "corporeal contradiction" that reveled in the anomaly of a woman's body costumed (or culturally draped) in masculinity "yet retaining putatively inherent womanhood" (170).

A Return to George Mandeville

To augment this discussion on how conceptualizations of gender and sex are challenged through representations of literary celebrity, it is helpful to consider again Robins's *George Mandeville's Husband*, particularly the figure of fame created through Robins's embodiment of her author-character Lois Wilbraham/ George Mandeville, as well as some of the American and British reviews commenting on the novel, since they highlight the cultural tensions mapped out in the relation between transatlantic literary professionalism, gender, and celebrity. As I detail in Chapter 5, Robins's writing (anti)-heroine, George Mandeville, is drawn as obese and overbearing, suggesting that the physical form of the woman is a direct result of her writerly practice (and sometimes vice versa), an idea inversely similar to the conflation of text and character in Oliphant's *The Athelings* discussed in Chapter 3. In *George Mandeville's Husband*, Ralph Wilbraham, the husband the title refers to, offers the point of view from which the reader is invited to observe the character of the famous author, George Mandeville. Ralph looks at his wife's "large florid face and shrewd yellow eyes" and wonders "that eight years should have made such a difference in the fine young woman he had married. 'It's that damned writing that has changed her! Women weren't made to spoil their eyes and their figures scribbling idiotic yarns'" (14). The fact that this famous author's behavior is focalized through Ralph and then told through an implied male author who might also be male, suggests a masculine authority that is (seemingly) justifiably outraged at a female author-character who refuses to submit to gender appropriate behaviors.

---

[3]   Literal cross dressing was actually a strategy devised for greater mobility by many actresses and authors, as well as a featured element of stage performance. See Daphne Brooks's *Bodies in Dissent*.

A reviewer for the London-based *Lady's Pictorial*, clearly unnerved by the repulsiveness of George Mandeville, asked in print, "But where has C.E. Raimond [Elizabeth Robins] come across such a woman? Not in the best society in London, surely, for in it, George Mandeville would not be tolerated for an hour; and, as each literary clique in London claims to be *the* very best, the logical inference is that George Mandeville does not exist."[4] Ann Ardis's theorization of the New Woman suggests such obvious fictionalizing offered an important distanciation to the figure of the empowered woman, who possessed extra-domestic interests and capacities. Ardis argues that to identify an idea or image as "literary" rather than as something "real" is to "quarantine it, in effect: to isolate it in a special corner of life, to box it off as a special kind of phenomenon, not something one encounters in society at large" (*New Women* 12). She cites an 1895 article in London's *Athenaeum* arguing that the "'New Woman' is a product oftener met with in the novels of the day than in ordinary life, where, fortunately, she remains so rare as to be seldom seen in the flesh at all" (*New Women* 12–13).[5] Though the New Woman, then, might have seemed more fictional than actual, when it came to *George Mandeville's Husband*, a newspaper like The *Dundee Courier* (of Dundee, Scotland) praised the novel's portrait of feminized fame, saying George Mandeville was not exaggerated but a faithful portrait. The Dundee reviewer, moreover, also praised C.E. Raimond's courageous punishment of obnoxious literary women: "The worship of the New Woman is so universal in fiction now that it is quite refreshing to come across a book like C.E. Raimond's *George Mandeville's Husband*, which places the Woman Writer in anything but a favourable light."[6]

The Lady's Pictorial, considering C.E. Raimond a man, equally applauded him for creating such an "obscene portrait" of a famous authoress, which this reviewer

---

   [4] *Lady's Pictorial*, August 25, 1894. One reviewer's derision of George Mandeville bordered on the paranoid. He wrote, "We are all like the wretched husband who painted furtively in the box-room, to the great wonder of his own daughter, while the terrible woman who called herself George Mandeville was writing the third volume below …. It seems to us that we are in the box-room too, writing this article in a panic … [T]he satire is a savage retaliation, to be appreciated only by men who have been put into their proper places by the irresistible enlightenment of woman about all the mysteries of life" (*Illustrated London News*, September 8, 1894). Unless otherwise indicated, reviews of *George Mandeville's Husband* come from the Elizabeth Robins's scrapbooks, housed in the Robins archive at the Fales Library at New York University. Materials relating to *GMH* are found in the 1894 scrapbook, Series Eleven, Subseries A, Folder 8. All subsequent citations will give the dates of the reviews and the names of the periodicals only.

   [5] Sally Ledger similarly reads the New Woman as a plural signifier. She writes, "The New Woman as a category was by no means stable: the relationship between the New Woman as a discursive construct and the New Woman as a representative of the women's movement of the fin de siècle was complex and by no means free of contradictions. The gap between ideological projection and social praxis was often considerable. Even within discourse the New Woman was not a consistent category" (23).

   [6] *Dundee Courier*, August 1894.

perceived to be an important restoration of male authority. Other reviewers, also perceiving the author of *George Mandeville's Husband* to be male, praised the corrective representation offered by the book. The *Gazette*, for instance, lauded the "reason" in the novel, claiming, "Readers who have become tired of the predominance of 'the New Woman' in modern fiction will lay down *George Mandeville's Husband*, by C.E. Raimond, with a sense of gratification that at last that erratic and unloveable creature will be able to see herself as others see her."[7] The *General* of Providence, Rhode Island, concurred, noting the novel "is a scathing arraignment, and a well-deserved one. We respectfully commend it to Mrs. Sarah Grand and others of her kind; though nothing will do them good."[8] In these responses to *George Mandeville's Husband*, we can see the ways in which the figure of the famous author (lightly veiled as the New Woman) is both contained and amplified, George Mandeville's "obscene portrait," produced in London by an American-born Robins, greedily gobbled up on both sides of the Atlantic and made to discipline the excesses of that New Woman extraordinaire, Sarah Grand.

The enigma of the author's sex, hidden as it was behind the pseudonym C.E. Raimond, heightened the gendered tensions connected to the reception of the book. As we can see above, if C.E. Raimond were a man, the book clearly rebuked the aggressive and publicity-seeking authoress it depicted, a stand-in for the New Woman. If C.E. Raimond were a woman, however, the novel could not so easily be read as a wholesale condemnation of the New Woman, and reviewers were at a loss as to how to explain the unsympathetic portrait of George Mandeville. The San Francisco *Argonaut* dealt with such concern by attributing to C.E. Raimond ontological femaleness but a rare form of masculine talent:

> It may be that *George Mandeville's Husband*, by C.E. Raimond, marks the beginning of a reaction against the New Woman, and the "Heavenly Twins," and the rest of it .... Curiously enough, the thought obtrudes itself that the non-commital pseudonym, "CER" – it is acknowledged to be an assumed name – conceals a woman, but a woman of rare qualities: a masculine breadth of view, a masculine admiration for the womanly woman, and a power of satire such as is given to a few of the fairer sex, but withal a delicacy of sentiment and an intimate knowledge of the emotions and workings of the feminine heart such as woman only could possess.[9]

In this review there is praise for Robins's gender mimicry of conventional codes (in her "masculine" appreciation of a "womanly woman") that is predicated on a reluctance to relinquish cultural designations of masculine and feminine, but we also see a willingness to allow a female C.E. Raimond the possession of masculine powers of discernment and satire. In this case, to imagine C.E. Raimond as capable

---

[7]   *The Gazette*, July 31, 1894.
[8]   *General*, September 2, 1894.
[9]   *Argonaut*, August 27, 1894.

of literary hermaphroditism, is to code him/her as exceptional (not like the rest of us) and so non-threatening because rare.

Some of the reviews of the period, however, show the manner in which the caricatured representation of the famous author in George Mandeville allowed for the articulation of a feminist message. I quote a rather long passage from a review in the London-based *The Chronicle* called "Pioneering Backwards" because it nicely demonstrates the degree to which George Mandeville's excessive embodiment made of her a most alarming figure of fame:

> As a work of art [*George Mandeville's Husband*] suffers by the author's determination to be a satirist first, an artist only in the second place. There is a touch of positive ferocity in the portrait of Mrs. Lois Wilbraham, the lady novelist and champion of the New Womanhood, whose husband is, if we may put it so, the passive hero of the story …. So persistently are the dice cogged against the hapless "George Mandeville" that one comes at last to sympathise with her and rather to take her part. She "already weighed twelve stone six" before her marriage; as to her later years statistics are not vouchsafed, but we are given to understand that "her bulk" was elephantine. She is seldom mentioned without some epithet designed to make her grotesque or repulsive. She is "a large uncorseted woman in a faded flannel dressing-gown," a "stout, frowsy, blowsy vision." She has "shrewd yellow eyes," and in moments of emotion her "large florid face" turns "a fine brick-red." Even her hands are not spared; they are "fat and boneless." Her novels, of course, are utterly contemptible, her play a dismal absurdity. Never once in the whole course of the narrative is she suffered to say or do anything kind, dignified, "seemly" or even sensible. She is egoism, vanity, and obtuseness incarnate. The author may perhaps reply that she is always looked at through the eyes of her suffering husband, and that the very purpose of the story is to show how, through her "strong-minded" neglect of the small decencies of life and her absorption in the struggle for petty social and literary notoriety, she has "got upon his nerves" until he sees her as something dehumanised and almost monstrous. To this plea one can only answer that, whatever may have been the intention, she is not, in effect, always seen through Wilbraham's eyes, and that at best we can never entirely dissociate Wilbraham from the narrator.[10]

In this passage the critic urges an underdog advocacy among readers, who instead of following the narratorial lead that defiles the woman writer, will take her part as an act of justice and sympathy. Indeed, this reviewer suggests that the more invective heaped onto the figure of George Mandeville, the greater the hyperbole in the descriptions of her corpulence, the more likely the reader will be to champion her. The reviewer actually leads the way in a resistant reading by suggesting that subversion can be encoded into cooperation.

[10]   W.A., "Pioneering Backwards," *The Chronicle*, July 24, 1894. The Pioneer Series is the name Robins's publisher, Heinemann, gave to its new series of one-volume novels. The idea that W.A. may have been Robins's friend, William Archer, is a tantalizing notion, though I have found no information to corroborate such a link.

Although this reviewer reads George Mandeville's excessiveness as evidence of C.E. Raimond's faults, I consider the hyperbole to be evidence of Elizabeth Robins's rhetorical savvy. Robins sets up a caricatured version of a wildly maligned cultural figure, the virago author who claims a manly name, physical size, and popular fame, and who thus dwarfs "common" men. Yet, she launches the attack on this "egoism, vanity, and obtuseness incarnate" in a way, and through a potentially male pseudonym, that encourages the reader to castigate the "real" author's attack as a too-harsh and excessive campaign against the fictional George Mandeville. In other words, Robins can be read as encouraging readers to defend the famous female author-character (George Mandeville) by resisting the implied and unknown male implied-author (C.E. Raimond).

I can't help but imagine Elizabeth Robins's chuckle as she pasted these entries into her scrapbook, for the reviewers' confusion affirms a most extraordinary power: as novelist she can parrot the voice of the dominant masculine culture in a way that evokes praise for her "courage" to offer a "realistic" portrait of that which she is herself, a famous and female literary professional. By depicting characters such as George/Lois and Ralph, who vacillate between the effeminate and the masculine, and by obscuring the novel's (gendered) mode of production, Robins underscores a fluidity of gendered possibilities that could manifest through literary product and celebrated producer. Within the novel, somewhat ironically, though professional writing has transformed George Mandeville's healthy body into a monstrous presence, her robust body is, in fact, sturdier than the delicate weakness of either her slight husband Ralph or her fragile daughter Rosina. This famous author possesses a "female" identity, Lois, now shrouded by a "male" name, George, and in the process has abandoned "innate" maternal and wifely instincts in order to enact a man's behavior in the public sphere. By all accounts, if George Mandeville is not a literary hermaphrodite, it is only because she explodes the gender and sex-based categories that form such a model.

As author, actress, playwright, activist and transatlantic celebrity, Robins demonstrated a keen awareness that a woman's sex places her at a disadvantage in terms of the perceived credibility of her ideas, a fact that compels women to employ, as Robins says, "the old rule of feminine dissimulation" ("Woman's Secret" 4). Robins's feminine dissimulation, much like Fanny Fern's "Uriah Heep policy," involved the elaborate enactment of a gendered femininity seemingly congruent with dominant mandates about women's passivity and subordination, only to use the freedom such underestimation ultimately yielded to grab as much decision-making agency as possible. We can see a further extension of the way that representation served political ends linked to women's rights by turning to a closer examination of two pieces Mary Cholmondeley and Elizabeth Robins would publish in the early years of the twentieth century.

Incommensurate Role Reversals

Would changing positions right the gendered wrongs of the world? Both Cholmondeley and Robins saw the matter in more complex terms than those satirized in these cartoons from adjoining pages of the American political magazine *Puck* (see Figures C.2 and C.3). In 1909 Mary Cholmondeley wrote a satire for the *The Cornhill Magazine* (published in America in *Harper's Bazar*) called "Votes for Men" in homage to Elizabeth Robins's famous 1908 suffragist play *Votes for Women*.[11] Cholmondeley's mini-play is set 200 years in the future, "possibly less," when a woman Prime Minister, Eugenia, kindly condescends to her "little husband," Henry, who eagerly watches the Men's Reinfranchisement League march by their window. "I really can't see," Henry complains to Eugenia, "though you often tell me I do, why men should not have votes. They used to have them. You yourself say that there is no real inequality between the sexes" (748). Cholmondeley's goal seems, as does Robins's in *George Mandeville's Husband*, to be a straightforward role reversal, a way of demonstrating to men what it would be like to be in the position of women. Indeed, Eugenia has a key line in the dialogue in which she informs Henry, "What women must have endured in the eighteenth and early part of the nineteenth century makes me shudder. For if they did not marry they were never spared the ridicule or the contemptuous compassion of men. It seems incredible looking back to realise that large families of daughters were kept idle and unhappy at home, after their youth was over, not allowed to take up any profession, only to be turned callously adrift in their middle age at their father's death, with a pittance on which they could barely live" (753). We hear the echoes of Cholmondeley's own circumstances as well as the arguments put forward in the 1890s by daughters in revolt that I will discuss in the next section.

It is Henry, though, who offers the most incisive commentary on inequity. In contrast to Eugenia's belief that turnabout is fair play, he argues that power systems built on a model of dominance and submission can never be equitable. "Those who have the upper hand cannot be just to those who are in their power. They don't intend to be unfair but they seem unable to give their attention to the rights of those who cannot enforce them.... It seems to be an inevitable part of the rule of 'top dog'" (755). Though Henry and Eugenia resolve not to discuss the matter further, Cholmondeley succinctly lays the issue before the reader: there can be no justice in a system that is committed to binaries of power. As I have noted, ending *Red Pottage* in a non-conventional pairing between Hester and Rachel is one way for Cholmondeley to take a stand against patriarchal values. But it allows her to do so in a way that underscores her gendered credibility by seeming to work in accord with culturally acceptable feminine values. Rachel and Hester

---

[11] "Votes for Men." *Harper's Bazar* 44 (January 1910): 10–12, with original illustrations by F.C. Yohn. It is anthologized in Cholmondeley's final book, *The Romance of His Life*, 1921. Robins's *The Convert* (1909) is a novelization of *Votes for Women*.

NOT BUILT FOR IT.

MRS. LEANDER.— I should be ashamed to be seen in such a suit.
MR. LEANDER.— Well, I should think you would be!

Fig. C.2   "Not Built For It." *Puck*. August 1882, 6.

do, after all, allow Rachel's love interest, Dick, to be part of their twosome, and
Cholmondeley mentions "many children" as part of their collective shared future.

For Robins's part, her 1913 essay, "Woman's Secret," may well offer the best
clue of how to interpret the power dynamics and role reversals that are perceived
as concomitant with women's increasing cultural power and visibility. In this
essay she criticizes the notion that men are solely to blame for women's plight.
To assume "that men have consciously and deliberately initiated all the injustices
from which women suffer … is at once to suppose men more powerful than they
have ever been, and more wrong-headed" (1). As Robins trenchantly notes, laying
the blame of oppression strictly at the feet of men instantiates masculinist power.
Instead, if one suggests that men are also "victims of circumstance" (2), it is
possible to explode the binary that gender essentialism constructs. She suggests a

"TURN ABOUT IS FAIR PLAY."

Fig. C.3   "Turn About is Fair Play." *Puck*. August 1882, 7.

similar idea in *George Mandeville's Husband* in the way that Lois and Ralph are positioned relative to each other. For indeed, both possess and manifest strong, albeit stereotypical, masculine/male and feminine/female qualities. I use this awkward construction to suggest the way that Robins played both with social categories (the feminine or masculine) and with biological sex (the male or female), hence complicating a notion of the natural that underscores such categories as the hermaphroditic. As an example, Lois clearly possesses a biological capacity for motherhood, and Ralph a biological ability to father. In a late-Victorian culture in which an idealized biological determinism held great sway in prescription if not in reality, these are not small factors. Had Lois/George been barren or Ralph been sterile, their manifestation of cross-gender qualities would have more fully cemented them in a role-reversal scenario.

Robins similarly complicates gender codes in "Woman's Secret." "Let us remember," she writes, "it was only yesterday that women in any number began to write for the public prints. But in taking up the pen, what did this new recruit conceive to be her task? To proclaim her own or other women's actual thoughts and feelings? Far from it. Her task, as she naturally and even inevitably conceived it, was to imitate as nearly as possible the method, but above all the point of view, of man" (4). According to Robins, then, it is a pragmatic decision for public authors to choose to give the dominant ideology what it expects. "Contrary to popular impression," she writes, "to say in print what she thinks is the last thing the woman-novelist ... is commonly so rash as to attempt. In print, even more than elsewhere (unless she is reckless), she must wear the aspect that shall have the best chance of pleasing her brothers" (5). And in a line from "Woman's Secret" that must surely be a key to reading *George Mandeville's Husband*, Robins expounds:

> What she is really doing is her level best to play the man's game, and seeing how nearly like him she can do it. So conscious is she it is his game she is trying her hand at, that she is prone to borrow his very name to set upon her title-page. She does so, not only that she may get courage from it to talk deep and go a-swashbuckling now and then, but for the purpose of reassuring the man. Here is something quite in your line, she implies; for lo! my name is "George." (6–7)

Robins suggests here a more complicated version of gender and celebrated authorship than in *George Mandeville's Husband*: the position of the woman literary producer is not the literary hermaphrodite, in which male and female become forged together in one body, but a literary transvestitism that engages in a public and deliberate performance, a willful cross-dressing necessitated in a culture that makes it too dangerous for a woman to tell the truth about her own experience. Note here that the logic is still essentialized in terms of an identity that correlates between sex and gender, so this is not an example of the kind of gender performativity we theorize in a twenty-first-century context but of a gender masquerade, where innate sex/gender identity exists but can only manifest through deliberate artifice. In Robins's construction, the famous woman can only send out messages through the dissimulation of the male game, using the forum that celebrity affords to pretend to play according to the rules so that she might eventually alter them.

The need for this elaborate proficiency for and fluency in the "male game" as a means of securing artistic credibility, is voiced best through the biases of Ralph Wilbraham, who tells Rosina:

> There's never yet been a woman who deserved the name "great." The Shakespeares, the Miltons, the Goethes, the Dantes were men. No woman has ever written a great epic, composed an immortal piece of music or given the world a new idea. If women were ever going to do great, original work, they'd have done it long ago. It's very clear they were not sent into the world for that purpose. There's nothing that a woman can do in art that a man can't do better, and with one-tenth the fuss. (80)

Ralph here imports a common transatlantic Victorian argument espoused in particular by Social Darwinists, such as Henry Maudsley and Francis Galton (Darwin's cousin), who contended in blithe disregard of social conditions that women "suffered no other hindrance to the exercise and evolution of their brains and their intellect than those that are derived from their constitution and their faculties of development" (qtd. in Russett 47). In other words, if women would be geniuses, it was their own physical form, not "superior" men, who held them back.

Since there had been no female Dantes, no "Shakespeare's sister," as Virginia Woolf would term it, logic dictated, just as Ralph here dictates to Rosina, that women were incapable of artistic merit because of their ontological embodiment, in many ways mirroring Elizabeth Barrett Browning's epic poem *Aurora Leigh* (1856), where the budding authoress's cousin, Romney Leigh, tells Aurora that women do not have the passion or intellectual capacities to be serious artists. In Robins's depiction, and as with most of Ralph's statements, these comments are loaded with irony since he is the exemplum of masculine effeminacy and inefficacy.[12] Indeed, though Lois/George clearly assumes the role of villain in the novel, it was Ralph's passive inertia that generated the greatest cultural derision.[13] Rosina tries to suggest that perhaps an exceptional woman like George Eliot is proof that her father is mistaken.[14] "Yes, yes, all women say George Eliot," Ralph responds contemptuously, "and think the argument unanswerable. As if to instance one woman (who, by the way, was three parts man) did more than expose the poverty of their position! I could bring up five times as many examples to prove that female babies were born with two heads" (80–81). Ralph's comments indicate that an exceptional and famous woman, such as George Eliot, is no woman at all, but freakishly both female and male, the form of hermaphrodite we see repeatedly referenced. Ralph is incapable of appreciating the possibility that the kind of hard work needed to produce a piece of art, the very same toil Cholmondeley depicts Hester as doing in the cramped spaces of her attic

---

[12] Five months after the publication of *GMH*, *Vanity Fair* published a long editorial ridiculing a small and timid man in government. Their final insult? He was derided as a "George Mandeville's Husband," a fact Elizabeth Robins noted, circled with her blue china pencil, and pasted into her scrapbook (*Vanity Fair*, October 4, 1894). In 1896, Robins's contemporary, Marie Corelli, suggested that "lazy noodle" men who depended on women for their support were precisely the sort to "run down women's work, women's privileges, women's attainments and women's honour" (*The Murder of Delicia*, vii, viii).

[13] Edward Anthony Spitka underscores the Victorian code against passive men, who are not vigorous members of the working sphere, in his 1908 "Study of the Brains of Six Scientists." In it he forms a hierarchy of the male brain that links to social codes of appropriate masculine behavior, so that those most debased are they who "never remain steadily employed," a conclusion clearly damning to Ralph (qtd. in Russett 223–4). In fact, the only positive response I've read to Ralph Wilbraham has come from twentieth-century scholars, such as Penny Boumelha, who calls him "deserving" and "talented" (166–7). It is perhaps one indication of the lasting pervasiveness of the idea that men are made weak by women's fame and talent that a 2008 biography of Arthur Bell Nichol, Charlotte Brontë's husband of nine months, is titled *Mr. Charlotte Brontë*.

[14] For a helpful rumination on George Eliot and the figure of the exceptional woman, see Deborah Heller's *Literary Sisterhoods* and Jennifer Cognard-Black's *Narrative in the Professional Age*.

bedroom, is within womanly parameters.[15] He intones, "No woman understands the patient, inexhaustible joy of work for the sake of the work. That's masculine my child" (82).[16]

In "Woman's Secret" Robins reveals the transparency of these twin arguments that passionate work is masculine and that it requires a patient fortitude women lack. She raises the encomium heaped upon Anglo-American Victorian women to "Be patient; be patient; and again and always, and down to the dark, mysterious end, be patient" (13). In so doing, she critiques the cultural imperative for female long-suffering (the same self-sacrifice we see Oliphant resisting) at the same time as she inextricably connects to women rather that to men the exacting work ethic Ralph celebrates. The piece as a whole also excoriates the rhetorical move of calling an exceptional woman "sexless" because such a label functions as a warning and reinforces the notion in all "non-exceptional" women that it is "by sex you live." As I've noted in the introduction to this book, Robins here exposes the slippery slope logic of a woman's quick slide out of femaleness that is brought on by talent and fame: "Take heed lest in some unwary hour you, too, become exceptional, and so, by a well-known philological necessity, decline through 'singularity' to 'egregiousness' and 'insolence'" (15). We can hear Robins laughing through the lines of her hyperbole, but the point is a lucid and valid one. The representational backlash against women who move outside of their scripted spaces, making of themselves the exceptional, the freakish, the hermaphroditic, is enough to frighten all other women into submission. Given this, Robins's best attack against the politics of representation is mockery. In this case, these metaphors may not provide us with a direct mirror on historical events and attitudes, but they do reflect the ways in which ideas about gender, artistry, labor, and value were being negotiated.

Both Robins and Cholmondeley would go on to write other pieces that called upon the figure of the famous female author, and these other portraits continue to raise important ideological debates about the professional woman's "nature." As one example, in 1909 Robins wrote, but never published, a novel she called *White Violets* that depicted one woman's desire to become a renowned author.[17] At wits

---

[15]   By all appearances, or in print anyway, Eliza Lynn Linton might have agreed with Ralph Wilbraham. She wrote, "When we think of the length of time it has taken to create all masterpieces—and, indeed, all good work of any kind, not just masterpieces—it is food for wonder to see the jaunty ease with which the scarce educated in art throw off their productions, which then they fling out to the public as one tosses crumbs to the sparrows" ("The Wild Women: As Social Insurgents" 601).

[16]   Ralph's championing of artistic labor for its masculine dividends provides an interesting contrast to Max Nordau's controversial, yet popular, treatise on social evolution, published in *Degeneration* (1895). Nordau categorically denounces most artistic and "criminal types" as degenerate, but he particularly dooms people who are hyper-emotional or grotesque in appearance.

[17]   For an extended discussion of this novel, see Weber "Channeling Charlotte: Woman's Secret, Great Powers, and the Cult of Celebrity in Elizabeth Robins's *White Violets*."

end and in need of cash, Selina Patching calls upon the spirit of Charlotte Brontë to inspire her literary production.[18] Selina is a writer of simple tales for the popular press, but she holds within her the desire to write something bigger, more classic, and more meaningful, the "new *Jane Eyre*." Robins allows for the possibility that Charlotte does indeed commune with her earthly sister Selina, leaving five to six pages of cramped script on Selina's desk every morning. But Robins also interjects a New Woman writer, Barbara—the Wild Child—who does not follow the rules, flirts with whomever catches her fancy, and has a capacious imagination. *White Violets* evokes the span of Robins's own life as it crosses from a Victorian period into Modernism, but perhaps more importantly, it depicts in some detail what it takes for a woman, and her consequent text, to be exceptional in the public eye.

Two scenes bear this out. Selina, the Victorian woman writer, much like her literary grandmothers Elizabeth Gaskell and Jane Austen, works under a model of discretion and invisibility. Rather than adopting the public role of writer, as does George Mandeville, Selina eschews bravado, and believes modesty betokens talent. Robins writes:

> She had heard how it is the little talents that put on the great airs. She knew how especially obnoxious this tendency was when illustrated in the person of a woman. She had not failed to mark in her discursive reading those innocently frequent admissions, scattered so liberally throughout Literature, of men's impatience at women's preoccupation with matters of Art and Learning. She would guard herself against the tendency (supposed to be purely feminine) to magnify her office, or in any way to obtrude the practice of her art; to speak of "my Work" with a capital W; to bristle with pens, to brandish a galley as it were an oriflamme, to go, like some, ink-stained and unashamed. Never should she do any of these things. No room in the Vicarage open to the general eye betrayed the occupation of the woman-writer. Selina raised concealment to a fine art. She covered her tracks as though in writing a story she committed an act of questionable taste. Or at best a deed – it might be, necessary, but unseemly to transact openly, like washing one's body or cutting one's nails. (55)

That Selina restricts her movements and her very identity largely due to "men's impatience" with women's literary involvements is again a way for Robins to raise and critique the representational backlash accorded to "exceptional women."

---

[18]   In 1895 Robins, still writing under the pseudonym C.E. Raimond, authored a short piece called "Miss de Maupassant," whose protagonist woman writer is lovely, enticing, and mesmerizing; she looks like a "Dresden China Shepherdess" (236) and beguiles with her tinkling bracelets (237). In a scene that could be taken from Gaskell's *Life of Charlotte Brontë*, Miss de Maupassant arrives at the offices of her editors, only to find them shocked and amazed that the writer of such bold and daring literature is a woman. This story ends with a twist, though, because the authoress is revealed as a plagiarist and so her textual product is discredited. Though Robins undermines the ethos of her female author figure, she simultaneously raises some compelling issues about imagination and experience while critiquing the publishing profession for its sexist preconceptions.

It also strikes me as significant that the text becomes associated with the stigmatized acts of bodily hygiene that one performs in private, "like washing one's body or cutting one's nails." The text and its construction, in this case, becomes a kind of abject bodily excess that cannot be suppressed but equally cannot be exposed.

Barbara, on the other hand, is nothing if not exceptional and non-private. Our first exposure to her is as she stands, knee-deep in a muddy river, fighting boys to keep them from drowning a puppy. "Miss Patching stared horror-struck at the unseemly spectacle of this girl, with streaming hair, and the visage of an immature Maenad fighting like Fury incarnate. Her pinafore half tore off, mud to the middle – and giving off streams and sprayings of water like some erratic and half-choked fountain" (115). The Wild Child is clearly a brave and willful girl who will stand her ground against masculine brutality. Selina stands impotent on the banks, trying to coax the boys away with the bribe of a penny, and thus suggesting the stark contrast between the decorous Victorian writer and the impulsive physicality of the writer for the coming age. Though one could read the text as a suggestion of Selina's hopelessly old-fashioned ideas, the reader is encouraged to sympathize with her as well as the Wild Child, giving the sense that both writers fulfill important functions. Yet, Selina dies in a swoon at the end of the novel, indicating that it is only Barbara's reckless and masculinized individualism that has the staying power for the twentieth century. In this respect, the Wild Child is no literary hermaphrodite but Fanny Fern's "Coming Woman."

By contrast, Cholmondeley's other extended portrait of a professional female author is one that she constructs of her 18-year-old sister Hester in her family memoir *Under One Roof* (1918). Sometimes assumed to be the model for Hester Gresley in *Red Pottage*, Hester Cholmondeley was also weak in body and strong in intellectual fortitude. Though admitting to often being tempted to draw her characters from life, Cholmondeley disavowed that she used Hester as the model for any of her characters because the "fragile little form had not the strength to stand alone" (xvi). Amazed at her sister's prodigious literary output, Cholmondeley writes, "After her death we discovered that she had left an enormous mass of manuscript, including a diary in many volumes. All her papers she left to me. We were aware in her lifetime that her weak health had diverted part of her indefatigable energy to pen and paper. But only after she was gone did I realize with amazement the vast amount of her literary work, which in bulk would have done credit to an octogenarian" (xiii). It is telling that Cholmondeley prefaces her sister's ideas with these reminders of her ill-health, for Hester's writing itself is strong, opinionated and decidedly "exceptional." Indeed, were she to have lived, she very likely would have rivaled her elder sister's literary fame and production. In the emphasis she puts on the weak writer's body as compensatory to the vigorous properties of the text, Cholmondeley's representation is much like Elizabeth Gaskell's portrait of Charlotte Brontë. Cholmondeley represents her writing sister as a powerful mind made sympathetic through a delicate (and markedly feminized) body. So, as we see her doing in *Red Pottage*, Cholmondeley displaces the threat posed by literary hermaphroditism by erasing Hester's physicality altogether, creating for her not a textually conceived "actual" body but a culturally imagined ideal that borders on complete disembodiment.

It's noteworthy that Percy Lubbock would reinforce a similar trope of the weakened body in his representation of Mary Cholmondeley. "She was," he notes, "a brave woman, helped by no care-free indifference, encouraged by no easy hopes – above all hampered perpetually by a grievous burden of ill-health" (14). Though he makes of her an enigmatic, powerful, removed, and amused woman who bordered on genius, he takes great pains to underscore her physical delicacy, which for him is as much a factor of her class as her gender. For Lubbock Cholmondeley's noble bloodlines cannot be separated from her personality or her profession. He writes:

> The daughter of her race she was indeed to the core of her being. She belonged, she never ceased to belong, to her stock, her county, her England – an England of the English, far beyond earshot of the many strange accents in our hearing today. This tall grave lady, plain-faced, delicately robed, with her thin hands and angular movements, England had made her and had taken long to make her; she had a quality, native, ancestral, that is not to be improvised in brief time. (15)

We can clearly see Lubbock's investment that Cholmondeley's appearance and demeanor be saturated by her Englishness, yet he also seems frankly titillated that given Cholmondeley's ancestral bearing, she would address such controversial issues as adultery and religious hypocrisy. Lubbock wrote of her success with *Red Pottage*, her fifth published book (of eleven), "She was the author of *Red Pottage*; and what did that mean? I think it would still mean much; but it meant at that time a fine cackle of the public, rounds of warm exhilarating notes of dissent, of disapproval and horrification. 'Have you Read Pottage?" we said to each other brightly .... Wasn't she clever, wasn't she cruel? – but wasn't she wise and just? – she was very amusing at all events, and very hard on the clergy: but then – but consider, remember – !" (24). Just what it is precisely that Lubbock would have the reader remember is not clear, but soon after this description of Cholmondeley's fame, he notes what a scandal it was for her to tamper with Britain's "backbone," its middle class (27–8). In his treatment of her, I would argue, the fact of her "noble blood" is made to diminish the possibility of any indiscretion; it's a way for class standing to trump gender indiscretion, but it also inextricably links Cholmondeley to her class. Given this, it's telling that Lubbock divests her with a "large aboriginal simplicity, in which her imagination slowly grew and flowered" (16). The metaphor is apt, for it locks Cholmondeley in seemingly mutually exclusive identity locations: the patrician and proper British woman with the undomesticated mind of the aboriginal. It's a way of making her acceptable and exotic, a conflation of qualities that Cholmondeley may not have been flattered by, but would surely have employed for a character in a book.

This image of the famous author as aboriginal subject confined within the strictures of appropriate womanhood amplifies a number of concerns that women at the end of the century challenged in their published writings. The fact that not all women could or would conform to the mandates of the marriage market was pretty clearly established, but the pressures of that ideology were still operative, as we see in the public dialogue between mothers and daughters that I discuss in the following section.[19]

The Revolt of the Daughter

In January 1894, *The Nineteenth Century* ran "The Revolt of the Daughters," an essay on a phenomenon that began the autumn before: a group of young women, "daughters," had publicly "detailed their intimate and personal home grievances" (23). These complaints were responded to by "mothers," angry at the young women's "burning ingratitude" and eager to set them in their place (23). The "Daughters" essay, authored by Blanche Althea Crackanthorpe, a friend and confidante of Elizabeth Robins, set off a flurry of responses because it took the side of youth and argued against automatic middle- to upper-class conventions (such as sending a boy to university and a girl to dance lessons). At the same time, Crackanthorpe chastised young women for becoming a "hideous product, a non-human thing," which is to say a strident and stubborn campaigner (26). In March 1894, four essays ran in succession, two from "mothers," two from "daughters," all speaking to and around the theme of women's independence and the need for self-determination and self-representation. The last of the four, called "A Reply from the Daughters, II," by Alys Pearsall Smith, succinctly lays out the issues that we see addressed throughout *Women and Literary Celebrity in the Nineteenth Century*, in particular in *Ruth Hall, Red Pottage*, and *George Mandeville's Husband*. Pearsall Smith writes:

> The suffering endured by many a young woman [living as a dependent in her father's household] has never yet been told. Possessing no money in her own right, and obliged to beg, too often from an unwilling father, for all she gets, a girl of character, as she grows into maturity and lives on as a woman in her father's house, suffers from a sense of bitter humiliation that no one who has not experienced it can understand. Many young women under these circumstances would gladly engage in any honourable labour, however menial, that would enable them to be independent and to own themselves. But this, of course, "is not to be thought of for a moment." Could the parents of these daughters ... get a glimpse into the hearts of their quiet, uncomplaining daughters, they would be astonished and perhaps horrified. "What can our daughters want more than they have now?" they would ask .... To such parents I would reply: Your daughter

---

[19]   The anxiety about insufficient numbers of men to uphold a code of marital domesticity is pronounced in the 1890s but present on both sides of the Atlantic throughout the entire nineteenth century. See, for example, Miss Bessie Rayner Parkes's "The Market for Educated Female Labour," published in the November 1, 1859, *English Woman's Journal*, and "Queen's Bees or Working Bees?" an anonymous response published in the November 12, 1859, *Saturday Review*.

wants herself .... She wants to belong to herself. The revolt of the daughter is not ... a revolt against any merely surface conventionalities, ... but it is a revolt against a bondage that enslaves her whole life. In the past she has belonged to other people, now she demands to belong to herself .... She asks simply and only for freedom to make out of her own life the highest that can be made, and to develop her own individuality as seems to her the wisest and best. She claims only the ordinary human rights of a human being, and humbly begs that no one will hinder her. (446–50)

In rhetoric that employs tropes of the abolitionist, Pearsall Smith hammers home several important ideas: daughters have long suffered a "bitter humiliation" in their dependence on men, young women are revolting not against trivial circumstances but against a "bondage" that has robbed them of control over their lives, and a woman is owed, as any "ordinary human being" is owed, the freedom to develop her sense of identity "as seems to her the wisest and the best." That she still "humbly begs" no one to hinder her would strike some as stepping back from the demand for independence and autonomy, but I would suggest Pearsall Smith here demonstrates the use of compromise formation tactics: as Fanny Fern said in the 1850s, it is more efficacious to "pursue the 'Uriah Heep' policy; look 'umble, and be almighty cunning. Bait 'em with submission, and then throw the noose over the will" (Parton 211). Though they may be advocating humbleness, neither Fanny Fern nor Alys Pearsall Smith, in her ardent appeal for emancipation, backs down from her public role as a woman who can and must influence readers.

This form of public influence as manifested in these particular texts through the representation of literary professionalism and transatlantic celebrity is, I would argue, precisely the point of possessing fame at all. For, indeed, though celebrity brings rewards of attention, money, and (perhaps) affirmation, for all of the writers considered here, it also provides a very specific public platform through which to influence conditions for women. At once, these books announce not only a resistance to a standard viewing apparatus but the need for a more heterogeneous gaze that is not circumscribed by its own limited focalization. And though I would consider the counter-hegemonic moves to be insistent and decided through all of the books considered in *Women and Literary Celebrity in the Nineteenth Century*, none of them glorifies nor overtly romanticizes the revolt of women against patriarchal systems. Indeed, as demonstrated in *George Mandeville's Husband*, women who go too fully against the grain are caricatured into gross monstrosity. Instead, these daughters/sisters/lovers speak of a desire to please and even to placate an old guard in rather conventional terms. But when that older regime fails them, these authors become active—learning to negotiate their copyrights and their public image with remarkable savvy. This, in turn, both allows for and requires that the female characters develop skills for their own economic survival as well as new epistemologies that can accommodate complex identity locations where male strength and characteristics are not taken as a given.

These collective representations of the famous woman—her body, her behavior, her ideas—serve to broaden the transatlantic sense of who and what the professional female author might be. The composite representation, in turn, challenged a conventional ideology predicated on the notion of two-part divisions and clear hierarchical governance. Their work interrupted a patriarchal logic by allowing women author-characters to evade the categories that marriage, class, and body size and skin color are "supposed" to establish for them. Though the authors examined here do not erase the category of the gender/sex deviant, they do obscure its meaning, and thus shrug off the damning marginalization implied through the images used to police them, in turn showing quite graphically that a woman has a right to call herself famous.

Afterword:
In Search of the Cult of Charlotte

Throughout this consideration of gender and celebrity in a transatlantic context, Charlotte Brontë figures prominently as a guiding presence. It is, after all, the charge of her own gender/sex anomaly (a woman's body housing a man's passion and genius), as well as a reconstitution of the "exceptional woman," which makes salient the contradictory paradigm that can only be resolved by expanding the capacity to re-imagine what maleness, femaleness, and famous authorship can mean. Because of Charlotte Brontë's continuing influence and presence throughout this reflection on fame, it seems fitting to end this book with a rumination drawn when visiting her home in Yorkshire.

* * *

I have twice been to Haworth, the small Yorkshire town where the Brontës lived and died—the first trip in August 2001 when I was writing a dissertation, and the second journey in July 2008, when I was revising that dissertation into this book. I hardly knew, when I first decided to visit Haworth, how many other literary pilgrims had made a transatlantic journey to gaze upon the Brontës' burial markers in the church or walk upon the moors that gave rise to Heathcliff and Cathy's tempestuous love affair. I only knew that I wanted to see "Brontë-land" with my own eyes, and if in the bargain I could channel literary brilliance, like Selena in Elizabeth Robins's *White Violets*, so much the better.

On my first trip, I started in Manchester, where Elizabeth Gaskell had lived and worked. When inquiring about how to find the place of a museum honoring either Gaskell or Brontë, I was amazed at the repeated blank stares I received from Mancucians. (I received a similar reaction in Norwich when asking for the birthplace of Harriet Martineau. "I've lived here my whole life, and I've never heard of her," said an indignant hotel clerk, as if I were making this Miss Harriet up out of the clean blue air.) In Manchester, though people had certainly heard of the Brontës, none recognized Haworth, less than 100 miles away, giving evidence to Alexis Easley's characterization of literary women as "ghostly" presences who haunt the geographical spaces they used to occupy (see Chapter 2 of *Literary Celebrity*). Elizabeth Gaskell's name rang no bells among the B & B owners, information desk clerks, and money changers with whom I spoke. This is perhaps not a complete surprise given that Victorian literature isn't on the forefront of the average contemporary person's mind, but I was astounded to discover that BritishRail doesn't even run to Haworth directly. If you refuse a bus or taxi, to get to Haworth from Manchester, it is necessary to journey to Keighley and then to climb on a nineteenth-century novelty steam engine, operated by a non-profit collective of train enthusiasts that visits scenic spots in the Yorkshire dells. Arriving in Haworth by steam engine makes for a concrete sense that one is literally traveling backwards in time. Things came to a head on my journey when, finally in Haworth, I overheard a woman at the entrance to the Parsonage Museum identifying Caroline Brontë as the author of "lots of great books. Like *Pride and Prejudice*, for instance." I began to wonder if I were in the right place, and if literary celebrity were as pervasive as I believed. For though distortion is always a part of cultural transmission, I was astounded by the sheer inaccuracy of hearing that Caroline Anybody had written *Pride and Prejudice*! Or that Jane Austen had lived in Haworth.

If you look under B in the Haworth phone directory, you're likely to find a flurry of Brontë-inspired (and Brontë-irrelevant) shops and services before coming to the Brontë Parsonage Museum. Brontë Caravan and Storage, Brontë Aromatherapy, Brontë Home for Old Age Pensioners—each reminds the literary pilgrim, for such I was on that warm summer's day, of both the significance and the banality of fame. A traveler's story often details the contrast between expectation and experience, and mine is no different. Having seen countless pictures and read sentimentalized accounts, I was prepared for the overfull Haworth cemetery, where gravestones crowd together like big crooked teeth in a small mouth. I was less prepared for standing inside the house, in Tabby's room in particular, and seeing tombstones that could easily be touched from the windowsill. But still, the sight didn't rewrite my sense of Brontë-lore, though it did function as a powerful reminder to me that Anne, Emily, Branwell, and Charlotte's weak bodies were probably equally due to a water source contaminated by rotting bodies than the weight of the phallogocentric pen.

Indeed, most of what I witnessed on my 2001 journey to the house and the adjoining museum perfectly meshed with my overall sense of the Brontës, their lives, and their literary works. Of course, it helps that the curators of the museum then leaned so heavily, and so uncritically, on Gaskell's construction of Brontë. If Gaskell were trying to hitch her wagon to a star, as many scholars claim, she surely succeeded in a material fashion at this English tourist attraction where the curious flock to read her documentary accounts of the frail Charlotte, which were blown up into four-foot posters and mounted at key sites in the exhibit. On my return to the museum in 2008, however, Gaskell's influence had been decidedly diminished. I believe Gaskell's lesser role is the consequence of a new curator and several recent books on the Brontës, including Lucasta Miller's *The Brontë Myth*, which is none too enchanted with Elizabeth Gaskell's rendition of Charlotte. Indeed, signs posted in the museum announced that Gaskell "made the most of the tragic aspects of Charlotte's life" and her portraits of Charlotte's father and brother were "unkind" and too frequently accepted as fact.[1]

---

[1]   In 1960, Daphne DuMaurier attempted a similar exoneration of Branwell Brontë, whose own brilliance, she believed, had been unfairly eclipsed by his sisters. She concludes

Under a sign reading, "Who was Charlotte Brontë?" the curator pointedly tells the curious museum patron that, "[Mrs. Gaskell] described a tragic heroine who lived a life of duty and suffering"; whereas, the explanatory note continues, "the real Charlotte was more complex. Her letters reveal her sense of humour and even a bitchy side. She was also strong-minded and ambitious. She was the driving force behind publishing the sisters' poems and braved many rejections before her novels were published." It occurred to me when reading this new signboard attesting to Charlotte's "bitchy side," that the statement actually spoke to a twenty-first-century valor put on professional assertiveness and celebrity. From behind the protection of her great and long-lasting fame, Charlotte is now allowed to be seen retrospectively as having deliberately cultivated such celebrated stature in her own lifetime.

The museum now also puts the lie to Gaskell's contention that Patrick Brontë malnourished his children by displaying an enormous photo-magnification of a piece of Emily's hair, which had been plaited by Charlotte soon after Emily's death into the kind of Victorian memorial hair-jewelry that is both creepy and fascinating. The placard (dated 2006) reads, scientists at Bradford University proved that the Brontë children had a "healthy and balanced diet." But even this is not enough. Conflating the body of the author with the vibrancy of her novel and the electricity of genius, Cornelia Parker, an artist who rendered the slides into photographs, described Emily's hair, saying, "Looking at that plait through an electron microscope, it had such a surprising vitality and energy, as if it were alive."

On both trips, it was only when I exited the museum, re-entering the back garden cemetery, that I experienced a thrill of surprise. There before me were strings of laundry hanging from long lines to all sides of the parsonage: the flapping reds, yellows, and whites of t-shirts and underthings were a powerful reminder of lives still lived practically on top of this second-most visited literary tourist site in Britain (after Shakespeare's home in the Cotswolds). My 2008 journey to Haworth made this sensation of lives and times lived on top of each other all the more visceral. Since on this trip I had three days in which to experience the town and to engage in a writer's retreat (fostered, I hoped, by the spirits of four genii wafting through the winds), I treated myself with a stay at the Old White Lion Inn, not more than 50 feet from the heart of Brontë-central—the Black Bull pub where Branwell drank, the Apothecary where he bought laudanum, the church where all of the Brontës save Anne are buried (she lies along the Yorkshire coastline in Scarborough where she died). And, of course, the Inn is within yards of the house where they lived and worked. All of this is set at the top of a very steep hill, and if the Brontë children were weak of heart and lung, they must surely have had most impressive calf and thigh muscles, for it is truly a hike to get up to their home.

On the third night of my stay in Haworth, I was awakened around 2 a.m. by a piercing siren, which turned out to be the hotel's fire alarm. Grabbing my passport

---

The Infernal World of Branwell Brontë, however, resigned to the fact that he possessed nothing near the talent of his siblings.

and my laptop computer, I rushed into the cobbled streets of a desolate Haworth, the chilly midsummer night air thick with an acrid smoke. Directly beside the inn—and not more than a hundred feet from the Brontë Parsonage, there sat a car engulfed in flames, which shot up easily 20 feet. Tired, disoriented, and many of us literary pilgrims from foreign lands (who did not know how to reach emergency services on our rented mobile phones), we watched helplessly as the flames licked closer to the hotel, threatening all other nearby residences. Would this be the end of Brontë-philia as we knew it? Would I be the last in a long line of literary pilgrims who had come to be inspired by the Brontës' combined triumphs and failures?

Suddenly, from one of the row houses along the side of the road, out burst the proprietor of Mrs. Beighton's Sweet Shop in a flowing magenta and orange caftan, her hands shaking as she lit a cigarette. I have to admit, for a moment I was shocked to see her smoking and in modern dress. Indeed, while the sweet shop does not resort to period costumery, "Mrs. Beighton" does her level best to approximate an old-world ambience where Victorian sweeties are handed down to deserving children. Perhaps even Anne, Emily, and Charlotte tried these lemon drops, you can't help thinking as you suck merrily on their tangy sweetness. In her middle-of-the night twenty-first-century-guise, Mrs. Beighton came rushing out of her shop, frantically calling for the fire brigade. "My car is parked right behind that flaming mass," she exclaimed to us all (expletives here deleted). "It's made of plastic. It'll dead melt." In my middle-of-the-night grogginess, if I were surprised to see Mrs. Beighton smoking and wearing lounge wear, I was even more baffled about her owning a plastic car that was in imminent danger of melting, no doubt running down Haworth's steep streets and alley ways in one sticky glob and finally coming to a steaming halt in the river below the town. By now, joined by others in their night dress, I could hear people complaining in broad Yorkshire dialects, "Where is aught in this poxy place? 'tis no wonder the Brontës died of boredom. We'll all be dead in our beds before long." And, indeed, the fire brigade, like the staff of the hotel where I stayed, had to come all the way from Keighley four miles away, since Haworth, to all but the literary supplicant, held few charms.

Grasping my computer to my chest and watching people sort out the emergency by the light of the burning car, it all brought to mind a scene Eliza Potter describes in *A Hair-dresser's Experience*. Also in the middle of the night, also due to a hotel fire, Potter watches as all of the ladies whose hair and make-up she brilliantly created each day come running into the streets as a hotel burns behind them. Never, she says, had she seen such a mass of ugly and witch-like creatures, aghast at how the façade of beauty slipped in the night. For me, it was not the image of beauty but the façade of a rustic nineteenth-century charm that went up in smoke. In truth, I was more responsible for creating that image of the cozy past than was the woman playing Mrs. Beighton, but these moments of seeing laundry snap in the wind or watching frightened people crowd into the streets of Haworth underscored for me the fragile continuity between now and then, between moments in time laid over one another and experienced in simultaneity.

On both trips, I had come to Haworth expecting to witness unbridled adulation at the force and power of the Brontës' writings, and I did see much of this. But on the whole, the entire experience was remarkably understated. I did feel a shiver run up my spine when looking at the couch on which Emily died, but honestly, the most outrageous thing I saw on either trip was a plaque outside the old apothecary that bragged of being the supplier of Branwell Brontë's opium. This was less shocking to me than the fact that it is now an aromatherapy emporium (where I bought some lovely lavender bath oil). I started both trips looking for pithy insights into the Cult of Charlotte; I ended both trips in total capitulation to my surroundings, rummaging through vintage clothing stores and trying on Edwardian hats; later sitting in the green grass of the village park while children played nearby and I repeated in whispers the inflection of the Yorkshire accent spoken all around me.

All of this adds up to more than a sobering reminder that academic work sets you in a world apart, for this twenty-first-century context offered me an important message of nineteenth-century heterogeneity. After spending years thinking through the complexities built into the representation of the female literary celebrity in the Victorian periods of Britain and America, as I have, it's easy to develop a form of tunnel vision that makes these writers and these ideas seem a dominant element in history. If this experience of flapping laundry and burning stolen cars, of erroneous Caroline Brontës and jam-packed tombstones, did nothing else for me, it underscored a new appreciation for the intensely crowded, and even contradictory, sign systems that are a part of any cultural moment.

Such hybridity was furthered all the more when I had the opportunity to look closely at one of Branwell and Charlotte's tiny juvenilia books. Interspersed in their tales of heroic splendor was a perfectly replicated broadsheet for a horse auction, mimicking the language, style, and form of Victorian periodicals to the level of offering "fine ebony stallions" to "men of force and character." Never having really imagined the Brontës as a particularly jovial lot, I was delighted to see this clear evidence of humor. But more, I was intrigued by the notion that young teenagers trying to create a literary product would include an advertisement as a critical element of that product, thereby blending discourses of the literary and the marketplace, as if to suggest that one is not possible without the other.

Against this backdrop of nineteenth-century heterogeneity and the blending of the creative and the commercial, the achievement of the authors I examine seems all the more noteworthy. For though a general public may look puzzled when a visiting academic asks for Fanny Fern or Margaret Oliphant, suggesting that their respective literary stardom may have dimmed, the work they accomplished by means of their use of celebrity lives on. In these Anglo-American Victorian writers and their crafting of a public sense of what it meant to be both feminine and famous, we see the grounds for constituting what Luce Irigaray has called a female "elsewhere." This "elsewhere" disconnects from a dialectics of power that balances on a fulcrum of domination and submission, instead allowing for difference in both power relations and gender codes. These portraits of literary celebrity suggest that "elsewhere" is not silenced, marginalized, or purely semiotic.

It can be uttered through dominant languages and imagined through dominant epistemologies. The difference we seek is not, therefore, supernaturally conferred or obtained but immanent within any given culture. And the exceptional woman of talent and fame is not a freakish anomaly coded as a gender/sex aberrant, but wholly a part of the culture in which she resides. Sensitive to the registers of the language and ideas that were central to their respective historical moments, the authors I have examined crafted representations that altered ideological codes. In so doing they were not miraculously ahead of their time, but fully enmeshed within it.

Works Cited

Printed Primary Sources

Alcott, Louisa May. *Jo's Boys*. 1886. New York: Bantam Books, 1995.

Allen, Grant. "The Girl of the Future." *Universal Review*. May 7, 1890: 49–64.

Anon. "A few words about Jane Eyre." *Sharpe's London Magazine* Vol. 5 (June 1855): 339–442.

Anon. "Mrs. Sigourney and Miss Gould." *North American Review* 41 (1835): 441–3.

Archer, William. "Introduction to Elizabeth Robins [and (Lady) Florence (Eveleen Eleanor Olliffe) Bell]. *Alan's Wife: A Dramatic Study in Three Scenes*." London: Henry, 1893.

Baker, H. Barton. "Great Writers at Work." *Argosy* 2 (Nov. 1881): 378–82.

Brontë, Anne. *The Tenant of Wildfell Hall*. 1848. London: Oxford University Press, 1982.

Brontë, Charlotte. *Jane Eyre*. 1848. London: Oxford University Press, 1973.

———. *Villette*. 1853. New York: St. Martin's Press, 1992.

Broughton, Rhoda. *A Beginner*. London: Bentley and Son, 1894.

———. *A Fool in Her Folly*. London: Bentley and Son, 1921.

Brown, William Wells. *Clotel, or, The President's Daughter*. 1853. New York: Carol Publishing Group, 1995.

Browning, Elizabeth Barrett. *Aurora Leigh*. 1856. New York: Oxford University Press, 1993.

Byron, Baron George Gordon. *The Works of Lord Byron, Volume 1*. New York: E. Duyckinck and G. Long, 1821: 185.

Caird, Mona. *The Daughters of Danaus*. 1894. New York: The Feminist Press, 1989.

Carpenter, Edward. "The Indeterminate Sex." Rpt. in *The Fin de Siècle: A Reader in Cultural History c. 1880–1900*. Ed. Sally Ledger and Roger Luckhurst. New York: Oxford University Press, 2000.

Castle, Cora Sutton. *A Statistical Study of Eminent Women*. New York: The Science Press, 1913.

"Charlotte Bronte." *Ohio Farmer* (July 11, 1857): 4.

Child, Lydia Maria. *Romance of the Republic*. 1867. Lexington: University Press of Kentucky, 1997.

Cholmondeley, Mary. *Red Pottage*. 1899. New York: Virago Press, 1985.

———. "Votes for Men." *The Cornhill Magazine* (July 1909): 34–43.

———. *Under One Roof: A Family Record*. London: John Murray, 1918.

"Clever Married Women." *Chambers's Journal of Popular Literature, Science and Arts* 853 (May 1880): 284–6.

Coghill, Mrs. Harry (Annie). *The Autobiography and Letters of Mrs. M.O.W. Oliphant, arranged and edited by Mrs. Harry Coghill*. New York: Dodd, Mead and Co. 1899.

Colver, Anne. *Mr. Lincoln's Wife*. New York; Toronto: Farrar and Rinehart, 1943.

[Cooke, Nicholas Francis]. *Satan in Society* (by "A Physician"). 1870. Cincinnati: C.F. Vent, 1876.

Cooke, W.H. "A Winter's Day at Haworth." *St James's Magazine* 21 (December–March 1868): 161–71.

Corelli, Marie. *The Murder of Delicia*. London: Skeffington & Son, 1896.

Crackanthorpe, B[lanche] A[lthea]. "The Revolt of the Daughters." *The Nineteenth Century* 35 (1894): 23–31.

———. "The Revolt of the Daughters I: A Last Word on 'The Revolt.'" *The Nineteenth Century* 35 (1894): 424–9.

Cuffe, Kathleen. "A Reply from the Daughters I." *The Nineteenth Century* 35 (1894): 437–42.

Cullinan, Thomas. *Mrs. Lincoln*. New York: Dramatists Play Service, Inc., 1969.

Curtis, George W. "Charlotte Bronte and the Jane Hyre [sic] Novels," *New York Daily Times*, 1856: 10.

———. "Three Gifted Sisters." *New York Evangelist* (March 6, 1856): 38.

Dall, Caroline Healey. "Ruth Hall." *The Una: A Paper Devoted to the Elevation of Woman* (March, 1855): 42–3.

"Death of Mrs. Oliphant." *Chicago Daily* (June 27, 1897): 10.

"Death of Mrs. Oliphant." *The New York Times* (June 27, 1897): 13.

D'Esterre-Keeling, Elsa. "Charlotte Bronte and her Circle." *Dublin Review* 22 (April 1897): 319–33.

Devotion. Warner Brothers, 1946.

Dickens, Charles. *David Copperfield*. 1850. New York: W.W. Norton & Co., 1990.

"Dog to be a Star in Suffrage Play: Miss Jane Austen to Show How to Gather Contributions at Benefit Matinee." *The New York Times* (March 11, 1911). Sports 9.

Egerton, George. *Discords*. Boston: Roberts Bros.; London: John Lane, 1894.

Eliot, George. "Silly Novels by Lady Novelists." 1856. In *George Eliot: Selected Critical Writings*. Oxford: Oxford University Press, 1992.

"English Realism and Romance." *Quarterly Review* 173 (1891): 486–8.

Fern, Fanny. *Fern Leaves from Fanny's Port-folio*. Auburn, NY: Derby and Miller, 1853.

———. *Fern Leaves from Fanny's Port-folio, Second Series*. Auburn, NY: Miller, Orton and Mulligan, 1854.

———. "Ruth Hall: A Domestic Tale of the Present Time." 1855. In *Ruth Hall and Other Writings*. Ed. Joyce Warren. New Brunswick, NJ: Rutgers University Press, 1992.

———. *Rose Clark*. New York: Mason Brothers, 1856.

———. *Fresh Leaves*. New York: Mason Brothers, 1857.

————. *Folly as it Flies; Hit at By Fanny Fern.* New York: G.W. Carleton and Co., 1868.

————. *Ginger-Snaps.* New York: G.W. Carleton and Co., 1870.

————. *Caper Sauce: A Volume of Chit-Chat About Men, Women and Things.* New York: G.W. Carleton and Co., 1872.

————. "Gail Hamilton – Miss Dodge." In *Eminent Women of the Age: Being Narratives of the Lives and Deeds of the Most Prominent Women of the Present Generation.* Ed. James Parton. Hartford, CT: S.M. Betts & Co., 1872.

Ford, Michael Thomas. *Jane Bites Back.* New York: Ballantine Books, 2009.

————. *Jane Goes Batty.* New York: Ballantine Books, 2011.

Gaskell, Elizabeth. "'My Diary:' The Early Years of My Daughter Marianne." London: Privately Printed by Clement Shorter, 1923 (by permission of copyright holder, Brian Holland, Esq. and his sister).

————. *The Life of Charlotte Brontë: 1857.* Intro by Winifred Gerin. London: Everyman's Library, 1970.

————. *The Life of Charlotte Brontë: 1857.* Intro by Angus Easson. New York: Oxford University Press, 1996.

Gaskell, Meta. "Mr. Brontë Alone, a letter from Meta Gaskell to Mrs. Shaen (EmilyWinkworth), 1857." In *The Brontës: Their Lives Recorded by Their Contemporaries.* Ed. E.M. Delafield. London: Hogarth Press, 1935.

Gaskell, William. "Statement of Public Apology after Publication of *The Life of Charlotte Brontë.*" *Times* (May 26, 1857). Athenaeum May 30, 1857.

"The Gazette on Hair Dressing." Rev. of *A Hairdresser's Experience in High Life* by Eliza Potter. *Cincinnati Daily Commercial* 22 Oct. 1859: n.p.

"The Genius of George Eliot." *Dublin Review* 5:2 (April 1881): 371–94.

Gissing, George. *New Grub Street.* 1891. Oxford: Oxford World Classics, 1998.

Grand, Sarah. *The Heavenly Twins.* London: W. Heinemann, 1893.

————. *The Beth Book.* New York: D. Appleton, 1897.

Greenwood, Grace. *Haps and Mishaps of a Tour in Europe.* 1853. Boston: Ticknor, Reed, and Fields. 1854.

Grein, J.T. "Editor's Preface to Elizabeth Robins's [and (Lady) Florence (Eveleen Eleanor Olliffe) Bell] *Alan's Wife: A Dramatic Study in Three Scenes.*" London: Henry and Co., 1893.

Grimké, Charlotte Forten. *The Journals of Charlotte Forten Grimké.* Ed., Brenda Stevenson. New York: Oxford University Press, 1988.

Hale, Sarah Josepha. *Woman's Record: or Sketches of All Distinguished Women, from "The Beginning" till AD 1850.* Harper & Brothers, Publishers, 1853.

Hamilton, Gail. "Fanny Fern—Mrs. Parton." In *Eminent Women of the Age: Being Narratives of the Lives and Deeds of the Most Prominent Women of the Present Generation.* Ed. James Parton. Hartford, CT: S.M. Betts & Co., 1872.

Harper, Frances E.W. *Iola Leroy, or, Shadows Uplifted.* 1892. New York: Oxford University Press, 1988.

Haweis, M.E. "The Revolt of the Daughters II: Daughters and Mothers." *The Nineteenth Century* 35(1894): 430–36.

Herbert, Paul. "George Eliot." *Nineteenth Century and After, a Monthly Review* 51:304 (June 1902): 932–46.

Jacobs, Harriet A. *Incidents in the Life of a Slave Girl*. 1861. Cambridge, MA: Harvard University Press, 1987.

Jewett, Sarah Orne. *The Country of Pointed Firs*. New York: Houghton Mifflin Co. 1896.

Keckley, Elizabeth. *Behind the Scenes, or, Thirty Years a Slave and Four Years in the White House*. 1868. New York: Oxford University Press, 1988.

Keeling, Anne E. "The Real Charlotte Bronte." *Wesleyan-Methodist Magazine* 120 (Jan 1897): 38–45.

Kickley, Betsey (pseud.) *Behind the Seams: By a Nigger Woman Who Took in Work From Mrs. Lincoln and Mrs. Davis*. New York: The National News Co. 1868.

Larison, C.W., M.D. 1884. *Sylvia Dubois, A Biografy of the Slav Who Whipt her Mistres And Gand her Freedom*. New York: Oxford University Press, 1988.

Lewes, G.H. "The Condition of Authors in England, Germany, and France." *Fraser's Magazine* 35 (March 1847): 285–95.

———. "The Lady Novelists." *Westminster Review* 58 (July 1852): 129–41.

———. "The License of Modern Novelists." *Edinburgh Review* 206 (1857): 155.

Linton, Eliza Lynn. "The Girl of the Period." *Saturday Review* (March 1868): 339–41.

———. "The Wild Women: As Politicians." *The Nineteenth Century* 30 (July 1891): 79–88.

———. "The Wild Women: As Social Insurgents." *The Nineteenth Century* 30 (October 1891): 596–605.

Lubbock, Percy. *Mary Cholmondeley: A Sketch from Memory*. London: Jonathan Cape, 1928.

Lyall, Edna. "Mrs. Gaskell." *Women Novelists of Queen Victoria's Reign: A Book of Appreciation*. London: Hurst & Blackett, Ltd., 1897.

Macdonald, Fredericka. *The Secret of Charlotte Brontë*. London: TC and EC Jack, Book Publishers, 1914.

Mackay, Angus Mason. *The Brontës: Fact and Fiction*. London: Service & Paton, 1897.

Martineau, Harriet. "Death of Currer Bell." *The Daily News* (April 6, 1855): 5.

———. "Obituary Notice" from *The Daily News*, 1855. In *The Brontës: Their Lives Recorded by their Contemporaries*. Ed. E.M. Delafield. London: Hogarth Press, 1935.

"Miss Brontë." *National Review* 5:9 (July 1857): 127–64.

"Mrs. Margaret Oliphant." *Christian Observer* (July 28, 1897): 18.

"Mrs. Margaret O. Oliphant." *The Chautauquan; A Weekly Newsmagazine* (August 1897): 569.

"Mrs. Oliphant as a Novelist." *Blackwood's Edinburgh Magazine* (September 1897): 305–19.

"Mrs. Sigourney and Miss Gould." *North American Review* 41 (1835): 441–3.

Moberly, L.G. "The Reign of Woman." *Argosy* (Feb. 1901): 130–44.

Moore, George. "A New Censorship of Literature." *Pall Mall Gazette* XL (1884): 1.

[Moulton, William U.] *The Life and Beauties of Fanny Fern*. New York: H. Long and Brother, 1855.

"The Mystery of Jane Eyre." *New York Daily Times* (May 15, 1857): 2.

"New Books." Rev. of *A Hairdresser's Experience in High Life by Eliza Potter*. *Cincinnati Daily Commercial* (Oct. 19, 1859): 1.

"New Publications." *The Saturday Evening Post* (May 23, 1857): 3.

Noble, Julie. *Talli's Secret*. Leicester: Matador, 2004.

Nordau, Max. *Degeneration*. Trans. from 2nd ed. of German work. New York: D. Appleton, 1895.

"Notes on Books and Booksellers." *American Literary Gazette and Publishers' Circular* (April 15, 1868): 314.

"Notices of New Works." *The Southern Literary Messenger* (April 1853): 253–356.

Nussey, Ellen. "Reminiscences of Charlotte Brontë." *Scribner's Monthly* 2 (May 1871): 18–31.

Oliphant, Margaret. "Modern Novelists – Great and Small." *Blackwood's Edinburgh Magazine* (May 1855): 554–68.

———. *The Athelings, or, The Three Gifts*. New York: Harper and Brothers, 1857.

———. "The Condition of Women." *Blackwood's Edinburgh Magazine* (Feb. 1858): 139–54.

———. "Novels." *Blackwood's Edinburgh Magazine* (Sept. 1867): 25–80.

———. "Review – *George Eliot's Life as Related in Her Letters and Journals*. Arranged and edited by J.W. Cross." *Edinburgh Review* (April 1885): 514–53.

———. *Janet*. Hurst and Blackett, 1891.

———. *The Victorian Age of English Literature*, Vols I and II. Philadelphia: David McKay, Publisher, 1892.

———. "The Sisters Brontë." *Women Novelists of Queen Victoria's Reign; A Book of Appreciation*. London: Hurst and Blackett, Ltd., 1897.

———. *The Autobiography of Mrs. Oliphant*. 1899. Ed. Laurie Langbauer. Chicago: University of Chicago Press, 1988.

———. *The Autobiography of Margaret Oliphant: The Complete Text*. 1899. Ed. Elisabeth Jay. Oxford and New York: Oxford University Press, 1990.

Parton, Ethel. "Fanny Fern at the Hartford Female Seminary." *New England Magazine* (1901): 94–8.

———. "A Little Girl and Two Authors." *The Horn Book Magazine* 17 (March– April 1941): 81–6.

Parton, James. *Fanny Fern: A Memorial Volume, Containing her Select Writings and a Memoir*. New York: G.W. Carleton and Co., Publishers, 1874.

Pearsall Smith, Alys. "A Reply from the Daughters II." *The Nineteenth Century* 35 (1894): 443–50.

Phelps, Elizabeth Stuart. "A Plea for Immortality." *Atlantic Monthly* 45 (February 1880): 277–80.

————. *Our Famous Women: An Authorized Account of the Lives and Deeds of Distinguished American Women of Our Times*. Hartford, CT: A.D. Worthington & Co., Publishers, 1884.

Potter, Eliza. *A Hairdresser's Experience in High Life*. 1858. New York: Oxford University Press, 1991.

Prideaux, James. *The Last of Mrs. Lincoln: A Play in Two Acts*. New York: Dramatists Play Service, Inc., 1973.

"Revelations of a Fashionable Hairdresser." Rev. of *A Hairdresser's Experience in High Life* by Eliza Potter. *Cincinnati Daily Gazette* (Oct. 19, 1859): 3.

"Review of *A Beginner*." *The Athenaeum* 3471 (1894): 574.

"Review of *The Three Brothers*." *The Contemporary Review* (1870): 316–17.

"A Reviewer Reviewed." Rev. of *A Hairdresser's Experience in High Life* by Eliza Potter. *Cincinnati Daily Commercial* (Oct. 20, 1859): 2.

Riddell, Charlotte E. *A Struggle for Fame: A Novel*. London: Robson and Sons, 1883.

Rigby, Elizabeth (Lady Eastlake). "Jane Eyre by Charlotte Brontë from the *Quarterly Review*, December 1848. In *Notorious Literary Attacks*. Ed. Albert Mordell. Freeport, NY: Books for Libraries Press, 1969.

Robins, Elizabeth. "Woman's Secret." *Way Stations*. New York: Dodd, Mead, 1913.

————. *Whither and How* (unpublished biography) in Fales Collection, New York University. No date.

Robins, Elizabeth (as C.E. Raimond). *George Mandeville's Husband*. New York: D. Appleton and Co., 1894.

————. "Miss de Maupassant." *New Review* 13:72 (January 1895): 233–47.

————. *Below the Salt*. London: W. Heinemann, 1896.

————. *White Violets, or, Great Powers*, 1909. Unpublished manuscript in the Fales Special Collections Library, New York University.

Robins, Elizabeth [and (Lady) Florence (Eveleen Eleanore Olliffe) Bell]. *Alan's Wife: A Dramatic Study in Three Scenes*. London: Henry, 1893.

"Romance of Charlotte Bronte and Her Father's Curate." *New York Times* (Dec. 9, 1906): SM3.

Rowland, Laura Joh. *The Secret Adventures of Charlotte Brontë*. Woodstock, NY: The Overlook Press, 2008.

————. *Bedlam: The Further Secret Adventures of Charlotte Brontë*. Woodstock, NY: The Overlook Press, 2011.

Shelley, Mary. *Frankenstein: The Modern Prometheus* (1818). New York: W.W. Norton & Co., 1996.

"Shirley." *Fraser's Magazine for Town and Country* 55:329 (Mary 1857): 569–82.

Sinclair, May. *The Three Brontës*. London: Hutchinson, 1912.

"Sing at Your Work." *Democratic Standard* (May 13, 1858): 1.

Smith, George. "Charlotte Brontë." *The Cornhill Magazine* (December 1900): 778–95.

Spitzka, Edward Anthony. "A Study of the Brains of Six Eminent Scientists and Scholars Belonging to the American Anthropological Society, Together with a Description of the Skull of Professor E.D. Cope." *Transactions of the American Philosophical* Society 21 (1908): 223+.

Spofford, Harriet Prescott. *Harper's Bazaar* (July 10, 1897): 571.

Stanton, Elizabeth Cady. "Review of Ruth Hall." *The Una: A Paper Devoted to the Elevation of Woman* (Feb. 1855): 29–30.

Stead, William Thomas. "A Life Tragedy: Mrs. Oliphant's Autobiography." *The Review of Reviews* 19 (1899): 498.

Stephen, Sir Leslie. "Studies of a Biographer – Southey's Letters." *National Review* 33 (March–August 1899): 740–57.

Stowe, Charles Edward. *Life of Harriet Beecher Stowe, Compiled from Her Letters and Journals*. Boston: Houghton Mifflin Co., 1889.

Stowe, Charles Edward and Lyman Beecher Stowe. *Harriet Beecher Stowe: The Story of Her Life*. Boston; New York: Houghton Mifflin Co., 1911.

Stowe, Harriet Beecher. *Uncle Tom's Cabin, or, Life Among the Lowly.* Boston: John P. Jewett & Co., 1852.

———. *Sunny Memories of Foreign Lands*, Vols I and II. Boston: Phillips, Sampson, and Co.; New York: JC Derby, 1854.

"Table-Talk." Round Table. *A Saturday Review of Politics, Finance, Literature, Society* (April 11, 1868): 236.

"The Twenty Most Famous Women of the World." *New York Times* (June 15, 1913): M7. *The Washington Post*. Nov 15, 1989: 4.

Willis, Nathaniel Parker. Letter to Sarah Eldredge Farrington, n.d., Sophia Smith Collection, Smith College, no date.

Wilson, Augusta Jane Evans. *St Elmo: A Novel* (1867). New York: Arno Press, 1974.

Wilson, Harriet. *Our Nig, Or, Sketches From the Life of a Free Black: A Novel*. 1859. London: Allison and Busby, 1984.

Woodberry, George E. "Mrs. Ward and the Brontës." *Harper's Bazaar* (Nov. 18, 1899): 979.

Woolf, Virginia. *A Room of One's Own* and *Three Guineas*. 1929. New York: Oxford University Press, 1998.

———. "Professions for Women." *The Death of the Moth and Other Essays*. 1942. New York: Harcourt Brace and Co., 1971.

Zion's Herald. June 30, 1897: 1.

Secondary and Theoretical Sources

Abel, Elizabeth. "Introduction to Writing and Sexual Difference." In *Writing and Sexual Difference*. Ed. Elizabeth Abel. Chicago: University of Chicago Press, 1982.

Adams, Florence Bannard. *Fanny Fern, or, A Pair of Flaming Shoes*. West Trenton, NJ: Hermitage Press, Inc., 1966.

Adams, James Eli. "The Banality of Transgression?: Recent Works on Masculinity." *Victorian Studies* 36:2 (Winter 1993): 207–13.

Adams, Katherine. "Freedom and Ballgowns: Elizabeth Keckley and the Work of Domesticity." *Arizona Quarterly* 57.4 (2001): 45–87.

Adamson, Alan H. *Mr. Charlotte Brontë: The Life of Arthur Bell Nichols*. Montreal: McGill-Queen's University Press, 2008.

Allen, Robert C. *Horrible Prettiness: Burlesque and American Culture*. Chapel Hill: University of North Carolina Press, 1991.

Allot, Miriam. *The Brontës: The Critical Heritage*. New York: Routledge, 1995.

Almeida, Joselyn M. *Reimagining the Transatlantic, 1780–1890*. Aldershot, UK and Burlington, VT: Ashgate Publishing, 2011.

Althusser, Louis. *Lenin and Philosophy and Other Essays*. Trans. Ben Brewster. London: New Left Books, 1971.

Altick, Richard. *Lives and Letters: A History of Literary Biography in England and America*. New York: Alfred A. Knopf, 1965.

———. *Punch: The Lively Youth of a British Institution, 1841–1851*. Columbus: Ohio State University Press, 1997.

Ammons, Elizabeth. *Conflicting Stories: American Women Writers at the Turn into the Twentieth Century*. New York: Oxford University Press, 1992.

Andrews, William L. *Introduction to Six Women's Slave Narratives*. New York: Oxford University Press, 1988.

———. "Reunion in the Postbellum Slave Narrative: Frederick Douglass and Elizabeth Keckley." *Black American Literature Forum* 23:1 (1989): 5–16.

———. "The Changing Moral Discourse of Nineteenth-Century African American Women's Autobiography: Harriet Jacobs and Elizabeth Keckley." In *De/Colonizing the Subject: The Politics of Gender in Women's Autobiography*. Ed. Sidonie Smith and Julia Watson. Minneapolis: University of Minnesota Press, 1992.

Applegate, Debby. *The Most Famous Man in America: The Biography of Henry Ward Beecher*. New York: Doubleday, 2006.

Ardis, Ann. *New Women, New Novels: Feminism and Early Modernism*. New Brunswick, NJ: Rutgers University Press, 1990.

———. "'Retreat with Honour:' Mary Cholmondeley's Presentation of the New Woman Artist in *Red Pottage*." In *Writing the Woman Artist: Essays on Poetics, Politics and Portraiture*. Ed. Suzanne W. Jones. Philadelphia: University of Pennsylvania Press, 1991.

Armstrong, Nancy. *Desire and Domestic Fiction: A Political History of the Novel*. New York: Oxford University Press, 1987.

Auerbach, Nina. "Artists and Mothers: A False Alliance." *Women and Literature* 6 (Spring 1978): 1–17.

———. "Review of The Madwoman in the Attic." *Victorian Studies* 23 (1980): 506.

Bailin, Miriam. *The Sickroom in Victorian Fiction: The Art of Being Ill.* Cambridge: Cambridge University Press, 1994.

Baker, Jean H. *Mary Todd Lincoln: A Biography.* New York: W.W. Norton & Co., 1987.

Baker, Thomas Nelson. *Sentiment and Celebrity: Nathaniel Parker Wills and the Trials of Literary Celebrity.* New York: Oxford, 1999.

Banner, Lois. *American Beauty.* Chicago: University of Chicago Press, 1984.

Barker, Deborah. *Aesthetics and Gender in American Literature: Portraits of the Woman.* Cranbury, NJ, and London: Associated University Presses, 2000.

Barker, Juliet R.V. *The Brontës.* New York: St Martin's Press, 1994.

———. "Saintliness, Treason and Plot: The Writing of Mrs. Gaskell's The Life of Charlotte Brontë." *Brontë Society Transactions* 21:4 (1994): 101–15.

Battersby, Christine. *Gender and Genius.* London: Women's Press, 1989.

Baty, S. Paige. *American Monroe: The Making of a Body Politic.* Berkeley: University of California Press, 1995.

Baym, Nina. *Women's Fiction: A Guide to Novels by and about Women in America, 1820–1870.* Ithaca: Cornell University Press, 1980.

Beer, Janet and Bridget Bennett. *Special Relationships: Anglo-American Affinities and Antagonisms, 1854–1936.* Manchester: Manchester University Press, 2002.

Bellamy, Joan. "A Lifetime of Reviewing: Margaret Oliphant on Charlotte Brontë." *Brontë Studies* 19 (March 2004): 37–42.

Belsey, Catherine. "Constructing the Subject: Deconstructing the Text." *Feminisms: An Anthology of Literary Theory and Criticism.* Ed. Robyn R. Warhol and Diane Price Herndl. New Brunswick, NJ: Rutgers University Press, 1996.

Benjamin, Lewis Saul. *Victorian Novelists.* London: A. Constable and Co., Ltd., 1906.

Bennett, Paula Bernat. *Poets in the Public Sphere: The Emancipatory Project of American Women's Poetry, 1800–1900.* Princeton: Princeton University Press, 2003.

Berg, Maggie. "Escaping the Cave: Luce Irigaray and Her Feminist Critics." In *Literature and Ethics.* Ed. Gary Wihl and David Williams. Kingston: McGill-Queen's University Press, 1988.

Berlant, Lauren. "The Female Woman: Fanny Fern and the Form of Sentiment." *American Literary History* 3:3 (Fall 1991): 429–54.

Bick, Suzann. "Clouding the 'Severe Truth': Elizabeth Gaskell's Strategy in The Life of Charlotte Brontë." *Essays in Art and Sciences* 11 (1982): 33–47.

Birman, Michele. *Dark Intimacies: The Racial Politics of Womanhood in the 1890s.* PhD Diss., U of Washington, 1992.

Blair, Emily. *Virginia Woolf and the Nineteenth-Century Domestic Novel.* Albany: State University of New York, 2007.

Booth, Alison. *Greatness Engendered: George Eliot and Virginia Woolf.* Ithaca: Cornell University Press, 1992.

———. *How to Make It as a Woman.* Chicago: University of Chicago Press, 2004.

————. "Introduction." Emily Brontë's *Wuthering Heights*. New York: Longman, 2009.

Boumelha, Penny. "The Woman of Genius and the Woman of Grub Street: Figures of the Female Writer in British Fin-de-Siècle Fiction." *English Literature in Transition* 40 (1997): 164–90.

Boyd, Anne E. *Writing for Immortality: Women and the Emergence of High Literary Culture in America*. Baltimore: Johns Hopkins University Press, 2004.

Bradshaw, David and Suzanne Ozment, eds. *The Voice of Toil: Nineteenth Century British Writings About Work*. Athens: Ohio University Press, 2000.

Braudy, Leo. *The Frenzy of Renown: Fame and Its History*. New York: Oxford University Press, 1986.

Braxton, Joanne. *Black Women Writing Autobiography: A Tradition Within a Tradition*. Philadelphia: Temple University Press, 1989.

Brickhouse, Anna. *Transamerican Literary Relations and the Nineteenth-Century Public Sphere*. Cambridge: Cambridge University Press, 2004.

Brock, Claire. *The Feminization of Fame, 1750–1830*. New York: Palgrave Macmillan, 2006.

Brodhead, Richard. *Cultures of Letters: Scenes of Reading and Writing in Nineteenth-Century America*. Chicago: University of Chicago Press, 1993.

Brody, Jennife DeVere. *Impossible Purities: Blackness, Femininity, and Victorian Culture*. Durham: Duke University Press, 1998.

Brooks, Daphne A. *Bodies in Dissent: Spectacular Performances of Race and Freedom, 1850–1910*. Durham: Duke University Press, 2006.

Brown, Gillian. *Domestic Individualism: Imagining Self in Nineteenth-Century America*. Berkeley: University of California Press, 1990.

Budge, Belinda. "Joan Collins and the Wilder Side of Women: Exploring Pleasure and Representation." In *The Female Gaze: Women as Viewers of Popular Culture*. Ed. Lorraine Gamman and Margaret Marshment. Seattle: The Real Comet Press, 1989.

Buell, Lawrence. "Rethinking Anglo-American Literary History." *Clio* 33 (Fall 2003): 65–72.

Butler, Judith. *Gender Trouble: Feminism and the Subversion of Identity*. New York: Routledge, 1990.

————. *Bodies That Matter: On the Discursive Limits of "Sex."* New York: Routledge, 1993.

Capper, Charles. *Margaret Fuller: An American Romantic Life: The Public Years*. New York: Oxford, 2007.

Carby, Hazel. *Reconstructing Womanhood: The Emergence of the Afro-American Woman Novelist*. New York: Oxford University Press, 1987.

Carroll, Traci Reed. *Subjects of Consumption: Nineteenth Century African American Women Writers*. PhD Diss., Northwestern University, December 1992.

Castle, Cora Sutton. *A Statistical Study of Eminent Women*, 27. *Archives of Psychology*, ed. R.S. Woodworth, Columbia Contributions to Philosophy and Psychology 22.1. New York: Science Press, 1913.

Cervetti, Nancy. *Scenes of Reading: Transforming Romance in Brontë, Eliot, and Woolf.* New York: Peter Lang, 1998.

Chapple, J.A.V. and Arthur Pollard, eds. *The Letters of Elizabeth Gaskell.* Cambridge, MA: Harvard University Press, 1967.

Chesler, Phyllis. *Women & Madness.* New York: Avon Books, 1973.

Christian, Barbara. *Black Women Novelists: The Development of a Tradition, 1892–1976.* Westport, CT: Greenwood Press, 1980.

Clarke, John Stock. "The Paradoxes of Oliphant's Reputation." Ed. D.J. Trela. *Margaret Oliphant: Critical Essays on a Gentle Subversive.* London: Associated University Presses, 1995: 33–48.

Claybaugh, Amanda. "Toward a New Transatlanticism: Dickens in the United States." *Victorian Studies* 48.3 (Spring 2006): 439–60.

Cognard-Black, Jennifer. *Narrative in the Professional Age: Transatlantic Readings of Harriet Beecher Stowe, George Eliot, and Elizabeth Stuart Phelps.* New York and London: Routledge, 2004.

Colby, Vineta. "'Devoted Amateur': Mary Cholmondeley and *Red Pottage*." *Essays in Criticism: A Quarterly Journal of Literary Criticism* 20 (1970): 213–28.

Coleman-Bell, Ramona. "Droppin' it like it's hot: The Sporting Body of Serena Williams." In *Framing Celebrity: New Directions in Celebrity Culture.* Ed. Su Holmes and Sean Redmond. London and New York: Routledge, 2006.

Collins, Patricia Hill. "Comment on Hekman's 'Truth and Method: Feminist Standpoint Theory Revisited': Where's the Power?" *Signs* 22:2 (Winter 1997): 375–81.

Colloms, Brenda. "Thoughts on Mrs. Gaskell's The Life of Charlotte Brontë." *Gaskell Society Newsletter* (March 1992): 2–9.

Conboy, Katie, Nadia Median, and Sarah Stanbury, eds. *Writing on the Body: Female Embodiment and Feminist Thinking.* New York: Columbia University Press, 1997.

Conor, Liz. *The Spectacular Modern Woman: Feminine Visibility in the 1920s.* Bloomington: Indiana University Press, 2004.

Coombe, Rosemary J. "The Celebrity Image and Cultural Identity: Publicity Rights and the Subaltern Politics of Gender." *Discourse: Journal for Theoretical Studies in Media and Culture* 14.2 (Summer 1992): 59–88.

Cooper, Anna Julia. *A Voice From the South by a Black Woman of the South.* 1892. New York: Oxford University Press, 1988.

Corbett, Mary Jean. *Representing Femininity: Middle-Class Subjectivity in Victorian and Edwardian Women's Autobiographies.* New York: Oxford University Press, 1992.

Cordell, Sigrid Anderson. *Fictions of Dissent: Reclaiming Authority in Transatlantic Women's Writing of the Late Nineteenth Century.* London: Pickering & Chatto, 2010.

Coultrap-McQuinn, Susan. *Doing Literary Business: American Women Writers in the Nineteenth Century.* Chapel Hill: University of North Carolina Press, 1990.

Courtney, W.L. *The Feminine Note in Fiction*. London: Chapman and Hall, 1904.

Crawford, Robert. *Devolving English Literature*. Oxford: Clarendon Press, 1992.

Creswell, Julie. "How Suite it Isn't: A Dearth of Female Bosses." Sunday Business, *New York Times*. December 17, 2006. Section 3: 1, 9, 10.

Crisp, Jane. *Mary Cholmondeley: A Bibliography*. Victorian Fiction Research Guides VI. Queensland, Australia: English Department, University of Queensland, 1981.

Cutter, Martha J. *Unruly Tongue: Identity and Voice in American Women's Writing, 1850–1910*. Jackson: University Press of Mississippi, 1999.

Cvetkovich, Ann. *Mixed Feelings: Feminism, Mass Culture, and Victorian Sensationalism*. New Brunswick, NJ: Rutgers University Press, 1992.

D'Albertis, Deirdre. "'Bookmaking out of the remains of the dead': Elizabeth Gaskell's *The Life of Charlotte Brontë*." *Victorian Studies* 39 (1995): 1–31.

———. *Dissembling Fictions: Elizabeth Gaskell and the Victorian Social Text*. New York: St. Martin's Press, 1997.

———. "The Domestic Drone: Margaret Oliphant and a Political History of the Novel." *Studies in English Literature, 1500–1900* 37 (1997): 805–29.

David, Dierdre. *Fanny Kemble: A Performed Life*. Philadelphia: University of Pennsylvania Press, 2007.

Davidson, Cathy N. *Revolution and the Word: The Rise of the Novel in America*. New York: Oxford University Press, 1986.

Davidson, Cathy N. and Jessamyn Hatcher, eds. *No More Separate Spheres!* Durham: Duke University Press, 2002.

Davis, Deanna L. "Feminist Critics and Literary Mothers: Daughters Reading Elizabeth Gaskell." *Signs: Journal of Women in Culture and Society* 17 (1992): 507–32.

Davis, Rynetta. "Performing Beauty: Allegories of Social Passing in Eliza Potter's *A Hairdresser's Experience in High Life*." *Arizona Quarterly* 65.1 (Spring 2009): 34–54.

Dean, Sharon G. "Introduction to Eliza Potter's *A Hairdresser's Experience in High Life*" (1859). New York: Oxford University Press, 1991.

Delafield, E.M. *The Brontës: Their Lives Recorded by Their Contemporaries*. London: Leonard and Virginia Woolf at the Hogarth Press, 1935.

DeMoor, Marysa. "Women Authors and Their Selves: Autobiography in the Work of Charlotte Yonge, Rhoda Broughton, Mary Cholmondeley and Lucy Clifford." *Cahiers victoriens et édouardiens* 39 (April 1994): 51–63.

Dijkstra, Bram. *Idols of Perversity: Fantasies of Feminine Evil in Fin-de-Siècle Culture*. New York: Oxford University Press, 1986.

Dobson, Joanne. *Dickinson and the Strategies of Reticence: The Woman Writer in Nineteenth-Century America*. Bloomington: Indiana University Press, 1989.

Donoghue, Frank. *The Fame Machine: Book Reviewing and Eighteenth-Century Literary Careers*. Cambridge: Cambridge University Press, 1996.

Douglas, Mary. *Natural Symbols: Explorations in Cosmology*. New York: Pantheon Books, 1970.

Du Maurier, Daphne. *The Infernal World of Branwell Brontë*. 1960. London: Virago Press, 2006.

DuCille, Ann. "The Occult of True Black Womanhood." In *Female Subjects in Black and White: Race, Psychoanalysis, Feminism*. Ed. Elizabeth Abel, Barbara Christian, and Helene. Berkeley: University of California Press, 1997.

DuPlessis, Rachel Blau. *Writing Beyond the Ending: Narrative Strategies of Twentieth-Century Women Writers*. Bloomington: Indiana University Press, 1985.

Dyer, Richard. *Stars*. 1998. London: British Film Institute, 2004.

Eagleton, Terry. *Myths of Power: A Marxist Study of the Brontës* (1975). New York: Macmillan Press, 1988.

Eakin, John Paul. *Fictions in Autobiography: Studies in the Art of Self Invention*. Princeton: Princeton University Press, 1985.

Easley, Alexis. *Literary Celebrity, Gender, and Victorian Authorship, 1850–1914*. Newark: University of Delaware Press, 2011.

Easson, Angus. "Substantive Misprints and a Deletion in Mrs. Gaskell's *The Life of Charlotte Brontë*." *Notes and Queries: For Readers and Writers, Collectors and Librarians* 23 (1976): 61–2.

———. "Thackeray in Elizabeth Gaskell's *The Life of Charlotte Brontë*: Some Manuscript Evidence." *Victorian Newsletter* 54 (1978): 19–21.

———. "Domestic Romanticism: Elizabeth Gaskell and *The Life of Charlotte Brontë*." Durham University Journal 73:2 (1981): 169–76.

Easson, Angus, ed. *Elizabeth Gaskell: The Critical Heritage*. New York: Routledge, 1991.

Easthope, Antony. *Poetry as Discourse*. London: Methuen, 1983.

Eberwein, Jane Donahue. "'Is Immortality True?' Salvaging Faith in an Age of Upheavals." In *A Historical Guide to Emily Dickinson*. Ed. Vivan R. Pollak. New York: Oxford University Press, 2004.

Elbert, Monika, ed. *Separate Spheres No More: Gender Convergence in American Literature, 1830–1930*. Tuscaloosa: University of Alabama Press, 2000.

Elfenbein, Andrew. *Romantic Genius: The Prehistory of a Homosexual Role*. New York: Columbia University Press, 1999.

Epstein, Julia and Kristina Straub, eds. *Body Guards: The Cultural Politics of Gender Ambiguity*. New York: Routledge, 1991.

Epstein, Norrie. *The Friendly Dickens*. New York: Viking, 1998.

Fanon, Frantz. *The Wretched of the Earth*. New York: Grove Press, 1963.

Fausto-Sterling, Anne. *Sexing the Body: Gender Politics and the Constitution of Sexuality*. New York: Basic Books, 2000.

Feltes, N.N. *Modes of Production of Victorian Novels*. Chicago: University Press of Chicago, 1986.

Fetterley, Judith. *Provisions: A Reader from 19th-Century American Women*. Bloomington: Indiana University Press, 1985.

Finkelstein, David. *The House of Blackwood: Author-Publisher Relations in the Victorian Era*. University Park: Pennsylvania State University Press, 2002.

Fish, Cheryl J. *Black and White Women's Travel Narratives: Antebellum Explorations*. Gainesville: University Press of Florida, 2004.

Fishburn, Katherine. *The Problem of Embodiment in Early African American Narrative*. Westport, CT: Greenwood Press, 1997.

Fiske, John. *Media Matters: Race and Gender in U.S. Politics*. New York: Routledge, 1992.

Fleischner, Jennifer. *Mastering Slavery: Memory, Family, and Identity in Women's Slave Narratives*. New York: New York University Press, 1996.

———. *Mrs. Lincoln and Mrs. Keckly: The Remarkable Story of the Friendship Between a First Lady and a Former Slave*. New York: Broadway Books, 2003.

Foreman, P. Gabrielle. *Activist Sentiments: Reading Black Women in the Nineteenth Century*. Carbondale: University of Illinois Press, 2009.

———. "Introduction to Harriet E. Wilson's *Our Nig, or, Sketches from the Life of a Free Black*." 1859. Ed. P. Gabrielle Foreman and Reginald H. Pitts. New York: Penguin, 2009.

Foster, Alison. "A Personal View of the First Joint Brontë/Gaskell Conference." *The Gaskell Society Journal* 5 (1991): 77–83.

Foster, Frances Smith. "Introduction to Octavia V. Rogers Albert's *The House of Bondage, or, Charlotte Brooks and Other Slaves*." 1890. New York: Oxford University Press, 1988.

———. *Written by Herself: Literary Production by African American Women, 1746–1892*. Bloomington and Indianapolis: Indiana University Press, 1993.

Foucault, Michel. *Discipline and Punish: The Birth of the Prison*. Trans. Alan Sheridan. New York: Vintage Books, 1979.

———. *History of Sexuality, Vol. 1: An Introduction*. Trans. Robert Hurley. New York: Random House, 1980.

Fox-Genovese, Elizabeth. *Within the Plantation Household: Black and White Women of the Old South*. Chapel Hill: University of North Carolina Press, 1988.

Frank, Katherine. *A Chainless Soul: A Life of Emily Brontë*. New York: Random House, 1990.

Frawley, Maria H. "Elizabeth Gaskell's Ethnographic Imagination in The Life of Charlotte Brontë." *Biography* 21:2 (1998): 175–9.

Frederickson, George M. *The Black Image in the White Mind: The Debate on Afro-American Character and Destiny, 1817–1914*. New York: Harper Torchbooks, 1972.

Frederico, Annette R. *Idols of Suburbia: Marie Corelli and Late Victorian Literary Culture*. Charlottesville and London: University Press of Virginia, 2000.

Friedman, Susan Stanford. "Creativity and the Childbirth Metaphor: Gender Difference in Literary Discourse." In *Speaking of Gender*. Ed. Elaine Showalter. New York: Routledge, 1989. 73–100.

Gaines, Jane M. *Contested Culture: The Image, The Voice, and the Law*. Chapel Hill: University of North Carolina Press, 1991.

Gallagher, Catherine. *The Industrial Reformation of English Fiction: Social Discourse and Narrative Form, 1832–1867*. Chicago: University of Chicago Press, 1985.

———. "George Eliot and Daniel Deronda: The Prostitute and the Jewish Question." In *Sex, Politics, and Science in the Nineteenth-Century Novel*. Ed. Ruth Bernard Yeazell. Baltimore: Johns Hopkins University Press, 1986.

———. *Nobody's Story: The Vanishing Acts of Women Writers in the Marketplace, 1670–1820*. Berkeley, University of California Press, 1994.

Gallagher, Catherine and Thomas Laquer, eds. *The Making of the Modern Body: Sexuality and Society in the Nineteenth Century*. Berkeley: University of California Press, 1987.

Gamson, Joshua. *Claims to Fame: Celebrity in Contemporary America*. Berkeley: University of California Press, 1994.

———. "The Assembly Line of Greatness: Celebrity in Twentieth-Century America." In *Popular Culture: Production and Consumption*. Ed. C. Lee Harrington and Denise D. Bielby. Malden, MA: Blackwell Publishers, 2001: 259–82.

Garrison, Dee. "Immoral Fiction in the Late Victorian Library." *American Quarterly* 28:1 (Spring 1976): 71–89.

Gates, E. Nathaniel, ed. *Cultural and Literary Critiques of the Concepts of "Race."* New York: Garland Publishing, Inc., 1997.

Gates, Henry Louis, Jr. "Introduction to Harriet Wilson's *Our Nig, Or, Sketches from the Life of a Free Black: a Novel*." London: Allison and Busby, 1984.

———. "Foreword: In Her Own Write." Schomburg Series of Nineteenth-Century African American Women Writers. New York: Oxford, 1993.

Gates, Joanne. *Elizabeth Robins, 1862–1952, Actress, Novelist, Feminist*. Tuscaloosa: University of Alabama Press, 1994.

Geary, Susan. "The Domestic Novel as a Commercial Commodity: Making a Best Seller in the 1850s." *Papers of the Bibliographical Society of America* 70 (1976): 365–93.

Gerin, Winnifred. *Elizabeth Gaskell: A Biography*. Oxford: Oxford University Press, 1976.

Giddings, Paula. *When and Where I Enter: The Impact of Black Women on Race and Sex in America*. New York: William Morrow and Co., Inc., 1984.

Gilbert, Pamela. *Disease, Desire, and the Body in Victorian Women's Popular Novels*. Cambridge: Cambridge University Press, 1997.

Gilbert, Sandra M., and Susan Gubar. *The Madwoman in the Attic: The Woman Writer and the Nineteenth-Century Literary Imagination*. New Haven: Yale University Press, 1979.

Giles, Paul. *Virtual Americas: Transnational Fictions and the Transatlantic Imaginary*. Durham: Duke University Press, 2002.

Gilman, Sander. "Black Bodies, White Bodies: Toward an Iconography of Female Sexuality in Late Nineteenth-Century Art, Medicine, and Literature." In *"Race," Writing and Difference*. Ed. Henry Louis Gates, Jr. Chicago: University of Chicago Press, 1986.

Gilmore, David D. *Manhood in the Making: Cultural Concepts of Masculinity*. New Haven, CT: Yale University Press, 1990.

Glass, Loren Daniel. *Authors Inc.: Literary Celebrity in the Modern United States, 1880–1980*. New York: New York University Press, 2004.

Gorsky, Susan. "Old Maids and New Women: Alternatives to Marriage in the English Woman's Novel." *Journal of Popular Culture* 7 (1973): 68–85.

Graber, Susan P. "*A Hairdresser's Experience in High Life* by Mrs. Eliza Potter: Cincinnati in the Mid-Nineteenth Century." *Bulletin of the Historical and Philosophical Society of Ohio* 25:3 (1967): 215–24.

Graff, Gerald. *Professing Literature: An Institutional History*. Chicago: University of Chicago Press, 1987.

Green, Laura. "'Long, Long Disappointment': Maternal Failure and Masculine Exhaustion in Margaret Oliphant's Autobiography." In *Other Mothers: Beyond the Maternal Ideal*. Ed. Ellen Bayuk Rosenman and Claudia C. Klaver. Columbus: Ohio State University Press, 2008: 36–54.

Greenblatt, Stephen and Giles Gunn, eds. *Redrawing the Boundaries: The Transformation of English and American Literary Studies*. New York: MLA, 1992.

Griest, Guinevere L. "A Victorian Leviathan: Mudie's Select Library." *Nineteenth-Century Fiction* 20:2 (1965): 103–26.

———. *Mudie's Circulating Library and the Victorian Novel*. Bloomington: Indiana University Press, 1970.

Grosz, Elizabeth. *Volatile Bodies: Toward a Corporeal Feminism*. Bloomington: Indiana University Press, 1994.

Grubin, David. *Abraham and Mary Lincoln: A House Divided*. Produced for *The American Experience*, Public Broadcasting Service, 2001.

Gruesz, Kirsten Silva. *Ambassadors of Culture: The Transamerican Origins of Latino Writing*. Princeton: Princeton University Press, 2002.

Haley Bruce. *The Healthy Body and Victorian Culture*. Cambridge, MA: Harvard University Press, 1978.

Halttunen, Karen. *Confidence Men and Painted Women: A Study of Middle-Class Culture in America, 1830–1870*. New Haven: Yale University Press, 1982.

Hammill, Faye. *Women, Celebrity, and Literary Culture Between the Wars*. Austin: University of Texas Press, 2007.

Haney-Lopez, Ian. *White By Law: The Legal Construction of Race*. New York: New York University Press, 1996.

Harding, Sandra and Merill B. Hintikka, eds. *Discovering Reality: Feminist Pespectives on Epistemology, Metaphysics, Methodology, and Philosophy of Science*. Dordecht (Holland), London and Boston: R. Reidel Publishing Co., 1983.

Harker, Jaime. "'Pious Cant' and Blasphemy: Fanny Fern's Radicalized Sentiment." *Legacy* 18:1 (April 30, 2001): 52–64.

Harlow, Alvin Fay. *The Serene Cincinnatians*. New York: E.P. Dutton and Co., 1950.

Harris, Susan K. *19th-Century American Women's Novels: Interpretive Strategies.* Cambridge: Cambridge University Press, 1990.

Hart, James D. *The Popular Book: A History of America's Literary Taste.* New York: Oxford University Press, 1950.

Hartman, Saidiya V. *Scenes of Subjection: Terror, Slavery, and Self-Making in Nineteenth-Century America.* New York: Oxford University Press, 1997.

Hartsock, Nancy C.M. *The Feminist Standpoint Revisited and Other Essays.* Boulder, CO: Westview, 1998.

Hastie, Amelie. *Cupboards of Curiosity: Women, Recollection, and Film History.* Durham: Duke University Press, 2007.

Hedrick, Joan D. *Harriet Beecher Stowe: A Life.* New York: Oxford University Press, 1994.

Heilmann, Ann. "The 'New Woman' Fiction and Fin-de- Siècle Feminism." *Women's Writing* 3:3 (1996): 197–216.

———. *New Woman Fiction: Women Writing First-Wave Feminism.* New York: St. Martin's Press, 2000.

———. *New Woman Strategies: Sarah Grand, Olive Schreiner, Mona Caird.* Manchester: Manchester University Press, 2004.

Hekman, Susan. "Truth and Method: Feminist Standpoint Theory Revisited." *Signs* 22:2 (Winter 1997): 341–65.

Heller, Deborah. *Literary Sisterhoods: Imagining Women Artists.* Montreal: McGill-Queen's University Press, 2005.

Helms, Gabriele. "The Coincidence of Biography and Autobiography: Elizabeth Gaskell's *The Life of Charlotte Brontë.*" *Biography* 18:4 (1995): 339–59.

Herbert, Christopher. *Culture and Anomie: Ethnographic Imagination in the Nineteenth Century.* Chicago: University of Chicago Press, 1991.

Hickok, Kathleen. *Representation of Women: Nineteenth-Century British Women's Poetry.* Westport, CT: Greenwood Press, 1984.

Higgins, David. *Romantic Genius and the Literary Magazine: Biography, Celebrity, and Politics.* London and New York: Routledge, 2005.

Hoffert, Sylvia D. "Jane Grey Swisshelm, Elizabeth Keckley, and the Significance of Race Consciousness in American Women's History." *Journal of Women's History* 13.3 (Autumn 2001): 8–33.

Holmes, Su. "All you've got to worry about is the task, having a cup of tea, and doing a bit of sunbathing': Approaching Celebrity in *Big Brother.*" In *Understanding Reality Television.* Ed. Su Holmes and Deborah Jermyn. New York and London: Routledge, 2004: 111–35.

Homans, Margaret. *Bearing the Word: Language and Female Experience in Nineteenth-Century Women's Writing.* Chicago: University of Chicago Press, 1986.

hooks, bell (Gloria Watkins). *Ain't I a Woman: Black Women and Feminism.* Boston: South End Press, 1981.

———. *Feminist Theory: From Margin to Center.* Boston: South End Press, 1984.

————. "Representations of Whiteness in the Black Imagination." In *Cultural and Literary Critiques of the Concepts of "Race."* Ed. Nathaniel E. Gates. New York: Garland Publishing, Inc. 1997.

Horowitz, Helen Lefkowitz. *Rereading Sex: Battles Over Sexual Knowledge and Suppression in Nineteenth-Century America.* New York: Alfred A. Knopf, 2002.

Huf, Linda. *A Portrait of the Artist as A Young Woman: The Writer as Heroine in American Literature.* New York: Frederick Ungar Publishing Co., 1983.

Hughes, Linda. "Review of [Laurie Langbauer] *Novels of Everyday Life."* *Victorian Studies* 42.3 (Spring 1999/2000): 505–7.

————. "A Club of Their Own: The 'Literary Ladies,' New Women Writers, and Fin-de-Siècle Authorship." *Victorian Literature and Culture* 35:1 (March 2007): 233–60.

Hughes, Linda K. and Michael Lund. *Victorian Publishing and Mrs. Gaskell's Work.* Charlottesville and London: University Press of Virginia, 1999.

Hull, Gloria T., ed. *The Works of Alice Dunbar-Nelson.* New York: Oxford University Press, 1988.

Hutchings, Kevin and Julia M. Wright, eds. *Transatlantic Literary Exchanges, 1790–1870: Gender, Race, and Nation.* "Aldershot, UK and Burlington, VT: Ashgate Publishing, 2011.

Irigaray, Luce. *Speculum of the Other Woman.* Trans. Gillian C. Gill. Ithaca: Cornell University Press, 1985.

————. *This Sex Which Is Not One.* Trans. Catherine Porter. Ithaca: Cornell University Press, 1985.

Ives, Maura. "Introduction." In *Women Writers and the Artifacts of Celebrity in the Long Nineteenth Century.* Ed. Ann R. Hawkins and Maura Ives. Aldershot, UK and Burlington, VT: Ashgate Publishing, 2012: 1–12.

Jaggar, Allison M. *Feminist Politics and Human Nature.* Totowa, NJ: Rowman and Littlefield, 1983.

————. "Feminist Practical Dialogue and a Third World Feminism." Speech at Miami University of Ohio. Oxford, Ohio. October 6, 1995.

James, Henry. *Literary Criticism.* 2 vols. Ed. Leon Edel. New York: Library of America, 1984.

JanMohamed, Abdul R. "Negating the Negation as a Form of Affirmation in Minority Discourse: The Construction of Richard Wright as Subject." *Cultural Critique* 7 (1987): 245–67.

Jarratt, Susan C. and Nedra Reynolds. "The Splitting Image: Contemporary Feminisms and the Ethics of Íthos." *Ethos: New Essays in Rhetorical and Critical Theory.* Ed. James S. Baumlin and Tita French Baumlin. Dallas: Southern Methodist University Press, 1994.

Jay, Elisabeth. "Introduction to *The Autobiography of Margaret Oliphant: The Complete Text.*" Oxford and New York: Oxford University Press, 1990.

————. *Mrs. Oliphant: "A Fiction to Herself": A Literary Life.* Oxford: Clarendon Press, 1995.

Jenkins, Rebecca. *Fanny Kemble: A Reluctant Celebrity*. London and New York: Simon and Schuster, 2005.

John, Angela. *Elizabeth Robins: Staging a Life: 1862–1952*. London and New York: Routledge, 1995.

Jones, Ann Rosalind. "Writing the Body: Toward an Understanding of *l'EcritureFéminine*." In *Feminisms: An Anthology of Literary Theory and Criticism*. Ed. Robyn R. Warhol and Diane Price Herndl. New Brunswick, NJ: Rutgers University Press, 1993. 357–70.

Jones, Jacqueline. *Labor of Love, Labor of Sorrow: Black Women, Work, and the Family from Slavery to the Present*. New York: Basic Books, 1985.

Jones, Suzanne W., ed. *Writing the Woman Artist: Essays on Poetics, Politics, and Portraiture*. Philadelphia: University of Pennsylvania Press, 1991.

Jump, Harriet Devine, ed. *Mary Wollstonecraft and the Critics 1788–2001*. London and New York: Routledge, 2003.

Jusova, Iveta. *Fin de Siècle Feminisms: The Development of Feminist Narratives Within the Discourses of British Imperialism and Czech Nationalism*. PhD Diss., Miami University of Ohio, 2000.

———. *The New Woman and the Empire*. Columbus: Ohio State University Press, 2005.

Kaplan, Amy. *The Social Construction of American Realism*. Chicago: University of Chicago Press, 1988.

Kaplan, E. Ann. *Motherhood and Representation: The Mother in Popular Culture and Melodrama*. New York: Routledge, 1992.

Karcher, Carolyn L. "Lydia Maria Child's Romance of the Republic: An Abolitionist Vision of America's Racial Destiny." In *Slavery and the Literary Imagination*. Ed. Deborah McDowell and Arnold Rampersad. Baltimore: Johns Hopkins University Press, 1989.

Kelley, Mary. *Private Woman, Public Stage: Literary Domesticity in Nineteenth-Century America*. New York: Oxford University Press, 1984.

Kerber, Linda, Alice Kessler-Harris, and Kathryn Kish Sklar, eds. *U.S. History as Women's History: New Feminist Essays*. Chapel Hill: University of North Carolina Press, 1995.

Kershaw, Alison. "The Business of a Woman's Life: Elizabeth Gaskell's *Life of Charlotte Brontë*." *Brontë Society Transactions* 20 (1990): 11–24.

Kilgour, Maggie. *From Communion to Cannibalism: An Anatomy of Metaphors of Incorporation*. Princeton: Princeton University Press, 1990.

Kirkpatrick, David D. "On Long-Lost Pages, A Female Slave's Voice." *The New York Times*. November 11, 2001: A1+.

Kohn, Denise, Sarah Meer, and Emily B. Todd, eds. *Transatlantic Stowe: Harriet Beecher Stowe and European Culture*. Iowa City: University of Iowa Press, 2006.

Lane, Margaret. *The Brontë Story: A Reconsideration of Mrs. Gaskell's* Life of Charlotte Brontë. London: Heinemann, 1966.

Langbauer, Laurie. "An Ordinary Woman: Forward to *The Autobiography of Mrs. Oliphant.*" Chicago: University of Chicago Press, 1988.

———. *Novels of Everyday Life: The Series in English Fiction, 1850–1930.* Ithaca and London: Cornell University Press, 1999.

Leavis, Q.D. "Introduction to Margaret Oliphant's *Miss Marjoribanks.*" London: Hammon and Sons, 1966.

Ledger, Sally. "The New Woman and the Crisis of Victorianism." In *Cultural Politics at the Fin de Siècle.* Ed. Sally Ledger and Scott McCracken. Cambridge: Cambridge University Press, 1995.

———. *The New Woman: Fiction and Feminism at the Fin de Siècle.* Manchester: Manchester University Press, 1997.

Ledger, Sally and Rogert Luckhurst, eds. *The Fin de Siècle: A Reader in Cultural History c. 1880–1900.* Oxford and New York: Oxford University Press, 2000.

Letherby, Gayle and Catherine Williams. "Non-motherhood: Ambivalent Autobiographies." *Feminist Studies* 25(1999): 719–28.

Levine, Caroline. "Strategic Formalism: Toward A New Method in Cultural Studies." *Victorian Studies* 48.4 (Summer 2006): 625–58.

Levine, George, ed. *Constructions of the Self.* New Brunswick, NJ: Rutgers University Press, 1992.

Levine, Lawrence W. *Highbrow/Lowbrow: The Emergence of Cultural Hierarchy in America.* Cambridge, MA: Harvard University Press, 1988.

Loeffelholz, Mary. *From School to Salon: Reading Nineteenth-Century American Women's Poetry.* Princeton: Princeton University Press, 2004.

———."Mapping the Cultural Field: *Aurora Leigh* in America." In *The Traffic in Poems: Nineteenth-Century Poetry and Transatlantic Exchange.* Ed. Meredith L. McGill. New Brunswick, NJ: Rutgers University Press, 2008. 139–59.

Logan, Deborah A. "'An Unfit Subject for Fiction': Elizabeth Gaskell and the Duty of Silence." *The Gaskell Society Journal* 9 (1995): 27–42.

Lonoff, Sue. "An Unpublished Memoir by Paul Heger." *Brontë Society Transactions* 20 (1990–92): 344–8.

Lootens, Tricia. *Lost Saints: Silence, Gender, and Victorian Literary Canonization.* Charlottesville: University Press of Virginia, 1996.

Lorber, Judith. *Paradoxes of Gender.* New Haven: Yale University Press, 1994.

Lott, Eric. *Love and Theft: Blackface Minstrelsy and the American Working Class.* New York: Oxford University Press, 1993.

Lueck, Beth L. "'A little private conversation … in her boudoir': Stowe's Appearance at Stafford House in 1853." In *Transatlantic Women: Essays on Nineteenth-Century American Women Writers and Great Britain.* Ed. Beth L. Lueck, Brigitte Bailey, and Lucinda L. Damon-Bach. Lebanon, NH: University of New Hampshire Press, 2012. 89–103.

Lydon, Mary. "Calling Yourself a Woman: Marguerite Yourcenar and Colette." *Differences: A Journal of Feminist Cultural Studies* 3:3 (1991): 26–44.

Manning, Susan. *Fragments of Union: Making Connections in Scottish and American Writing.* London: Palgrave Macmillan, 2002.

Manning, Susan and Andrew Taylor, eds. *Transatlantic Literary Studies: A Reader*. Edinburgh: Edinburgh University Press, 2007.

Marcus, Jane Connor. *Elizabeth Robins*. PhD Diss., Northwestern University, 1973.

Marshall, P. David. *Celebrity and Power: Fame in Contemporary Culture*. Minneapolis: University of Minnesota Press, 1997.

Martin, Emily. *The Woman in the Body: A Cultural Analysis of Reproduction*. Boston: Beacon Press, 1992.

McDayter, Dhislaine. *Byromania and the Birth of Celebrity Culture*. Albany: State University of New York Press, 2009.

McDowell, Deborah E. "Introduction to Emma Kelley-Hawkins' *Four Girls at Cottage City*." 1898. New York: Oxford University Press, 1988.

McFadden, Margaret H. *Golden Cables of Sympathy: The Transatlantic Sources of Nineteenth-Century Feminism*. Lexington: University Press of Kentucky, 1999.

McGill, Meredith L., ed. *The Traffic in Poems: Nineteenth-Century Poetry and Transatlantic Exchange*. New Brunswick, NJ: Rutgers University Press, 2008.

Meer, Sarah. *Uncle Tom Mania: Slavery, Minstrelsy, and Transatlantic Culture in the 1850s*. Athens: University of Georgia Press, 2005.

Melville, Lewis (Lewis S. Benjamin). *Victorian Novelists*. 1906. London: Archibald Constable and Co., Ltd., 1970.

Merish, Lori. *Sentimental Materialism: Gender, Commodity Culture, and Nineteenth-Century American Literature*. Durham, NC: Duke University Press, 2000.

Mermin, Dorothy. *Godiva's Ride: Women of Letters in England, 1830–1880*. Bloomington: Indiana University Press, 1993.

Meynell, Alice Christiana. *Hearts of Controversy*. London: Burns & Oates, 1917.

Michie, Helena. *The Flesh Made Word: Female Figures and Women's Bodies*. New York: Oxford University Press, 1987.

Midgley, Clare. *Women Against Slavery: The British Campaigns, 1780–1870*. London: Routledge, 1996.

Miller, D.A. *The Novel and the Police*. Berkeley: University of California Press, 1988.

Miller, Lucasta. *The Brontë Myth*. New York: Alfred A. Knopf, 2003.

Minh-ha, Trinh T. *When the Moon Waxes Red: Representation, Gender and Cultural Politics*. New York: Routledge, 1991.

Moran, Joe. *Star Authors: Literary Celebrity in America*. London: Pluto Press, 2000.

Morrison, Toni. *Playing in the Dark: Whiteness and the Literary Imagination*. Cambridge, MA: Harvard University Press, 1992.

Morrow, Honore Willsie. *Mary Todd Lincoln: An Appreciation of the Wife of Abraham Lincoln*. New York: William Morrow and Co., 1928.

Mullen, Harryette. "Optic White: Blackness and the Production of Whiteness." *diacritics* 24.2–3 (Fall 1994): 71–89.

Mulvey, Christopher. *Transatlantic Manners: Social Patterns in Nineteenth-Century Anglo-American Travel Literature*. Cambridge: Cambridge University Press, 1990.

Mulvey, Laura. "Visual Pleasure and Narrative Cinema." *Screen* 16.3 (1975): 6–18.

Murray, Janet, ed. *Strong Minded Women & Other Lost Voices from 19th-Century England*. New York: Pantheon Books, 1982.

Nadel, Ira Bruce. *Biography: Fiction, Fact, and Form*. New York: St. Martin's Press, 1984.

Nelson, Dana D. *The Word In Black and White: Reading "Race" in American Literature, 1638–1867*. New York: Oxford University Press, 1993.

———. "Introduction to Lydia Maria Child's *Romance of the Republic*." 1867. Lexington: University Press of Kentucky, 1997.

Newbury, Michael. "Eaten Alive: Slavery and Celebrity in Antebellum America." *ELH* 61:1 (Spring, 1994): 159–87.

Nicholson, Linda. "Introduction." In *Feminist Contentions: A Philosophical Exchange*. By Seyla Benhabib, Judith Butler, Drucilla Cornell, and Nancy Fraser. New York: Routledge, 1994.

Okruhlik, Kathleen. "Gender and the Biological Sciences." *Canadian Journal of Philosophy* 20 (1994): 21–42.

Olney, James. "Introduction to Elizabeth Keckley's *Behind the Scenes, or, Thirty Years a Slave and Four Years in the White House*." 1868. New York: Oxford University Press, 1988.

Orgeron, Marsha. *Hollywood Ambition: Celebrity in the Movie Age*. Middletown, CT: Wesleyan University Press, 2008.

Ostendorf, Lloyd and Walter Olesky, eds. *Lincoln's Unknown Private Life: An Oral History by his Black Housekeeper Mariah Vance, 1850–1860*. Mamaroneck, NY: Hastings House Book Publishing, 1995.

Parker, Rozsika and Griselda Pollock, eds. "New Introduction to Marie Bashkirtseff's *I am the Most Interesting Book of All: The Diary of Marie Bashkirtseff, Vol I*." Trans. Phyllis Howard Kernberger and Katherine Kernberger. San Francisco: Chronicle Books, 1997.

Parkins, Wendy. "Home and Away: The New Woman and Domesticity in Mary Cholmondeley's *Red Pottage*." *Women: A Cultural Review* 10.1 (1999): 47–55.

Pattee, Fred Lewis. *The Feminine Fifties*. New York: D. Appleton, 1940.

Peters, John G. "Inside and Outside *Jane Eyre* and Marginalization through Labeling." *Studies in the Novel*. 28:1 (1996): 52–64.

Peterson, Carla. "Foreword: Eccentric Bodies." In *Recovering the Black Female Body: Self-Representations by African American Women*. Ed. Michael Bennett and Vanessa D. Dickerson. New Brunswick, NJ: Rutgers University Press, 2001.

Peterson, Linda H. *Becoming a Woman of Letters: Myths of Authorship and Facts of the Victorian Market*. Princeton: Princeton University Press, 2009.

Petrochenkov, Margaret Wise. "Pregnancy and Birth as a Metaphor for Literary Creativity." PhD Diss., Indiana University, 1992.

Poovey, Mary. *The Proper Woman and the Woman Writer: Ideology as Style in the Works of Mary Wollstonecraft, Mary Shelley, and Jane Austen*. Chicago: University of Chicago Press, 1984.

———. *Uneven Developments: The Ideological Work of Gender in Mid-Victorian England*. Chicago: University of Chicago Press, 1988.

———."Exploring Masculinities." *Victorian Studies* 36:2 (Winter 1993): 207–13.

———. *Making a Social Body: British Cultural Formation, 1830–1864*. Chicago: University of Chicago Press, 1995.

Price, Leah. "The Life of Charlotte Brontë and the Death of Miss Eyre." *SEL, 1500–1900* 35:4 (1995): 757–68.

Price-Herndl, Diane. *Invalid Women: Figuring Feminine Illness in American Fiction and Culture, 1840–1940*. Chapel Hill: University of North Carolina Press, 1993.

Pykett, Lynn. *The "Improper" Feminine: The Women's Sensation Novel and the New Woman Writing*. London and New York: Routledge, 1992.

———. "Portraits of the Artist as a Young Woman: Representations of the Female Artist in the New Woman Fiction of the 1890s." In *Victorian Women Writers and the Woman Question*. Ed. Nicola Diane Thompson. Cambridge: Cambridge University Press, 1999. 135–50.

Rainwater, Catherine and William J. Scheick. "Aliens in the Garden: The Re-Vision of Mary Cholmondeley's *Red Pottage*." *Philological Quarterly* 71.1 (Winter 1992): 101–19.

Raitt, Suzanne. *May Sinclair: A Modern Victorian*. New York: Oxford University Press, 2000.

Ransom, Teresa. *The Mysterious Miss Marie Corelli: Queen of Victorian Bestsellers*. Thrupp, England: Sutton Press, 1999.

Reisen, Harriet. *Louisa May Alcott: The Woman Behind Little Women*. New York: Henry Holt and Co., 2009.

Robbins, Sarah. *The Cambridge Introduction to Harriet Beecher Stowe*. Cambridge: Cambridge University Press, 2007.

Robinson, Solveig C. "Expanding a 'Limited Orbit': Margaret Oliphant, Blackwood's *Edinburgh Magazine*, and the Development of a Critical Voice. *Victorian Periodicals Review* 38.2 (2005) 199–220.

Rodden, John. *The Politics of Literary Reputation: The Making and Claiming of "St. George Orwell."* New York: Oxford University Press, 1989.

Rojek, Chris. *Celebrity*. London: Reaction, 2001.

Romero, Lora. *Home Fronts: Domesticity and Its Critics in the Antebellum United States*. Durham: Duke University Press, 1997.

Roper, Michael and John Tosh, eds. *Manful Assertions: Masculinities in Britain Since 1800*. London and New York: Routledge, 1991.

Rosenman, Ellen Bayuk. *Unauthorized Pleasures: Accounts of Victorian Erotic Experience*. Ithaca and London: Cornell University Press, 2003.

————. "Gender Studies in the Twenty-first Century: An Interview with Christopher Lane and Alison Booth." *Nineteenth-Century Gender Studies* 3.1 (Spring 2007). http://ncgsjournal.com/issue31/rosenman.htm. Accessed June 8, 2009.

Rosenman, Ellen Bayuk and Claudia C. Klaver. "Introduction." In *Other Mothers: Beyond the Maternal Ideal*. Ed. Ellen Bayuk Rosenman and Claudia C. Klaver. Columbus: Ohio State University Press, 2008: 1–22.

Royster, Jacqueline Jones. *Traces of a Stream: Literacy and Social Change Among African American Women*. Pittsburgh: University of Pittsburgh Press, 1994.

Rubik, Margarete. *The Novels of Mrs. Oliphant: A Subversive View of Traditional Times*. New York: Peter Lang, 1994.

Russett, Cynthia Eagle. *Sexual Science: The Victorian Construction of Womanhood*. Cambridge, MA: Harvard University Press, 1989.

Sabiston, Elizabeth. *Private Sphere to World Stage from Austen to Eliot*. Aldershot, UK and Burlington, VT: Ashgate Publishing, 2008.

Saintsbury, George. *Corrected Impressions: Essays on Victorian Writers*. New York: Dodd, Mead and Co., 1895.

Sanchez-Eppler, Karen. *Touching Liberty: Abolition, Feminism, and the Politics of the Body*. Berkeley, University of California Press, 1993.

Santamarina, Xiomara. "Behind the Scenes of Black Labor: Elizabeth Keckley and the Scandal of Publicity." *Feminist Studies* 28.3 (Autumn 2002): 515–37.

————. *Belabored Professions: Narratives of African American Working Womanhood*. Chapel Hill: University of North Carolina Press, 2005.

————. "Black Hairdresser and Social Critic: Eliza Potter and the Labors of Femininity." *American Literature* 77.1 (2005): 151–77.

Schaffer, Talia. "'A Wilde Desire Took Me:' The Homoerotic History of Dracula." *English Literary History* 61:2 (1994): 273–95.

Schor, Hilary. *Scheherezade in the Marketplace: Elizabeth Gaskell and the Victorian Novel*. New York: Oxford University Press, 1992.

Schwyzer, Philip. *Archipelagic Identities: Literature and Identity in the Atlantic Archipelago, 1550–1800*. Aldershot, UK and Burlington, VT: Ashgate Publishing, 2004.

Scott, Anne Firor. *Making the Invisible Woman Visible*. Carbondale: University of Illinois Press, 1984.

Sharps, John Geoffrey. *Mrs. Gaskell's Observation and Invention: A Study of Her Non-Biographic Works*. Fontwell, Sussex: Linden Press, 1970.

Shockley, Ann Allen. *Afro-American Women Writers, 1746–1933: An Anthology and Critical Guide*. New York: Meridian, 1988.

Showalter, Elaine. *A Literature of Their Own: British Women Novelists from Brontë to Lessing*. Princeton: Princeton University Press, 1977.

————. "Feminist Criticism in the Wilderness." *Critical Inquiry* 8 (1981): 179–205.

————. *The Female Malady: Women, Madness and English Culture, 1830–1980*. New York: Penguin Books, 1985.

————. "Introduction to Mary Cholmondeley's *Red Pottage*." 1899. New York: Virago Press, 1985.

————. *The New Feminist Criticism: Essays on Women, Literature, and Theory*. New York: Pantheon, 1985.

————. *Speaking of Gender*. New York: Routledge, 1989.

————. *Sexual Anarchy: Gender and Culture at the Fin de Siècle*. New York: Penguin, 1991.

————. "English Fruits and Yankee Turnips: A Literary Banquet." Address given at Transatlantic Women: Nineteenth-Century American Women Writers in Great Britain, Ireland, and Europe. July 18, 2008. Rothermere American Institute, University of Oxford, England.

Sinclair, May. "Introduction" to *Jane Eyre*. London and Toronto: J.M. Dent & Sons; New York: E.P. Dutton & Co., 1908.

Smith, Shawn Michelle. *American Archives: Gender, Race, and Class in Visual Culture*. Princeton: Princeton University Press, 1999.

Smith, Sidonie. *A Poetics of Women's Autobiography: Marginality and the Fictions of Self-Representation*. Bloomington: Indiana University Press, 1987.

Smith-Rosenberg, Carroll. "Their Writing Was Suspect." *The New York Times*. January 22, 1984. http://query.nytimes.com/gst/fullpage.html?res=9907E7D A1138F931A15752C0A962948260&sec=&spon=&pagewanted=2 Accessed July 7, 2008.

————. *Disorderly Conduct: Visions of Gender in Victorian America*. New York: A.A. Knopf, 1985.

Sorisio, Carolyn. "Unmasking the Genteel Performer: Elizabeth Keckley's *Behind the Scenes* and the Politics of Wrath." *African American Review* 34.1 (Spring 2000): 19–38.

Spenser, Jane. *The Rise of the Woman Novelist: From Aphra Behn to Jane Austen*. Oxford: Basil Blackwell, 1986.

Spielmann, Marion Harry. *The History of Punch, Vol 1*. New York: The Cassell Publishing, Co., 1895.

Spillers, Hortense J. "Mama's Baby, Papa's Maybe: An American Grammar Book." *diacritics* 17.2 (Summer 1987): 65–81.

Stallybrass, Peter and Allon White. *The Politics and Poetics of Transgression*. Ithaca: Cornell University Press, 1986.

Steedman, Carolyn. "Culture, Cultural Studies and the Historians." In *Cultural Studies*. Ed. L. Grossberg, C. Nelson, and P. Treichler. London and New York: Routledge, 1992.

Sterling, Dorothy, ed. *We Are Your Sisters: Black Women in the Nineteenth Century*. New York: W.W. Norton & Co., 1984.

Stern, Madeline B. *Louisa May Alcott: A Biography*. Norman: University of Oklahoma Press, 1971.

————. "Introduction" to *The Selected Letters of Louisa May Alcott*. Ed. Joel Myerson and Daniel Shealy. Assoc. ed. Madeleine B. Stern. Boston: Little, Brown, 1987.

Stevenson, Brenda, ed. *The Journals of Charlotte Forten Grimké*. New York: Oxford University Press, 1988.

Stevenson, Louise L. *The Victorian Homefront: American Thought and Culture, 1860–1880*. New York: Twayne Publishers, 1991.

Stoneman, Patsy. *Elizabeth Gaskell*. Bloomington: Indiana University Press, 1987.

————. *Brontë Transformations: The Cultural Dissemination of* Jane Eyre *and* Wuthering Heights. Hertfordshire: Prentice Hall, 1996.

Storace, Patricia. "Toni Morrison's Utopia." *The New York Review of Books* XLV:10 (June 11, 1998): 64–9.

Suleiman, Susan Rubin. "Writing and Motherhood." In *The (M)other Tongue: Essays in Feminist Psychoanalytic Interpretation*. Ed. Shirley Nelson Garner, Claire Kahane, and Madelon Sprengnether. Ithaca: Cornell University Press, 1985. 352–77.

Sussman, Herbert. *Victorian Masculinities: Manhood and Masculine Poetics in Early Victorian Literature and Art*. Cambridge: Cambridge University Press, 1995.

Sutherland, John. *Mrs. Humphry Ward: Eminent Victorian, Pre-eminent Edwardian*. Oxford: Clarendon Press, 1990.

Swindells, Julia. *Victorian Writing and Working Women: The Other Side of Silence*. Minneapolis: University of Minnesota Press, 1985.

Tate, Claudia. *Domestic Allegories of Political Desire: The Black Heroine's Text at the Turn of the Century*. New York: Oxford University Press, 1992.

Taylor, Sandra Lynn. *Becoming Conduct: Victorian Women Writers Negotiating Gender: Charlotte Brontë, Elizabeth Gaskell, Elizabeth Barrett Browning, George Eliot*. Dissertation Abstracts International 57:6 (1996): 2498A.

Terry, Jennifer and Jacqueline Urla. "Introduction: Mapping Embodied Deviance." *Deviant Bodies: Critical Perspectives on Difference in Science and Popular Culture*. Ed. Jennifer Terry and Jacqueline Urla. Bloomington: Indiana University Press, 1995.

Theweleit, Klaus. *Male Fantasies Vol I: Women, Floods, Bodies, History*. Minneapolis: University of Minnesota Press, 1987.

Thomas, Sue. "Elizabeth Robins and the New Review." *Victorian Periodicals Review* 28:1 (Spring 1995): 63–6.

Thompson, Nicola Diane. "Responding to the Woman Questions: Rereading Noncanonical Victorian Women Novelists." In *Victorian Women Writers and the Woman Question*. Ed. Nicola Diane Thompson. Cambridge: Cambridge University Press, 1999.

Tomisch, John. *A Genteel Endeavor: American Culture and Politics in the Gilded Age*. Stanford: Stanford University Press, 1971.

Tompkins, Jane. *Sensational Designs: The Cultural Work of American Fiction, 1790–1860*. New York: Oxford University Press, 1985.

Tong, Rosemarie. *Feminist Thought: A Comprehensive Introduction*. Boulder, CO: Westview Press, 1989.

Tonkovich, Nicole. *Domesticity with a Difference: The Nonfiction of Catharine Beecher, Sarah J. Hale, Fanny Fern, and Margaret Fuller*. Jackson: University of Mississippi Press, 1997.

Trela, D.J. "Introduction: Discovering the Gentle Subversive." In *Margaret Oliphant: Critical Essays on a Gentle Subversive*. Ed. D.J. Trela. London: Associated University Presses, 1995: 11–27.

Tuchman, Gaye. *Edging Women Out: Victorian Novelists, Publishers and Social Change*. New Haven: Yale University Press, 1989.

Turner, Graeme. *Understanding Celebrity*. London and Los Angeles, CA: Sage, 2004.

———. *Ordinary People and the Media: The Demotic Turn*. London and Los Angeles and London: Sage, 2010.

Uglow, Jenny. *Elizabeth Gaskell: A Habit of Stories*. London: Faber and Faber, 1993.

Vicinus, Martha. *Intimate Friends: Women Who Loved Women, 1778–1928*. Chicago: University of Chicago Press, 2004.

Viswanathan, Gauri. "The Beginnings of English Literary Study in British India." In *Race, Culture and Difference*. Ed. James Donald and Ali Rattansi. London and Los Angeles: Sage, 1992.

Vrettos, Athena. "Body Science." *Michigan Quarterly Review* (Winter 1991): 211–20.

———. *Somatic Fictions: Imagining Illness in Victorian Culture*. Stanford: Stanford University Press, 1995.

Wald, Patricia. *Constituting Americans: Cultural Anxiety and Narrative Form*. Durham: Duke University Press, 1995.

Walker, Nancy A. *Fanny Fern*. New York: Twayne Publishers, 1993.

Walkowitz, Judith. *Prostitution and Victorian Society: Women, Class, and the State*. Cambridge: Cambridge University Press, 1980.

Waller, Philip. *Writers, Readers, and Reputations: Literary Life in Britain, 1870–1918*. Oxford: Oxford University Press, 2008.

Ward, Mrs. Humphry and C.K. Shorter, eds. *The Works of Charlotte Brontë and her Sisters, in Five Volumes*. London: The Chesterfield Society, 1900.

Warren, Joyce W. "Introduction to Fanny Fern's *Ruth Hall*. 1855." New Brunswick, NJ: Rutgers University Press, 1986.

———. *Fanny Fern: An Independent Woman*. New Brunswick, NJ: Rutgers University Press, 1992.

———. "Domesticity and the Economics of Independence: Resistance and Revolution in the Work of Fanny Fern." *The (Other) American Traditions: Nineteenth-Century Women Writers*. Ed. Joyce W. Warren. New Brunswick, NJ: Rutgers University Press, 1993.

———. "Introduction: Canons and Canon Fodder." *The (Other) American Traditions: Nineteenth-Century Women Writers*. Ed. Joyce W. Warren. New Brunswick, NJ: Rutgers University Press, 1993.

Washington, John E. *They Knew Lincoln.* New York: E.P. Dutton & Co., Inc., 1942.

Washington, Mary Helen. "Introduction to Anna Julia Cooper's *A Voice From the South by a Black Woman of the South.*" 1892. New York: Oxford University Press, 1988.

Weber, Brenda R. "'Were Not These Words Conceived in Her Mind?': Gender/Sex and Metaphors of Maternity at the Fin de Siècle." *Feminist Studies* 32:3 (Fall 2006): 547–72.

———. *Makeover TV: Selfhood, Citizenship, and Celebrity.* Durham: Duke University Press, 2009.

———. "Always Lonely: Celebrity, Motherhood, and the Dilemma of Destiny." *PMLA* (*Publication of the Modern Languages Association*) (October 2011): 1110–17.

———. "Channeling Charlotte: Woman's Secret, Great Powers, and the Cult of Celebrity in Elizabeth Robins's *White Violets.*" *Women's Writing* 18.4 (November 2011): 486–504.

———. "Reluctant Celebrity: Harriet Beecher Stowe, Fanny Fern, and the Transatlantic Embodiment of Gender and Fame." In *Transatlantic Women: Nineteenth-Century American Women Writers and Britain.* Ed. Beth L. Lueck, Brigitte Bailey, and Lucinda L. Damon-Bach. Lebanon, NH: University of New Hampshire Press, 2012: 193–217.

Weber, Ronald. *Hired Pens: Professional Writers in America's Gold Age of Print.* Athens: Ohio University Press, 1997.

Weisbuch, Robert. *Atlantic Double-Cross: American Literature and British Influence in the Age of Emerson.* Chicago: University of Chicago Press, 1986.

Weiss, Gail and Honi Fern Haber, eds. *Perspectives on Embodiment: The Intersections of Nature and Culture.* New York: Routledge, 1999.

Welter, Barbara. *Dimity Convictions: The American Woman in the Nineteenth Century.* Columbus: Ohio State University Press, 1976.

West, Lisa. "Foreword." *Popular Nineteenth-Century American Women Writers and the Literary Marketplace.* Ed. Yarington, Earl and Mary De Jong. Cambridge: Cambridge Scholars Publishing, 2008.

Wexler, Laura. "Seeing Sentiment: Photography, Race, and the Innocent Eye." In *Female Subjects in Black and White: Race, Psychoanalysis, Feminism.* Ed. Elizabeth Abel, Barbara Christian, and Helene Moglen. Berkeley: University of California Press, 1997.

Wiegman, Robyn. *American Anatomies: Theorizing Race and Gender.* Durham: Duke University Press, 1995.

Wiley, Catherine. "Staging Infanticide: The Refusal of Representation in Elizabeth Robins's *Alan's Wife.*" *Theatre Journal* (December 1990): 432–46.

Williams, Linda, ed. *Viewing Positions: Ways of Seeing Film.* New Brunswick, NJ: Rutgers University Press, 1995.

Wilson, Christopher P. *The Labor of Words: Literary Professionalism in the Progressive Era.* Athens: University of Georgia Press, 1985.

Wilson, R. Jackson. *Figures of Speech: American Writers and the Literary Marketplace, from Benjamin Franklin to Emily Dickinson*. New York: Alfred A. Knopf, 1989.

Wise, Thomas James and John Alexander Symington, eds. *The Brontës: Their Lives, Friendships & Correspondences*. Oxford: Basil Blackwell, 1932.

Wohl, A.S. *Endangered Lives: Public Health in Victorian Britain*. London: Methuen, 1983.

Wolfson, Susan J. "'Romantic Ideology' and the Values of Aesthetic Form." In *Aesthetics and Ideology*. Ed. George Levine. New Brunswick, NJ: Rutgers University Press, 1994.

Wood, Ann Douglas. "The 'Scribbling Women' and Fanny Fern: Why Women Wrote." *American Quarterly* 23:1 (Spring 1971): 3–24.

Wright, Elizabetha A. *Fern Seeds: The Rhetorical Strategies of ((Grata) Sara(h) Payson Willis Eldredge Farrington Parton)*. PhD Diss., Rensselear Polytechnic University, 1997.

Yarington, Earl and Mary De Jong, eds. *Popular Nineteenth-Century American Women Writers and the Literary Marketplace*. Cambridge: Cambridge Scholars Publishing, 2008.

Yeazell, Ruth Bernard. *Fictions of Modesty: Women and Courtship in the English Novel*. Chicago: University of Chicago Press, 1991.

Zafar, Rafia. *We Wear the Mask: African Americans Write American Literature, 1760–1870*. New York: Columbia University Press, 1997.

Zandy, Janet, ed. *Calling Home: Working-Class Women's Writings: An Anthology*. New Brunswick, NJ: Rutgers University Press, 1990.

Ze Winters, Lisa. "More desultory and unconnected than any other": Geography, Desire, and Freedom in Eliza Potter's *A Hairdresser's Experience in High Life*. *American Quarterly* 61.3 (2009): 455–75.

Index

Note: Bold page numbers indicate figures.